D1237341

SCARDED

Diplomats and Demagogues

Diplomats and Demagogues

THE MEMOIRS OF

Spruille Braden

ARLINGTON HOUSE
New Rochelle, New York

Library of Congress Catalog Card Number 76-154410

ISBN 0-87000-125-6

MANUFACTURED IN THE UNITED STATES OF AMERICA

To my multitude of friends throughout the Western Hemisphere, whose confidence and kindness, wisdom and friendship, encouraged the writing of this book.

Introduction

TO paraphrase Schopenhauer: If we were not all vain and so excessively interested in ourselves life would be so dull none of us would be able to endure it. Accordingly, it is a reasonable presumption that anyone bold enough to publish his memoirs has at least a goodly share of vanity; although I prefer to call it pride. I hope not to appear too conceited nor unduly boastful, irrespective of whether it be pride or pride coupled with vanity. In any case, I am convinced neither has played any tricks with my memory. Moreover, for any thinking man advancing years tend to undercut vanity and moderate pride. In short, the reader may rely on the accuracy of my account, which has been checked against my files.

The most important reasons that led me to write the pages that follow have been the people, events, and ideas that composed my life in its different periods. They were spirited, often exciting, and not infrequently dramatic, and I did not want their essence to be concealed under a too academic manner. Therefore in writing DIPLOMATS AND DEMAGOGUES—WITH NO HOLDS BARRED I have deliberately refrained from using the scholarly apparatus of footnotes that has become customary in such recollections as this.

I have trusted my memory to supply the direction and main features of my narrative, on the theory that what had remained vividly with me into later years certainly must have been of living significance to me. Also, it may even assist such scholars as may peruse this volume, by casting a more searching and illuminating spotlight on the occurrences themselves and this behind-the-scenes background to events that rarely, if at all, appear in official records. The relevant documents through official channels are accessible to the serious student, and others who wish further to explore the matters I touch upon.

The design of DIPLOMATS AND DEMAGOGUES derives from the working of some deeper, less conscious sense of selectivity. I regard the stopping of the ferociously fought war in the Chaco between Bolivia and Paraguay and the establishment of a complete peace for those two nations as perhaps my most important achievement. Here my pride comes to the fore as the only living citizen of the United States who has negotiated and signed a peace treaty that has now endured for more than 32 years. That treaty is in the Washington archives, where the scholar easily may find it. He does not need me to supply a copy.

Nor does the general reader require from me an exhaustive recitation in minutiae of all the events, despatches, and other documents involved in the over three years of intensive negotiations that finally resulted in a Peace Treaty. I believe he will prefer and find it more instructive that I tell him something about the people who fought for the treaty, obstructed its passage, or were indifferent to it. I feel a debt to that reader, as well as an affinity to him, that urges me to think of him before the scholar. More interesting for the general reader will be the egomania of a famous Nobel Peace Prize winner, who helped bring on that war and who as Foreign Minister and Chairman of the Peace Conference prevented the attainment of a peace treaty for nearly 36 months.

By signaling out the Chaco War for this brief comment, I do not intend to belittle in the slightest other accomplishments or the many equally stirring happenings in which I participated but they best can be left for the body of the book.

I do not impugn the worth of scholarship. But, after all, this is my personal record. Also, I think the fascination of history in the making deserves a wider appreciation and lighter touch than a more scholarly book would give.

In bringing DIPLOMATS AND DEMAGOGUES to completion I have leaned upon many people, among them several colleagues who worked indefatigably to bring a measure of order and coherence into my gush of recollections. The final manuscript passed through the capable, and smoothing, editorial hands of Robert Ostermann. I am particularly grateful that he was made available for this service by Fordham University. My thanks go to my old and cherished colleagues Ellis (Ambassador) and Lucy Briggs. I cannot forget the boundless encouragement given me by John A. Mulcahy, a dear and esteemed friend and fellow member of The Metropolitan Club. And of course the self-reliance stimulated by the feminine and therefore intuitively discerning counsel of my two beloved, beautiful, and charming wives. They inspired and aided me during times when I was perplexed and deeply worried although never really discouraged, when often I was less than patient, annoyed, and irritated, by some of the holds that were not barred.

Always I shall appreciate those who read, and I trust approve of this memoir.

Contents

CONTENTS

Diplomats and Demagogues

Chapter I

NEVER have I expected to occupy the White House but I qualified for occupancy by being born in a log cabin. Not one of presidential legend, however, for it had four small rooms with board floors. Still, it was a log cabin and, being in Elkhorn, a Montana mining camp, was certainly in primitive surroundings.

My mother, ordinarily a family-conscious woman, chose to give birth to her first (and only) child in such unsophisticated circumstances because she did not trust her doctor in Helena, preferring my father's brother-in-law, Will Riddell, the mine doctor in Elkhorn. She had the cabin on loan from him, and there, on March 13, 1894, I was born.

My parents, William and Mary Kimball Braden, were living in Helena at the time. My father, a mining engineer, had a consultant's and assay office with his brother Eugene. During this period my father acquired considerable reputation as chief technical witness in a famous lawsuit between the Amalgamated Copper Company (now the Anaconda) and Frederick Augustus Heinze. Millions of dollars were involved, and the litigants paid premium prices for lawyers, engineers, and geologists from all over the world. Father was brought in to such an important position at so early an age because he was regarded as a local engineer and Amalgamated thought the fact would have a good effect on the jury. But he did such distinguished work that at twenty-eight he could decide to set himself up in New York.

Butte at that time was a very festive place, a boom town flooded with money from the mining operations, with a 24-hour air of carnival. I remember with particular excitement and joy the daily balloon ascension, which included a parachutist diving forth to perform tricks on the ropes of his chute as it sailed down from the gondola. I was also impressed by a tallyho that would drive through the raucous streets, with a Negro in a high silk hat blowing a horn.

My father's success did not come without personal risk. There was the night he went down into the Amalgamated mines with an assistant, to check on some geological feature which would be important in the technical testimony. They went out through some drifts into a crosscut, came into a big stope, and ran into a lot of Heinze's men hard at work taking out the enormously rich chalcocite ore. Knowing they would be killed if caught, Father and his companion ran for their lives. They were seen and recognized, but managed to outrun their pursuers.

Two nights later, Heinze's brother was married, and the people on both sides of the case were invited to the wedding reception. It was an Arabian Nights affair, with a lavish supper served on solid gold plate. Heinze walked up to Father and asked. "What do you think of this wedding?"

"It certainly is magnificent," answered Father.

Heinze smiled. "Now you see why we have to steal your ore," he remarked.

My father took a dim view of his five-year-old son smoking, so having caught me one day puffing on corn silk, he said, "If you're going to smoke, smoke like a man. Smoke cigars."

He made a deal with me that he would keep me in cigars and I was to smoke nothing else. Then he went off to the Montana Club and bought the biggest, blackest, meanest cigar he could find. I had had my supper and was in bed when he brought it in. I lit it and started to smoke. Father and Mother went off to dress for dinner. When they returned I had smoked about a third of it, laid it aside, and was sleeping in angelic peace, to the discomfiture of my father and agony of my mother, who chided him with being obliged to honor his rash agreement.

Early next morning I fished out the cold, stale butt and went over to show off to my cousins. In an hour or so my aunt telephoned Mother.

"For heaven's sake, the next time you give your young hopeful cigars keep him at home. He and my four have just ruined my house."

We were so sick that even my little wire-haired terrier threw up in sympathy.

I was twenty-three when I smoked my next cigar. As president of the American Society in Chile I was presiding at a dinner in honor of Admiral William Banks Caperton and his staff at the Club de la Union in Santiago. To ease my embarrassment at sitting at the head table surrounded by ambassadors, cabinet ministers, and other dignitaries, I took a cigar. Fortunately the dinner was nearly over and I lived only three blocks from the club. I was able to get home and get rid of my silk hat and overcoat. Then, in full dress, I lay down on the bed in a cold sweat. I have never since been able to smoke cigars.

2

My father was a man of tremendous ability. I think he inherited his great strength of mind and his whole approach to life from his mother, a formidable character who ruled her family with an iron hand. I always dreaded having to visit her as a child, because she was so strict. I delighted in going to Brooklyn to see my maternal grandmother, who worshipped and spoiled me. I got along magnificently with her.

My paternal grandfather had been in the printing business in Indianapolis, in the firm of Braden and Burford; my grandmother, his second wife, was a Burford. Grandfather endorsed someone's note, and when the principal defaulted was pretty well wiped out. He died when my father, his youngest child, was a boy. There was a much older brother, Spruille, for whom I was named and whose portrait hangs over my mantel.

When this older brother was about sixteen, my grandmother having heard what fine training cadets received on the British training ship H.M.S. Worcester gathered up her teen-ager and set off for England, where she contrived to get him enrolled as a cadet on that ship. During his first few days one of the officers ordered him aloft. My uncle, displaying a characteristic typically Braden, asked, "Why?" History does not record if the officer was seized with apoplexy or fainted, how badly Her Majesty's Navy was shaken, and if the timbers of the good ship *Worcester* were shivered to its very keel.

Despite this somewhat inauspicious beginning to a naval career, Uncle Spruille not only finished the course of training, he came out of it with the Queen's Gold Medal, the highest prize a cadet could win for overall proficiency. American flags were draped all over London the day he graduated. He was offered an ensignship in Her Majesty's Navy (this would have required a change of citizenship) and in our own. He declined both opportunities and went on to the University of Freiburg, whose mining college was world-famous. There he won more honors and prizes. Later on he became Cecil Rhodes' consulting engineer.

A cadet colleague on the *Worcester* was Heihachiro Togo, who won fame in the Japanese Navy as an admiral during the Russo-Japanese War.

At one point Father was convinced I should follow in my uncle's footsteps as a *Worcester* cadet. I had enough sense to know that if I did not win the Gold Medal—by then it was the King's—if even I came out second, I would be adjudged a flop. I staged a revolution, which was successful, and went to Yale instead. A decided improvement in every way, as I could be seasick in a row boat on a millpond.

My father was brought up by his mother with the help of his brother Spruille, and I have no doubt that their stern discipline had much to do with his early success as well as his extreme reserve. He always tried to conceal the great sweetness of temper he had inherited from my grandfather. He seemed to feel it was effeminate or weak to show it. But down deep he was the kindliest of men.

And he was extremely generous, with complete integrity, and in financial matters was the soul of honor. He always made a point of giving his associates a share in his enterprises. In consequence of his many mining successes he made the fortunes of such men as Messmore Kendall, Tom Hamilton, and on a lesser scale some others who were connected with him.

Few men were gifted with Father's ability to size up a mineral deposit. He loved the work, and his genius as an engineer and geologist inspired him to develop the Braden Copper Company, the Andes Copper Company, and other great mining properties—the greatest in the world. He had the rare gift of being able to bring together material resources, men, and capital.

My mother was born Mary Kimball, and she liked to boast she was related to half the statuary in New England. When she came to Chile to attend my wedding to Maria Humeres Solar she called one day on some aunts of my bride, the Valdiviesos. They had in their home an old Valdivieso family tree that included nine kings of Spain. Not long after we were married, she told Maria she had seen it, remarking that any children we might have would also inherit good blood on their father's side, as through her family I was descended from the Holmeses, Adamses, Clements, and Hoares of Massachusetts.

When we were alone Maria said, "You may have them in your family, but why boast about them?"

Mother had the most tremendous fund of knowledge I've ever known anyone to have, with the possible exception of her own mother. Both were walking encyclopedias of history, literature, art, all manner of subjects. Mother's memory for dates was superb, which enabled her to do an extraordinary job of correlating the histories of France, England, and the other European countries.

One day Father, whose mother was a Burford, came home with a book on the Burford genealogy that traced them back to the Earls of Burfort. Father, having listened for some years to Mother's boasting about her ancestors, was disposed to crow. "Now, you see," he said, "we're descended from the Earls of Burfort."

"Well," answered Mother, "that's very interesting. You know, Will, that the Burford line ran out and the title lapsed. Charles II revived it for Nell Gwynn's son. So you must be descended from Nell Gwynn."

Father could only reply, "Well, she was a good girl and got along," and was never again heard to mention his descent from the Earls of Burfort.

At sixteen, Mother took and passed the Harvard entrance examinations, just for the fun of it. I am a poor speller and I like the story about how she could not for the life of her remember where to put the "d" in "college." Fortunately she glanced through the open window and saw an advertisement for the YMCA College, which solved the problem for her.

She had a keen intelligence, an excellent sense of humor. But her wit was often biting and she was capable of a sarcasm that sometimes hurt and angered people unnecessarily. Her courage was indomitable. On one occasion when Father was starting the Braden Copper Co., high in the Andes, she was with him at the mine when a snow slide took out one of the flume lines to the mill. The mill superintendent went out with a gang of 15 or 20 to fix it and another slide caught and killed them all. It took some 48 hours in a driving blizzard to dig the bodies out of the snow. Then Father and Mother, with the mine superintendent and some workers, got them down to the Valley, strapped one on either side of a mule, in snow up to the horses' chests. She took such dangerous hardships in her stride.

Father had great respect for her opinion on business matters, which was in some ways, I think, better than his own. He sometimes disregarded it when it would have been better not to, as in the case of the 1929 crash, which she predicted more than a year before it happened. She would judge such things on minor indications. When a friend who owned houses in Norwalk, Connecticut and Sioux City, Iowa, told Mother of her difficulty selling either one, Mother linked that with several other things she had heard and decided the end of the boom was in sight.

During the 1948 election campaign she insisted, in spite of all indications of a Dewey victory, that Truman would be elected. "The American people," she said, "like a fighter, and Dewey is not fighting. Therefore Truman will win."

She endured suffering with great stoicism. Her death, due immediately to a heart attack, followed an operation for cancer. During the last months she and I played a macabre game. I pretended I didn't know she had cancer and she pretended not to know either, although of course we both knew perfectly well that the other knew. When I went through her checkbook after her death I found that her biggest contributions had been to the Cancer Fund.

3

I was a reckless, confident boy. In New York we lived in what was then a fashionable neighborhood, just off Fifth Avenue on 28th Street. Our apartment house had some ten stories with a prominent parapet. One day, with a playmate, I climbed up and began running back and forth along the parapet. (My penchant for high level risks had an early start.) The greater the watching crowd below, the more enthusiastically we performed, until at last two policemen appeared on the roof and very cautiously coaxed us down.

My father, who believed children should be helped to develop self-reliance, gave me a bicycle on which I used to pedal up Fifth Avenue past the reservoir where the Public Library now stands, then all the way around Central Park and back. The trip was long, but as the city practically ended with the park, not particularly hazardous. Only once did I have a narrow escape, when on the hill below 41st Street and Fifth Avenue (then very steep) I had to maneuver so that my pedals would not hit the protruding axles of two huge horse-drawn trucks passing on either side of me in opposite directions. It was before the days of the brake pedal, and had I fallen I would have been crushed under the iron-shod wheels.

At last I began to get bored. I decided to look for a job. Applying at the most fashionable leather goods shop on Fifth Avenue, I was immediately hired as office boy for mornings at twenty-five cents a week. I was a funny looking office boy, for my mother used to dress me in little pink or white sailor suits, socks, and patent leather pumps. The employees took to sending me with messages to their girl friends, and by the end of the week I had added $7.50 in tips to my modest wage. With the pickings so rich, I tried to expand operations by taking on the Armenian carpet shop next door for afternoons. That ended badly. The proprietor got angry and rolled me in a carpet. Furious at the indignity, I quit.

Even so, I ended my first week with $7.75, and began to strut as the newly rich so often do. Pride was my undoing. My mother demanded to know the source of my wealth and at last I had to confess. The next morning Father accompanied me to my place of employment and resigned for me. At seven-and-a-half I joined the unemployed.

Chapter II

MY first experience of Latin America came before I was eight years old, when we went to Velardeña, a mining, milling, and smelting center in Mexico, then under the regime of Porfirio Diaz. We lived near the smelter and some of the mines. The other mines were scattered for miles around.

I remember vividly the religious festivals, particularly that of Holy Week. They were an odd mixture of Catholic and Indian observances. Two tribes, as they were called, took part, the Matochines and the Fetochines, each with its colorful costume of Indian design in reds and blues, liberally sprinkled with small bits of mirror and other baubles. There were also the most impudent clowns in traditional costumes—the Devil, for instance, whose dress seemed hardly suitable for the fires of Hell. He was all over feathers—body, legs, arms, head. Death was the usual skeleton, surprisingly convincing for the work of simple peons—except that their anatomy was a bit awry: the ribs were continued right down the legs.

The two "tribes" and the clowns went around in these costumes throughout the festivities. And no matter how solemn the ceremony, the clowns were prompt to ridicule it. Even during the celebration of Mass they would go around the church, interrupting people in the midst of their prayers and pretending to be signing them up for perdition. During the blessing of the crosses that stood on every hill in the neighborhood, when many worshippers were climbing painfully on their knees, Death, the Devil, and the other clowns would lock arms as schoolboys sometimes do, back to back, and bow alternately with mock respect; that is, one would bow with the other lying on his back, legs in air.

At the end of Holy Week came the ceremony, quite general throughout Latin America, of blowing up Judas. They had a figure of Judas and literally blew it to smithereens, using dynamite stolen from the mines. Candles used in the mines for illumination were also removed in large numbers for these ceremonies. Father changed to green candles for company use so that he could identify them. The green candles duly showed up in the processions and in the church, and that was that.

I have seen the same combination of Catholic and Indian ceremonies in Bolivia and Guatemala. One of the wisest things the Catholic Church did among these primitive peoples, I believe, was to permit this mixing of religious rites instead of trying to force a drastic change. By following this policy, which it had established in converting pagan Europe, the church gradually raised the level of religious belief and made Catholics of the Indian populations of South America.

One had to be impressed in those days by the Mexican federal police force (*rurales*). Diaz had decided that the best way to cope with the bandits terrorizing the country was to make use of them. He made the most notorious bandit his chief of police, with some of the other top bandits as aides. The scheme worked. He had a police force comparable with the Texas Rangers or the Canadian Mounties or any of the other great police forces of the world.

But they were cruel. One day as Father and I rode into a mining camp we saw a man dragging his wife around by the hair, stopping only now and then to give her a kick. Of course the *rurales* arrived; they usually went in pairs. They led him off, we thought to jail. Only later did we learn what had happened. They had tied one of his arms to the pommel of each saddle, then ridden at full gallop for about three kilometers, beating him with the flats of their swords whenever he tried to lift himself up and drag his feet instead of running.

On another occasion the mine superintendent, Tom Hamilton, was inside one of the mines, and a carpenter for some reason attacked him with a chisel. Hamilton was no man to tangle with. He wrested the chisel from the man's hand and brushed him off. When the *rurales* arrived they asked, "What shall we do with him?" and Hamilton, being a happy-go-lucky sort, answered, "Oh, take him outside and shoot him." By the grace of God he finished his work and himself got outside in time to prevent their doing just that.

Whenever I went out riding in Velardeña an armed *rurale* went along to protect me. He wore a handsome gray uniform with a huge wide brimmed silver decorated sombrero and packed an arsenal of weapons: a sabre, a rifle, a bayonet, and two revolvers. It wasn't enough for him that the peons, when they saw us coming, would scramble into the ditch or up the bank and doff their hats; he would dash ahead to drive them off the road as I came riding by. Being treated like a little prince gave me such an exalted opinion of myself that when we got back to the States I was sent to a school that soon took it out of me.

My arm was broken in a compound fracture during a long ride with my father to visit a mine in a neighboring valley. It is still crooked, although I think that is the result of a second accident rather than the clumsy setting of the mine doctor. With my arm in a cast, I went riding, using an English saddle with small stirrups instead of the McCleland saddle I normally preferred. I was thrown and dragged, the break in the arm this time occurring at the elbow. The doctor's decision, after several x-rays, to cut off a piece of bone was fortunate, for the broken end was so near the surface it crumbled in his hands like sand.

I was also fortunate in having x-rays. Durango City, where I was taken for medical treatment, had a most unreliable electric power supply. As a safeguard, the doctor had devised his own amateur power generator. A peon would mount a stationary bicycle and pedal furiously, driving the rear wheel of the bicycle from which a belt ran to the power generator. The combination of primitive energy and sophisticated equipment is provocative to contemplate even today.

2

The school my parents decided would best cope with my self-importance was Ridley College, a High Church of England school at St. Catherine's, Ontario. (My mother, who was innately religious, was also High Church; my father called himself a non-believer although I always doubted that he really was.) I was now nine years old, but had never been to school because of a theory of Father's that I should develop physical fitness before undertaking classroom work. I therefore had to begin at Ridley with my ABCs.

So far as discipline was concerned, my parents were right. Ridley had a sort of semi-fag system. If some of the older boys threw shoes at us and ordered us to clean them, we were supposed to do so. The older boys also used to beat up the younger ones, and I got my share of that. I really took a lot of physical punishment during the first few months. Ridley used the strapping and caning system that is common in English schools. I was never caned, but strappings were plentiful.

The straps were about a little over a foot long, two inches across the flat, and over a quarter of an inch thick. The punishment would be so many strappings on each hand and no boy could get along with his mates if he pulled away.

In spite of all this it was an excellent school, although at first I was miserable, and held out for one homesick month before breaking down and agreeing to clean shoes. Then I began to like the place. In the classrooms students were lined up and a question was put to the first boy. If he failed to answer, the next in line received it, and so on down the line. The one answering correctly would go to the head of the class. I found the competition so stimulating that after having flunked in all my studies (excepting religion and Bible class) the first term, I was at about the head of all my classes by the end of the year.

A great affliction for the American boys at Ridley was the obligation to wear Eton suits. When we went home for our holidays we made a regular ceremony of tossing our derbys through the window into the Niagara as the train crossed the bridge above the rapids. My mother never could understand how every time I came home she had to buy me a new "derby," as it was called. She was proud, alas! of that Eton suit I so hated. We were living at the old Waldorf-Astoria, and she expected me to put the thing on and come down to Peacock Alley every evening. My embarrassment was acute.

The first Christmas vacation I spent in Washington with my paternal grandmother, who also had with her my cousin Marsa Riddell, a year younger than I. One morning I thought it might be well to call on President Theodore Roosevelt. Leading Marsa by the hand I appeared at the door of the White House and announced we were there to see the President, explaining that I had been born in Montana and knew that he liked all Far Westerners. We not only were given an appointment for 2:30 that afternoon but also a guided tour of the White House.

Fearing my grandmother would disapprove of my social impertinence, I kept quiet about it and made Marsa do likewise. We returned at 2:30 and were cordially received by President Roosevelt, who chatted with us for a bit and gave us each a red rose. Marsa ate hers on the way home. I kept mine for many months, but it finally crumbled into dust.

Chapter III

AFTER one year at Ridley I was out of school for over a year. My father was expecting to go to Chile, but repeatedly had to postpone our departure. At last we sailed on the old *Alianza* of the Panama Railway Steamship Company. It was small—only 1600 tons—and I was almost continuously seasick from New York to Panama. My parents became quite worried at my inability to take nourishment. One day Mother offered me a menu, saying, "Now there must be something you can hold on your stomach. Just look over this menu and pick out anything you think you can eat."

With slight enthusiasm I made my choice. A grape. One grape. But even that I was unable to retain.

We reached Panama just as the first U.S. Army officers were arriving to start work on the Canal. It still excites me to think that I was a close spectator of this important historical engineering achievement. In my life, I have crossed the Isthmus before the Canal was begun, during its construction, upon its completion, and many times since; and by every kind of transportation.

Breaking our journey down the West Coast at Guayaquil, we learned that the presence of bubonic plague or yellow fever, both practically endemic to the Ecuadorian coast, would restrict our movements to the area immediately around our hotel. That offered entertainment enough. It was Sunday, and ceremonies were scheduled to inaugurate the town's new high-pressure water system.

In Latin America amateur fire brigades were and often still are a popular sort of social club. In Santiago, Chile, one brigade was most exclusive. The same was true in Guayaquil; all the young men belonged to fire companies, each having its own distinctive uniform. The brigades were resplendent for the opening of Guayaquil's water system, in new uniforms bought for the occasion: white trousers, huge brass or silver gladiator type helmets, and all the colors of the rainbow in their gaudy coats.

The fire hydrants were placed around the central plaza. For the ceremony, a hose had been attached to each hydrant and a fire company placed in charge of each hose. The mayor would turn a key to start the flow of water and all the streams were to be directed to meet over the plaza to form a pyramid of water cascading down. It was a beautiful conception.

The mayor turned his key; the water came. But the brigades had never handled high-pressure streams. The hoses bucked from their hands and thrashed about, knocking the men heels over head. They rolled about the pavement with the hoses whacking them and water gushing out in all directions. Alas, the rainbow jackets soon looked like scrambled Easter eggs, for the dyes used to color them were not fast and all those reds, purples, and blues had run together. Soon the poor boys were struggling in eddies of tinted water to regain control of the hoses.

My father had come to Chile to begin the development of the great copper mine that became famous as the Braden Copper Company. After our move to New York he became consulting engineer for E. W. Nash, at that time the first president of the American Smelting and Refining Company, and the two men had become close friends. One day Nash called Father in and told him he had been offered a property in Bolivia, the Coro Coro (it later played a part in my own mining career). He thought Father should go down and have a look at it.

In those days it took a long time to get to the West Coast of South America. Father had spent a year there when I was a baby, in charge of an American mining machinery exhibit, and had met an Italian mining engineer, Marco Chiapponi. Now he suggested to Nash that they wire Chiapponi and ask him to find out whether the property was any good. Chiapponi answered, quite erroneously, in the negative. (In 1915 we had an option on the property amounting to some six million dollars, but at that time it could have been had for almost nothing.) Chiapponi, however, called Father's attention to "a small but very rich" property in Chile and urged him to see it.

When Father reached Chile he found that this "small, rich property," known as *El Teniente* (the Lieutenant), had been examined and turned down by engineers of various nationalities. Several rich veins had been worked in both colonial and pre-colonial times; we found there the old copper hammers made by the early Indian miners. But my father had a brand new inspiration; to work the mine as a huge mass of low-grade ore—not much more than 2 per cent. At that time there was no place in the world where copper of less than 5 per cent was being mined; it was not considered profitable. Father climbed the mountain opposite and viewing the property from there realized that the deposit lay around the whole circumference of an extinct volcano. He decided that it could, and should, be worked on a mass-production basis by pillar-stoping and caving.

The idea was revolutionary. Up to that time mass production had never been attempted, and even to conceive of it required a high order of imagination. Nash was deeply impressed by Father's report. "If this thing is as good as you say it is," he said, "let's keep it to ourselves."

He invested his own money and brought in a few friends. Father wanted to call the enterprise the Rancagua Mining Co., Rancagua being the place one left the main line of the Chilean State Railways to ascend to the property. Nash, however, insisted on calling it the Braden Copper Company; no one, he contended, could ever pronounce Rancagua. What he really wanted, I think, was to tie Father firmly into the undertaking so that as main associate he would be under pressure to assure the mine's successful operation.

When Father sent his first annual report on the Braden Copper Company to the *Engineering and Mining Journal* for printing, the editor said Father's estimate of a minimum of one hundred million tons of ore running better than 2 per cent and yielding a substantial profit was absurd.

In the years since, more than 400 million tons have been mined and there are a billion tons left.

Chiapponi's unreliability proved a great misfortune for my father. Twice he dissuaded Father from going to see the Chuquicamata property in northern Chile, the last time when he was in Calama, only a few miles away. "Chuqui" as it is generally known, is one of the greatest mines in the world. Father would certainly have had that, too. Even I, when I saw it, could tell what it was. It didn't require any genius. You just looked at it and knew. But Chiapponi did not. He had no appreciation of mass mining possibilities.

2

The Central Valley of Chile, with quite a bit of rain, gets fairly cold in winter; occasionally the thermometer drops to freezing. Even when it remained in the 40s and 30s, life wasn't too comfortable for the peons in their thatched adobe huts, filled with smoke and with children, dogs, pigs, and chickens all mixed up together. To the shivering Chilean miner, the thought of winter work at 6000 feet in the Cordillera, where there is as much as 50 feet of snow, was nothing short of appalling. Father faced a serious problem. The mines had to be operated 365 days a year. Yet to work them in winter would be impossible unless he could find a way to hold the miners.

The first winter was the big challenge. What Father did was to appeal to the Chilean passion for gambling. He covered the mining sections of Chile—practically all the country—with huge placards showing the goddess of plenty, her cornucopia pouring out an avalanche of gold. Then he set up a lottery with many handsome prizes. Every miner who went into the mines in the autumn (our spring) and worked until September 1 received one or two free tickets, depending on the time he began to work. The drawing was to be on the Chilean national holiday, September 18, at the mines.

The Chileans could not resist the inducement; Father had a complete working force the whole first winter. After that he needed no lottery. Wages at the Braden mine were the highest in Chile; instead of wretched adobe huts, most of the workers had snug frame houses with central heating; schooling was free; and the necessaries were sold at or below wholesale cost in the company store. (For the luxuries, the fancy Parisian soaps and perfumes that the Chilean miner strangely insists on having, prices were plenty high.) Above all, no liquor was permitted at the mines, and the miners—prodigious drinkers when opportunity offers—had no choice but to remain sober. These conditions solved the labor problem at the Braden mine, for the miners' wives found them so pleasing that they insisted their husbands work for the company right through the winter and stay on thereafter.

Enforcing prohibition at the mine was literally a bloody business, with actual battles in the surrounding mountains with men wounded and even killed. The stakes were high; the mining crews could have been decimated because of drunkenness. As a boy, I saw Chilean miners come into one of the Central Valley stores, which are also roadhouses and bars, and order the bartender to start pouring the *chocoli* or *chicha*. The drink was served in huge glasses called *potrillos,* and the drinker would try to empty his glass as fast as the bartender filled it. They didn't always succeed; streams of liquor would often be seen running out into the roadside. It was a matter of grim necessity to keep booze away from the mines.

3

Holding a working force and keeping it sober was only one of Father's problems. Others arose that would have defeated a less resourceful and tenacious man.

All supplies had to be brought in: the machinery; timber for the mine, power plant, mill, houses; food; medicine; everything. Enormous quantities of timber were needed. Father arranged for an entire shipload of timber to be bought from W. R. Grace & Company and transported on a Grace Line ship to Chile. The big shipment would arrive in Valparaiso.

Valparaiso at that time was practically an open roadstead. The timber would have to be off-loaded onto barges, brought ashore, and unloaded onto the piers. The Grace Company told Father there would certainly be substantial additional charges (demurrage) due to delay in unloading. "We can't possibly," a Grace spokesman said, "unload this ship in the time specified in the charter."

Discovering that no firm would undertake to unload the ships within the scheduled time, Father put his assistant George McCann on a tug and had him meet the ship practically in mid-ocean. As an officer of the company, McCann had access to the bridge. There he got the captain into a heated argument over just how close he could bring his ship to the shore. McCann would say, "Oh, you can't get it that close," and the captain would insist that he damn well could. The upshot was a fifty-dollar bet.

The captain won the bet, and nearly beached his ship, bringing it in close enough for a crew of men to board it, haul out the huge beams, some more than two feet square, lashing them together into rafts. Then they set up a cable system, with pulleys that kept the rafts circulating from ship to shore and back just as fast as the timber could be loaded onto the rafts and unloaded on shore. The ship was unloaded in even less time than the charter allowed, and Father was able to collect the handsome premium guaranteed under this condition.

Every foot of that timber, as well as all machinery and other equipment, had to be moved by oxcart from the main railway line up to the mine. Father had to build wagon roads over the mountains from a level of 1,500 feet up to about 4,000, then down another 500 to 600 feet and up again to 6,000. Three hundred oxcarts were kept moving continuously to the mine with all that heavy material.

Then, with the death of E. W. Nash, calamity struck. He was a man of great courage and daring, but the people handling his estate were timid about putting more money into the Braden Copper Company. And additional investment was essential. A railroad from Rancagua to the mine was essential. It had to be built from scratch through the Andes.

To finance it, the company sold first mortgage bonds to the Guggenheim Brothers. Barton Sewall, a vice president of American Smelting and Refining, had succeeded Nash as president of the Braden Company. If Sewall had used the proceeds of the bond issue to buy rails at the price then current, all would have been well. He decided, however, to try to make money for the company by waiting for prices to fall. Instead, rails went up, and at last Sewall was obliged to buy some Belgian re-rolled rails. They were 100 per cent defective. A blow from a sledge hammer would split any of them from end to end.

The road bed was ready; equipment for the railroad was there; only the rails were needed. Neither was there any more money for operations. The mine was producing, but the ore had to be brought out before it could be sold. It was an impasse.

Word came that the Guggenheims were about to foreclose on the bonds. All seemed lost and the Guggenheims would pick everything up for an insignificant sum on those first mortgage bonds. But while everyone sat in New York waiting for Father to admit defeat, he acted in Chile. He bought some old iron and an old furnace and put together a new furnace that would produce about a 45 per cent matte. It may not have been the most efficient or modern smelting plant in the world but it did produce.

That was all he needed to present a request to the German Bank for a loan against his concentrates and the matte. The request went all the way to Hamburg. The answer was negative: No loan. Father would not concede. He brought the two bank managers up to the mine, showed them the ore concentrates and the matte, estimated the production by the end of winter, and waited. The loan was approved.

In the spring, Father brought the concentrates and the matte out by oxcart. He paid off the German Bank loan and had sufficient funds remaining to continue operations and to meet the interest on those bonds. Then the Guggenheims, having failed to lick him, joined Father and arranged for adequate financing. But my father had gone through hell to get it.

I know of nobody in the mining game comparable to my father. His nerve in developing that property despite the enormous obstacles and his genius in overcoming the obstacles have no need of encomiums. The achievement stands. What he did was very great, and a tremendous thing for Chile, too.

When I returned to Chile in 1914 the Braden Copper Company had already paid out in that country more than the total Chilean currency issue. Since then its contribution to the national wealth and the betterment of Chilean living conditions has been colossal. None of the much-discussed—and extravagant—Point Four or other taxpayer-financed projects of our day can approach the effects for Chile of my father's development of that one property, not to mention all the others he developed. Without Chilean copper we would have lost both World Wars. Yet today, with taxation as it is, no individual but only the great corporations (and they would find it extremely difficult) could procure the financing from private sources to do what my father did in Chile on a scale and in a manner that no government giveaway enthusiast could even conceive. And I venture to say that no government engineer would ever be able to see what my father saw in the formation around the crater of that extinct volcano.

4

When we arrived in Chile my formal education had consisted of one year at Ridley College. My parents put me in the *Instituto Ingles,* an English Presbyterian missionary school in Santiago. The *Instituto Ingles* required children in the lower school to wear pinafores, as they did in France. It had never been faced with the problem of getting a ten-year-old American boy into pinafores. I staged such a violent rebellion that the headmaster at last offered to admit me to the higher school if I could pass the examinations. Tutored for three weeks by my mother and spurred by the horrifying prospect of a pinafore, I passed. The result was that I had no training in penmanship, spelling or geography after that one year at Ridley. However, the world's political geography has changed twice since I left school; and I have traveled so much that I probably know physical geography better than most people who have had to pass examinations in it. My spelling and penmanship would probably have been bad anyhow by inheritance from my mother and grandmother.

In the beginning I was miserable at the *Instituto Ingles.* The building was cheerless, my room on the top floor cold and bleak. The second year I had a pleasant room on a lower floor and got some warmth from the headmaster's quarters immediately below me. I began really to enjoy the school when a new teacher arrived from England. He had been an Oxford "blue" and had won all kinds of prizes for scholarship.

I spent most of my vacations with my parents; but always in the summer a month with Tom Hamilton at the mine. And of course the mine was fascinating. One fascination was a bucket tramway that brought the ore from the mines down to the mill site. The tramway towers were perched up on steep slopes—even the edges of precipices. Oiling the wheels that carried the cable was extremely hazardous; if the oiler lost his footing he might fall a thousand feet. He would ride a bucket up to a tower, jump off, stand on the lower of two big beams, grab the upper beam, and oil the wheels. Then he would climb over to the other side of the tower, hop another bucket and ride on to the next. The oil splashed and the beams were slippery.

I must have been about eleven years old when I had the bright idea of taking over from the oiler. He was glad enough to turn over his can to me and have a long rest while I rode the buckets and oiled the wheels. Once my hand was nearly caught between the cable and a wheel. But I managed to get away with the job for ten days or two weeks, until someone told Hamilton what I was doing and once more I found myself without work.

5

Chile, I need hardly say, is a land of earthquakes. When we first arrived there I took a child's delight in the small shocks that knocked over lamps, shook the house, and rattled anything loose. The great earthquake of 1906 put an end to that. According to the experts, the actual shock was much more severe than the San Francisco earthquake. It was far less severe, of course, than the calamitous quake of 1960, which caused the subsidence of the whole southern Chilean coast. Nevertheless it was terrible, and it was years before I got over being nervous when a building shook, no matter what the cause.

We were having a dinner at the *Instituto Ingles* to celebrate some athletic event. It had been raining all day; it was what the Chileans call "earthquake weather," a certain kind of rainy and cloudy winter weather that seems to presage an earthquake. No doubt the scientists would scoff at the idea of earthquake weather, but their scorn would not impress the Chileans.

We were applauding a speech. As the applause died down it seemed to start up again. This was the earthquake hitting.

The walls started to come in. A teacher showed both courage and presence of mind by making for a door and holding it open. One of the greatest dangers in an earthquake is that of doors slamming to and jamming. The safest place in an earthquake is supposed to be a doorway or arch, when walls are crumbling and the earth outside may open up at any moment. But we could not all stand in one doorway. The teacher stood there holding the door open and we passed out under his arm into the patio. Between the main shocks—two severe ones and a lesser one—it was like standing in a rowboat in a heavy swell. The rain was torrential, the earth rolled under our feet. Some of the walls went down, but the building was not too badly damaged. Indeed, we were able later to enter some of the classrooms and remove mattresses and blankets.

The damage in Santiago was not nearly so bad as that in Valparaiso, especially among the houses built on filled-in land at the base of the hill on which the city stood. The quake had smashed open the Valparaiso prisons and a horde of criminals was released in the city. Civilian officials were anything but courageous. But a young Captain of the Port, Commander Gomez Carreño, was equal to the occasion. He declared martial law in the most severe terms, and ordered it applied with deadly effectiveness. Before long you could leave your coat on a park bench and find it safe upon your return—provided you had told the patrolling policeman it was your coat. But God help you if you had not identified it, you might be shot when you picked it up. It was said that Commander Carreño took advantage of the situation to kill off a number of well known dangerous criminals. However that may be, he certainly made crime unhealthy in Valparaiso after the earthquake. He later became a distinguished admiral and Minister of Marine. We could use such a hardheaded man in some of our cities today.

The earthquake travelled in waves. One town would be completely destroyed, its neighbor unshaken. At the Braden mines nothing under the ground was damaged; not a beam was out of place. Above ground, houses, tramway towers, and almost everything else suffered severely.

At the *Instituto Ingles* everything was at sixes and sevens. Two days after the earthquake I left for Graneros, some 60 miles distant where my parents were living. I had not heard from them or they from me. It was one of the points from which the oxcarts started to the mines before the railroad was built from Rancagua.

There being no other means of transport, I walked. At the Maipu River the trestle was somewhat damaged but still up, and I crossed the river on it. I walked a long way farther and finally came to a place called San Francisco. There some kindly peons picked me up and one of them put me on his horse. I got home at about three in the morning after a long, wearying day. I had left Santiago early the previous morning and had walked a total of 30 or 40 miles.

I found my father and mother living in a tent in the garden. The house was unsafe due to the continuing shocks. There were 20 or 30 a day, not severe but sufficient to make it dangerous to be around buildings weakened by the main shocks.

6

After I had been in the *Instituto Ingles* two-and-one-half years, Father took us north out of Chile. Along the way he had to inspect some mines in Bolivia, and chartered a private train for the journey from Antofagasta to the important Bolivian mining center Oruro. The engine pulled only a baggage car and the sleeping car occupied by ourselves and the Chiapponis. Waking our first morning, some 10,000 feet above sea level, we found our two cars attached to the end of a long freight train. The maneuver was completed during the night, we were told, to prevent our sliding back down the rails.

Father's investigations took two weeks. Our next leg would take us to La Paz, the Bolivian capital, and as no rail line ran there we rented a special stage coach to convey us across the *altiplano,* a complete desert about 14,000 feet above sea level. Inns were few and primitive on this journey of three days and two nights, never being composed of more than one large room, and on the second night we did not reach an inn but were forced to seek lodging in Chacacamayo, which was only a little Indian hut and stable. The owners denied having any food, even chickens, and the sight of money failed to change their answer.

While my elders argued the matter I went over and sat down on a pile of sacks in the corner, from which there immediately issued a loud chorus of cackling. The deception was not based on hostility to us. The Spaniards had treated those poor Indians so badly that not even actual cash could still their fear that in the end they would be cheated if they dealt with us. That night all of us slept in the stable, which was cleaner than the hut.

In La Paz the hotel delighted me because the partitions were of paper, through which so many inquisitive fingers had been thrust that they all looked pockmarked. We had some difficulty getting baths, because the only bathtub had been filled with soil and the soil was filled with growing plants which the proprietors were loath to disturb.

From La Paz we went to Lake Titicaca and took the boat trip of nearly twenty-four hours across the highest big body of water in the world. On the train to Arequipa a man who had established what he liked to call "a dwelling house for single gentlemen" passed out cards on which a printer ignorant of English had rendered the words, "devilling house for angel gentlemen." From Arequipa we went on to Mollendo to catch the weekly steamer, only to see it, as we descended from the final hills, steaming away without us.

During our week at Mollendo waiting for the next steamer, I entertained myself in the surf. I was always a strong swimmer, and this week it was fortunate for me that I was. One day, cavorting off an isolated beach, I was caught in a powerful undertow that started to suck me out to sea. In some fashion I fought my way diagonally across the treacherous current to gain the security of a finger of rocks extending out into the ocean. I was about 12, but more than 60 years later my memory of that desperate struggle for life remains undimmed.

Chapter IV

AFTER several years in a Chilean school that put pinafores on its lower grade students, with instruction punctuated by earthquakes, it was pleasant to return to the United States.

The pleasure soon dimmed, however, because my father lodged me in Betts Academy, a preparatory school he had attended before entering the Massachusetts Institute of Technology. Old Bill Betts, who ran the school, had changed it since my father's time into a school for expert tutoring. He was a genius at that. He had studied the college board and Yale examinations for years back (Yale then did not accept the college boards) and could almost forecast the questions. For example, he told us, "Now this year you're going to get the famous 'Building of the Bridge,' in Caesar." We all studied the passage, and, sure enough, it was required. So able was he at coaching that in that first year I passed my preliminary examinations for Yale.

But the school was a pretty bad influence. Bill Betts' genius for tutoring attracted many backward students. When I went there I was 13, and the next youngest boy was 15. The others ranged in age from 18 to 24. In order to advertise his school Betts, who was ahead of his time in this, fielded excellent athletic teams by cleverly including several so-called scholarship students who were really almost professional football and baseball players.

One of his teachers was a husky 230-pound tackle from Colgate University. He would play on the team against other prep schools. It was rough on the opposing teams but good advertising for Betts Academy.

Thus, Betts students were on the whole a pretty tough lot. They became even tougher after the school burned down in the middle of the year and the students were divided into groups and domiciled in separate houses near the former site. Their drinking and carousing and the great difference in ages set me apart from them and augmented a certain timidity in me that was no doubt due to my having spent so much of my childhood with adults. It took me some time after I entered Yale to learn how to be companionable with boys my own age.

My father, I need hardly say, had no idea how greatly Betts Academy had changed. He had chosen it for me because he had gone there and liked it. He had also recommended it to Tom Hamilton, for whom of course it was ideal. It was just as well that at the end of my one year at Betts my parents, who were going back to Chile, sent me to Chester, Vermont, to Dr. Charles N. Morris, an Episcopal clergyman and an excellent tutor. They felt that with Betts Academy having burned down, I might be falling behind in my studies. They need not have worried, because in the end I passed all my entrance examinations and at 16 entered Yale. I registered in the Sheffield Scientific School ("Shef"), majoring in mining engineering.

2

Mine was a three-year course. I had expected to play football, but my schedule of studies was so heavy it left me no afternoons off. I proposed to my father the scheme of stretching the work over four years. His reply was composed of sarcastic remarks directed at my motives for coming to Yale. So I abandoned football and went in for water polo and swimming; they could be practiced and played at night. In my junior and senior years I was all-American on the water polo team and was once selected as an all-time all-American choice.

One of my teammates was the poet Archibald MacLeish, and our competition for the team captaincy taught me my first lesson in politics. Arch was a forward, I a goal. The team was divided over which of us should be captain. All the Academic players supported Arch; the Shef Players supported me. After several deadlocked meetings, the decision finally went to Arch. The politicking was elementary but effective.

After our days as teammates in water polo I saw nothing of MacLeish until years later when I was in the Rehabilitation Corporation and *Architectural Forum* magazine was preparing an article on our work. Meeting for luncheon at the Yale Club with the editor and the writer who was to do the article, I discovered the writer was Archibald MacLeish. He intended, however to use a pseudonym because, he said, it would ruin his reputation as a poet to have an article on architecture appear over his name. We next met when a South American trip brought him to Buenos Aires, where I was ambassador at the Chaco Peace Conference. Our conversation during luncheon for the most part concerned our disagreements over the Roosevelt New Deal, on which he waxed enthusiastic. MacLeish had two close friends at Yale who also made great reputations: Dean Acheson and Cole Porter.

Porter I knew only slightly then and not at all later. Acheson and I had a rather close association in later years in my diplomatic career and I shall say more about him at that place in this record. For now let me say he did have a measure of intellectual arrogance mixed with considerable charm and intelligence. The speech he made to the nation in 1950, immediately after the Chinese had hit our forces hard in South Korea and were driving them back at a terrific pace, came at a grave moment, an occasion to which Churchill or even Roosevelt, though he was no Churchill, would have risen eloquently. For some reason President Truman turned the moment over to Acheson. I was one of many people who broke appointments to hear Acheson on the radio. He let us down. He became very highbrow, talked over everyone's head, and when he was through hadn't really said anything. On the other hand, Dean grew greatly with the years so that today I consider him to be one of our abler statesmen.

It was on a question of information that MacLeish and I last communicated. In May 1960 I wrote Arch, taking exception to a statement he had made in *Life* that the Castro regime had not been proved to be Communist.

"Actually," I wrote, "it is blatantly Communist and of the many errors committed by the State Department in recent years, the coddling of this enemy government is one of the worst."

Arch came back with a rather astringent letter reminding me that he had been trained as a lawyer and had used the word "proof" in the legal and positive sense.

"A number of people, for example," he wrote, "talk as though Alger Hiss had been proved to have been a Communist. This, of course, is not true. As for the Cuban Government, some of the best informed people I know in the State Department and among American businessmen in Cuba regard the question as still highly debatable. You, of course, know all about this debate."

His letter continued: "The serious fact about the Cuban situation—far more serious than the question of Castro's politics—is the apparent preference of the vocal part of the Cuban people for the Russian solution of their problems. That, quite frankly, scares me."

Since the "vocal part of the Cuban people" was the part Castro would allow to be vocal, in support of Castro, I had to assume Arch could believe Castro was offering Cuba a Russian solution not "proved" to be a Communist solution. It hardly seemed worthwhile to continue the discussion. Whether he has ever considered Castro's actual Communism proved or not, I have never heard.

3

During my freshman year I enjoyed my studies, got good marks, and won my numerals and swimming "Y." The following year I interrupted my studies, going West to work in the Nevada mines. The decision was not exactly voluntary.

The episode to blame began one Sunday night after a week-end in town with my parents. I was supposed to take an early train to New Haven. Instead, I kept a date with some friends to go to Bustanoby's, a popular dancing place. I intended to catch the midnight train to New Haven. My companions urged me to stay with them and take the milk train, which would get us there just in time to go bleary-eyed to class.

"Nothing doing!" I declared. "I want to get some sleep."

I should have remained with them. To pass the time on the train I took up with a couple of Princeton students and two attractive chorus girls. The quartet was going to New Haven for one couple to be married. They had been drinking heavily. I tried to dissuade them, with no success. So I decided to save them, as it were, from themselves.

At New Haven, I said, "Now don't worry about anything. I'll help with the details. But first, of course, you'll want to go to a hotel and get ready."

I took them to White's Tontine House, on the green, and told White their plans, assuring him that none of them was in any state to behave responsibly. I told him to put the boys on one floor and the girls on another.

"Tomorrow they'll wake up sober and everything will be all right —I guess," I said.

He said, "Fine, I'll do that."

I went home feeling like a good Samaritan. Sure enough, the would-be marrieds awakened sober and returned, unmarried, to New York. But on the way the girls told someone that one of them was going to marry one of the young men, who happened to belong to a prominent family. The story circulated and the next night a reporter accosted me and asked whether the wedding had taken place.

"I don't know anything about it," I answered. "They said they were going to be married, but I don't know."

The next morning the headline over this report read:

"Braden Doesn't Know Whether He is Married or Not."

The story was accurate enough, but the headline was seen by my father's attorney who showed the paper to my father. I had quite a little explaining to do. And it was decided that a year away from the New Haven area was recommended.

First I worked for the Steptoe Valley Smelter of the Nevada Consolidated in McGill, in the concentration mill and later in the smelter on the experimental gang. Then, wanting some actual mining experience, I worked in the old Cumberland Ely mine, near Copper Flat, where I began as a mucker and miner and timberman.

When I returned to college I had had almost 18 months of practical experience, which helped me greatly in my technical courses. I had, of course, the added advantage of having been around mines enough in my life to acquire a lot more mining knowledge than the average student. One boy took the mining course at Yale because he had read Richard Harding Davis' novels and thought the career would be romantic. Very few such students remained in the mining profession.

In the chemistry laboratory in my first year I had found irksome and unnecessary the delays getting to the laboratory equipment. When I started my courses in qualitative and quantitative analysis I decided to improve the situation for myself by going to the laboratory occasionally on Saturday afternoons and doing enough work to keep ahead of the class.

It worked out even better than I had expected, for with the others two, three, and four experiments behind me the professor in charge had to give me special instruction—a private lecture during which I could ask all the questions I wanted. The further ahead I moved, the more quickly I advanced still further. The result—entirely unforseen—was that my mark in qualitative and quantitative analysis was the highest ever given at Yale. I finished the course so far ahead that the professors, not knowing quite what to do with me, put me at post-graduate work.

This gave me something of a reputation. I even began to have a pretty high opinion of myself as a chemist. Fortunately I worked the following summer at the Chile Exploration pilot plant located at the American Smelting and Refining Co. plant in Perth Amboy, New Jersey. There I had to do my own chemical analyses and it took just 48 hours to learn how little I knew about chemistry.

Other laurels withered as quickly. In the engineering courses it was customary each term to write an article on a technical subject that would be judged on both subject matter and English. I decided to write on the flotation process, which Father was then putting in at the Braden copper mine.

Unfortunately, Father was in Chile at the time. I researched as much information as I could on the brand new process, and wrote the paper. My success was dramatic. Not only was mine the highest possible mark; I was excused from all further work on term papers.

On my first week-end in New York after Father's return from Chile I brought along my thesis, of which I was proud, and with careful casualness placed it on the library table where I knew he was bound to see it. When I came in that evening, rather late, Father remarked, "I've been reading this article of yours, and I've made several comments."

Comments! There was hardly a line he hadn't blue penciled. The margins were full of corrections. And he said, "If you'll make these changes I've suggested, I guess you'll get by."

"What do you mean, get by?" I said. "I've already won the highest possible mark."

He was flabbergasted. Apparently no one on the Yale faculty in the mining and metallurgical courses had any knowledge of flotation. It was such a startling discovery to them. I learned later, that they sent a copy of my paper to the office of Guggenheim Brothers, where it provoked hilarious amusement.

4

In June 1914, at the age of twenty, I graduated from Yale and sailed for Europe with my mother. We were in Paris when the war broke.

Historians of World War I have been reserved to the point of deception in their treatment of the popular French reaction to the beginning of that war. I have seen no mention in any book on the war—and I have examined many—of the scenes we witnessed on the streets of Paris, scenes that filled us with dread not of German invasion but of French insurrection.

The night before war was declared I was out on the *grands boulevards* in a fiacre with two friends. At every crossing troops with fixed bayonets were forcing the crowds off into the side streets and dispersing them. And the crowds were yelling defiantly, *"A bas la guerre! A bas le gouvernement! A bas . . . ! A bas . . . !"*

With the people in this ugly mood, foreigners stranded in the city quickly turned panicky. I remember returning to our hotel one afternoon and finding my mother in tears. She had just come from a visit with dear friends, the Donald Bacons (he was president of the Tennessee Coal and Iron Corporation), where Bacon had put his arm around his wife and said, "Well, we'll just stay here and die. This is the end."

He, it seems, had been talking to Judge Elbert H. Gary, chairman of the board of U.S. Steel, who was of the same opinion: There was nothing for it but to die.

Our situation was certainly not reassuring. In those days no one dreamed of traveling with passports and visas; and suddenly proof of identity was imperative. I succeeded in penetrating the mobs thronging the Embassy and procured identification papers. Then Mother and I stood in line at the prefecture of police for some eight hours to be issued permits to remain in Paris or to leave it.

Every telephone call and visitor produced a new batch of rumors, alleging that mobs were sacking the major hotels. The streets were unsafe. Paris had gone mad.

A small group of friends at the Hotel between us had quite a little gold, which was indispensable; without it one could do nothing. A truth, incidentally, that has been forgotten since the 1930s and is an important cause of our present economic troubles. This precious gold was almost lost in an impulsive effort of my mother and these friends to book passage on an Atlantic steamer. All ports were inaccessible from Paris; the investment in reservations was wasted; I raced to my friend at the Embassy and was able to recover the gold.

Finally, Mother and I, with Barton Sewall's son and his family, made it to London, which was as overcrowded and almost as unsettled as Paris. Hotels were full; we were fortunate to find lodgings in a small establishment not far from the Chilean embassy out in Queen's Gate.

While we were making plans to leave London, I developed my part in a business deal that had begun in Paris with Marco Chiapponi. I saw myself becoming a millionaire at twenty, for Chiapponi, at dinner one night in Paris, had lamented my father's absence from the scene in view of a grand opportunity he had come on.

With the confidence of a twenty-year-old Yale graduate I said, "You don't need my father. What is it?"

Chiapponi said he and several others had an option on a deal to raise a loan against all the assets of the *Mont de Piete,* the French government pawnshops. The negotiators for this loan of between

$200,000,000 and $300,000,000 would make a handsome commission.

Through friends of my parents I was introduced to London bankers who agreed to make the loan. All I had to do was produce the required figures and authorization. Triumphantly I notified Chiapponi, urging him to come to London at once. What a disappointment. He actually didn't have the option he had boasted of. I wrote him an indignant letter, to which he replied with a dressing-down for my being sassy. Later, showing my father this correspondence, I defended my action. Father in part agreed, but cautioned me to understand that people would repeatedly let me down and such letters as I had written Chiapponi would prove not only to be ineffective but a waste of energy. I have learned he was right.

England at this time was suffering a severe shortage of wool and mutton. I soon became aware of this and telegraphed my father in Chile. If he had been able to round up some of the southern sheep and wool, we could have made several mililons. Nothing came of the opportunity, however, so I went back to Chile and started to work for $100 a month.

It wasn't easy to get passage. We had to be satisfied with accommodations on a ship of the Nelson Line that had carried Argentine beef to England. Our suite de luxe consisted of two microscopic cabins. Fortunately for our stomachs the ship called at Vigo and La Coruña in Spain, where it was possible to eat well. Thereafter, until we reached Montevideo we nearly starved. The food was infested with maggots and impossible to eat.

After a brief sojourn in Buenos Aires we traveled as far as Puente del Inca on our way to Chile, to join my father. The road over the Andes was snowbound. We crossed on muleback. Theoretically in my case, for my mule was so lively he threw me three times. I rashly vowed to walk if he threw me again. The mule accepted the challenge and I ended by literally walking across the Andes. By the time we reached the descent on the other side the snow had burned all the skin off my face. It was only the first time.

Chapter V

BEFORE I went to Chile as a graduate mining engineer, Father offered me $100 a month to work for the Andes Exploration Co., which Anaconda had formed jointly with Father to locate and acquire new mining properties. I refused until I had been offered twice as much to work elsewhere. He agreed to let the other people in the organization know that I could earn twice as much as he was paying me, so that no one could accuse him of nepotism.

Father discovered what was known as the Potrerillos mine, in the northern desert region of Chile, inland from Chenaral. Despite its rejection by earlier engineers, the mine struck my father as extremely valuable and he at once started exploration.

After three years of exploration Anaconda proceeded to form the Andes Copper Mining Company to work the Potrerillos property, in which, as discoverer, Father had an interest—one-third, I believe, was the agreement. Anaconda said his interest was too high for them to handle the financing, and asked if he would be willing to reduce his interest. They knew it would take an investment of some $36,000,000 before ever a pound of copper came from the mine. Father agreed.

The negotiations reached an impasse finally and it was suggested that my father and Anaconda President John D. Ryan sit in on the conversations. At the meeting Mr. Ryan turned to my father and said, "Our spokesmen are stalled on what amounts to $500,000. What do you suggest as a settlement?"

Father replied, "Mr. Ryan, I'm willing to do any one of three things: We can split the difference. Or toss a coin for it. Or you take it."

Mr. Ryan smiled. "That's certainly a sporting offer," he said. "*You* take it."

Father said, "I will." And he did.

The incident is typical of Anaconda men who were later libelled by the Roosevelt administration and such gossip columnists as Drew Pearson. They were hard-boiled; they didn't throw money away. But they were fair men. My father had rights far beyond the half-million. If he had stood on them, the mine couldn't have been developed. Anaconda has continued to have executives of the finest character.

One of the first locations I went to was at Sulfatos. It was an extraordinarily interesting deposit; the whole center of an extinct volcano. The ridge above it—snow-capped the year round—is visible from Santiago. The center has been eroded and one side of the crater taken out entirely by a glacier which is still there. Tom Hamilton was my companion. We had to make our camp on the morainal detritus on top of the glacier, 15,000 feet above sea level. Some of our tunnels were as high as 17,000 feet.

To get there we reconstructed a wagon road to Villa Paulina, a pretty place between 5,000 and 6,000 feet up, where there was a little farm. We took over the farm buildings, and from there started making a trail. When we reached the snow we found it too deep to dig through, and had to make our trail by putting rock and dirt on top. It would gradually sink in, of course, but we knew it would support the mules because of the extreme cold at that altitude.

We finally got our camp set up. It was anything but easy because the wind blew a constant furious gale down the canyon over the glacier. It was so strong that although I was heavy and Hamilton at that time weighed 230 pounds, we usually had to crawl on hands and knees to cross a little ridge. The skin was not only burned off our faces, but reburned off. My face became a mass of yellow blisters, a repulsive sight, with blood trickling from almost every pore where the blisters had broken.

We had tents for Hamilton, myself and an office; and for a kitchen and dining room. The only way we could keep our tents up was to erect shields of corrugated iron on four-by-four timbers braced by other four-by-fours. At night the pebbles blowing against the iron sounded like machine gun fire.

Unfortunately we had not tents for the men, and the poor devils had a really hard time. They would build little huts three or four feet high and put sheet iron across the top with boulders to hold it in place. One night eight or nine sheets of iron blew off and we never did find them. The men would also build fires in the huts. It was a disastrous comfort. The fires would melt the icy detritus and the huts would collapse as their occupants cried out in dismay.

Our cook was a German from one of the ships interned during the war at Valparaiso. After the kitchen tent had blown down twice and the chimney once as he was getting breakfast, he quit. Hamilton drew his revolver, laid it on the table, and said, "If you try to leave I'll shoot you." Tom had the look of a man who would. The cook stayed on the job. It is not, however, a method I would recommend to the Park Avenue hostess faced with her cook's resignation.

While we were in that snowbound camp Hamilton and I took turns returning to the Villa Paulina every two weeks. It was mainly a bathing trip. And one we badly needed when the time came round. At the mine, our custom on retiring was to heat the stove red hot, remove our shoes and trousers (we were never without our heavy woolen underwear), don an extra sweater and a toboggan cap, and then into bed with seven or eight additional blankets and ponchos on top of us.

On Christmas Day I went down to Villa Paulina to check on some needed equipment and have my semi-monthly bath. It was springlike down there, and just before I left I placed a lovely little rose under my sweater. When I reached the mine, Hamilton was out surveying. I found him up on a ridge having difficulty keeping his transit from blowing away. Before handing him a letter from Father I tossed him my little rose and said, "Merry Christmas." His profanity in response was unparalleled.

Hamilton had written Father grousing about the situation. Father, in answer, reminded him that the boys in the Belgian trenches were a lot worse off than we were. Hamilton wrote back that he'd be glad to trade Sulfatos for the trenches of Belgium any day.

It wouldn't have been such a bad bargain at that. We had some two hundred men in our crew. Over half of them, Hamilton and I included, were snowblind at one time, an affliction that causes extreme pain along with the blindness. What was worse, during the three months we were there five men went insane from the altitude. We had to catch one of them who was brandishing a knife and threatening to kill everybody in sight, bind him, and tie him on a mule in order to get him out. As nearly as I could determine, all five had been drinking pretty heavily down in the valley before they came up. There may have been some connection between the drinking and the insanity.

The crew were a lot of cutthroats. A group of them broke into and robbed our store. When the carabineros came to arrest the thieves, the captain told us that every man of the crew had either been in jail or was wanted. We persuaded him not to arrest them all, as it would leave us short-handed.

These thugs gave me my first experience in handling an ugly situation. Some fifty of them went on strike. That meant that the rest would strike, and we just could not afford any work stoppage. Our tunnels had to be prepared during the summer so that we could see what grade the ore was and get samples out to be analyzed. Yet I had to sympathize with the men. We were paying them high wages, but their living conditions were impossible.

The strikers surrounded me one day as I came along the trail on horseback, and one of their leaders began to harangue me about their sufferings. When he dared put his hand on my knee, I flung it off angrily, chastening him. But he pleaded, "It's so cold I've had to double up with Juan over here, and sleep with him."

I seized the opportunity for a vulgar and not very funny joke about his poor taste in bed companions. The others started laughing at him. And the strike was over. So was he as ringleader. The men kept hounding him with the joke until he quit a few days later.

The only time in my life I ever felt I was going to die was up there. I had started an inspection of the workings, which I made twice a day, and was going up hill at a dog trot when a sudden feeling of weakness forced me to stop and sit down. I have a tremendous lung capacity and had never suffered from altitude before but that day I sat for half an hour, convinced that if I made a single move it would be my last.

The ore turned out to be so low-grade that we never worked the property although we had invested over eighteen thousand dollars exploring it. The Utah Copper Company is today working ore of three-quarters to eight-tenths of one per cent, but they had everything —railroads, plant, etc.—installed and paid for when they were working higher grade ore in the same location. To start from scratch in a location like Sulfatos to work ore of one-half per cent would have been folly.

Had we been able to work it, we would have gone in through tunnels at about 10,000 feet, struck the deposit 5,000 feet under the surface, and worked up from there to get out the ore. But at the 10,000-foot level there was a lake. A jacknife dipped in it became copper-plated almost instantly; this will suggest how much copper was being leached out by the water flowing through that deposit. There are other such deposits in Chile of that extremely low grade of ore.

At the end of those three gruelling months I was taken into the Santiago office as an assistant to my father. He was going to the States, and in his absence I would be in charge of the office. Our scouts and engineers were going out and reporting back all the time. All the reports from Potrerillos, where Hamilton was in charge, were coming through the office. I supervised the Lo Aguirre property, which later became the Santiago Mining Co. A young engineer could not hope for better training. Besides, it was there that I met Maria.

Chapter VI

THE start was inauspicious. I had just come back from an inspection trip to Sulfatos, and I had been in the saddle fourteen hours. At the Club de la Union for dinner, I ran into a friend, Dr. Amenabar. Pleading fatigue, I declined his invitation to accompany him to the operetta playing that evening at the Comedia Theater.

Departing the club, we passed the Comedia. "Oh, come on in," said Amenabar. "You don't have to stay if you don't like it."

We went in. The show had already started. Theaters in South America were then built with tiers of boxes all the way around, like the Diamond Horseshoe. At the first intermission Dr. Amenabar bowed to a woman sitting in a box with three young girls. One of them, much more blond than myself, I had met at a party, but it was another who attracted my attention. I asked, "Who is that girl?"

"Maria Humeres Solar," said he, and I said, "I want to meet her."

"We'll go up in the next intermission."

"No, we'll go up *this* entre-acte."

I dragged him up. As we entered the box Maria looked up at me from under her big picture hat and I decided then and there that I was going to marry her. I had had my twenty-first birthday on March 13 and this was March 17. Our youngest daughter is named Patricia because we met on St. Patrick's Day.

At the end of the intermission Dr. Amenabar wanted to return to our seats. I turned to my future mother-in-law and asked, "Do you mind if we stay here?"

What could the poor woman say? We stayed there. Then we saw them home and I asked if I could call the next day. They were a bit dumbfounded by such impetuosity but I received permission.

I called the next day. I called every day. I would show up at the *paseos* (the daily promenades on the Alameda where the young men flirted with decorously chaperoned young girls, who were not inhibited from responding in kind). There I would at least see my future wife.

One evening Maria's mother asked me to a party. I started proposing and being turned down—at that first party. Maria later confessed she had been told that "Yankees" liked to come to South America, get engaged, kiss a girl, and then run away. She wasn't going to have that happen to her.

I kept on proposing. I sent flowers and candy. Finally I asked her to a *tanda*—a matinee, though it began at 5 o'clock. Her sister came along as chaperon; no Chilean girl went out alone with a young man in those days. At the *tanda* I proposed again and was told I had been calling too much. The whole family was upset about it, and I was not to come around so often.

I stayed away from Thursday to Monday afternoon. Sunday was the day everyone went to the paseos. I must have put on my hat and overcoat a dozen times, each time removing them by sheer will power.

But I called on Monday. That day when I proposed I was accepted.

Maria's father was in San Felipe, where the family owned two big ranches. The news came to him over the telephone. He replied, "What on earth happened to her? Has she lost her mind, or what?"

It wasn't long, however, before we were getting on famously. And when Maria timidly told me her family was shocked because I kissed her and her mother had said it must stop, I asked to see her father.

I explained to Dr. Humeres that in the United States it was customary to kiss one's fiancee; therefore I had kissed mine and expected to continue. I proposed, however, since her family seemed so wrought up about it, that I be allowed half an hour alone with her each day during which I could kiss her without embarrassing anyone, and I engaged to refrain from kissing her at any other time. He agreed this was a perfectly fair proposition, and the deal was made. My mother-in-law never did get over it. She told her husband he was getting senile.

A couple of weeks after receiving my engagement ring Maria told me, again very shyly, that in Chile it was customary for the fiance to give his betrothed a medal. She meant a religious medal honoring the Virgin Mary but she said only *"una medalla"*—a medal.

I replied, in blissful ignorance, "Oh, you want a medal! I'll give you a medal that *is* a medal," and the next day brought her one of my Yale swimming team medals—a large gold plaque with an oversized enamelled blue "Y" on the face and the seals of Harvard, Princeton, Columbia, and what-have-you on the back. The poor girl bravely wore it and when her friends would say, "What on earth is that thing hanging around your neck?" she would answer, "Oh, that's a Yankee custom."

We weren't married as quickly as engaged. We met on March 17 and became engaged on April 12. Such haste was unheard of in Chile. It usually took at least a couple of years just to get engaged. There were all kinds of formalities—a special call from the young man's father in all the dignity of a cutaway, then an exchange of formal calls by the two families, then formal application for the girl's hand by the boy's father on behalf of his son, and so on. The nearest approach to family I had in Santiago at the time was Tom Hamilton. So I had him pinch hit for Father, as it were, by calling on Maria's family.

The substitution was not always comfortable. One night we went to an operetta together, Maria, her family, Tom, and I. At all the risque jokes Hamilton would nudge my future mother-in-law with his elbow and roar with laughter.

My mother was extremely upset when she learned I was engaged, and to a girl whom she and Father had never met. They were preparing to dine with some friends, and Mother was in the tub, when Father came home with my letter announcing the engagement. He barged right into the bathroom, letter in hand, and said, "Here's what that damn fool son of yours has done."

Her hostess told me later that when Mother arrived she had to go upstairs and dress again. In her agitation she had put on her corset upside down.

The first time Maria met her future in-laws, they invited her to dinner at the Santiago Restaurant, complete with snails (which she loathed) and other gourmet's delights. And Mother, with all the instincts of a mother-in-law and all her talent for sadistic irony, during dinner cut loose on the poor little thing, who gave her back as good as she sent and then some. Maria always had a gift for turning away barbed words and leaving their sender completely devastated, but doing it in an amiable and sweet way.

Under Chilean law at that time young people could not marry without parental consent until they were twenty-five years old. Our families were disposed to take advantage of the law. The law, however, declared there had to be justification for refusal and granted the couple in question the right of appeal to have the parents overruled.

Maria's grandfather had left her the bulk of his fortune, and I knew I could earn at least twice as much as my father was paying me. We were pretty cocky. We threatened to take our families into court if necessary. Whereupon Father caved in (a good looking girl was bound to make him cave in anyhow) and said, "If you have only twenty-four hours of the happiness you think you're going to have, it's worth it. Go ahead."

But mother resisted right up to the end.

We were married. Maria's uncle, Alberto Solar, was so devout he had mass said in his own chapel every day. Because of his standing with the Church we were married by the Papal Nuncio and had the Pope's blessing, although because I was not a Catholic we could not be married in Church.

I had left Yale a convinced atheist, I thought. But as Maria wanted me to become a Catholic if I could, I agreed to try. Her Uncle Alberto arranged for me to take instruction from a Jesuit priest who had been educated at the Universities of Louvain and Dublin. For eight or nine months I went to see him three times a week and spent from half-an-hour to three or four hours with him. It was no use. When it came to matters that have to be taken purely on faith I couldn't go along with the Catholic doctrine. Therefore I have never become a Catholic.

We were married on a Sunday and left that night for Viña del Mar. Father had agreed to my taking a week off for our honeymoon. But his ideas about discipline inopportunely asserted themselves, and on Tuesday night he sent me a telegram insisting that I was urgently needed in the office. Our honeymoon ended after two days.

A fine old Santiago residence, the *Palacio Urmaneta,* which had belonged to one of Maria's great-grandparents, had just been converted into a hotel. The management, thinking it would be good publicity to have us there, offered us a very low rate, not unimportant, for Maria, at my insistence, had turned her inheritance back to her family (who lost it a few years later in a bank crash). We moved in, and lived there in luxury. It lasted just a month.

2

Father and the Andes Company had taken an option on the Coro Coro properties in Bolivia, the first on which Chiapponi had misled him. Their ownership was about evenly divided between a Chilean and a French company. The optional purchase price for the Chilean Company was around two million dollars. But the option to buy the French company, negotiated in Paris, settled at near six million. Ten years earlier those properties could have been bought for almost nothing. Even in 1915 taking the options was good business. The European war was running up the price of copper, and as war needs increased we could no doubt have paid off the whole purchase price and made 100 per cent profit before the end of the war. However, on any reasonable basis the price looked too high; so we finally dropped the options.

We first sent a young engineer up there with some assistants to investigate and sample the properties and determine whether or not they were promising enough to justify the price. His reports caused certain suspicions, so it was decided that I should go up there and try to find out what was going on.

Maria and I took a coast line vessel to Arica, traveling the remaining distance to Coro Coro by train. On the ship, as on the smaller coastwise ships in those days, we had become thoroughly infested with fleas and bed bugs. But as these pests cannot live at 14,000 feet, they dropped off and died on the way.

The manager of the Chilean company had a very comfortable house with floors and kerosene stoves. But suspecting he was con-conspiring against us with the engineer, and also because he had his Indian mistress living there, to his great joy we bypassed the administration house. Special accommodations were arranged for us at the town of Coro Coro's lone hotel. Our room was about twenty-six feet long and twelve wide, furnished with a double bed, a single bed, one chair, a washstand with basin, and pitcher. To make it more habitable the management covered the dirt floor with newspapers and laid carpet over them. They also hung canvas under the eaves to keep the straw and such bugs as might survive at that altitude from dropping off on us.

I had brought with me a thoroughly reliable Chilean shift-boss. He was not only chief sampler and guard of the samples, which I intended to analyze as a further check—but also a kind of general handyman. Travel-soiled after our long, dirty trip from Arica, I told him to bring us the biggest receptacle he could find, and arrange for plenty of hot water, so that we could bathe before going to bed.

He returned with the biggest washbasin I have ever seen as well as two old Standard Oil tins filled with hot water. The sponge baths this made possible were not particularly comfortable as the one door to the room was so warped that even with a wooden brace it only came within twelve inches of closing.

The next morning the landlord requested our basin. "Nothing doing," I said. "It's our private bath and nobody else is going to have it."

"Perish the thought," said he. "Nobody wants to bathe in it. We have to knead the bread in it."

Even for that I wouldn't let him have the article.

We had to develop most discriminating dietary rules. One day

Maria explored our hostelry's kitchen, where she found the cook nursing two children with smallpox. From that moment we restricted our diet to eggs, bananas—indeed anything protected by a shell or skin.

The house adjoining ours was the busiest bordello in town. The noise of carousing was sometimes so objectionable I had to threaten to fire my revolver through the wall if it wasn't reduced. One morning Maria, who was completely alone all day, saw two rather attractive girls sitting on the hillside. To the Indian maid with her braids down her back and the many petticoats the Bolivian Indians wear, she said, "Those look like rather nice girls. I'd like to talk to them."

"Oh no!" answered the maid. "You can't talk to them! They're *Chilenas* (Chileans)!"

This seemed all the more reason to Maria for talking to them—until she learned that in Bolivia prostitutes were known as *Chilenas*. In Chile, on the contrary, they were called *las Francesas* (the Frenchwomen).

Social life in Coro Coro wasn't. There was a nice Frenchwoman, Mme. Dorion, whom we saw once or twice, but she was worlds apart from Maria. And off in one of the outlying mines was an engineer's wife, a little Englishwoman, whom Maria saw now and then. There wasn't another woman within hundreds of miles to whom she could talk, except the Indian girl who made up our room.

In a conversation it came out that this chambermaid had several children; and she was not married to the father. Maria, her Catholic scruples outraged, exclaimed, "You ought to marry the man!"

"Oh, no!" said the other. "If I marry him he won't work any more and I'll have to support him along with the children. As it is, he works, and helps out some with them; I work, and we get along. If I marry him, he's going to sit down and let me do the work for everybody."

"Well, then," said the logical Maria, "you shouldn't have children at all."

"But I *must* have children," the girl explained. "Out near a certain river there's a chapel, and in the chapel is a picture in which mules are giving birth to baby mules. The moral is that every female must give birth to her kind. If I don't have babies in this life, in the next I shall have to carry loads of wood forever. So it's much better to have babies here."

Maria could not even turn to her church for companionship and comfort. When she had told her Father Confessor in Santiago that we were going to Bolivia, he forbade her while she was there—no matter if it were for years—ever to confess to a Bolivian priest. She was nonplussed by the injunction, but understood it later, after learning about Coro Coro's priest. A pleasant enough man, he was quite openly the father of seven. His youngest child was born not long before we arrived, and he had asked the manager of the French company, M. Dorion, and his wife to act as godparents.

The mine foreman we had sent in first, wanted a girl. He was referred to the priest, who acted as procurer. It sounds shocking but I'm not at all sure that the priest didn't do a kindly thing for the girl and her family, for what the foreman gave her in dollars was a fortune in Bolivianos. And as for marrying, she probably had the same scruples against it as Maria's Indian maid. We saw several weddings in the little church during our stay. Chains would be hung around the necks of bride and groom and joined. In Bolivia, as in some other parts of Latin America, Catholicism has a large admixture of the pagan.

3

One day while sitting by the window, knitting or sewing, Maria observed a man walking up and down outside, eyeing her as he came closer and closer. She was sure he would try to enter the room through the warped-open door. I had left a revolver with her. At last she got it out (she afterwards said it was the most difficult thing she ever did) and held it in view of the approaching man. But, she was so unnerved that she almost fired the gun at him anyway. For a girl brought up in luxury, life at Coro Coro was a drastic change.

Her constant concern for my welfare aggravated matters. I had taken her out to show her the mines. We came into a big stope and at once the superintendent said, "Don't stand there. You can see the roof is about to come." Several times he repeated his warning as Maria moved about.

Ten days later the whole roof in that particular stope did cave in, killing seven or eight men.

The mines *were* extremely dangerous; at least one death a week occurred while we were there. I shall never forget the ordeal of going down the shaft in one of the bigger mines. It was quite deep. We would stand on planks placed over the ore bucket, and down we would go. But the shaft was out of plumb, and the timbers had warped. Suddenly the bucket would stick with the cable piling up on top of us. As the cable increased our weight, the bucket would break through the impasse and drop with a mighty jerk, while the boards jumped and we held on for dear life, wondering if the cable would hold.

Often I would go down to cut samples. I remember this day going round a curve in a drift that turned, fortunately for me, about 30 degrees. The miners were just starting work at another cross-cut. They knew we were in there; they had seen us go in. But they weren't deterred. Having drilled their holes, they tamped in the dynamite and exploded the charge. The blast was shattering. Though we were situated around the curve some of the dirt and rocks were blown against us; we were fortunate our eardrums remained whole. This kind of stupidity imperilled one's life as much as the imminence of cave-ins from improper stone wall supports. It was good for Maria's peace of mind that she had no idea how dangerous the place actually was.

4

The Indians were treated with cruelty. Centuries of exploitation had bred terror of the Spanish in them. They were abjectly humble. I recall an occasion while waiting at the junction between the main rail line and the branch to Coro Coro. An Indian tried to buy a ticket. The station master who was a *cholo*—a higher class Indian often having Spanish blood—came out and for no apparent reason began to cuff him and pull his hair. The Indian was big enough to wipe the earth with his tormentor. Instead, he began to cry. An Indian woman happened to be standing near by, and he went up to her like a small boy, put his head down on her breast, and sobbed while she consoled him.

On Sundays the Indians had a market outside the church. They would spread little cloths on the ground for a display of frozen potatoes, corn, and other delicacies. The policeman on duty would go among these poor little heaps and take anything he wanted. He carried a thick strap like those I knew so well at Ridley College, and used it freely, but on Indian heads not hands. His victims took the maltreatment as a matter of course.

Small wonder that they loved to get drunk on *chicha*. In Chile, *chicha* is boiled grape juice fermented. But in Bolivia it was made by chewing up corn, spitting it into a bowl, and letting it ferment. The flavor was supposed to be better if the chewing were done by toothless old women. I never found the courage—or the interest—for research on the point. But I had to keep my laboratory alcohol under strict guard, for the Indians mixed 40-degree alcohol with their *chicha* and would not have known that mine was wood alcohol, until too late.

All Indians drank. I have seen men, women, and children drunk. I have seen nursing mothers and expectant mothers so drunk they couldn't stand up. On All Souls Day the whole town went to the cemetery, taking along *chicha* and alcohol; also frozen—really rotten—potatoes, a great delicacy with them but so repulsive looking I never had the nerve to taste them. They would arrange for blessings from the priests for the graves, and for enough holy water to get them soaking wet. Then they staged a perfect orgy of drinking until all had passed out on top of the cold, wet graves. That is how they celebrated All Souls Day.

But special-occasion drinking did not prevent the Indians from getting drunk every week and in between. They got drunk regularly on Saturday night after work, stayed drunk all day Sunday, and were hung over on Monday. It happened rather frequently that an intoxicated Indian would fall down a mine shaft, which at best had only 18″ x 18″ timber around it to guard against such accidents. And that would be the last seen of him, for a peculiar reason.

Years before, the people working the Chuquicamate mine came into an old working that had caved back in pre-Colonial times. There they found the completely petrified mummy of an Indian woman. She had been caught in the cave-in, and the cupriferous waters filtering through for centuries had petrified her. She had a little basket, also petrified, of the ore samples she had picked up. They removed the mummy and began to exhibit it. Whereupon the Chilean government said, "We gave you a concession to mine copper, not women."

"This," answered the finders, "is not a woman; it's copper."

However, realizing that they probably would not win an argument with the government, they smuggled her out of the country. She next appeared in a dime museum in New Orleans, and was subsequently bought by the Natural History Museum in New York for a handsome price. She has deteriorated somewhat since I first saw her there as a boy. Then her thumbnails were perfect. Now there has been some erosion; evidently the petrifaction was not totally effective. But there she is, and of course everyone in the mining districts of Chile and Bolivia knows the story of this mummified woman.

That is why the mine superintendent at Coro Coro refused to yield up to their sorrowing families the remains of those who had fallen down the shaft. He didn't know how long it takes to petrify a body, and he had visions of setting up a profitable wholesale business in mummies with the American Museum of Natural History.

Sometimes these Indians, so long suffering under outrageous mistreatment, would go on the rampage for no apparent reason and subject any whites they caught to exquisite tortures. At a property we were later exploring between Arequipa and Cuzco the Indians suddenly went wild, and our people caught by surprise, had to beat them off with clubs or any other weapons they could lay hands on. No one could explain the attack. The Indians were being paid higher wages than they could earn elsewhere, and were apparently satisfied.

In the Chaco War these same abject, downtrodden people proved to be extraordinarily valiant fighters. I had it from their adversaries, the Paraguayans, who are Guarani Indians and just love to fight. But when it came to actual combat, they paid tribute to the fighting qualities of the Bolivians of the Altiplano.

The Bolivian Indians are either Aymara or Quechua, but more Quechua in our area. The women wore short dresses and a series of petticoats each shorter than the one beneath, so that all were visible. Of course the poorer Indians wore no more than three or four petticoats. But the costumes of the *Cholas* were worth five or six hundred dollars even in those days. They consisted of very high boots, as many as twenty-five petticoats, expensive shawls fastened with silver pins, and pearls—not fine pearls, but pearls nevertheless. All the grandeur was topped by funny little hats like derbies perched on their heads above braids falling down the back. The men wore their hair in a sort of Buster Brown bob. Their trousers were black on one side and white on the other. The black, they would tell you, was mourning for Atahualpa, last of the Incas. The trousers were rather like riding britches at the top, then narrow at the knee and flared out below it like a sailor's.

The Spanish language as spoken in Bolivia has an admixture of Quechua words. One is *guagua,* meaning baby. It is easy to understand why a baby would be called *guagua* (wahwah), yet so far as I can find out the only other language in which the word occurs is that of a tribe of Indians in Alaska.

These memories of course go back to 1915. I was last in Bolivia in 1938, and then only in La Paz and in luxury. Yet I doubt whether that part of it is greatly changed. There is still the desert, and it is still 14,000 feet high; and the combination may help to account for the habitual abjectness and occasional wildness, the extreme timidity and martial boldness of the inhabitants. It is a depressing region. I have ridden out to look at remote properties through miles of desert where the only sign of life was the occasional skeleton of a llama, burro, or other animal, even a man. Then suddenly, miles away from civilization, I would hear the doleful notes of the *quena*—an instrument resembling the pipes of Pan. And sitting there all alone on a knoll—always on a knoll would be an Indian, playing what I suppose was music, but unlike any other music ever heard; at once alluring and repellant, and so mournful it was all one could do to keep from bursting into tears. Nothing could have summed up half so well the character and feeling of the Bolivian *altiplano*.

Chapter VII

A LETTER my father wrote me while I was at Sulfatos illustrates his attitude toward exploration for minerals. He and the Anaconda Company had sent two distinguished geologists to Lo Aguirre to make a survey of the property. Naturally, interested in their findings, I wrote Father for details. His reply was epic:

> The two engineers are having a heated argument as to whether the deposit is epigenetic or syngenetic. In the meantime we'll go ahead with our drilling and our tunnels and find out whether there's any ore.

I have often had occasion to quote that letter. Father was all for the scientific approach; but he was also thoroughly practical.

Because of this reputation, judgment and financial backing, everyone who had, or thought he had, a mining prospect wished to interest him. Our office received an average of ten properties a day for possible exploration. Frequently we already knew about them. I remember the occasion our attorney interrupted my discussion with a petitioner presenting a property I knew to be no good because our engineers had already examined it. When we were alone the attorney said, "Here is a property that's being presented." It was the same prospect. One man had been in my office and another in his, each claiming to have the owners' authorization to sell it.

Epitomizing this zeal to interest us in mining properties was a man who repeatedly brought in a number of prospectuses, each if possible worse than the last. One day he appeared with two men, each carrying a pile of papers as high as his chin. They were all dumped on my desk with the comment, "Well, among them there must be at least one good mine."

For our genuine exploration work we employed a corps of engineers and geologists. We would send out a scout, one of our younger engineers, to perhaps one in 10 or 20 of the properties presented. These were arduous trips. The scout started by train and automobile, switched to horseback or muleback, and most often made his final ascent by foot over dangerous mountain terrain. In such preliminary examinations, from 90 to 95 per cent of the properties showed no valuable mineralization. Geologists or engineers of greater experience would follow up the few favorable reports. Again the rate of rejections was high, but there would always be a couple of properties worth investigating further.

The amount of investigation varied, sometimes no more than spending several thousand dollars to run a tunnel in to test the mineralization. On the other hand, expenditures in drilling and tunnels could run over $1,000,000, as they did at Potrerillos.

Father often went off on long expeditions to examine a property. One such trip took him to Hinde Island, 200 miles south of Punta Arenas, the southermost city in the world. He chartered a whaling vessel for the journey. After the Chileans came to know his achievements at Braden Copper Company and the Andes Copper Mining Company, they no longer tried to sell only the very rich veins. They would come in and say, "We've got a mountain of copper."

That was their favorite expression. The "mountain" of copper usually turned out to be a little stringer of mineralization, on a hillside that had eroded and crumbled, leaving loose rocks with a little copper in them to be picked up at various places on the slope. The Chileans picking them up began to dream of copper mountains and instant wealth.

Just the same, the Chilean miner has a wonderful nose for ore and Chileans generally are born prospectors. Every one of them with a hole in the ground somewhere brought it to our attention. Copper mining in the Andes, to be sure, goes back to pre-colonial times. The prospectors' centuries-old instinct for finding ore plus 60 years of intensive work by American engineers add up to a great deal of exploration in the Andes.

2

A subject on which there is a great deal of uninformed discussion is investment by Latin Americans and other foreigners in our enterprises abroad. Of course any foreigners can come right up to the New York Stock Exchange and buy the securities of Anaconda, Kennecott, or of any of the American enterprises in his country. But in this matter of foreign participation my father was a pioneer. His experience is revealing.

When the Braden Copper Company was formed, Father did his best to persuade the Chileans with an interest in the property to keep the stock that had been part of their payment. Only one did and he made a killing. The stock, which was worth perhaps $5 a share when he got it in 1906, was selling at the equivalent of $500 a share by 1914.

El Teniente, which became the Braden Copper Company, had enough workings and enough surface indications to prove at once that it was worth buying. An option was unnecessary. However, in exploring the Potrerillos property, where it was necessary to do a lot of drilling and other work, a favorable judgment wasn't immediately available. Father talked with the owners. "I need an option," he told them, "in order to go ahead. It will take at least a couple of years to drill this property and to put in some tunnels and find out whether there is sufficient ore of an adequate grade."

The price agreed upon was five times the value of the owners' authorized stock. They had paid in less than twenty cents on the dollar, so it was about a 25 to one deal. He offered payment in cash. They accepted.

Then Father said, "I'm going to do something better for you. I want all of you to remain as stockholders in this company and to participate with us if we decide to exercise our option and develop the property. So for each dollar you're getting in cash I'm going to give you a dollar of the par value stock of the company we'll form eventually to operate the property if we find the ore."

They were enchanted. We went ahead with our drilling, a costly process because the property was between 75 and 100 miles inland from Chañaral, through desert, up 10,000 feet in the middle of the Cordillera. There was absolutely nothing on the property. Everything had to be brought in—every stick of wood, every bit of charcoal to burn, every scrap of food. Even the water was piped in from the higher Cordillera. We spent over a million dollars.

At the end of three years we decided there was enough ore blocked out, of sufficient grade, although the high-grade ore was only 1.43 per cent as compared with better than two per cent at the Braden Mine. But improved methods of mining and treatment meant we could profitably handle lower grade ores.

We invested another $2,500,000 experimenting to see whether the ores could be treated profitably. After that came the installation of housing for the workers, stores, schools, church, moving picture theater, all of the utilities, the power plant, and the railroad to bring in all of this equipment and haul out the ore. This involved the expenditure of an additional $35,000,000 by the Andes Copper Mining Company before a pound of ore could be produced at a profit.

When the time came to exercise the option, Father went to New York and arranged to have cash sent down to the Chilean banks. The stock was delivered to the stockholders. On the day we delivered the cash and the stock we all went over to the club and had champagne; everybody was happy. But within 48 hours more than half those Chilean stockholders asked us to buy their stock. It had cost them nothing; it was a bonus they never had expected. Having received a handsome cash profit on their original investment, they well could have afforded to retain an interest in the enterprise.

We pointed this out to them, but they said, "It's all right for you people to go ahead. You're going to have a lot of difficulties in developing the property. But we won't wait several years for our stock to yield dividends."

That was fairly representative of the Latin-American attitude. Now it has changed considerably. Some Latin-Americans are ready to go along with investments of North American capital; but they are not prone to do so. A friend of mine in the power business in Brazil once told me of his experience with a leading Brazilian businessman. This man was protesting the outrageous profits the power company was making in Brazil. When my friend reminded him the company was making three per cent at most on its investment, the Brazilian replied, "Well, that's all you're entitled to."

Ironically, the Latin did not hesitate to maintain that a minimum "fair rate" on a bank loan was 8 or 10 per cent and preferably 20 to 25 per cent. In any business they go into, Brazilians consider 30 per cent a fair rate of return. Yet many of them think 4 per cent should be the absolute maximum return on foreign capital.

Moreover, it should not be forgotten that the risks foreign investment incur have multiplied—not excluding that of outright confiscation. In Chile there has not only been great inflation, but the Chilean government has exercised exchange controls in such a way as to tax the mining companies many ways in addition to their regular income tax.

During my father's Chilean years few restrictions on foreign companies existed. My father always dealt with the Chileans frankly and openly; he was admired and trusted. One illustration of their cooperation involved a Chilean law permitting machinery for a new enterprise to enter the country duty free. Father pointed out that all his imports comprised one big machine, including timber and cement for construction, indeed everything required to set up mining operations. He argued it should all come in duty free.

The Chileans were persuaded, but said they didn't think the phrasing of the law covered such a conclusion. "We'll have to have a special Act to give you that permission," they told my father.

They proceeded to put through such an Act. But time was passing and Father could not wait while the debates dragged along. By the time the law was finally enacted he had already paid $250,000 in duties to the Chilean government on equipment imported. Within 24 hours after the law was passed the money was returned to him. Would that modern governments were so comprehending. But then the U.S.A. sets a miserable example in such matters.

The Chilean government at that time had a very keen sense of responsibility. My favorite example is an incident that took place during the so-called Balmaceda Revolution, fought to determine whether the form of government was to be presidential or congressional, President Jose Balmaceda being a very strong president. In the midst of the revolution some government obligations fell due to the House of Rothschild in London. On the due date both sides showed up to make payment. What a tragedy it is for our time that such integrity is gone with the winds of war and revolution!

My father never had any difficulty. Up to his time Chile had been governed by an oligarchy, more or less, of the so-called "forty families," who had supplied the presidents and high officials. The gold standard was still in force and there were no exchange difficulties. But by the time I went to work different types of men were coming to power and the Chilean government had started to speculate in its own exchange. Father was enraged by the practice. Any government, he maintained, that played with its own exchange in such fashion was dishonest.

Nevertheless he continued on the best of terms with the Chileans and retained his influence with them. In 1928 the government of Carlos Ibañez del Campo began to legislate with respect to taxation and exchange, and tried to force the copper companies to convert from oil to southern Chilean coal. The changeover would have been both uneconomic and ruinously expensive, but company representatives in Chile were getting nowhere with the government. Father was asked by Anaconda executives to go to Chile and adjust the matter.

Father spent two weeks in Chile. Finding Pablo Ramirez, the minister of finance, difficult to deal with, he went over his head to President Ibañez. He explained the facts of the case to Ibañez, who agreed with him and summoned the finance minister to witness the agreement, which was embodied in a memorandum written by Father. Subsequently Ramirez tried to renege and Father said, "All right, let's go right back to the President."

He had no further trouble.

Chapter VIII

MARIA and I left Coro Coro after about a month. My father had telegraphed he was leaving for New York and wanted me to operate the Santiago office. Maria, who was in bed with fever the day his wire arrived, had seen enough of Bolivia. She said, "Let's get out."

There was the additional factor of my having confirmed the dishonesty of the company's young engineer. Maria was particularly apprehensive that my unfavorable reports might provoke retaliation against me. Our first child was on the way. More worry for Maria was not needed. We left immediately, meeting Father in Valparaiso just as his ship was leaving for the States.

Part of the fun of those days in Santiago lay in the constant warfare one maintained with the native taxi drivers. I was always able to maintain my own because of the Lozier limousine my father had left behind him. The car had huge Westinghouse air springs; and later on a lighter body than the limousine was substituted. A friend of mine described it not inadequately when he said the vehicle looked like a World War I tank. It had no windshield so I could not be cut by flying glass.

The taxicabs in Santiago were original Model T Fords; indeed, one ordered a Ford, not a taxi. The drivers handled them exactly as Chilean riders handle their horses.

Chilean horsemen are superbly skilled daredevils. One of their stunts was to draw a line across the road, then approach it at a dead gallop. At the line the rider would give a little jerk to the rein, whereupon the horse would abruptly stop, rear up, pivot, and take off at full gallop in the opposite direction. In its original form, so the story goes, this game required the riders to rein up their mounts on the very edge of a cliff. Once out riding I unwittingly gave my horse (just given me) the signal for this maneuver. He reared and was instantly off in the opposite direction. I, however, continued straight ahead. Riding in Chile was full of the unexpected.

Another favorite stunt of the *huasos* (the equivalent of cowboys), particularly on Sunday when they had been drinking too much, was to face one another bareback a few hundred yards apart, put their horses at a gallop, and collide at top speed to see who would be unhorsed. The result was a kicking mass of horses and men. No one ever died from these encounters, though it was very hard on the horses. I have seen many a drunken *huaso* and his horse staggering down the road, the rider lurching in the saddle as his mount instinctively shifted in order to keep under his weight so he wouldn't fall off. The effect was of a drunken man on a drunken animal.

In that same devil-may-care spirit the taxi drivers maneuvered the Model T. They raced through the narrow streets of Santiago at top speed, with total disregard of safety, including their own. I would say that over a period of four-and-a-half to five years never a week went by without our hearing, on one corner or another, brakes screeching, shouts, a crash, complete silence for a few seconds, then an uproar as each driver accused the other.

On the corner opposite my father-in-law's house there was a telegraph pole. One day a pedestrian jumped behind it to escape an onrushing Ford. To no avail; it got him. On the night my first daughter was born I took a Ford to go for the doctor, telling the driver why I was in a hurry. He not only went around every corner on two wheels; the two wheels were right up on the sidewalk.

When stop-and-go signs began to appear in the United States, some one decided they would be a fine thing for Chile. The Chileans improved on our simple installation by putting a small, round cement base in the middle of intersections. On this stood the traffic policeman, protected from the sun, which never gets very hot in Chile, by a huge parasol above which rose the sign. On the very day the system was inaugurated a speeding Ford zoomed up over a cement base and took parasol, sign, and policeman off together. Thereafter the policemen would busily try to keep the signs going with the traffic, not an easy job because the traffic totally ignored them.

Ford drivers thought it great sport to crowd all good cars or carriages against the curb. They would speed up beside you, force you over, and as likely as not damage your car. When I appeared in my stripped-down Lozier, they started coming for me as they had for our handsome Marmon limousine. I turned their game against them. One day I chased a Ford around the block. He was speeding as fast as he could, with the poor passenger leaning out of the window praying and imploring me not to run them down. Of course I could have run right over the Ford. From that time on I had no trouble with the taxi drivers. They kept their distance because they knew I could demolish them—and even might.

2

After a couple of years in the Santiago office I began to lose weight and my family grew worried. I was merely tired from overwork and heavy responsibility, but my father insisted I come to the United States for a medical checkup. Nothing loath, I booked passage for Maria and myself and our eight-months-old daughter, on the *Huasco* of the Compania Sud Americana de Vapores.

During the trip there was a fight among the crew—not unusual on those ships—with the result that the cook came up missing. Investigation revealed a little blood and a small piece of his clothing in one of the portholes down in the crew's quarters. It was discovered that one or more of the crew had killed him, hacked him up, and pushed the pieces out through the porthole.

Ships traveling up and down the coast in those days stopped at almost every port to load and unload passengers and freight. They were the only means of communication with the outside world for many a small port that did not even have a telegraph office. On the other hand, ports that were then thriving centers of trade today almost never see a ship. Before and during World War I, a ship could barely edge its way into Iquique so crowded was the harbor with vessels loading nitrate. Today Iquique is a dead city that sees only a few ships a year.

The sea air and the rest on board ship had brought about an improvement in my health even before we arrived in New York. However, my medical checkup set at rest my parents' fears that I might have some serious ailment. We had a marvelous time in New York. It was Maria's first trip to the United States, and she charmed everyone she met.

During our 1917 visit, I decided to make a tour of all the principal Western mining camps. We took the Lake Shore Limited and were speeding along at seventy or eighty miles an hour when our train crashed head on into a freight train and ripped it to pieces. Our car wound up about one hundred feet off the track in the middle of a field, telescoped at either end. Maria, who was facing forward, was thrown against the table between us (we were playing cards) and rather badly injured internally, from which she developed pleurisy. That ended our Western tour. Maria had medical treatment in New York before we returned to Chile, on a ship that had to run at night with all lights out because the United States had entered the war.

Once in Chile I registered for military service. At that time our ambassador in Chile was Judge Joseph H. Shea, a nice old chap who had been a circuit judge in Indiana and for political service of one kind or another was rewarded with an ambassadorship. As I was the only American in Chile on a friendly footing with society and government people, he continuously opposed letting my service application go through. I finally adopted the device of applying for engineering officers' training camp in the States and sending the application through my father in New York. My arm, which had been badly broken and set in Mexico, delayed matters. I was accepted just as the war ended, so I didn't get out of Chile.

Chapter IX

IN New York, after we entered the war, Father worked very closely with the Naval Consulting Board, of which Benjamin Bowditch Thayer, a vice-president of Anaconda, was a member. Some 300,000 tons of German shipping lay in Chilean harbors; the United States wanted it; Father naturally took advantage of his and my connections in the attempt to persuade the Chilean government to turn it over to the United States.

The matter was handled with typical government efficiency. The Embassy was trying to get the shipping; the War Shipping Board sent down representatives to get it; some miscellaneous business interests, thinking to make a good profit, wanted the ships. Admiral Reginald Fairfax Nicholson, a distinguished retired officer who had commanded the Pacific Fleet, was sent down as naval attaché. His efforts soon so embroiled him with the Ambassador that they couldn't be invited to the same parties. The British and French also had designs on the shipping. Each person involved, including our own government representatives, seemed more concerned lest someone else get credit for the deal than actually obtaining the ships. Fortunately I was in no position to seek kudos. I just kept busy behind the scenes pulling every wire I could.

The negotiations were extremely delicate. The Chileans have great national pride; and they didn't want it to appear that they were being pressured into violating their neutrality. Yet they wanted to help. Finally we arranged an appointment at four o'clock one afternoon between President Juan Luis Sanfuentes and Ambassador Shea. The Ambassador, unfortunately, liked his cups too well; so we urged the second secretary to keep him sober and get him to the palace at the appointed time.

Four o'clock came, but not the Ambassador. He wasn't in the Embassy; he wasn't in the club or any of his usual haunts. The President of Chile was waiting to turn over 300,000 tons of German shipping and the U.S. Ambassador was incommunicado. Finally, toward eight o'clock, in one of the private rooms of the Club de la Union, we found His Excellency peacefully snoring in an overstuffed chair. That is why we never got the German ships.

2

Two Allied committees were formed in Chile. The Central Allied Committee was composed of two representatives each from Britain, France, Belgium, Italy, and the U.S. That committee did very little except handle all the festivities after the Armistice was signed. The important one was the Allied Commercial Committee, with representatives of these same powers. Each nation had two representatives and one vote. This committee was responsible for the black list, a directory of companies not to be dealt with commercially because of their involvement with the enemy.

In this matter of the black list, the British attitude was unexpected and disturbing; and not only in this. When we came into the war a curious thing happened in Chile; an immediate outburst of anti-United States propaganda. We traced it not to the Germans but to the British. The British attitude toward our entering the war impressed me at the time as extraordinary. Many Britishers, including the Minister, Sir Francis Strong, thought our coming in was a mistake. Their explanation was that our entry would only prolong the war. I would reply, "That means that you had already lost the war to Germany, and if we prolong it we'll win it."

At that time I could only assume they thought it would be lost even with us in it. Years later I came to believe that Sir Francis, who was especially insistent on the error of our entry, really meant that if we had stayed out, the war must soon have ended in a stalemate and a negotiated peace, with neither side strong enough to impose conditions destructive of European equilibrium. This I now realize might have prevented the disastrous Versailles peace negotiations, the ruin of Germany, and the rise of Nazism and Communism.

In Chile at that time I first observed the way the British live up to the saying that they are a nation of merchants. Then, and again in World War II, many times I saw them apparently more dedicated to their commerce than to winning the war. I suppose it was because for generations foreign trade has been vitally important to their existence. Whatever the reason, it is something we have to recognize in them, no matter how friendly we may feel toward them.

Some of the American firms in Chile had Englishmen or Germans in charge of their operations. But wherever an American was in charge, our committee had no trouble in getting patriotic compliance with the black list, and no dealings with the enemy at any time. But the British, in that war and in the last, appeared to regard the black list as a way to eliminate competitors and to favor clients they might later want to sell. Repeated cases arose of leading British firms dealing with the Germans.

The pattern three decades later was unchanged. At the time of Dunkirk, surely the darkest period for Britain in World War II, the British Minister to Colombia approached me (I was U.S. Ambassador) for help. I immediately expressed my sympathy for his country's plight, but he soon showed he had little interest in the Dunkirk disaster, the war, or anything but selling textiles. He hoped to sell several hundred thousand dollars worth of cloth to the Colombian army. Assuring me that the textiles did not compete with textiles from the United States, he urged me to intervene on his behalf with the Colombian Minister of Defense, a great friend of mine. And this was all he could think about on that black day of the Dunkirk evacuation.

My experience with black lists proved very useful to me when I went to Colombia as Ambassador just before World War II. In 1935, as Ambassador at the Chaco Peace Conference, I had become convinced that war was inevitable and that we would eventually become involved. A friend of mine, David Matson, one of the chief engineers for the American and Foreign Power Co., had gone to the Krupp Works in Germany to inspect some turbines his company had ordered. He had been an artillery officer in World War I, and as he was led through the Krupp plant to the section where his turbines were he was able to recognize parts of artillery that would have meant nothing to the uninformed observer. He saw thousands of them, and realized the extent of Hitler's preparation for war.

This discovery, reported by me to Washington along with a number of other signs that came to my attention, led to my having black lists prepared as soon as I arrived at our Colombian Embassy. The result was that when all ambassadors received orders from Washington (before we entered the war) to prepare black lists, I had only to turn to Merwin L. Bohan, my commercial attaché, and say, "Merwin, send them in."

My extensive experience in Chile during World War I in composing black lists and making their prohibitions stick was of much value in World War II. On at least one occasion I helped under Secretary Sumner Welles see the folly in a plan proposed by the Brazilian government. The idea was to substitute a list of companies it was proper to deal with for the conventional list of proscribed companies. A white list for a black list, in other words.

By describing how the black list worked in practice, I was able to persuade Sumner (facts always impressed him) that a white list would be absurd and inoperable. I think there was no one else in Washington who could have done it, because no one remained in the State Department who had played an important part in handling black lists during World War I.

3

Among the Americans sent to Chile after we entered World War I was Seymour Ransom, who later became an editor of the *Birmingham News*. He was there as an intelligence officer, and he approached Father and me at once because he realized our knowledge of Chile could be of value to him.

Ransom was in his late forties or early fifties, gaunt, with sparse red hair; not at all prepossessing looking. But he had a good mind and a fantastic memory. His passions were two, equally strong: argument and the ponies. He would bet everything he had on the races, and he usually lost. Often he would eat on pay day and not again for a week unless we fed him.

In argument he could be equally persuasive on either side, and equally ready with accurate citations from the relevant authorities. He argued for the sake of argument. One day my father interrupted him in the midst of a warm defense of an unlikable character, and said, "If you'll defend that fellow, I suppose you would defend Benedict Arnold."

"Absolutely. Benedict Arnold was a very fine character; the best in the Revolutionary period." And Ransom proceeded to develop an elaborate argument.

Father remarked, "Well, that certainly is something. What about Judas Iscariot?"

"There you have it!" exclaimed Ransom. "The real hero of the New Testament."

His argument was that for generations the prophets had foretold the denial of the Savior. Many heroes throughout history had sacrificed their lives for one cause or another. But Judas, to make sure that the Biblical prophecy came true, not only laid down his temporal life but his eternal life as well; and that took a far higher order of heroism.

One night I tried him out when he had been going on for an hour or two, with long verbatim quotations, and was obviously winning the argument. I said, "Wait a moment. Let's reverse. You take the other side."

Like a Chilean pony he wheeled abruptly and tore off in the opposite direction.

One day Ransom came into my office, threw a batch of telegrams down on my desk, and said, "Look at those! We've got something here."

The telegrams consisted of a series of business transactions between a small, rather insignificant Yugoslav firm, Petrushkin and Segal, in Santiago and some firms in Argentina. They were selling so many drums of carbide, so much leather, so much rice, and so on. I asked, "Are these legitimate transactions, or is this a code?"

"It's a code, but they're legitimate transactions."

"How can you tell? Take this telegram, about five drums of carbide shipped to Mendoza. Were the five drums shipped, and paid for at this price?"

"Yes, the whole transaction went through."

But when he began to check up on all those wires, he found subsequent telegrams concerning shipment from Mendoza across the Andes to Chile of five drums of carbide. The companies appeared to be trading the same commodities in both directions, and it didn't make sense. Ransom proceeded to break down the code. That was one of the steps leading to the discovery of the large scale plot involving the German Minister to Argentina, which led in turn to the disclosure of the attempt by some Mexicans and Germans to get the Japanese into the war against us, and to the Peninsula of Southern California scandal.

One of the times my life has been threatened was during that period. Because of my various activities, particularly concerning the black list, some of the Germans threatened that they would "get" me. One night Maria and I were coming home when we saw a shadowy figure step up into the lobby of our house. Maria was terrified; she was sure it was a German about to shoot me. When we entered we found Seymour Ransom, who hadn't eaten anything in two or three days. We took him upstairs and there watched him wash down a big deep dish blueberry pie with sherry wine. That pulled him through until the next day, anyhow.

Chapter X

FROM the early years of the century there had been talk about electrifying the Chilean State Railways between Valparaiso and Santiago, and the branch line running up to Los Andes. In 1919 a group of my wealthy Chilean friends got together to promote the project. They were led by a brilliant engineer of English descent, Ricardo Simpson. Their idea was to form a Chilean company that with my influence in the U.S. would get the Westinghouse agency for Chile and with theirs in Chile a contract from the Chilean government to electrify the railroads.

By that time I had been in mining a little over five years and had gone about as far as I could in Chile. I had never really expected to stay in mining. Father, who had always hoped I would, wanted me to go out to the Western mining camps and get some more practical experience. But I didn't like the work, or living in mining camps. The Santiago and Braden mines were near big cities, but most mines are in remote, inaccessible and uncomfortable areas. I had roughed it enough to know that I preferred the amenities of civilization. In short, I was ready for a change, and this seemed a good opportunity to make it.

While in college I had known the chairman of the Westinghouse board, General Guy Tripp, through his daughters, Molly and Olive. In my youthful self-confidence I considered the acquaintance practically a guarantee of success in getting the Westinghouse agency. After much discussion we agreed that I, though not becoming a partner in the Chilean company—Errazuriz, Simpson & Co., it was called—would have 25 per cent of their profits. They were to finance all overhead and other expenses in New York, and I was to get them the Westinghouse agency.

In July 1919 I came to New York and at once got in touch with General Tripp. I gave him an enthusiastic sales pitch—really quite a show. He said, "Spruille, this thing's been pending for many years. I've followed it. I know more about it than you do. Let me just sum up the situation by telling you that you're a damn fool to fuss with it. You won't get anywhere."

I was somewhat dashed by his remarks. And Father's comment when I repeated them was hardly reassuring: "Well, I'll differ a little bit from General Tripp. I'd say you were a goddam fool."

Whether I was one or the other or neither, I was so persistent, and made life so miserable for General Tripp and other officers of Westinghouse, that I finally got the agency and their agreement to prepare a bid on the electrification contract. Under Chilean law there had to be competitive bidding.

I tried to get an American engineering firm to bid on the construction work, but not one was ready to make a firm bid. Having been spoiled by government cost-plus contracts during the war, they were convinced that the postwar world was too unsettled to warrant taking on such a big contract on any but a cost-plus basis. So we decided to bid on the construction work ourselves—Errazuriz, Simpson and I working together on it. Getting plans, specifications and estimates took a great deal of time, so that we were not ready to make our bid until 1921.

2

There was no reason, I decided, why we should limit ourselves to this one project. So, in addition to Westinghouse, I persuaded the Pressed Steel Car Co., the Worthington Pump Co., and a number of other leading U.S. concerns to appoint Errazuriz, Simpson & Co. as their Chilean agents. Just at that time I met the head of the Archibald McNeil Co., Willis Townes, a very wealthy coal operator and treasurer of the Democratic National Committee. His attorneys were Joseph E. Davies of *Mission to Moscow* fame and Homer Cummings, then chairman of the Democratic National Committee and later for six years Roosevelt's Attorney General. Cummings and I became good friends.

The war had left a world-wide shortage of coal. Chilean coal was never very good, and even that ran short. Errazuriz, Simpson telegraphed me, and I bought the coal from Willis Townes. One order alone was for $1,500,000, and the profits were handsome indeed. Errazuriz, Simpson were more modest in their demands than Townes; even so we made a lot of money.

We sold 25 engines for the American Locomotive Co. and 100 freight cars for the Pressed Steel Car Co. A number of the minor companies manufacturing couplings, brake gear, and so on made us their agents and we sold their products in Chile.

I also brought Chilean products to the United States. I was the first importer of Chilean fresh fruit. Only two ships had refrigeration at that time—the *Ebro* and *Essequibo* of the Pacific Steam & Navigation Co. We brought up some fresh fruit under refrigeration; other fruit was picked almost green and ripened on the way up. We brought in canned fruit. Some of the Chilean peaches were so large that a single peach filled a can. Those brought premium prices at the Ritz Carlton.

We brought in chick peas—*garbanzos*—split peas and beans. We brought in honey—a risky import because we never knew when a paving block would be added for weight. But our biggest killing came when I learned by chance from my barber that Italians loved to get dried cherries, from which they made an especially potent wine (that was during Prohibition). We immediately bought up all the dried cherries in Chile, and made several hundred per cent profit on them. The next year we did less well because other people began to bid for the cherries.

Our business grew to the point where we were beginning to be serious competitors of W. R. Grace & Co., and I didn't like to be too dependent on their ships, which were the most numerous in the Chile trade. This was especially true because W. R. Grace had teamed up with General Electric and the Foundation Co. to bid on the Chilean railways electrification. I wanted to get our own ships, but I didn't want to go into setting up and managing a shipping line.

Percy Chandler of the banking firm of Chandler & Co. had brought together various shipping lines, and also the famous Cramp Shipyard of Philadelphia, in the American Ship and Commerce Corporation, one of the biggest shipping combinations in American history. The nucleus of its fleet were the ships acquired during the war by Kerr and Clegg, two Britishers doing business in the U.S.; and Kerr and Clegg were managing all the corporation's ships. It was to Percy Chandler, as banker for American Ship and Commerce and chairman of its board, that I took our shipping problem.

"I can work that out for you," he said. "If you will invest $45,000 (a token amount) in American Ship & Commerce, we can put ships on the Chilean run, making Errazuriz, Simpson our agents down there. And we'll put you on the board and executive committee of the Corporation so that you'll know what's going on every minute."

It looked like an ideal setup and I promptly made the investment and joined the board and the executive committee, the list of whose members read like a Who's Who in Financial America. There was Joseph Wright Harriman of the Harriman National Bank, Jacob Leonard Replogle of the Replogle Steel Co., one of the Roeblings and so on down the list. President of the company was General George Washington Goethals. Kermit Roosevelt was secretary.

It didn't take more than a couple of board and committee meetings to scare me half to death. The corporation owned the ships that Kerr and Clegg were managing, but Kerr and Clegg owned the companies servicing those ships—a dock company, a tug company, a stevedoring company, and so on. I had no figures on their charges, but I got a strong feeling that they were absorbing all the profits, and American Ship and Commerce the losses.

I went to Chandler and said, "Percy, count me out. I don't know what's going on and I can't make any accusation, but I do know that I don't want to go to the penitentiary; and that's what I'm afraid of from what I suspect is going on."

Percy Chandler said, "Spruille, please stay on for one more meeting. I know exactly what you mean. We're going to take care of that situation. All I ask of you is to bear with me. If, at the end of the next meeting, which is coming in just a few days, you're not entirely satisfied, you resign from the board and the executive committee and I'll buy back your stock at what you paid for it."

That was fair enough; I couldn't refuse. I went to that meeting, and it was dramatic. Percy Chandler opened up on Kerr & Clegg with the most insulting accusations, reciting the facts to back his statements. At last poor old General Goethals turned to him and said, "I'm the president of this corporation and I'm presiding at this meeting. You're accusing these people, and saying that crookedness is going on; and that's accusing me."

"No," said Chandler, "I'm not accusing you."

But Goethals insisted until Chandler said, "All right. If that's the way you want to take it, go ahead!"

Whereupon Kerr and Clegg promised to resign as soon as the legal papers could be drawn. Goethals and Roosevelt both resigned then and there, and all four left the room.

There we sat. One of the most prestigious boards the country had ever seen, directing a corporation with thousands of tons of shipping in operation, but no management.

There I shall leave us long enough to take up a stitch in the thread of my narrative. The great Hamburg-American Line had come out of the war with very few ships and was in the market for a management contract. There was keen rivalry among American shipping concerns over the contract, for they all felt that management by so efficient and experienced an organization would be *ipso facto,* guarantee of success.

Back to our baffled board. With one accord we turned to Chandler, who said, "I have the answer for you. Averell Harriman is waiting down the hall of these offices with his associates. They have signed a contract with the Hamburg-American for management. Mr. Harriman and his associates have agreed to buy the controlling interest in American Ship & Commerce if that is agreeable to you. He will take over and become chairman of the board. He has with him Mr. Richard Hallett Robinson, his top shipping man, who will be president of the corporation."

Thereupon he brought in Harriman and Robinson, also Samuel F. Pryor, a partner of Percy Rockefeller who was interested in the deal; Charles Hayden of Hayden-Stone; and others of Harriman's associates. They were elected to the offices that had just been vacated, and to the board. Then they transferred the Hamburg-American contract to the American Ship & Commerce Corporation.

Next we had to get rid of Kerr & Clegg. For days we had board and executive committee meetings several times a day while we bargained for their stock interest in the company. At last they and their lawyers put over a clever bit of timing.

At a directors' meeting on a late Friday afternoon Kerr and Clegg appeared and formally tendered their stock at $5,500,000. We agreed to buy it. Hidden away in the original contract with them was a provision that once such an offer was accepted they were to be paid in full within twenty-four hours; otherwise they would have a prior lien on the company and could take over everything. At six o'clock Friday afternoon we woke up to the fact that we had exactly half a day and Saturday at that to scare up $5,500,000 in cash—for it was cash they demanded. They would accept no check.

Even in New York, to get that amount of cash on a Saturday morning is not easy. However, the thing was somehow done through the Chase National Bank. Kerr and Clegg presented themselves at the bank that morning. There, laid out on tables, was $5,500,000 in bills. The money was counted into their hands and they stowed it in valises they had brought along. In front of the bank a car was waiting to take them to one of the big transatlantic liners, due to sail at 12:30 P.M.

The payment was made and we were in the clear. But a former and unfriendly associate of theirs tipped off the Treasury Department. Kerr and Clegg took their valises and started to leave the bank. Up stepped Internal Revenue agents and handed them a Federal claim for $7,500,000 in taxes, which the pair had hoped to elude by getting their money to England, out of U.S. jurisdiction. The Federal agents took over their $5,500,000 and placed it in escrow in the Equitable Trust Co. There it remained for years while the tax claim was fought out in the courts.

3

While I was developing our incidental import-export business we were of course preparing to put in our bid on the electrification. Our preparations required an organization of engineers both in Chile and the United States, with whom the Westinghouse people worked very closely from 1919, when we began to get organized, to the job's completion in 1925. My associates and I had to bid for the overall contract: to put in the overhead lines, build the sub-stations, put Westinghouse equipment in sub-stations and locomotives, and so on; so that Westinghouse would be in a way our subcontractor. I have been told that this still is the biggest electrification outside the U.S.A.

The original bid was on delivery to the Chilean State Railways of a completely finished and operating electrification of its lines. One other bidder—a combination of General Electric, W. R. Grace & Co., and the Foundation Co., would agree to deliver the complete job but insisted on a cost-plus contract. Siemens-Schuckert and Braun Boveri also were in competition.

We therefore had an advantage in the fact that we offered to undertake the electrification at a fixed price. The opposition made an attempt to discredit Westinghouse with the Chilean government, on the ground that the company had been through a receivership some years before. That was true; indeed, General Tripp had gone in originally as the receiver. He had pulled the company out of bankruptcy, put it on its feet, and made it a sound and prosperous concern.

I was in Chile when this tactic was tried out. Chilean congressmen began to make speeches questioning whether Westinghouse was financially able to swing such an important job. At once I cabled Ed Kilburn, vice president of the Westinghouse International Co., who was in charge of the Chilean project. I also cabled my father, asking him to go to Washington with Kilburn and see the Chilean ambassador, a good friend of ours. Kilburn was able to furnish the ambassador with all the evidence of the company's solvency that he needed in order to cable his government refuting the slanders.

Our next hurdle was set up by Westinghouse itself. No sooner was it agreed that we were to get the contract than Westinghouse stipulated that for their part in it, which came to some $5,500,000 out of something over $7,500,000, they must have an irrevocable letter of credit. (In those days a dollar was worth two and a half to three times what it is now.) The Chilean government resented this reflection on its credit, about which it was extremely sensitive and which, as I have already said, was excellent. Moreover, it did not have the cash on hand to put up full payment in advance on a contract which would require about four years for completion.

Obviously it was necessary to get a loan for the State Railways. That loan would have to be guaranteed by the government; but the government, which had borrowed some $20,000,000 only a year earlier, was out of money again and there was the danger that it would take over any money loaned the railways and use it for other purposes than electrification. It was therefore imperative that we get two loans.

Let me go back a distance. When I had started to work on the plan for electrification my father had presented me with $250,000 in the preferred stock of Blair & Co., which was a merger of the old banking firm of Blair & Co. with Wm. Solomon & Co. During the 1921–1922 depression he had found himself hard pressed and asked me to return it, which I did. That stock ownership had given me an association with Blair & Co., and I had tried to interest them in the previous Chilean loan. My friends in Chile were so influential that if I had been successful they could have secured for us the profitable business of negotiating the loan. At that time the commission was half of one per cent.

But Blair & Co. were too timid; so that earlier loan was made through what was known in Wall Street as the South American group, which included pretty much everybody who was anybody in the financial world—J. P. Morgan & Co., Kuhn Loeb & Co., Lee Higginson, the National City Bank, the Guaranty Trust Co., the First National Bank of Boston, and a number of others.

Blair & Co. were interested in the new loans. But there was still another hurdle. Joe Swan, vice president of the Guaranty Trust Co. in charge of securities, had very cleverly inserted in their loan contract with the Chilean government a clause obligating Chile to offer the South American group a first option on any further financing. Moreover J. P. Morgan and other members of the South American Group were close to General Electric and wanted the electrification contract for that company.

Once more I had to make the trip to Chile. Fortunately my father-in-law was the largest single stockholder in the Banco Nacional. Although the Banco de Chile was the more important bank it had been involved in the loan from the South American Group, so we couldn't deal with it.

With the help of the Banco Nacional we got the Chilean government to go through the necessary forms. We practically had to break the South American Group contract by inducing the government to notify the Group that it needed and wished to borrow more money. As soon as the government was turned down by the Group, we stepped into the picture with Blair & Co. and arranged for the two loans totalling $20,500,000. They were paid in full within a very few years. We got our contract and Westinghouse its irrevocable letter of credit. We were on our way.

4

Some rather amusing problems kept cropping up. The Chilean government agreed with us that there should be regeneration of power on the downgrades. From Santiago, about 1,500 feet above sea level, the road ran up some 500 feet to the summit, where it passed over and began the descent to the coastal area. That was quite a drop, and through braking apparatus on the cars and locomotives power could be regenerated at a substantial saving.

I also hoped we could do something about controlling the speed of locomotives. I had several times been badly scared on that route. The passenger trains were equipped with air brakes, but the engineers, true Chileans, liked to drive their engines the way the drivers in Santiago drove their Model T Fords. I had often made the run down to Valparaiso in a Pullman with the wheels on one side apparently not touching the rails as we raced round the frequent curves.

At that time freight trains had no air brakes. Instead, there were sidetracks at intervals, running upgrade. As a freight train gathered dangerous speed on its way down, the engineer would blow his whistle, signalling the switchman at the next sidetrack to throw his switch. The train would run onto the sidetrack, gradually lose speed, and come to a stop, then back slowly down to the main track and repeat the whole cycle.

Ideally that was what happened. But sometimes the switchman uncertain if he had responded to the signal, would fail to turn his switch. Then the train would go hurtling down to the next curve and jump the tracks. It was no uncommon sight to see a pile of freight cars down below a curve.

We also had problems in sending employees from North to South America. Americans often seem to suffer a sort of psychosis, or sea change on the way south. Even the normally best dressed women at home once south of the equator would look like frumps in contrast with the latest Parisian styles of the Latinas.

In making the overhead installations we needed an expert foreman. Westinghouse made a careful survey for us, and picked a man who had been with them for a number of years and had gone to the New York, New Haven & Hartford Railroad when it was electrified by Westinghouse.

I personally checked up on him and found he was a sober, hard-working, family man with no bad habits. So I put him on a ship and sent him off to Chile.

Two weeks later I followed him. When I asked my colleagues there how the new foreman was getting along, smiles appeared on their faces. The minute that man had boarded ship he had started to prove he could drink enough whiskey to float the vessel. He arrived in Valparaiso with delirium tremens and had to be shipped right back to the United States.

One little difficulty arose on a sub-contract. The Baldwin Locomotive Co. was supposed to make the chassis of the locomotives for which Westinghouse supplied the electrical parts. The head of Baldwin was Samuel Vauclain, a famous industrialist in his day. Westinghouse told me that Vauclain, knowing that Westinghouse had its contract and its money in the bank, had boosted his price so far above his original estimates that the Westinghouse profit would be seriously reduced.

Thereupon I went to see my friend at the American Locomotive Co., which was selling Chile the 25 steam locomotives I mentioned earlier. His company was delighted by the prospect of making the mechanical parts for Westinghouse.

"We'll meet the Westinghouse price on that very happily," said my friend. And that was all it took to bring Samuel Vauclain back into line.

The electrification was finished, delivered and paid for in 1925. Westinghouse was delighted. During the depression of 1921–22 the company's business had dropped off and the Chilean contract made the 5 per cent difference in the volume of their business that kept them operating at a profit—an excellent example of the importance of foreign trade. Moreover, it was the first time they—or any of the big companies—had made a profit on an original electrification. Competition for such a contract was so keen that a company would take a contract on which it knew it must lose, in order to get its equipment installed. The hope was that orders for replacements and spare parts would eventually turn the loss into profit. But Westinghouse made a very handsome profit on the Chilean electrification.

It came about through good planning, close association with the Chileans, and knowing how to do business in that country. When the job was finished Ed Kilburn, who had become first vice president in charge of both domestic and foreign work, invited me to lunch. Without preamble he told me that the directors of Westinghouse had met, and in view of the services I had rendered the company beyond my contractual obligations in this satisfactory and profitable undertaking, had voted to present me with $25,000 in token of their gratitude and esteem. And he handed me the check.

So I hadn't been such a damn fool after all.

Chapter XI

THE Chilean loans, as I have said, were repaid within a very few years. During that period I participated in some other South American loans, among them one for Santiago de Chile. From others I withdrew after preliminary negotiation disclosed that they involved graft. After 1926 I would not touch a South American loan because I knew that the Latin American governments would be unable to repay the loans being pressed—indeed, almost forced—upon them by U.S. banks and investment firms.

In 1919–1920 the Bolivian government decided to borrow some money in the New York market, and authorized its Consul General in New York, Carlos Gomucio, and its Minister in Washington, whose name was Ballivian, to negotiate. Both came to me and I turned down both. I would have nothing to do with the loan so long as authority to negotiate it was divided.

The affair didn't end there for me. Ballivian proceeded, through a St. Louis firm, Steiffel Nicolaus, to borrow a million dollars from the old Equitable Trust Co. (later merged with the Chase National Bank) on a short-term basis, and permitted a clause in the contract giving Equitable a stranglehold on his government. It provided that until the loan was repaid only the Equitable Trust Co. could handle further Bolivian financing. In 1922, when the Bolivian government wanted to float a long-term loan of $22,000,000, the Equitable offered only 88 for 8 per cent bonds. As this discounting of the bonds 12 points below par value indicated mistrust of the Bolivian government's ability to make good, no Wall Street investment house would touch them. The Bolivians could not pay the Equitable's million unless they sold the long-term bonds.

At that point the Bolivian Minister of Finance came to New York to see me. The minister brought with him S. Abbot Maginnis, a Salt Lake City lawyer who had been U.S. Minister to Bolivia and was now acting as an unofficial adviser to the Bolivians.

My idea was to bring the Bolivian official to the late Eli Bernheim, head of the Columbia Bank, in which my father and I had sizeable accounts. We all, including Father, went to Bernheim, who not only knew a good piece of business when he saw one, but was rather pleased to be named Financial Adviser to the Bolivian government. Bernheim visited the officials of the Equitable Trust Co., and told them he was about to lend the Bolivians the money to pay off their million-dollar loan. Thereupon they came to terms without further delay—reasonable terms, for they saw themselves in danger of losing a $22,000,000 bond issue. Bernheim, who was later decorated by the Bolivian government, got the Bolivians around 94 (a more optimistic figure) for their bonds and received a handsome commission, out of which he in turn paid commissions to Maginnis, to Father and myself.

He also wanted to reward Carlos Gomucio, who had been very helpful. Carlos was pitiably underpaid as Consul General, and needed the money. But he refused to accept it, either in his name or his wife's.

The Bolivian loan was paid off—refunded by Dillon Reed & Co., which at once floated a much bigger loan. I remember that on the day the refunding and the new loan were announced a friend telephoned me to ask whether he should buy the Bolivian bonds. My answer was that if he were to present some of them to me I would call my broker the minute he hung up and order them sold. I knew that $22,000,000 had been absolute tops for a Bolivian loan. But by this time we were approaching the period of speculative delirium before the 1929 crash, and anything in the way of securities could be sold.

2

At about the time I refused to have anything to do with the first Bolivian loan, I acquired a brief interest in Bolivian oil.

During World War I, when Admiral Nicholson and Ambassador Shea were feuding over the German shipping in Chilean harbors, Washington sent to Chile a man, Durell Gage, who appeared to be the only person able to get along with both contestants. We became acquainted, and several years later, in 1919, in New York he approached me about obtaining a South American oil property. He represented a group of bankers who had just cleaned up on a property in Colombia (later a part of the Tropical Oil Co., with which I had a lot to do while I was Ambassador there). Did I know of any oil property they might be able to buy?

I did. I knew that on the eastern slope of Bolivia, down near the Chaco, there were oil seepages, and that experts considered the region potentially rich in oil. Chilean interests controlled a large part of it.

Gage then brought George Kendrick III to see me—a Philadelphian and member of an old banking house that he was about to leave in order to found his own firm. Along with Michael L. Benedum and Joseph Trees, he had cleaned up millions on the Colombia oil deal, and he was eager to get the Bolivian properties at once.

My inquiries in Chile disclosed that five companies had five and a half million acres of oil land in that remote section of Bolivia. Kendrick authorized us to take options on the properties. We formed what was known as the Bolivian-Argentine Exploration Company. We had to act quickly as competitors were bidding for the five companies. By personal influence and authorizing our attorney, Javier Dias Lira, to use my father's power of attorney, we closed the deal within a few days. Kendrick put up the necessary money. But in the midst of our explorations Kendrick found himself in financial difficulties due to the 1922 depression.

He asked me to go with him to Atlantic City and meet with Michael Benedum. He had repeatedly assured me that in addition to his own money (we had checked and knew him to be worth several million) the fortunes of Benedum and Trees were behind the Bolivian deal.

Benedum had one of the hardest faces I have ever seen, and to go with it, a soft sweet voice. He wore black and looked like a sanctimonious curate. Kendrick, who regarded himself as almost an adopted son to Benedum, was confident of his support. But as he explained his difficulties and reminded Benedum of his promised support of the Bolivian oil venture the stony face did not soften by one line. Benedum did, however, say, "Yes, George, I'll support you through thick and thin. Anything I can do for you I'll do."

"Well, Mike, I've got to have so many hundred thousand dollars. I'm in hell's hole."

"Yes, George, I know. I'll support you through thick and thin; but I can't let you have any money."

I was never more sorry for a man than I was for George Kendrick.

In due course Kendrick went broke, endangering several hundred thousand dollars of my father because of my use of his power of attorney. The oil business had been badly hurt by the crash. We were faced with salaries and other company expenses to meet as well as payments due to our Chilean creditors.

By good luck (and I thought good selling) I was able to dispose of the Bolivian properties to Standard Oil of New Jersey. We were paid $1,500,000, which enabled us to meet all the company's obligations with $450,000 over. Kendrick, having defaulted, was out of the picture. Father and I could have taken the money as profit on the deal, but we felt that Kendrick had acted in good faith. His loss was about $450,000. So we turned our balance over to him, and he was deeply grateful.

I was to hear about this Bolivian oil deal years later, from Saavedra Lamas, Argentine Foreign Minister and chairman at the Chaco Peace Conference.

Chapter XII

MY commission on the Bolivian bond issue described in the preceding chapter was most opportune. We were about to buy a house.

After the summer of 1919, which we had spent at Cedarhurst, Long Island, we lived for two years in an apartment on Riverside Drive. The second was rendered miserable by the illness of our three children. There was one period of three months when among them aside from adenoids and tonsil operations, they had 26 ear punctures and the life of our son William, then only two, was endangered by a double mastoiditis involving the jugular vein on one side. At one time I was employing seven trained nurses and nine doctors.

During this ordeal our fourth child and third daughter, Patricia, was born. The following year she too had to be operated on for double mastoiditis unheard of now in this age of antibiotics. That year we lived in a house we rented at Kew Gardens, Long Island. But we were looking for a house to buy.

Maria had fallen in love with an old stone house in Riverdale that we had passed on our way to look at other places. But it was very large, and looked as if it might be beyond our means. It belonged to the widow of George W. Perkins, who had been a partner of J. P. Morgan and financed Teddy Roosevelt's Bull Moose campaign for the Presidency. The estate was called Stonehurst, and was for sale. My commission on those Bolivian bonds made it possible for us to buy the property in 1922.

There were approximately ten and one-half acres, with riparian rights, and that perfectly beautiful old house set high above the river with a superb view of the Palisades. The house was some 130 years old, built of hand-cut granite that had been floated on barges all the way from Maine. The music room and porch had curved walls, built with stones individually cut to fit. Installing the electric wiring (the house had only gas when we bought it), the contractor found seven layers of concrete between floors and ceilings, which broke the bits of drills as his workmen bored through it. We installed crystal chandeliers. Those in two of the drawing rooms were from Aaron Burr's house on Staten Island.

I remember showing the place with some pride to Paul Herzog, a close friend of my father's and mine, who knew a great deal about suburban real estate. When we came to the dining room he began to chuckle.

"This reminds me," he said, "of an old Jewish friend of mine who was doing just what you are doing: showing me around a house he just bought. When we came to the dining room, as big as this one, he turned to me and said, You see, Paul, it can seat fifty people—God forbid!"

An old stable was built of the same stone as the house; I converted it into a garage by knocking out the stalls and shoring up the floor. Next to it was a small cottage for the chauffeur. At one of the two gates was the gardener's cottage. There was a big greenhouse, and later I built a swimming pool. The trees were magnificent, including the most beautiful copper beeches I have ever seen, a remarkable old black cherry, and a gingko tree that experts told me was better than any they had seen in Japan. They came from all over the country to examine it.

The property was on three levels. From the upper gateway, at which we entered, the lawn sloped down to the house and greenhouse—the other buildings were on the upper level, then dropped off steeply to a lower level, and again down to the river. On this lower level I decided some years later to build a large, deluxe apartment house, whose roof located well below the level of our house would leave our view unimpeded. It was evident that as highways were built from Manhattan and the urban sprawl spread to our quiet countryside, we would eventually have to get out. The apartment house I planned would be the first step in a development that would some day include the upper levels of the property.

With my good friend Thurman Lee, then president of Duff & Conger, the real estate firm, I worked out the plan and arranged for architects and blue prints. When I went off to the Chaco Peace Conference in 1935, it was all settled. A Philadelphia bank had undertaken the financing. Thurman was to wire me in Buenos Aires when the steam shovels started working.

Then some of my neighbors began to protest vehemently. The Philadelphia bank withdrew. Thurman suggested I come back and apply to the Reconstruction Finance Corporation for the money to go ahead. Unable to leave the conference, I put him in touch with Cordell Hull and Homer Cummings, and they in turn spoke with the head of the RFC, Jesse Jones, who assured Thurman the Corporation would finance the undertaking.

I never learned just how Jones was persuaded to renege on his promise. But he did. Charles Evans Hughes, Jr., one of my protesting neighbors, assured me they had not tried to block the RFC, though they certainly had continued to protest to Thurman. Therefore I withdrew the suit Thurman had started against them on my behalf. I gave up my project and took a total loss on the preliminary work. The potential loss on the development of both levels of the property easily exceeded a couple of million dollars. Ironically, those same neighbors who were responsible only a few years later went on to build apartment houses, far inferior to my plans, on their own properties.

I am thankful that from 1922 until 1937, when I sold it, Stonehurst was our home—beautiful, comfortable, and an ideal place to bring up our five children.

2

Our move to Stonehurst led me into a curious involvement with the world of sport.

After our trip to the United States in 1917 on account of my health, I had taken up boxing as a regular exercise, and engaged an American Negro prizefighter to box with me. I continued to box after our move to the United States. When we bought Stonehurst I turned the top floor of my garage into a gymnasium with a regulation boxing ring, dummies, punching bags, and weights—all the required paraphernalia.

In the early twenties a lot of publicity was given to a new Chilean heavyweight champion of both South America and Europe, Quintin Romero Rojas. His predecessor, Luis Firpo, had come to the United States and had fought his way up to his bout with Jack Dempsey (who knocked him out in the most thrilling fight I ever saw). Firpo was doing too well to go back and defend his South American title; Rojas won it by default as it were. His backers, a group of wealthy young Chileans, took him to Paris, where he became heavyweight champion of Europe, and then they brought him to the United States.

His young Chilean manager arrived with letters of introduction to me from mutual friends. I observed Romero box, and even invited him and his gentleman manager out to Stonehurst one Sunday to spar with him myself. Romero knew nothing of the American style of boxing. His French trainer had taught him an awkward crouch with both arms up, so that he was wide open for an upper cut or body blow at any time.

They had arranged a match for him with Floyd Johnson, who was taking on some bouts in preparation for a probable title fight with Dempsey. He already had defeated Jesse Willard at the Polo Grounds. It was obvious that Johnson would simply cut Romero to pieces, and I said as much. I added that Romero should not be living in New York. "Even the trees don't grow in Central Park," I said. "Why don't you get a different trainer for him, and, if you like, send him out to my place? There's an extra room in the garage. He can occupy that and eat at the gardener's cottage."

The manager wouldn't hear of it. As I had guessed, the Johnson-Romero bout was a disaster. Romero had the courage of a lion, but Johnson cut him up so badly that the fight was called in the seventh round and Johnson won on a technical knockout.

Pleading business in Paris, Romero's manager asked me to take over the boxer. I said I would not, but would find someone for him.

Tex Rickard, who was then the grand panjandrum of boxing, recommended the firm of Woodman and Lawrence—Joseph Woodman and George Lawrence. I engaged them to manage Romero. His Chilean manager left him a little money, but he was completely discouraged. He thought Romero was through.

I dropped an old Irish heavyweight boxer I had been sparring with and began to train with Romero. The way George Lawrence worked with him was extraordinary. He would match Romero with a fighter having a good left hook—nothing else until Romero got his right hand up against that left hook. He repeated the tactic with other fighters until Romero overcame all his weaknesses.

Woodman had managed Sam Langford, the only boxer I'm willing to admit may have been better than Dempsey. He was so good that Jack Johnson was afraid to fight him a second time. Langford and Woodman would tour the country, and as purses were so small in those days the only way to make money was by betting. Woodman would wager on the minute and round that Langford would knock out his adversary. He sat there with a stopwatch and at exactly the right moment signalled Langford, who would knock the man out.

Lawrence had managed Sam McVey and Joe Jeanette. The four great Negro heavyweights of the period were Langford, McVey, Jeanette and Jack Johnson.

Maria accompanied me to Romero's first fight under Lawrence, at the Velodrome in Kingsbridge, on the Bronx side of the Harlem

River, where the bicycle races used to be held. Romero was doing all right but kept hitting his opponent in the head when it was evident he ought to hit him in the body. I heard Lawrence shouting in English. "Hit him in the belly!" and I began to yell, "Pegale en la barriga!" Evidently in the din he didn't recognize my voice, so Maria took up the cry. He heard her, hit as directed, and won the fight.

The Chilean consul-general was at the fight. He was so appalled to see a Chilean lady at a prizefight and to hear her yelling at Romero that on his next visit to Chile the story got back to Maria's mother. She never recovered from the shock.

Romero won several additional fights. In the meantime Floyd Johnson had fought Boston's favorite, Jack Sharkey, who knocked him out in the second round. Lawrence and Woodman came to me and proposed a match with Sharkey in Boston.

I was astonished. I protested that Romero hadn't come along far enough for that.

"He's ready for it," Lawrence assured me. "He'll lick Sharkey."

Lawrence was right. Romero was the first man who ever knocked out Jack Sharkey. Dempsey was the second. Later, Sharkey went on to win the world championship.

We went to Boston to the fight. Anxious to avoid any misunderstanding over his instructions, Lawrence had me sit in the front row right behind Romero and interpret for him between rounds.

It was quite evident that Sharkey was outpointing Romero through the first four rounds. I expressed my concern to Lawrence, who urged me not to worry. "He'll knock him out in four rounds more," he said.

Sure enough, at the end of the eighth round Romero caught Sharkey and knocked him flat. The bell saved him. His seconds jumped into the ring, hauled him over to his corner, revived him, and lifted him to his feet as the bell struck for the ninth round. Romero started across the ring, but Sharkey took only two steps and fell flat on his face, out cold.

The victory put Romero very much in the running. Rickard and Lawrence planned to have him meet Dempsey at the Polo Grounds in one of those fights that mean as much as $500,000 even to the loser. An enormous fortune to a Chilean peon who had come up from nothing.

Romero was a fine, decent chap. He was like a great big affectionate Newfoundland dog. I remember one day the governess was off duty and the nursemaid was ill. Maria had Romero take our two older daughters to a children's party. Riverdale was a very conventional place. All the other children were there with governesses and maids; and along came this great big husky prizefighter, shepherding two "prim little girls in party frocks."

Romero's career ended tragically. His Chilean manager, seeing his fighter right up at the top, returned and began at once to interfere with the training and management. He bickered with Lawrence and Woodman over the proceeds of the fights, and one day fired them. I have never seen anyone's morale drop vertically from 100 to below zero the way Romero's did. His next match was with a fighter he should have beaten in a few rounds. But he was beaten, and instead of fighting Dempsey he just disappeared.

Chapter XIII

AT about the time I came north to promote the electrification of the Chilean State Railways my fathei decided to retire. He was only forty-eight, but he had made several million dollars and saw no reason to burden himself further with the hardships and responsibilities of developing great mining properties. As I have remarked, mines have a way of being located in the most remote, inaccessible, uncomfortable places. He preferred the amenities of civilized life. He and Mother had many friends in New York; and naturally it was in New York that they settled.

Father bought the Ben Ali Haggin house on the southeast corner of Madison Avenue and 73rd Street, and my mother, who was quite equal to the task, took over the remodeling. Over the years she had brought together a collection of Spanish colonial antiques—furniture, pictures, carpets, silver—that was certainly the finest in this country, and indeed better than many single collections I know of in South America. She remodeled the house to make a setting for her collection. About all that remained of Ben Ali Haggin's was the lofty, two-story living room with its great organ, at the top of the house.

They lived there until my father lost his fortune in 1930. After that the house was sold and Mother sold most of her collection, chiefly to museums.

Father and I had large adjoining offices down town. He would arrive around noon, and leave several hours later to play bridge with such friends as Messmore Kendall and Coleman Dupont.

Dupont was an extraordinary character. A sort of poor cousin in the Dupont family, he went into the great Dupont company and worked his way up to become its head. Unwilling in World War I to participate in profits from the sale of munitions, he sold his multi-million dollar interest in the concern and went into other enterprises. The Equitable Building at 120 Broadway, one of the biggest buildings in down town New York, was his project. His builders were the Thompson-Starrett Company, headed by Louis J. Horowitz. When the building was finished Dupont, as a token of appreciation, presented

Horowitz with a million dollars. He liked that kind of gesture. Along in the middle twenties my father walked into his office the day before Christmas. There sat Dupont's secretary, a man named Dunlap, with his feet on the desk, apparently in a coma. He didn't stir, even in response to Father's "Merry Christmas."

"What's the matter?" asked Father.

"Look at this," answered Dunlap, and handed him a piece of paper he had been holding. It was Coleman Dupont's Christmas present: a check for one million dollars.

Dupont would call up Father on the spur of the moment, perhaps as late as noon, and say, "I've decided to give a luncheon at the Waldorf (he owned the old Waldorf Astoria) at one-thirty, and I'd like you to come." Father would arrive to find a luncheon party of as many as fifty people. Or it might be an impromptu dinner party, with orchestra and dancing.

I remember one such party at Dupont's estate at Tarrytown on the Hudson. Father couldn't go, but I was there with a close friend from college days, Donald Markle. The guests numbered around two hundred—all men, and most of them prominent in banking, business, or politics. In one of the tents located on the lawn there was a big circular bar (yes, Prohibition was on) at which two bartenders kept busy with a cocktail shaker so big it took the two of them to shake it. In another tent luncheon was served, with more cocktails, highballs, wine, and champagne. Still another sheltered circus freaks and a variety of games. On the lawn a large brass band was playing, which the guests, none of them feeling any pain, took turns leading. All this had been arranged between Monday and Saturday. It had also been arranged for an identifying sticker to be placed on each car there. This exempted the driver from arrest between Tarrytown and New York, and considering the condition of all concerned it was just as well.

My father asked me to accompany him to an appointment he had one afternoon with Dupont, Messmore Kendall, Paul Herzog and others at Kendall's apartment above the Capitol Theater. Present was a young woman, Winifred Stoner, to whom Paul Herzog had taken quite a fancy. As an expert in Esperanto she was the youngest person to make *Who's Who*. She was very good looking, husky, and almost six feet tall. As Father and I came in the gentlemen there assembled, all in their fifties (they then seemed ancient to me) breathed audible sighs of relief. The young lady had been boasting of her prowess in jiu jitsu and was trying to persuade some one to offer himself for a demonstration of the holds. I was about twenty-eight and was boxing constantly so that I was hard as nails. With one accord those present nominated me to help her show what jiu jitsu could do.

I remembered having seen a frail little woman in an amusement park outside London throw great heavy men about with jiu jitsu holds; so when this girl came up and got her arm around my neck, her knee behind mine, and my arm twisted back under hers I was paralyzed with fright. I didn't at all relish the ignominy of having her toss me around—especially with sharp-cornered furniture on all sides. Fortunately for me I was literally scared stiff, for in stiffening I did something—I haven't the slightest idea what—that threw her off balance (she was standing on a small rug on a highly polished floor). Up went her heels and down came the Esperanto-jiu jitsu expert, smack onto the hardwood floor and her derriere. She looked up at me enraged.

"Why didn't you tell me you were a jiu jitsu expert?"

"You didn't ask me," said I, and got out of the place quickly as I could.

2

Father and Coleman Dupont were both investors in the Capitol Theater. In 1917 Messmore Kendall—whose original fortune, as I have said, was due to his association with my father—got a long-term lease on the property at Broadway and 51st Street where Loew's Cinerama, formerly the Capitol, now stands. Eddie Bowes, Major Bowes of the famous Amateur Hour, who had been an engineer but had gone into the theater and married the noted actress Margaret Illington, conceived and sold to Messmore the idea of building on the site a huge theater that not only could compete with the Strand, the Rialto, and the Rivoli—at that time the biggest movie houses on Broadway—but would be large enough to warrant combining motion pictures with such added attractions as stars from the Metropolitan Opera.

The construction of the theater, which seated 4,300, was novel in its day. Its balcony, capacity 2,000 persons, was the first to be cantilevered. Up to that time supporting pillars were used, which interfered with the view of a certain number of spectators. Father was responsible for the overstuffed armchairs—the so called "divans"—in the first three rows of the balcony. He said that when he came to the movie he wanted to come after dinner, sit in a comfortable chair, and smoke a cigar, with an ashtray easily available.

My father also inspired some of the murals in the upstairs lobby.

There was a huge expanse of wall there to be decorated, and the painter confessed he couldn't think of a subject. Father said, "Why don't you have a lot of red-haired Amazons being chased by satyrs?" The artist was enchanted.

When I reached New York in 1919, construction was nearing its end, but was soon halted by the financial collapse of the construction company. The owners took on James O'Day, the superintendent for the defunct company, and formed the O'Day Construction Company, with Father as president, in order to finish the job.

Father, being an engineer, took a keen interest in the building. He went there every day. I sometimes accompanied him, and we would climb the scaffolds to the very top. On the top floor Kendall had the apartment I spoke of, with a little stairway leading from his living room to a box at the back of the balcony.

The opening, in October 1919, was a spectacular affair. Everyone who was anyone entered the lobby under blinding lights to the clicking of cameras, and everyone who wasn't anyone gathered out front to watch the arrivals.

Under Eddie Bowes, the Capitol presented what I think was an ideal form of entertainment for such a house. In addition to the regular motion picture, the newsreel, and the shorts, he would offer one act of an opera, performed by the best Metropolitan singers. Audiences would see the first act of *Lohengrin* one week, the second act with the next picture, and so on through the opera. He developed a splendid orchestra; Eugene Ormandy was concertmaster in the beginning, and later conductor. The music at the Capitol became famous, and many people came regularly every week for that alone.

About a year after the opening the Goldwyn Company offered to buy a half-interest in the Capitol for the price of the whole initial investment. It looked like a wonderful deal, but it did not turn out so well. The Goldwyn people persuaded the initial investors to take a considerable part of their payment in Goldwyn stock at the market value of the moment. When the crash came, that stock collapsed along with all the rest.

Bowes was retained as manager, but he was joined by Goldwyn personnel. Later they insisted on having Samuel Rothafel as manager. He immediately began to boom himself as "the great Roxy." His management was inefficient, and he cheapened and vulgarized the entertainment offered. Even the house management deteriorated. My father was very critical of all this in directors' meetings, but to no avail.

He and Dupont had also put some money into the Goldwyn productions. Dupont became chairman of the board and Father of the finance committee. Father asked me to look into some of the Goldwyn activities. I soon found out that the amount actually spent on a production had no relation at all to the amount originally budgeted. Father suggested I come to a directors' meeting and relate the results of my investigations to the whole board. As I walked in the question under discussion was what actor they should get to play Ben Hur in the movie extravaganza they were planning to make in Italy. Someone exclaimed, "There's the man we want to play Ben Hur!"

I am sure they were doing it for my father's benefit. However, they kept on insisting for some time, much to Maria's alarm and my own amusement.

We retained our interest in the Capitol until 1950, when we sold our 50 per cent holding to Metro-Goldwyn-Mayer. It was a good investment and an interesting one. But an occurrence in connection with it during the depression shows how silly valuations can be. Father's Capitol Theater stock was part of the collateral for a loan with the Manufacturers' Trust Co., and I had the disagreeable chore every three months of arguing for extensions for his loans and mine. One day the bank examiner had been in and had appraised the Capitol Theater stock at only $11,000. I pointed out that even though the stock had not paid a dividend for a year or two, it had cost $200,000 and had paid a very good average dividend. But that was the bank examiner's appraisal.

From there I went up to the theater for a directors' meeting at which we decided, since business had improved, to pay a dividend. The amount applied to that stock was $12,000.

Chapter XIV

WHEN I ended my association with Errazuriz, Simpson & Company in 1922 I was offered a position as special assistant to General Tripp, chairman of the Westinghouse board. I could also have become a partner of Blair & Company. Indeed, I had a number of attractive offers at that time. I was twenty-eight, and already had behind me the successful promotion of the Chilean electrification and the sale of the Argentine-Bolivian Exploration Corporation to Standard Oil. My reputation in the financial world was good.

I was particularly attracted by the idea of becoming General Tripp's assistant. I felt that the position could eventually lead to my becoming—with an intermediate step or two—president and chairman of the board of Westinghouse. But my father opposed my taking any position. He argued that it was unnecessary for me, the sole eventual heir to his fortune of several millions, to get myself all tied up in corporate affairs where I would not be my own master. Moreover, he greatly enjoyed our close association and would miss it sadly if I went to Westinghouse, Blair & Company, or any other concern.

I always had great respect for my father's judgment, but this time I am convinced he made a grievous error and that I made one in taking his advice. At the end of each year up to 1929 we went through the discussion all over again. I was impatient and wanted to get out. We promoted some successful deals during the period, but I did not like promotion as a business. To be sure, we were promoting with our own money, as Father used to remind me. Nevertheless I became more and more unhappy.

At last, in order to get away from promotion I agreed to go into a new investment banking house being formed. We began our discussions in the summer of 1929. In September Maria and I were leaving for Europe for several weeks. The Saturday before we sailed I went over all my investments. The market was at its peak. Though I couldn't have told why, I had the feeling things were not right and I wanted to get out of the market. I made a complete list of my securities and resolved to sell everything I had.

On Monday I told Father of my intention. We were to sail the following Saturday. He was disposed to agree that it was a good time to get out. But he cautioned me:

"Don't be foolish. You've got some fairly large blocks of securities and you might depress the market if you tried to sell them all in a few days. I have your power of attorney. Leave it to me. I'll have you out of the market by the time you get back in November."

I began to sell that week, and my father continued—not as rapidly as I had been selling but steadily until the October crash. Maria and I were in Paris when it hit. I was worried, but Maria said, "We came over here to have a good time. The best thing you can do about this crash is to forget it. There's nothing you can do from here anyway; so let's go ahead and enjoy ourselves."

We did. Every day the stock prices were posted on the bulletin board of the Hotel George V, where we were staying. The Paris edition of the New York *Herald Tribune* also carried the quotations. I did not look at either. On Saturday after the calamity of Black Friday, Maria and I were lunching in a resturant on the rue de la Paix when Stanton Griffis, a partner in Hemphill Noyes, Inc., and subsequently one of my successors as Ambassador to Argentina, came in looking very dismal. He made some remark about the catastrophe of the day before.

I said, "I don't know. What happened?"

He was profoundly shocked that any American could sit there calmly eating lunch in ignorance of what had happened to the stock market. But Maria's advice was good. If I had followed the market, I would have dashed back to New York, ruining my vacation and finding myself powerless to do anything after I was there. I might or might not be broke; but I was going to finish my trip. However, my father's cables and letters became so desperate that we did sail for home a week earlier than our original plan.

Father and I did not suffer too badly in 1929. We suffered most when the market recuperated early in 1930. We had seen familiar stocks like Anaconda, which had been about 195, go crashing down to 30. Knowing they were worth that and more, we bought in again—of course on the customary margins with an excessive use of credit. It cost us both practically everything we had. We rescued very little from the debacle. But even worse than the losses was the possibility of actual bankruptcy as the Anaconda stock, which largely secured our substantial bank loans, plummeted to three dollars a share.

2

It was a dark period, and yet I think it was something of a blessing in disguise for my father. When he retired he had made the mistake of withdrawing entirely from his profession. He could have lived in New York and, as John D. Ryan and Cornelius Kelley of the Anaconda Company had wished, become president of the Andes Copper Mining Company and later the Chile Copper Company. Had he done so, with his ability he would no doubt have become one of the great mining magnates of the world.

Instead, he wasted his time on things he knew little about—real estate, for example, in which, excepting the Capitol Theater, his ventures proved none too fortunate. But the aimless way of living began to tell on him. He had never been ill a day in his life. Now he began to get colds, and stay home two days at a time. I was convinced his trouble was boredom, and tried to interest him once more in mining. His trip to Chile in 1928, of which I have already spoken, did him much good. He accomplished in two weeks what no other American could have done at all. And when he told the Anaconda people that he had enjoyed it and did not want to be paid, they sent him a check for $100,000. They knew the value of what he had done.

That convinced me I was right: my father needed to become active once more. I persuaded him to go and examine a property in the Dominican Republic. He began to take an interest in one or two other things.

But the depression was needed to spur him to a serious resumption of professional activity. A promising gold-mining prospect was offered for consideration in the Brazilian province of Goyas. Father assembled Tom Hamilton and an expert in gold dredging and went out to examine it. Typically, that property did not come up to the representations. But finding others that promised well he went to President Vargas, told him of his findings and of his successes in developing mass production of copper in Chile; that it meant large employment, the raising of living standards, huge revenues for the country.

"It also means an enormous investment," Father pointed out, "first of all for exploration. I'm willing to undertake that. But your laws in Brazil make it impossible for anyone here to do what I did in Chile."

After much discussion Vargas promised to have the laws changed. On the strength of his promise Father went ahead with his engineers and developed several likely gold-mining prospects. In the meantime

I had arranged with Averell and Roland Harriman to come in, giving us a backlog of financing far beyond anything Father or I could do.

Despite Vargas's promises the laws never were changed. Father went over to Chile, Ecuador, and even Peru, where he was also interested in gold-mining prospects. But he never found what he wanted —a property to warrant production on a vast scale, like the copper mines he had developed.

Finally the Harrimans dropped out of the picture, and Father renewed his association with the Anaconda Company. He transferred his operations to the Western part of the United States, where he was instrumental in developing properties that Anaconda has gone ahead to work.

Father died as I think he would have wanted to die—in the field looking at mines. He was stricken after examining a property outside Reno, Nevada, in July 1942. I was Ambassador to Cuba at the time, and Messmore Kendall telephoned me around noon to tell me that Father was in a Reno hospital. I was arranging to fly to Reno when Larry Duggan called me from the State Department and told me Father had died.

I have always felt that I was right in urging him to return to mining, away from the boredom of his New York life. Even though he felt keenly the loss of his fortune, I still think his last ten years were far happier than the preceding decade. He was too brilliant, resourceful, and energetic to be really content "to rust unburnished, not to shine in use."

3

The banking house in which I had agreed to become a partner never passed the planning stage. I arranged with Averell Harriman to become an associate of W. A. Harriman & Company, and to make my offices with them, occupying a desk in the partners' room with Averell and Roland Harriman and other partners in the firm. Although I was a partner not in but of the firm, I bought about $25,000 worth of stock; and about the same amount in the W. A. Harriman Securities Corporation, a very closely held investment trust.

If business had been anywhere near normal we might have made a lot of money. There were many opportunities. We had the chance to buy the entire Philco Corporation for some $12,000,000. It was still under the original, excellent management. To illustrate their ingenuity and resourcefulness, they had found that one difficulty of all shipping departments is oral instructions that end in changing the direction of shipments. Therefore, they employed only deaf mutes in their shipping department, to make sure that all orders would be in writing. Having some wiring to be done that required very small and delicate fingers, after careful research they put Filipino women to work on it.

W. A. Harriman and Company could have made enormous profits on the Philco deal, as Philco's subsequent history has proved, but they were too timid to undertake it, even though Walter Chrysler was to become chairman of the board. Another opportunity that in normal times they would have seized without hesitation was a proposal evolved by Ed Kilburn of Westinghouse and me to combine Allis-Chalmers, Brown Boveri, Landers, Frary & Clark, and some other important manufacturers to form a third big electrical company in competition with General Electric and Westinghouse.

Excessive timidity was the penalty of the speculative excesses that had led to the crash. There were many good business opportunities, but it was next to impossible to get them financed.

In 1931 I learned that the Chilean government wanted to end what it considered a too great dependence on some of the bigger oil companies, and was looking for help in building its own refinery, hydrogenation plant, and sales organization. The company acquiring the concession, with the government participating, would have a virtual monopoly.

John Lovejoy, president of the Mexican Seaboard Oil Company and a good friend of mine, very much wanted the concession. I agreed to go to Chile on behalf of his company and some individuals who were also interested—most importantly the late financier Ogden Mills. They agreed to pay me a retainer of $5,000 a month in addition to expenses for Maria and myself, and to give me an 8 per cent share in the business if the deal went through. At my request that the ablest petroleum engineer available be sent with me, Lovejoy engaged Roderic Crandall, who became a cherished friend of Maria and mine. He proved to be of great assistance in Chile because of the confidence he inspired among the government engineers with whom he dealt, including Walter Muller, an old friend and later ambassador in Washington.

At that time Carlos Ibañez del Campo was the dictator-president of Chile. As dictators go he was not bad; but everyone in Chile, especially my friends, detested him. The general sit-down strike that forced him out took place only a couple of days after we left Chile. He could have stayed on, I am convinced, if he had not shirked at shedding blood, for he had the army, the police, and the government workers with him. It is foolishly mistaken to assume that anything short of violent revolution or defeat in a foreign war can unseat a despot who is willing to shed any amount of blood.

Not wanting to base any deal I made in Chile on the favor of a dictator, either actually or seemingly, I engaged as my attorney Ernesto Barros Jarpa, a very able lawyer whom I had known intimately from young manhood. He was by no means in the good graces of Ibañez. He had been exiled for a short time, and was under constant surveillance. I soon found that I, too, was constantly and openly watched.

I went to Ibañez and told him why I was there, pointedly remarking that Ernesto was my attorney and that my sole interest was in an honest business deal. Ibañez was enthusiastic and promised every assistance. In a surprisingly short time I was able to wire Lovejoy that I had been able to get not only what we wanted but even rather more. I was elated.

But not for long. Confronted with success beyond their expectations, Lovejoy's backers, because of the continuing depression, went into a panic and quickly decided they dared not risk their money. Not only was I disappointed in my prospect of participating in an extremely profitable enterprise, I was placed in the difficult position of having to unmake the agreement with the Chileans while trying to retain my friendships and my standing in Chile. While we had not yet actually signed a contract, we had begun to draft it, and its provisions were all agreed to orally, with memoranda confirming them. It was much harder to unmake the deal then it had been to make it. I suppose it was also excellent training for my future diplomatic career, but I was unaware of that advantage as I strove successfully to get out of the affair with my reputation intact.

I got out with honor and came back to the United States. I was footloose. There was no use trying to get into one of the big corporations; they were all letting out even important executives.

One day Thurman Lee, whom I had requested to handle Father's real estate, said to me:

"You're interested in copper. The copper companies are having a hard time finding markets; yet here in New York from 80 to 90 per cent of the buildings have cast iron pipes which have rusted. (Copper tubing was just coming in at that time.) If you could devise a way to finance the installation of brass or copper pipes so that the owners could improve their buildings without having to pay down cash which they don't have at the moment, you might be able to do a big business."

I got in touch at once with my friends in the Anaconda Company, who put me in touch with Len Lilly, president of the First Bank Credit Corporation of St. Paul and Minneapolis, finance subsidiary of the First Bank Corporation, a wealthy group of Midwestern banks. He in turn suggested we also bring in the Crane Company. After much discussion that came to include other companies, Thurman's idea was expanded into the Rehabilitation Corporation. Its scope was precisely what the title implies, and we had graduated from mere replacement of pipes to the remodeling of whole buildings.

We did some minor jobs, but our showpiece was a building on Madison Avenue in the nineties, an old, badly deteriorated apartment house of railroad type flats. We had architects redesign the building, cutting up the long flats into small apartments. Otis put in new elevators and Crane the bathrooms and kitchens. Before a single apartment was ready for occupancy Thurman's company, Duff & Conger, had rented the whole building from the plans at rates that promised repayment of the total cost of renovation within less than three years.

The estate that owned the building had been able to finance the work. When it came to renovation that required outside financing, we encountered an insuperable obstacle in the attitude of the companies and individuals holding mortgages. For example, a savings bank, let us say, would hold a $500,000 mortgage on a building so run down that it was paying at most no more than taxes and a pittance on the mortgage. We proved by example that we could make it once more profitable. But when we asked for a prior lien to secure the financing of its rehabilitation they would draw back. Nothing could be allowed to come ahead of their mortgage, even if their mortgage was practically a total loss.

The extreme case was an old private house on East 72nd Street owned by four men who offered us $15,000 to take it off their hands and relieve them of a $50,000 mortgage they were personally guaranteeing. We were ready to take over the house and put in a further $10,000, remodeling it into small apartments. But the bank holding the mortgage preferred to rest on the personal guarantees of those four men—all hard pressed financially—rather than allow that vacant house to be converted into an income-producing property that, as Duff & Conger could demonstrate, could easily have provided a handsome profit above mortgage, taxes, and the cost of rehabilitation.

The Rehabilitation Corporation had to give up. But the idea was so good that a few years later the Federal Housing Administration began to make loans for the same kind of renovation we had tried. The difference was that where we worked on a sound, competitive business basis, the people who worked on FHA loans quite naturally saw to it that their renovations involved no financial risk for anybody except possibly at times the taxpayers.

Chapter XV

MY first official assignment was brief, easy and interesting. At the age of 26 I was named a member of the United States delegation to an inter-American financial conference in Washington, early in 1920. That does not mean I was one of the half-dozen delegates led by Carter Glass, who had succeeded William Gibbs McAdoo as Secretary of the Treasury. I make this assertion because in recent years everyone in a delegation, even a secretary, is carelessly called a delegate.

I was appointed an advisor particularly to help one of the delegates, Paul Warburg, distinguished as a principal architect of the Federal Reserve System, deal with the Chilean delegation. I knew Samuel Claro Lastarria, its chief, and his colleagues on the delegation. I was one of a dozen or so American advisors. We would all sit around the table with the delegates, who were supposed to be discussing inter-American financial problems following World War I. The problems hardly existed; and those that did develop were insignificant contrasted to the problems generated following World War II.

But if there was little real activity on the financial side, the social side was lively enough and Maria and I had a fine time. We became very friendly with Paul Warburg; also with John J. Raskob (one of my fellow advisers on the Chilean Committee), the Dupont official who later became national chairman of the Democratic Party. It was at a reception during the conference that I first met and briefly chatted with Franklin D. Roosevelt, then Assistant Secretary of the Navy. He was a magnificent looking man, still of course in full possession of his physical powers.

My participation in that conference made me automatically a member of the Inter-American High Commission, which had become a futile organization and expired in due course. I bore the title for some years and used to put it in *Who's Who.*

2

Thirteen years later I found myself once more at an inter-American conference and once more appointed by a Democratic Administration, this time as a delegate. At the time of the previous conference I was a Republican. I had cast my first vote a few months later for Warren G. Harding—a fact in which I take no special pride.

Even when I cast that vote I was already having discussions with Homer Cummings, a Democrat of course, about the differences between the two parties. I had great respect for him, and he influenced my political views. (Like most young people, I had inherited my party affiliation; my father was a strong Republican although he considered Teddy Roosevelt a dangerous radical.) At about the same time I heard Nicholas Longworth make a speech favoring high tariffs and maintaining that the tariff question was not only the most important but almost the only one before the country. That did much to cool my Republican ardor, as did Prohibition, which I considered an iniquitous, demoralizing law. I also preferred the Democratic ideas on foreign policy to the Republican. Besides, I liked Al Smith.

I began to vote Democratic while remaining a registered Republican, and continued this way until 1928, when I was asked to contribute to the Democratic campaign fund and to declare in favor of Al Smith for President. I did both.

At this time I met both Roosevelt and Raskob a second time, on a visit to the Democratic national headquarters in the General Motors Building on Broadway. Roosevelt was there—by that time a cripple. He took me in to talk with Raskob. I have never forgotten that conversation.

Raskob explained the program that he and his associates, including F.D.R. proposed to put in effect, once they gained power. They felt that the general direction of the country had to be put in the hands of the businessmen as the only group intelligent and competent enough to direct the destinies of the nation. In view of the fact that Al Smith was the Democratic presidential candidate and Roosevelt was going to run for governor of New York, the program seems rather startling in retrospect, although I was not struck by its incongruity at the time.

The outcome of that campaign was Hoover's election. And thinking of it, I am reminded of an amusing incident.

My close friend Carlos Davila, then Chilean Ambassador in Washington, invited Maria and me to a big dinner party he was giving at the Pan American Union in honor of a visiting Chilean Minister. The new Vice President, Charles Curtis, who was one-eighth Indian and showed it, was a widower; and official Washington was speculating whether Alice Roosevelt Longworth, as wife of the Speaker, would take precedence over Dolly Curtis Gann, the Vice President's sister and official hostess.

On the way to Washington I teased Maria by telling her she would probably be seated beside Mr. Gann. On one side of her at the table that night sat Lawrence Richey, one of President Hoover's secretaries and a delightful conversationalist. On the other sat a mousy little man who appeared tongue tied. There was some joking back and forth across the table about the Ganns, for Carlos had decided the question of precedence for the diplomatic corps by seating Mrs. Gann on his right. At last Maria turned to the little sphinx beside her, and asked, "Do you live in Washington?"

Oh, yes, he said, he lived in Washington. She glanced at his place card. It read, "Mr. Gann."

After dinner Maria and I circulated. Several times I saw Vice President Curtis talking to her. Suddenly she appeared before me in a perfect rage.

"There's a little *'so-and-so'* who tried to bother me before dinner, and he's been trying to bother me since dinner," she said. "I can't get rid of him!"

All ready to play the wrathful husband, I asked, "Where is he?"

She pointed to Curtis, and I said, "You're just trying to high-hat the Vice President of the United States. That's all."

3

Early in 1933, Samuel Claro Lastarria came to New York for the wedding of his youngest daughter Lucy. Among the wedding guests was the Chilean Chargé d'Affaires Benjamin Cohen (later Under Secretary of the United Nations for Public Relations), who was our guest for the week end. At dinner one evening I happened to mention that I was more or less footloose and wondering what to do next. Ben Cohen suggested diplomacy.

"You supported Roosevelt for election and his Administration is coming in very soon," he said. "You have a lot of friends in it, I've heard you mention William H. Woodin, Homer Cummings, and others. Why not get yourself sent to Chile as Ambassador?"

Why not? Well, what I knew about getting an ambassadorial post was nothing. And my political activity had been confined to one interview with Roosevelt and Raskob in 1928 and a contribution to the campaign fund. I had not even been able to afford a contribution to the recent campaign.

But I liked the idea. Things were completely dead in the business world. It might be very pleasant to go to Chile as Ambassador for a couple of years. The Chilean exchange had gone off badly, and living there would be extraordinarily cheap for Americans. While there in 1931 we had given a couple of extravagant parties and found the cost absurdly low. The United States Ambassador to Chile, I knew could maintain his embassy very creditably without using up his entire salary and bank account. As Maria and I talked over the possibility we became enthusiastic.

Will Woodin, when I spoke to him, thought the idea was a stroke of genius.

"You're just the man, of course. I'll talk to Frank immediately. Whom else do you know?"

"I know Homer Cummings very well. Cordell Hull I know slightly —not well enough to talk to him on this subject."

"Talk to Homer," said Will. "He knows Cordell. I'll speak to him about it."

Homer, too, was enthusiastic. Other friends began to work on my behalf. Jim Farley was ready to help. Then Homer Cummings telephoned me and to my astonishment—for there was really no political reason I should get the Chilean post—said the matter had been decided. "The President told me this morning that you're to go; so begin to make your plans."

Fortunately we were tardy in making plans. Jim Farley called up one noon in May and said, "Spruille, I'm sorry, but all bets are off for Chile."

It was the familiar story of patronage. Vice President John Nance Garner had demanded the Chilean post for Henry Hulme ("Hal") Sevier, who had been sent to Chile by George Creel during World War I to represent the Committee on Public Information. Sevier and Ambassador Shea did not hit it off well, and the Seviers were recalled. Apparently it had rankled; they were determined to go back. And since Mrs. Sevier—known as "Mother of the Alamo"—was the National Democratic Committeewoman for his native state of Texas, the Vice President could hardly be indifferent to their demand. The President, in turn, could hardly be indifferent to the demand of the Vice President. The Seviers went again to Chile, whence they were soon recalled again.

We all thought at the time that my having a Chilean wife and many Chilean friends especially qualified me to be the Ambassador to Chile. I have long known that the exact reverse is true. Far from proving advantageous, those connections must inevitably have proved embarrassing to me as Ambassador. We would have been inhibited in our official entertaining by the need to consider the feelings of relatives and friends. It was known that I had no connection with the Braden Copper Company, and I had sold the last of my Kennecott shares when the Chilean appointment seemed certain: I would have been pretty well immune to charges of favoring American business interests. But I might have been accused of partiality to Chileans and being influenced in their favor by my Chilean wife. I have always been thankful for that disappointment.

Roosevelt had given certain visiting Chilean officials to understand that I would be his Ambassador to Chile, and the probability had become a matter of public gossip. When the news leaked out that I would not be sent, a well-known columnist ran a paragraph about it in his newspaper column saying that both Maria and I had been counting on the appointment. Indeed, he wrote, Maria had been very busy trying to find out what kind of clothes to take to Chile, and in general what life in that country was like. So we had at least one good laugh out of our near-miss.

Naturally both Woodin and Cummings were deeply chagrined. I wrote almost identical letters to them, and I think also to Jim Farley. I said that although of course I was disappointed I accepted the President's decision without question, since it was certainly for him to decide who could best represent him in Chile. Woodin told me afterwards that the President had seemed pleased when shown my letter, and had remarked that I was a good sport. The fact may have had something to do with my appointment a few months later as a delegate to the Seventh International Conference of American States, held in Montevideo, Uruguay, from December 3 to December 23, 1933, and known as the Montevideo Conference.

4

The Montevideo Conference began my official career. Thereafter, until 1947, when I resigned as Assistant Secretary of State in charge of Latin American Affairs, most of my time was spent serving the United States in one or another official capacity—in the foreign field, of course; my disillusionment with Roosevelt's domestic policies began during his first term.

It did not begin as early as that of Will Woodin. Although a Republican, he had contributed generously to Roosevelt's campaign for the presidential nomination. He did not especially want to go into the

Cabinet; but when Carter Glass refused to become Secretary of the Treasury, Roosevelt prevailed on Will to accept the post.

It was said that Glass refused the Treasury because he had asked Roosevelt certain questions about our staying on the gold standard and had not liked the answers. If this was true, I have every reason to believe that Will Woodin knew nothing about it. Although the day before the inauguration he told me that the financial situation looked desperate and that some of the biggest banks in the country appeared about to close their doors, never once did he mention the possibility of our going off the gold standard. If Roosevelt had ever even hinted at such a thing to him, I am convinced he would never have consented to become Secretary of the Treasury.

His distress when the step was taken bears me out in this. By that time his signature was already on Treasury documents and currency, and he felt that his own personal word as well as the Administration's under the law was pledged to back currency with gold. That was not long before he became ill with the throat infection that brought about his resignation in November 1933 and his death the following year. It was the immediate cause of his death, but his doctor told me his chagrin over the abandonment of gold was a contributory cause.

Today I firmly believe that Will Woodin was right. At the time, however, I agreed with Homer Cummings, who as Attorney General advised the President that there was Constitutional authority for the step. (In this, be it said to Dean Acheson's credit, he took sharp issue with Cummings and the two had a nasty fight.) Homer, as I have already said, greatly influenced my thinking at that time, and Homer in turn was influenced in this matter of gold by the theories of Professor George F. Warren of Cornell. He derived the Constitutional right to abandon gold from the provision giving Congress the right to control the currency, and the economic justification from Warren, whose book he advised me to read. I had been so impressed by the spectacle of values wiped out during the depression that I fell for the idea of substituting government monetary controls for the automatic braking effect of the gold standard.

Indeed, I made a speech at the Montevideo Conference defending our abandonment of gold. The action was being criticized there as a purely selfish move to enable the United States to undercut competitors in the world market. I went to Secretary Cordell Hull and told him we were going to find ourselves in trouble if we did not explain. I gave him the reasons as I had heard them from Cummings and others, the President included, and suggested I make a speech. He did not think I should.

"But," he said, "this is such an important question that I think it should be put up to the President."

"Oh, no," I answered. "You make the decision."

"No," said the Secretary, "that's your right. You put it up to the President."

I had never realized before that if a delegate differed with the head of the delegation it was his right to appeal to the President. I told Mr. Hull I preferred not to exercise it, but he insisted that the President should decide. And the President decided I should make the speech. It had a remarkably soothing effect on the assembled delegations, and I was vindicated.

Today I am thoroughly ashamed of that speech. I believe the abandonment of the gold standard was morally wrong. It was an economic blunder that deprived the American people of their right to a redeemable currency, something strongly opposed by the Socialists and Communists. Yet today supposedly responsible bankers oppose our return to the gold standard and even advocate doing away with our gold certificate reserve. This is shocking. It would be like removing the foundation from under a house and expecting it to stand. Decisions these days are in favor of a anomalous self-contradiction called "paper gold."

It is my guess that Roosevelt, when he became President, had no idea of going off the gold standard. I believe he was sold that idea later. It was characteristic of him that the last person to talk to him—especially one with a spectacular idea—had the most influence on him. He loved to shock people; in that he was like a bad boy. I can remember saying to my friends, when they criticized the extravagances of the new Administration, "Franklin Roosevelt is instinctively conservative. It's his intellectual playing around and his desire for the spectacular that get him off on these tangents."

I sometimes wonder whether the tangents might not have been fewer and less harmful to the country if Thomas J. Walsh had not died on the very eve of becoming Roosevelt's first Attorney General. Walsh would almost certainly have considered it unconstitutional to abandon the gold standard. Or if Will Woodin had not been obliged to resign after a few months. Or if Roosevelt's political mentor—creator, rather—Louis McHenry Howe had lived. Or if Cordell Hull had not withdrawn into defensive actions against such extremists as Henry Wallace and Harold Ickes.

We can never know, of course. But we do know that Roosevelt became progressively irresponsible. I had my own experience of this in 1940 and 1941 in the course of visits to Washington from my ambassadorial post in Colombia. As we sat talking in his office, he invariably referred to the Allies as "we"—"We'll lose the Mediterranean, but that won't lose us the war." This from the head of an officially neutral state briefing an ambassador returning to his post with the responsibility of speaking for his chief to the head of the government to which he was accredited.

But at the time of the Montevideo Conference all this was in the future. I could not dream that the innovations due to the President's love of the spectacular might lead in the end to the destruction of the Republic.

Entr'acte

AS I review the notes, documents and records from which I have compiled this memoir, I am somewhat saddened by how much vitality has had to be suppressed in the cause of narrative continuity and brevity or even historical verisimilitude. So far, I have referred only superficially to the vitality of certain persons, some of them central and others peripheral to the main events of my own life and career. Their individuality and force of character have survived the years undiminished in my memory. So, I make room for them here. They deserve a better fate than oblivion. And though the existence I offer them is something less than immortality, it is inspired with my affection.

Perhaps the most prominent in my memory is Tom Hamilton, one of my father's most valued engineers, who appeared earlier in this chronicle. Hamilton was an extraordinary character. He was a year older than my father, and in the old Montana days had come to Father's office to interest him in a mining prospect on a ranch belonging to his mother's—the Fergus—family, who owned the whole of Fergus County. Tom had been raised as a cowboy on the enormous Fergus ranch. He was in his late twenties and, having developed a large herd of his own cattle, was quite affluent.

During Father's visit to the mine (it was no good), Hamilton was so taken with him that he called at the office again and expressed a desire to work for my father. "I want to become a mining engineer," he said.

Knowing Hamilton had had no schooling beyond the first few grades, Father tried to discourage the man. He said it couldn't be done without education.

"I want to do it anyway," Hamilton replied.

My father honored the determination, and put Hamilton to work at various menial chores around the office, as a messenger, cleaning the place up, and "bucking" samples, in which ore samples are broken down and mixed so they can be properly analyzed.

Hamilton refused to be discouraged. After some time he sold his cattle, went East, and put himself through preparatory school. He went on to Rensselaer Polytechnic Institute, where he was quite a football star, and then to Boston Tech. He spent his summer vacations wherever Father happened to be—Bruce Mines, Velardeña, anywhere—and after graduating he joined Father permanently. There were only two years he worked elsewhere, when my father, not being actively engaged in any specific development, loaned him to the Guggenheims. He became an excellent mining engineer.

During this two-year leave Tom was general manager at the Aguas Calientes plant of the American Smelting and Refining Company in Mexico. This was the Mexico of Pancho Villa and other bandit gangs roaming the countryside and marauding small communities.

Tom had about $35,000 in his company safe to pay wages. One gang of bandits learning of this, seized Tom in a raid on the plant and demanded the money. Despite an unmerciful beating, scars from which I saw on his back years later, Tom refused. Nothing would budge him. The bandit leader repeatedly held a revolver to Tom's temple, threatening to shoot. He just did not realize he was not dealing with a timid peon.

The Lord only knows how far the bandit chief would have taken his threats had not a rival gang rode into town. The second gang was made up of miners who had previously worked for Don Thomas but had turned to the more lucrative profession of banditry. They killed or drove off the first brigands and freed Hamilton.

Some days later my father remarked to Dan Guggenheim, who with his brothers controlled A. S. & R., "That was a pretty brave thing Hamilton did."

Guggenheim replied, "He was a damn fool. He should have let them have the money."

Apparently our Minister in Mexico City and the State Department held a similar opinion. They refused even to lodge a protest over this abuse of an American citizen.

Tom had more raw courage than any other man I have ever known. Following the great Chilean earthquake of 1906 external damage to the Braden Copper Mine was extensive and Hamilton set the miners to work on surface repairs. A group of eight or nine agitators saw this as an opportunity for troublemaking and set forth down the road shouting, "Huelga, huelga!" ("Strike, strike!") Tom wasn't about to tolerate a strike in the crisis. Alone and unarmed, he sailed into those tough rotos *(peons) and stopped the action right there, with his fists.*

Like the cowboy of Western lore, he was a dead shot. His skill was often put to the test but never more dramatically than in an episode involving claim jumpers. We had been warned to expect their arrival at an isolated part of the Company's property known as "The Devil's Box," a canyon so rough as to be nearly inaccessible. Hamilton camped out there before dawn, and waited gun in hand. When the gang, employed by a wealthy young Chilean of good family, showed up, Tom shot off their hats. They left in a hurry, giving us no future trouble. One of these hired thugs worked for me years later at another property.

In 1914, when I had just completed college, I was with Hamilton running a 200-man crew building a road and trail into the Andes. Three workers broke into our store through a four-foot adobe wall and stole a quantity of food, dynamite, fuses, and other things. No police were in the area. We soon learned the identity of the thieves and their probable location, not far down the road from our main camp. One of these men had been in an explosion earlier in his life and looked like a creature out of a horror movie. His mutilated face had two holes instead of a nose. He had no ears, just apertures in the skull. He was without hair, eyelashes, or brows. His skin was scar tissue, pink and mottled.

We sent a messenger off on horseback to summon a couple of carabineros (Federal police). The robbers intercepted him and drove him back. Another tried to make it over the range, but they caught him too and sent him back with word that the next messenger would be shot.

"There's only one thing to do," Hamilton said. "We'll take him out between us."

I was green with fear as we escorted the messenger past the spot where we knew the criminals were camped. Hamilton showed no fear at all; he almost seemed to be enjoying the experience. As soon as the messenger was free and clear, we rode back past the camp. Nothing happened. In a couple of days the three thieves, pretending innocence, asked for work. I put them in an isolated canyon, from which they could not escape without being seen, until a Carabinero captain and sergeant arrived to arrest them. The Captain informed us that all our 200 workers either were jail birds or "wanted" for some crime.

Tom was willing to fight with any kind of weapon. We had started exploration work at the Potrerillos property; it was a quiet scene. Until the day a miner came racing down to Hamilton's tent shrieking in fear. A man was hot on his heels brandishing a large knife. Hamilton wrapped a vicuna scarf around his arm, took up a carving knife from the table, and confronted the attacker. "Come on," he said. "Let's have it out!"

The man drew up, crying, "But, Don Thomas, I don't want to fight you. I want to kill him."

Tom replied, "Anybody who wants to fight or kill anyone in this camp has to kill me first!" After further discussion, the entire matter was dropped.

Tom had one defect that my father tried without success to overcome. He could flip a coin and make it land head or tail according as he chose. Father could never convince him that in buying mules for the company he should not take advantage of his art. Tom would bargain with the sellers to an agreed price, then say, "Good enough, but I'll flip you to determine the final price. If you win you get double the price for the mules. If you lose you sell the mules for half the price."

Chileans are born gamblers. They would take a chance every time. And they would always lose. Father repeatedly protested, but to no avail. Tom just could not understand why he was so squeamish.

I learned much from Tom Hamilton over the years. One lesson that rubbed off and stuck was to face up to any situation honestly and be prepared for the consequences. I needed that lesson the day a tough churn driller named Pete Raymond came to my office in Santiago full of anger and profanity. He was a couple of inches over six feet and husky. "I gotta talk to you," he snarled.

Observing the rage bubbling in him, I sat on the edge of my chair ready to jump at a second's notice to grab an ink well or anything to throw—no holds would be barred. Pete said, with curses and obscenities between every few words, "I've been up to the Braden Copper Company looking for work and they said they had checked with you about my work for you in Potrerillos. They said you told them not to hire me. I want to know what the hell this is all about."

"Pete," I replied, "you're just a no-good bum, a disgrace to the United States. You go around to all the bars getting drunk and picking fights. I wouldn't think of hiring you."

I braced myself for the attack. It didn't come. Instead he said, "Mr. Braden, I like an honest man who tells the truth. If I promise to go on the wagon and stop my carousing, will you let them take me on? I need the job."

I agreed to let him take the job if he reformed. He did, and, incidentally, lost an eye from a flying piece of stone. Pete was subsequently employed by Ingersol Rand as one of their principal salesmen and repairmen. He never got drunk again.

I had several memorable moments in connection with my investigations of a property, Lo Aguirre, shortly after going to work for my father in Chile. Accompanying me was an American diamond driller named Wilcox. The only other person there at the time was our Japanese cook.

Wilcox, a husky chap, asked the cook one night if he knew jiu jitsu "Yes," the cook replied, "but not too well. I only know the holds that kill. I don't use it for that reason. I might kill a man."

The reply set Wilcox back a bit but in a moment he continued, "How many people can you handle in jiu jitsu?"

The cook looked us over slowly, then answered, "About two."

Upon which I roared with laughter and Wilcox was thoroughly embarrassed.

As our explorations expanded we built some houses, and were soon joined by a number of American and Chilean assistants. We all ate at the mess served by the Japanese cook. One day rabbit stew was the main delicacy on the menu. I suspect no one would have felt any the worse for it had I not noticed, subsequently, the absence of a pet cat we kept in camp. Our suspicions spoiled appetites for days.

Lo Aguirre, as well as another mine called La Africana, was on a 19,000-acre ranch that we decided to buy to protect ourselves against possible damage suits due to smelter fumes and to provide space for disposal of tailings, i.e., waste material. The negotiations for the purchase of this ranch were bizarre, to be sure.

The ranch's owner, Don Ignacio Larrain Zañarto, was rich but a miser. We offered 400,000 pesos; at that time the Chilean peso was about 2.80 to the U.S. dollar. He refused. Each time we raised our offer to his figure, he would raise the target.

We went round and round this way until, one evening, Judge Elias de la Cruz, a friend of ours and a Supreme Court justice, offered to intervene. He said, "I know this man and I can close the deal with him definitely by noon tomorrow."

Don Ignacio was now asking 1,200,000 pesos. The terms were puertas cerradas, *or "gates closed," which meant that whatever is inside goes in the sale, whatever is outside doesn't. The sale had to be completed by noon the following day.*

It was Friday evening. To get 1,200,000 pesos on a Saturday morning was some job. Moreover, having met that figure, which was quite a jump from my father's offer, we could never settle for less in case the old man backed down again. We decided to take the gamble: we needed the ranch.

The deal was closed at the bank and Don Ignacio was paid his 1,200,000 pesos, in those days quite a fortune. Everyone had signed but the seller. To our consternation, with pen in hand, he hesitated and looked up. "I want it understood," he said, "that the two bags of potatoes and three bags of charcoal in the house are not part of the deal. They belong to me."

We agreed. And the purchase was completed.

Knowing not one thing about farming, I bought some books on agriculture the minute I found I was in charge of a going farm. Mostly, however, I bluffed my way. My method was to involve the different foremen in an argument until I saw them nearing agreement in a sort of Lyndon Johnson consensus, then announce my decision and walk off having concealed my ignorance.

It was perfectly evident to me as to everyone else that Don Ignacio had let the ranch's stock run down badly. My part in the purchase of breeding bulls is surely testimony to the prevalence of beginner's luck.

I had begged off making the purchase myself with the excuse of being tied up in Santiago for several weeks. I would come out and look over the animals after the farm superintendent and cattle foreman had made the purchase. I thought it would be safe to venture out to the farm, but on arriving I found some 30 bulls assembled before the central farmhouse.

The dismal explanation was soon made known to me. As we were buying eight bulls, the owner had sent over these 30, from which I was to make the final choice.

I looked at those animals. Not a glint of intelligence showed in their eyes. I hadn't a clue and might just as well have said, "Eeeny, meeny . . ." Then, getting an inspiration, I said, "I'm going to buy them in the Yankee way."

The "Yankee way" ? ! . . . I improvised madly. "Run a hundred of our cows into the corral," I ordered, "We'll buy on an efficiency basis. If the owner protests, we'll buy ten animals instead of eight."

The cows were run in and the bulls guided to join them. It was easy. Some bulls were ardently interested, others totally apathetic. I picked the active animals. I never did learn if my method was wrong or right.

Servants in Latin America are a rare combination of eccentric habits and intense loyalty. My parents had a mozo, *or general utility and handyman, who travelled with my mother whenever she accompanied my father on trips to the mines. He was devoted to Mother, and refused to spend the night anywhere but outside her door, where he would unroll a pancho and sleep. I am sure he would have given his life to protect her.*

My mother's personal maid was so good that Mother had her

occupy one of the guest rooms on the second floor. This girl's mother became ill, requiring her presence at home. She presently returned with the word that her mother had died, and requested a change in her accommodations. She asked if she could share one of the regular servant's rooms with another maid. This room was small and dark and in no way comparable in comfort to the one she had been occupying.

My mother said, "You don't mean to say that you're afraid of your mother haunting you?"

"Oh no," the maid replied. "She solemnly promised me on her death bed that she wouldn't haunt me. But, then you know, the old lady was such a liar!"

Pregnancies were dealt with in very summary fashion by such girls. During the period my father was developing the Braden Copper Company, my mother had a cook who usually served breakfast promptly at 7:30. One morning breakfast arrived fifteen minutes late. The cook apologized, and explained that during the night she had had a baby.

Petronilla, a nursemaid we brought up from Chile after Maria and I had lived for several years in the United States, handled the matter somewhat differently. Petronilla was a very attractive girl. Some time after her arrival I observed to Maria that our new nursemaid was growing in girth. I thought she was going to have a baby. Maria was shocked at my suggestion, but I insisted, and the event proved the accuracy of my diagnosis.

It was just before dawn on a May morning following a number of thunder showers. Sarah, an older nursemaid who had been Maria's nurse too, woke us with the news that Petronilla was in the butler's pantry preparing to walk to Yonkers Hospital to have a baby. I hurried downstairs. There was no doubt about it, Petronilla was having pains at least every five minutes. Our telephone was dead due to the thunderstorm. Still dressed in only a light silk Japanese kimono I dashed for the police booth just outside my gates and sought help from the two policemen on duty.

The police could not make the call for an ambulance without knowing the reason. As we talked, the rain began again. I was stranded in the booth. The call was made. The policemen exchanged good-natured vulgarities about the readiness of Chilean girls. One remarked to the other, "Mike, Chile's the place for you." "Oh," replied Mike, "New York's pretty good." The rain lifted and an ambulance arrived from Jewish Memorial Hospital.

I trotted back down the driveway to our house. A doctor, who could not have been more than five feet tall, insisted he had to examine the girl before collecting her. The shadows in our lower hall were dispelled by the crystal chandeliers, from which waves of light splashed along the tapestry hanging there and on the enormous stairway. The doctor stood startled. Outside, every blade of grass, every leaf was strung with drops of water like diamonds. The Palisades across the river were suffused with dawning light, and above them and hung across the Hudson was a magnificent rainbow. The little doctor turned around, looked at the house again, looked outside, and after repeating the series several times he cried, "What a house, what a day, what a case!"

Perhaps it was fortunate that the baby died in the ambulance. Maria took Petronilla back and fired the very handsome French butler who had been responsible. But then she hired another equally handsome French butler. One night as we were returning from the theater I saw a light in the basement, and discovered history being repeated. Hence, no more French butler, no more Petronilla.

Before the days of planes it was possible only to make a comfortable trip up the west coast of South America by boat. From these journeys, which I made many times, I recall a crusty old Norwegian sea dog named Captain Selmer. I sailed with him many times. He always had a huge cat seated on a taboret at his side. He loved to play deck golf and always used his own private small, very heavy, playing disk that could knock the competitors' far and wide.

The most remarkable tale told about him starts on a trip south from Panama, which was then filled with malaria. He had called in at Guayaquil, not the healthiest city in the tropics with its endemic bubonic plague and yellow fever. In those days, the ship would stop sometimes in as many as two or three ports a day so that the journey from Panama to Valparaiso could take between two and three weeks.

Towards the end of the voyage, about two days out of Valparaiso, the ship's doctor brought him alarming news. One of the passengers from Guayaquil had plague. He had no chance of recovery but might live another week. Selmer was panic-stricken. His ship could be held up indefinitely by the very strict Chilean quarantine officials. Something had to be done. In the company of the doctor Selmer went to the sick man and explained the situation to him. He laid particular emphasis on the costliness and inconvenience to the other passengers of a lengthy quarantine. And for what? The man was going to die anyway!

Selmer made a proposal that he believed was reasonable under the circumstances. What pleasures would the passenger like before weights were tied to his feet and he was slid overboard? The sick man cooperated splendidly. He said a couple of swigs of whiskey and a cigar would suffice. His requests were complied with and, presently, over the side he went.

I can't vouch personally for the truth of this story. It comes from credible witnesses and is supported by the character of Captain Selmer as I knew him. Moreover, it is characteristic of that long unsupervised period in Latin American history before mass communications and swift transport made neighbors out of the most remote places and the most separated peoples.

During the electrification of the Chilean State Railways, I sent a socially most agreeable young man to Chile on business connected with the project. In addition to acting for me, he became very friendly with a number of young men around Santiago of similar interests.

One weekend a group of them went to a seaside resort called Zapallar, about 80 miles north of Vina del Mar. Their beverage bore the name pisco but it was really agua ardiente, a potion composed of little more than straight alcohol. As the liquor took effect they decided it would be more fun to be in Vina del Mar. And immèdiately set forth in a Model T Ford, carrying two flagons of the agua ardiente for nourishment on the road.

In those days it was a dirt road, with no gasoline stations along the way. At about the half-way point, the motor sputtered and died. All efforts to start it failed until one young man more sober than the others suggested pouring in one flagon of their liquor. The engine leaped to life, and the joyful group was soon in Vina del Mar. The only harm done was to the finish of the Ford. Their hands in pouring the drink were somewhat unsteady and wherever the agua ardiente splashed it removed some of the paint.

Let me complete the roster with two highly individualistic personalities. My father's secretary, Don Carlos Michels, who retired at the same time as my father, was a most picturesque and remarkable man.

Don Carlos was born in Hoboken, New Jersey, of a French father and English mother. He went to Peru in his youth, married a relative of the famous Admiral Grau, and had two sons and three daughters. From Peru he moved to Chile, where he worked in the U.S. legation for a number of years, acquiring knowledge of just about everybody who was anybody. He was a walking encyclopedia of Chilean history from the time of his arrival in the eighties, a fact that greatly enhanced his usefulness to my father.

Father called Don Carlos his secretary; and that is what Don Carlos actually was. But his talents extended far beyond those implied in the *duties he performed. He was thoroughly cultivated, learned, and a linguist with a perfect working knowledge of English, French, Spanish, Italian, Portuguese, German, Greek, and Russian. He could take dictation in any one of these languages and read it back readily in any other. He also knew Quechua and Aymara, the Indian dialects of the Altiplano in Bolivia and Peru. He had taught Latin and Greek in the university. He played the organ in the cathedral; he composed music. He had written poetry and a novel. He was a fair civil engineer and the most beautiful draftsman I've ever seen; his maps were works of art.*

Winter and summer he wore a little collar not much wider than a collar band, and a black string tie that usually rode up under his left ear. He would have his typewriter on a table as high as my chest, and sat at it on a high stool or stood up while typing his letters and singing to himself. The songs were always on religious subjects and always blasphemous. He would type with perfect accuracy, often translating directly from his notes, and sing as he pounded the keys, "Oh, the Virgin Mary, the Virgin Mary . . ." No one knew why Don Carlos was rabidly atheistic and anti-Church, but he was. The fact, however did not prevent his being a great friend of bishops and priests or from being regularly in their company.

In his sixties Don Carlos, having been a widower for several years, remarried. Like everyone else, he had to fill out the required documents at the archbishop's palace. As he turned them in, the prelate's aged clerk, who had been there for decades, apparently forgetting that Don Carlos was not a female, looked up and asked, "Have you been a widower for nine months?"

Don Carlos' cup of happiness was thereby filled to overflowing.

He had a nervous habit of drumming with his fingers on a table or the arm of a chair. Once, sitting with Tom Hamilton behind Father and me on a train, he absentmindedly delivered his tatoos on Hamilton's knee. The outburst of profanity this provoked was unforgettable.

Tom would never dictate to Don Carlos if he could help it. Perhaps the older man had an inhibiting effect on him. Tom's letters were on the fantastic side because he would put in all his cussing, and he was the most ornate cusser I ever heard. His swearing was really something of an art, combining his early cowboy profanity with that of his later mining career. Any restraint on this, such as Don Carlos may have represented, would have been unwelcome.

Maria met an American original on her first trip to the United States. The lady was the mother of a family friend, known to her family and friends as Lady Elizabeth, a strikingly beautiful woman even in her old age. She had been widowed when her son was a small boy, and had never remarried. Her reputation for uninhibited eccentricity was exceeded only by the fact.

Shortly after our arrival in New York, Lady Elizabeth took my young wife of eighteen months to lunch. In the course of their conversation she completely shocked Maria by saying that as an elder woman she wanted to give her the most valuable advice one woman could give another: Do not have any but young lovers.

I was not shocked at all; I had known this Lady Philosopher too long.

Indeed, one of my earliest memories is of accompanying my maternal grandmother—prim and rather old-fashioned in a dress that buttoned up the throat, with a little lace cap—to Lady Elizabeth's home in Connecticut, a house of her own design consisting chiefly of a vast hall. The rain came at about the same time we did, and the roof began to leak. Our hostess immediately furnished us ladders, shingles, hammers, and nails and instructions to locate and repair the holes in the roof. I didn't mind but my grandmother was not amused.

At about this same time the son presented his mother with a one-cylinder Cadillac, known as a "one-lunger," that she would drive between her home in the rolling hills and Stamford. After more than a year, about to drive the car himself, he inquired if there was water in the radiator.

"Water!" she exclaimed. "What does a car need water for?"

When we moved to New York, Maria came to take Lady Elizabeth more or less in stride. But it wasn't always easy. One evening not long after we arrived, Lady Elizabeth telephoned our house in Cedarhurst to say she was at a roadhouse nearby with her present "young lover," a tall and very good-looking Major. She asked whether they might drop in for a nightcap. We assented, and waited. The interval extended; we decided she was not coming, and retired.

It was a hot night. I was in the shower when Lady Elizabeth and her Major arrived. Maria and her sister Laura, then staying with us, were not dressed. I half dried myself, drew on a silk robe, and descended. Maria and Laura shortly joined us. The robe was clinging obviously to my damp legs, and Lady Elizabeth demanded to know what I had on under it.

"None of your darn business," I answered.

Whereupon she made a grab for the robe, which led to a mad chase as I vaulted over chairs and sofas to keep out of her reach.

Some years later my mother, returning from a trip to South America, brought some beautiful old Indian gold bracelets for the aged eccentric. When she called to present them, she found Lady Elizabeth in bed. She had finished one bottle of gin and was well into the second. The tears flowed as she explained that the Major had left her for a famous retired opera singer, who also happened to be very much his senior. That particular "young lover" may possibly have read Benjamin Franklin's advice to young men to find their mistresses among ladies of advanced years.

Chapter XVI

THE Montevideo Conference took place at a discouraging juncture in inter-American relations.

It was generally known that Carlos Saavedra Lamas, the enormously egotistical Argentine foreign minister, intended to stir up as much trouble as possible for the United States. We were in trouble with the Nicarauguans and the Haitians. We had refused to recognize Grau San Martin in Cuba; therefore we knew we could expect trouble from the Cuban delegation. The only country in this hemisphere that had recognized Japan's puppet government in Manchukuo was El Salvador; we could count on difficulties there. Above all, the Mexican foreign minister, José Manuel Puig Casauranc, had been campaigning against this country through various Mexican embassies and legations for a good half-year. And he had left for Montevideo with a considerable retinue more than a month before the conference, travelling down the west coast of South America and visiting the capital cities to bring pressure to bear on the foreign ministries to oppose the United States. His active hostility was partly due to political ambition: if he could organize and .lead a successful opposition to the North American colossus his prospect of becoming President of Mexico would be greatly enhanced.

All grievances, real or imagined, were exacerbated by the depression. The Latin Americans had been forced to default on the bonds they had sold through United States banks, and yielded to the natural temptation to blame someone else—and with some reason—for their own foolishness. The banks that had made it easy for them to overborrow were also at fault. Still, the foolhardy borrowers were not thereby absolved.

Flaming up in the background was a renewal of the bitter dispute between Bolivia and Paraguay over the Chaco—this time with far more serious fighting than before. The two nations were carrying on a savage war in that disputed desert and swamp land. No wonder that State Department enthusiasm for the conference was—to understate—muted. Edwin C. Wilson, head of the American Republics

Division (whom I had known when he was third secretary in Chile) said frankly, "Spruille, I'm just praying to God every hour of the day that somehow, something will cause this conference to be cancelled before our delegation gets to Montevideo. Otherwise it's going to be an utter catastrophe."

My own optimism, which no one seemed to share, may have been partly due to ignorance. But I had my reasons. The first was the "good neighbor" policy the new President had announced. The second was his domestic platform of 1932, which, as now forgotten, was genuinely conservative and his early speeches, which I felt must have impressed the Latin Americans. The third was the appeal of the sincerity and what I may call the Lincolnesque quality of Cordell Hull.

2

The pessimists could also refer beyond Latin American attitudes to the failure of the London Economic Conference, held during the summer. Curiously, that failure had persuaded Hull he must go to Montevideo. James C. Dunn, Chief of Protocol in the State Department and Secretary to our delegation, told me that on the way back from London, when he and Hugh S. Cumming had urged Hull not to attend Montevideo, the Secretary said, "I am going to that conference because I've come out so badly on this one. I'm going down there to make up for the London fiasco."

And on the way to Montevideo, Hull said to me, "You know, this delegation is a great relief after the one I had in London. I was never able to finish a meeting in London because there was always a race among the other delegates to get to the reporters."

A great deal has been written about the London Conference and how Raymond Moley scuttled it. After I got to know Hull well he told me that when it became evident that Roosevelt was supporting Moley his own instinct was to get on a ship at the end of the conference and sail east instead of west, just dropping everything. Instead, when he got back to this country he drove up to Hyde Park to see Roosevelt before going to Washington. Homer Cummings, who drove with him and Mrs. Hull as far as Tarrytown, said when he left them, "stop in for a minute on your way back and tell me how your interview with the President came out."

As Homer later told the story, when the Hulls stopped on their return, the Secretary, pulling his forefinger across his own throat, said of Raymond Moley, "I cut the son of a bitch's throat from ear to ear."

"Jedge," protested Mrs. Hull, "don't use such language."

In the "Jedge's" conversation such language, I may say, was pallid.

A story then current about Hull's father was so characteristic of the son that I always felt it might well be true. The elder Hull was said to have been a Confederate soldier, captured early in the Civil War and sent to an Illinois prison camp where he was outrageously treated—actually beaten—by one Captain Smith. Before long the Captain was transferred to new duties. His victim remained a prisoner until the war's end. Three years later he found Captain Smith in California and shot him dead. Only then did Cordell Hull's father go home.

The Secretary had that same grim tenacity. I have sat in his office when one or another Roosevelt favorite was trampling on his official toes, and seen his lips thin to a slit in his face as he said, "I'm bidin' my time."

Raymond Moley had been the outstanding leader of the first "brain trust." He had gone into the State Department as Assistant Secretary at the time Roosevelt was inaugurated. He was much closer to the President than the Secretary of State. But when Hull got through, Moley was not only out of the government, he was out of Washington and estranged from Roosevelt. Later the story was repeated with Sumner Welles. Sumner, like Roosevelt, was a product of Groton and Harvard. He was a page at the wedding of Franklin and Eleanor Roosevelt. The President liked him, and Welles used to go over and discuss policy with Roosevelt, leaving the Secretary of State completely out of the picture. Moreover, when Hull was away Welles would make statements of policy that he knew to be contrary to the policy of his official chief. Knowing Hull, I told Sumner's friends several years before he went out that Hull would get him. He "bided his time," but he did it.

Hull was not only implacable, he was also powerful. I was convinced, from conversations with Roosevelt—his choice of a word, a fleeting expression—that he did not like his Secretary of State and would gladly have dispensed with his services rather than those of such favorites as Moley and Welles. But Hull was one of the most highly respected and influential figures in the Democratic Party. He was not to be eased out, and he was too self-respecting and strongwilled to be safely bypassed.

One member of the New Deal with whom he could hardly contain himself was Henry A. Wallace. I was in Hull's office one day when Henry telephoned to discuss a speech he was planning to make.

(Henry, of course, was Secretary of Agriculture, not State; but he loved to make little excursions into foreign relations.) I sat there at least ten minutes while Hull listened, nodding his head occasionally and saying, "Yes Henry. . . . Yes, it's all right for you to say that, Henry. . . . Yes, Henry, . . . [very sweetly] I'm very glad to have you make that speech. . . . Yes, I understand you perfectly. . . . Yes, it's all right, Henry."

At last he hung up the receiver and turned to me with, "Of all blankety blank fools, that fellow is the worst."

Under his surface hardness, however, and his frank and picturesquely profane distaste for fools in general and certain brightly stupid, over-assertive New Dealers in particular, there was much kindliness in Hull. Also great sincerity and singleness of purpose. His conduct at the conference completely vindicated my expectation that his personality would do much to win over the Latin Americans.

We had been in Montevideo only a few days when he said to me, "Do you think it would be appreciated as a courtesy if I were to go around and call on the chairman of each of the other delegations?"

I answered that I thought it would be a fine gesture. The next morning, a Sunday, he spoke of it again and again I expressed my enthusiasm for the idea.

"Come on," he said, and off we went.

One of the first chairmen we called on was from a smaller country. He was living with some distant relatives who were evidently in extremely modest circumstances. We arrived at about 10 o'clock; and before the man was even up and shaved he was being told that Secretary Hull and another U.S. delegate were calling. He was completely flabbergasted but at the same time tremendously impressed and grateful.

Hull proceeded to call on every chief of delegation. The only one showing any sign of frigidity was Saavedra Lamas of Argentina. All the others were deeply appreciative.

After our return from Montevideo it was decided to form an Advisory Committee to the State Department on Latin American Affairs, composed of all who had served as delegates at inter-American conferences. I was named chairman—an easy assignment, as the committee was never asked for advice and never had a meeting. However, Hull several times summoned me to Washington to discuss some aspect of our relations with Latin America. At other times when I was in town he would ask me to come to see him at his apartment in the Carlton Hotel. There, over our highballs, we discussed world affairs in general and Latin America in particular. He was always completely frank about his conversations with the President and about his opposition to some of the more extravagant New Deal measures, which he found appalling. I believe he was equally frank with anyone else he regarded as a friend. It was an association I always appreciated and enjoyed.

3

In addition to the Secretary of State, the U.S. delegates to the conference were: Alexander W. Weddell, Ambassador to Argentina; J. Butler Wright, Minister to Uruguay; J. Reuben Clark, former Ambassador to Mexico; Professor Sophonisba Breckenridge of the University of Chicago; and myself.

Weddell had been in the consular service long enough to attain the rank of Consul General. When it appeared he would not be promoted into the diplomatic corps, he resigned and went to live in Virginia, where he busied himself rebuilding an ancient monastery imported from England, stone by marked stone. With its gardens, the reconstructed building became a show place. But its owner still had diplomatic longings in him and having contributed to the Roosevelt campaign (his wife was very wealthy), he intimated he would be happy to be made Minister to Greece, of which he was fond. But the U.S. Embassy in Buenos Aires was notoriously expensive to run, and the Democratic Party of that day had few millionaires. To his astonishment, Alexander Weddell was offered the post of Ambassador. He was a fine looking man, tall, handsome, and well groomed, and invariably pleasant and courteous. His wife was disposed to be somewhat arbitrary and to command everyone around her.

The third delegate, J. Reuben Clark, was a high official of the Mormon Church. He was a former Under Secretary of State, and had been employed by Dwight Morrow, at a salary probably higher than Morrow's own, to go to Mexico with him as his political advisor. When Morrow retired as Ambassador, President Coolidge, on his recommendation, appointed Clark to succeed him. Clark was a lawyer, very conservative and conscientious, not spectacular but solid and dependable. Both Maria and I liked him, and our relations with him were always very friendly.

J. Butler Wright was a career diplomat. Indeed, Roosevelt might have had him in mind the day in Washington he defined to me the conditions for a successful civil service career: 1) never be late to the office; 2) always be sober on the job no matter how much you may drink in your off hours; and 3) live long enough.

Miss Breckenridge was added to the delegation at the last minute at Mrs. Roosevelt's urging. She was head of the woman's college and professor of Public Welfare Administration in the School of Social Service at the University of Chicago. She knew nothing of foreign languages nor of Latin American nor any other foreign affairs, and was completely out of her depth throughout the conference.

James C. Dunn, secretary to the delegation, was one of the ablest chiefs of protocol the State Department ever had. He later became special assistant to Secretary Hull, a position he held for several years. At the same time as I became Assistant Secretary for American Republics Affairs, Jimmy became Assistant Secretary for European Affairs. After that he served as Ambassador to Brazil, Italy, and France. He was a polished diplomat, and when he retired a few years ago he had behind him a long and distinguished career, in which he had been ably seconded by his wife, Mary.

The assistant to the chairman of the delegation was Hugh S. Cumming. His father, Dr. Hugh S. Cumming, was for years head of the Public Health Service in Washington and a most distinguished medical man. Hugh was a youngster at the time of the conferences. He went on to become a thoroughly able and competent career man. Among his posts have been those of Charge d'Affaires in Moscow and Ambassador to Indonesia.

Ernest Gruening, afterwards Governor and most recently Senator from Alaska, was general advisor to the delegation. He had recently resigned as an editor of the *Nation,* and right after the conference he was appointed head of the Division of Territories and Island Possessions in the Department of the Interior. Our morning conferences in Hull's suite on the ship to Montevideo were always enlivened by red hot debates between Gruening and Clark. Gruening, although quite inclined to the Left, is an intelligent and able man and I got along equally well with him and Clark, and mostly kept out of their arguments.

4

The *American Legion,* carrying four of the six delegates, sailed from New York on November 11, 1933. Weddell and Wright were at their posts and would meet us at the conferences. Mrs. Hull accompanied the Secretary of State, Maria was with me, Mary Dunn accompanied her husband, as did several other wives of men connected with the delegation.

The wife of a distinguished technical adviser caused quite a stir on board ship and later in Montevideo. At a party on our way down, a young Argentine politely invited her to dance. On the floor she asked him his nationality and being told he was from Argentina she gushed, "Oh, then you're one of those gigolos. I'm so glad! I've never seen a gigolo before."

She never understood why he left her standing in the middle of the floor.

Another time we met her on the stairs on the way to lunch. She stopped us and said to Maria, "Oh, Mrs. Braden, they tell me you have three children."

"No," Maria answered, "we have five children.

"You don't say so," exclaimed the lady. "How *did* you do it?"

"You're married, aren't you, my dear?" asked Maria.

"Yes."

"Then you know how it's done."

After we reached Montevideo this same misguided lady decided she wanted to live as the Uruguayans lived and to learn Spanish. She therefore would not stay at the hotel with her husband and other delegation members, but sought accommodations in a boarding house. Her way of locating one proved unsatisfactory. She instructed a taxi driver to take her to a boarding house, calling it *casa de fonda.* He took her directly to an assignation house. These are fashionable establishments where men can meet ladies not their wives. A butler opened the door to our courageous American and led her into a bedroom, where she found a naked man lying in bed with ice bags on his head. The lady beat a hasty retreat to the delegation's hotel, her enthusiasm for doing as the Uruguayans did considerably diminished.

On board the *American Legion* our companions were the Haitian and Honduran delegations, two advisors to the Mexican delegation, and one Venezuelan delegate. The ship stopped in Bermuda, and when we left we had on board two young Cubans, sent to oversee—practically dictate—the activities of the Cuban delegation. One was the student leader, Carlos Prio Socarras, who later became President of Cuba; the other was a medical student named Padilla. As we were expecting trouble with the Cuban delegation, I was glad of the opportunity to have some long talks with Prio, which later turned to our advantage.

Another passenger on the *Legion* was the late Doris Stevens, omnipresent lobbyist at international conferences on behalf of the equal rights, or extreme, wing of the women's movement. Miss Stevens was jailed for picketing the White House during World War I, and got a husband out of the episode: Dudley Field Malone, a promising young

Democratic politician, who indignantly resigned as Collector of the Port of New York and acted as lawyer for the pickets. The couple was later divorced. Miss Stevens proved to be a real, rough and tough politician, and did not hesitate to lead her cohorts right onto the floor of the Conference, breaking up discussions in the most rowdy fashion. All this to the horror of Miss Breckenridge, who like Mrs. Roosevelt belonged to the more moderately behaved wing of the movement, which wanted both rights and privileges—but gradually. The Stevens flying column invaded the secretariat at the close of the Conference and attempted to change the wording of resolutions in which they were interested.

All that was later, of course, and highly educational to a person like myself, who had never before had the slightest contact with any women's rights movement. On the ship Miss Stevens chiefly discussed her former husband, whom I knew, speaking about him with disconcerting frankness.

5

When we arrived off Montevideo we were requested to remain on board until the foreign minister, Dr. Alberto Mañe, could come aboard and welcome us in person. He arrived with a retinue of aides, one of whom was an army captain resplendent in a lavishly gold-braided white uniform with many decorations. This gorgeous creature came up to me, called me by name, and greeted me with evident delight. He then asked about Sra. Braden. I pointed Maria out to him.

He greeted her with the greatest cordiality, and asked about each of our five children by name, which wasn't easy—Maruja, Laurita, Pat, Bill, Spruilleito. He wanted to know whether we still lived at Stonehurst. All the time I was trying to place him, but found nothing in the least familiar about him except a peculiar rectangular cut in the pupil of one eye. I knew I had seen it somewhere, sometime, but where or when I couldn't remember.

"Of course you remember Dr. Pujol," he said. I saw that I should remember Dr. Pujol.

"Oh, yes, of course. How is he?"

"He's fine. You know he's a Minister now."

Suddenly I remembered seeing the name in a list of the Uruguayan Cabinet members. I said, "Oh, yes. I understand he's Minister of Education."

"No, he left that a couple of weeks ago." The gods were with me. He had left that post just about the time we sailed from New York.

"He's now Minister of Defense. He sends you his regards, and his apologies for not being down to welcome you this morning. He had to attend exercises at the military academy. But he is very eager to see you. When can I call for you and take you to the Ministry?"

Knowing that the first few days would be pretty busy, I suggested the fourth morning hence, and we arranged that he should call for me at eleven o'clock. He could not have been more effusively friendly.

All I knew was his name: Captain Godin. It meant nothing to me; no more than that of the new Minister of Defense. Discreet inquiries about them yielded nothing to connect them with the United States or with myself and my family. The mystery began to prey on my mind.

On the fourth morning Hull called a meeting of a couple of delegates. Among other things we discussed the Chaco War and the need for a permanent peace. He had certain ideas about it that he wanted to present to the Uruguayan President, Gabriel Terra. But J. Butler Wright pointed out that if Hull went direct to the President the Foreign Minister, Mañe, would be deeply hurt. On the other hand, if Hull tried to put his program up to Terra through Mañe, the Foreign Minister, being none too bright, was sure to bungle it. We all agreed with Hull's ideas, but how to get them before the President was not clear to anyone.

The meeting broke up a few minutes before eleven, and I was told that Captain Godin was waiting for me downstairs. We had a Presidential car, and off we were whisked, with a motorcycle escort, to the Ministry of Defense.

I could hear my name being echoed down the long corridors as we entered. We were ushered at once into the Minister's office. Dr. Pujol, a small man, greeted me cordially. I remembered having seen him somewhere. I even had a vague memory of sitting across a table from him; but that was all. I was becoming really distressed.

After a little conversation he summoned the Under Secretary and told him to give me his telephone number at the Ministry and his home number as well. Anything I requested was to be done; apparently if I wanted to call out the Uruguayan Army I just rang up the Under Secretary of Defense. Then he asked if I was still interested in athletics and when I answered in the affirmative he invited Maria and me to come to the equestrian and gymnastic exercises the following Sunday at the military academy. Dr. Pujol then inquired whether there was anything else I'd like to see while in Uruguay. Uruguay had won the soccer championship at the last two Olympic Games. I said I would greatly enjoy seeing one of their champion soccer teams.

Did I think the other delegates would be interested? I was sure of it. Once more he summoned the Under Secretary.

"I want you to arrange for an international soccer match between a picked team of Uruguayans and a picked team of Argentines. Ask all of the delegates."

The match, which was really quite a spectacle, was put on in a big stadium at night, under floodlights.

My conversation with Dr. Pujol ended with protestations of mutual esteem and promises to meet frequently during the Conference, as we did. As we left, Captain Godin introduced me to the officers and other gentlemen sitting in the anteroom. And one after another, like so many parrots, they said, "Ah, yes. Mr. Braden—the great friend and protector of South Americans in the United States."

At first I thought they were joking but they were perfectly serious; and still it did not stimulate my memory. Captain Godin said, "Now the President wants to see you."

At the Presidential palace Captain Godin left me with the President's secretary, who said, "The President is in the garden and would like to receive you there if you don't mind."

Of course I didn't mind. The President and I chatted for an hour and a half. Away in the back he had some chickens and dogs and an orchard that he showed me. We would saunter around, then sit on a bench and smoke. It was an ideal opening to present Secretary Hull's views on the Chaco War, with which I later became so closely connected.

When at last we went into the house he got out two pamphlets he had written and inscribed one to Maria and the other to me.

On the way in I had discreetly tried to learn something about Captain Godin from the President's secretary. All I got out of him was that Godin had been the first army officer to back President Terra in the palace coup d'état that had made him almost a dictator. When I left, Terra accompanied me to the door. As Godin came up, the President said to me, "You know, I love that boy as if he were my own son."

By this time "that boy" unwittingly had me about ready for a nervous breakdown. As we drove back to the hotel, preceded by our police escort, he turned to me and said, "You know, Mr. Braden, that I can never adequately thank you for all you have done for me. But I want to show you, in so far as I can, how deeply I appreciate it."

He produced a package wrapped in tissue paper. It was an old double-barrelled duelling pistol.

"This belonged to my great-grandfather," he told me. "It's a thing I've always treasured, and it would make me eternally happy if you would accept it as a small token of my gratitude."

I was simply overwhelmed with embarrassment and chagrin. How could I have so completely forgotten a man whom I had placed sufficiently in my debt to warrant such a proof of gratitude?

Then, to my enormous relief, I remembered.

One day when I had gone out to train with Romero at Stonehurst I found with him a down-at-heels, forlorn looking *Latino* whom he introduced as a veteran of the World War, a former sailor on a windjammer, and a former light heavy-weight fighter. Romero asked if I could help him. I gave him one of my suits and a few dollars. Then as an afterthought I said, "Until he gets on his feet he can occupy the other room here in the garage and take his meals with you at the gardener's cottage. And by the way, you might speak to Woodman and Lawrence about him. Maybe they can get a couple of fights for him so he can earn the money to get back home."

The newcomer settled down as a sort of sparring partner for Romero. Lawrence and Woodman did arrange some fights for him, and eventually he earned enough money to go home.

While he was there I decided one Saturday morning not to go to my office. Instead I went out to box with Romero and his companion. With them was a little man who was introduced as a friend of the down-and-out boxer, a university professor under whom the boxer had studied at one time. I found him a cultivated and interesting man.

Around one o'clock the professor asked how he could return to New York. There was no train, and the chauffeur happened to be away. I invited him to lunch with us and that accounted for my feeling that somewhere I had sat across a table from him.

For the boxer, of course, was Captain Godin, and his friend the university professor was the Minister of Defense, Pujol.

President Terra had personal as well as political reasons for being devoted to Captain Godin. He was troubled by water on the knee and had vainly sought relief in Buenos Aires, New York, Paris, Vienna—all over the world. Godin, by reason of his boxing experience, was able to relieve the condition through massage. The first thing he did every morning was to go to the palace and massage the president's knee.

Throughout the Conference he kept me informed of the President's state of mind about it. And every night he telephoned or saw me to ask if there was anything I would like him to mention to the President the next day. As for Terra himself, he couldn't have been kinder or more attentive.

He carried his friendliness to an embarrassing length on the last day of the Conference. Our Minister's wife, Mrs. Wright, failed to pass on to Maria and myself Terra's invitation to a lunch he and his wife were giving. Meanwhile, we had accepted a luncheon invitation from the Haitian delegation, which had been one of our special charges throughout the Conference.

"Don't forget that the President is expecting you and Mrs. Braden for lunch."

"I'm sorry, but we haven't been invited."

"Oh, but you have."

"No," I said. "No one has said anything about it. As a matter of fact we have an engagement with the Haitians and we can't hurt their feelings."

"Let me find out," said he, and hung up.

A few minutes later he called again.

"Absolutely you were asked. The invitation was sent through the Butler Wrights, and the President is expecting you. He will wait lunch until you come."

"But it's one o'clock now," I protested, "and the lunch is at one. The other guests must be there by this time. We haven't even finished dressing, and it will take us an hour to get out there."

"That doesn't matter. The President says he is going to wait for you."

Maria was more nearly ready than I. She made our excuses to the Haitians and invited them to dine with us that night—which meant our staying in Montevideo an extra day instead of leaving for Buenos Aires with Secretary and Mrs. Hull. We arrived at the President's palace after two o'clock. We had kept the United States Secretary of State, the Ambassador to Argentine, the Minister to Uruguay, and all his other guests waiting until Maria and I could get there, two reluctant and embarrassed lions but lions whether we would or no.

Throughout the Montevideo Conference, thanks to Captain Godin, the U.S. delegation enjoyed the cordial good will and cooperation of the host country. Never, I venture to say, did an amateur's interest in boxing pay off more handsomely in diplomacy.

Chapter XVII

AS I look back on the Montevideo Conference, I am impressed by the inadvisability of choosing delegates to international conferences for reasons having nothing to do with ability, experience, knowledge of international affairs or languages, or anything else but politics. Most international conferences do not last long enough for a delegate, even with the best of advisers—and our State Department used to, perhaps still does, provide excellent technical help—to learn his way about in time to make himself really effective.

It happened that I enjoyed several advantages over most political appointees honored with membership in such delegations. I was bilingual, and became the first United States delegate to an inter-American conference who made all his speeches and conducted all debate in Spanish. Every member of the Chilean delegation and its staff was my warm personal friend, and I also knew a number of the other Latin American delegates on a first-name basis. I had lived abroad and my business career had brought me into close touch with international affairs. Some of my experience had even verged on the diplomatic. Nevertheless, being new to the job of full delegate, I was a bit timid in the beginning.

Timidity prevailed in the first full meeting of the economic committee. I was sitting with my alternate, J. Butler Wright, when Alfonso Lopez, who soon became President of Colombia, indirectly attacked the United States. He said he didn't know why Colombia continued to send delegates to inter-American conferences, because the smaller countries were always brushed aside. Nothing was ever done about their wishes; indeed, they weren't even allowed to express them.

I turned to Butler Wright and said, "I'm going to answer, and tell him that so far as the United States is concerned, we want the smallest nation to express its views with complete frankness and will listen to them with as much respect as to those of the biggest nation."

Wright promptly went into a career man's dither of caution. "For God's sake," he urged, "don't say a word."

Unsure of myself I kept still, and lost an opportunity I afterwards regretted. A week later I wouldn't even have consulted Wright; I would have answered Lopez. Subsequently I made the statement as I had wanted to in the first place.

As the debates went on I learned that in these conferences the success of a proposal may not be determined by its merit. More important is the way it is handled. In a subcommittee of which Lopez was chairman, I found that our stand on the important issue of patents was opposed by a majority of the Latin Americans. I explained our position to Lopez in detail. He agreed we were right, but suggested that if I were to defend our position during the debate the effect might be to harden opposition. He offered to take the initiative, and I accepted.

He did a magnificent job. Only a couple of times did I have to break into the discussion with arguments he had forgotten. That experience taught me how helpful a "front" can be.

On another occasion the Mexican foreign minister Dr. Manuel Puig Casauranc, chairman of the fourth committee on economic and financial matters, was sponsoring a proposal concerning the organization of the conference that we did not like. With my intention of overcoming his antagonism to the United States, I did not want to oppose him in the discussion. My good friend Rodolfo Mezzera of the Uruguayan delegation agreed to front for me, knowing that as a delegate of the host country he would have great influence with the committee.

Rodolfo started his remarks by praising the wisdom and perspicacity of Dr. Puig Casauranc and spoke of his proposal in the most flattering terms. Being a novice, I thought he had changed sides and wondered what had happened. But as I sat there, Rodolfo began very skilfully to edge away from total approval. There were, he said, certain defects in the proposal—a most praiseworthy proposal, as he had said; still, there were defects. By the time he reached his eloquent peroration he had most politely riddled it, and when it came to the vote he won decisively. I wasn't obliged to open my mouth except to vote.

The lesson I learned from that experience was expressed in a few words during the later Chaco Peace Conference by the Brazilian Ambassador to that conference, José de Paula Rodrigues Alves, one of the ablest diplomats I have ever met and an intimate friend. I asked him, "What would you say is the fundamental lesson for a diplomat?" "Well," he answered, "it's the old saying we have in Brazil: *Tienes razon fero poco, y el poco qui tienes no vale nada.* [You have reason on your side, but only a little. And the little you have is worth nothing.] That is the precept above all that a diplomat must follow."

There, in a nutshell, is the art of diplomatic contradiction, in which Mezzera gave me an invaluable object lesson. I have used it repeatedly; and its usefulness is by no means confined to diplomacy. I improved on it as time went on, learning that in diplomacy one can get away with the most unlikely argument if one is careful to choose just the right approach, and just the right language.

The importance of knowing the language of other discussants can hardly be exaggerated. Even a simultaneous translation is a poor substitute. The interpreter may give a literal translation; but the best interpreters will make mistakes in the little nuances upon which so much of the meaning depends. Intonation and emphasis are lost; or a touch of humor, so that a delegation may think a thing has been said in ill temper that was really uttered in jest. All these pitfalls considered, I wonder that this country comes off as well as it does in those international conferences where its delegates do not understand the languages of the other countries represented.

In plenary sessions the language is not so important as in committee meetings. Often, sitting with other delegates around a table, I have overheard a remark that revealed another delegate's mind. At one meeting in Montevideo a vote was impending in which I very much wanted a majority. I was unsure of the Salvadorean vote. Overhearing an aside of the Salvadorean delegate on the matter under discussion, when I spoke I was able to include in my speech an apparently casual remark that reassured and satisfied him. In the division we got the Salvadorean vote.

2

The social side of the Montevideo Conference was typical, as I afterwards learned, of such international gatherings, even though Secretary Hull had asked that it be limited. It was limited only by the number of possible occasions for social affairs. Every lunch, every dinner was turned into a social function. There were afternoon receptions and evening receptions. Balls lasted all night. The Argentine embassy and grounds seemed to be permanently illuminated. They had three dance floors, with four orchestras for each, so that the music was continuous. Champagne bars were located strategically, with elaborate buffets. The Brazilians gave a magnificent ball in one of the big hotels; the Chileans in a restaurant and the park around it. These were enormously expensive affairs, with all delegations present, all of the diplomatic corps, all of the Uruguayan government officials, and all of Montevideo society—that is to say, hundreds of guests.

Maria and I drove back to our hotel at 6 A.M. from the Chilean affair with several Chilean delegates, including the Foreign Minister, Miguel Cruchaga Tocornal. On the way Gustavo Rivera, President of the Liberal Party and later a senator, asked me, "What did you think of the party?"

"It certainly was a good one," I answered. "You had everything."

"Of course," he remarked, "we're only able to do that because of the money we borrowed from you. Now you understand why we can't pay our debts."

I thought there might be something in it.

A conference is really about a twenty-hour job; it requires an iron physique. As much of its important work is done at lunches, dinners, receptions, banquets, and balls, the delegate has no choice but to attend these social functions. He must be prepared to take all the food, liquor, and late hours, then snatch a couple of hours sleep, rise, and shower before racing off to the next committee meeting or plenary session to see that the promises extracted at last night's banquet or ball are kept—including his own. If he isn't there to see to it, they sometimes won't be, and the defaulting delegate will be ready with a plausible excuse.

Because so much official business is transacted at these social affairs, the wives of the participants play an extremely important role. In general, a diplomat's wife can make the difference for her husband between success and failure. The contribution of my own wife, Maria, to whatever success I may have had in diplomacy was beyond calculation.

She was far more than a delightful and tactful hostess, although that she certainly was. Her charm, intelligence, and quick understanding made her enormously helpful in handling difficult situations and people; also in picking up information. In Montevideo I began, and developed during my subsequent diplomatic missions, a technique of working designedly through her.

Due to protocol, I always pretty well knew who would be at a given dinner and who would sit next to Maria, and I would make known to her the purposes that required her assistance. I always made a point of briefing her on anything of importance where I felt that she could put in a word. She was wonderfully clever about it, with an appearance of completely disarming innocence. She was very successful, both at finding things out and at putting things over. If there was any kickback, nothing official, after all, had been said; it was just a wife's gossip.

Maria also had a great advantage by being a *Latina*. She was told things by Latin American officials that would have shocked them if they had paused to reflect that she was also the wife of the United States delegate—or ambassador, as the case might be. They spoke to her much more freely than they would ever have spoken to me—or to her if she had been European or North American.

In passing, I may add that by the time I was ambassador in Cuba and Argentina, my three daughters were old enough to have a social life. I taught them, too, to keep their ears open, for their young friends might be juniors in the foreign office or under secretaries in other embassies who would gossip about subjects of interest to me. They frequently picked up bits of useful information.

3

Secretary Hull's charge to Maria and me to look after the Chileans and some other delegations included the Haitians—four delegates and a secretary, ranging in color from the coal black of Antoine Pierre-Paul to the near-white of Edmond Mangones. I mention color, because we learned that in Haiti there is as sharp a color and social line between the blacks and the mulattos as there is in this country between Negroes and whites. This division had a bearing on the strange patois spoken by Pierre-Paul, which his colleagues found difficult and sometimes impossible to understand. If addressed in either Spanish or English, he would respond with a blank stare, and his patois would, in turn, have to be translated into English or Spanish. This continued until my first speech, explaining our action on gold. When I finished I was immediately surrounded by delegates congratulating me both on the content of the speech and on having delivered it in Spanish. Among them was Pierre-Paul addressing me in perfectly good Spanish. He employed the strange patois, I learned, because it was the speech of the Haitian blacks, and Pierre-Paul wanted to dramatize his tie with them.

He was the delegation's firebrand. We had hardly left the ship in Montevideo when he gave an interview bristling with hostility to the United States. Maria spoke to Mangones about it (her French was much better than mine) and through him I received a promise from Justin Barau, chairman of the delegation, that it would not be repeated. Later the Haitian delegation met with Hull, Jimmy Dunn and myself, and gave further assurance that there would be no more attacks. Yet a few days later Pierre-Paul sounded off with another, which made headlines in all the Montevideo papers.

Maria was having people for tea that afternoon, among them Mangones. I got an evening paper to her before he arrived. When he came in she received him so coldly that he asked what was wrong. Maria answered, "You are always talking about discrimination against race and color. You must realize that what counts is the way people act, not what race or color they are. You and your associates gave your word that there would be no more attacks on the United States. Yet look at this newspaper. How do you expect to be respected and treated as equals if you will not live up to your obligations?"

Maria afterwards told me that Mangones blanched. He assured her that from that day there would not be another word out of Pierre-Paul. How they managed to silence him we never knew; but that time the promise was kept.

On board ship Maria and I had become friendly with two members of the Mexican delegation, an association that led to neutralizing Mexican hostility to the United States. Although no decision had been made, I was sure that the New Deal, having abandoned the gold standard, would raise the price of silver and that if we began to subsidize domestic producers of silver we would extend the subsidy to the Mexican producers. Knowing that the Mexicans wanted currency discussed at the conference, I held out this prospect to our Mexican shipmates. Before we left the ship they asked me whether I would be willing to discuss matters frankly with Puig Casauranc. Of course I was willing.

The second night after our arrival the two advisers, Maria and I had dinner with Puig and his wife, Maria Elena. We talked until the small hours, and during that time he showed me his telegraphic instructions from the President of Mexico while I went after him on the prospect of our purchasing silver.

There were three main points in the Mexican President's instructions, all opposed to our goals. That night I persuaded Puig to withdraw two of them, and later got him to modify the third. Later a misunderstanding developed about what our policy was to be, but Secretary Hull, with Saavedra Lamas and Miguel Cruchaga Tocornal, the Argentine and Chilean foreign ministers, listening, confirmed categorically the statement I had made to Puig. From that time on we had no difficulty at all with the Mexican delegation.

On the last day of the conference I went to Puig's office at his invitation, to pick him up for lunch. When I entered the outer room the door to his private office was open. With him were half a dozen delegates from other Latin American countries to whom he was talking emphatically as he paced the floor.

"You may think I don't know what's been done to me at this conference," I heard him say. "I know perfectly well. You did this, and you"—to someone else—"did that. The only friends we have had in this entire conference have been the United States delegation. They're the only ones we could count on and get along with."

He had been our avowed and most assiduous enemy before the conference. And his complete about face was largely due to the personal friendship I developed with him.

The Cuban delegation was headed by Angel Alberto Giraudy, a judge and an unprincipled radical who later, while I was Ambassador to Cuba, became a card-carrying member of the Communist Party. As the previous conference was held in Havana, it fell to Giraudy, according to custom, to make the opening address at Montevideo. Everyone was apprehensive about what he might say. His speech, as first written, was violently anti-United States, but Macedo Soares of Brazil, Cruchaga Tocornal, and even Saavedra Lamas managed to persuade him to reduce his anti-Americanism to less hysterical terms. A pretty ill-natured character at best, he managed to antagonize just about everybody by charging that Argentina, Chile, and Brazil were mere satellites of the United States. Whenever he really warmed to his subject his false teeth would drop and he would have to stop and push them hastily into place. This somewhat detracted from the effect of his eloquence.

So much for the delegations we had been most concerned about. Saavedra Lamas was also a potential trouble-maker, a role in which he was both expert and ingenious. Macedo Soares, chairman of the Brazilian delegation, and Cruchaga Tocornal of Chile took him in hand and saw that he did not become too troublesome. He came nearest to it in his demand that since the London Economic Conference had been such a fiasco there be held another world economic conference in Buenos Aires. He argued for it insistently and at length, and was finally satisfied by a resolution calling for a pan-American commercial conference at Buenos Aires in which financial matters might be discussed. When the time came, in 1935, I went to that conference as chairman of our delegation, largely because the State Department felt I might be able to handle Saavedra Lamas.

4

Perhaps the outstanding result of the Montevideo Conference was the general improvement it brought about in the atmosphere of inter-American relations. This was due in no small measure, as I indicated in the preceding chapter, to the sincerity and simple friendliness of Cordell Hull. The success of the conference was largely his personal triumph.

The most significant concrete achievement was also Hull's. His insistence on going to Montevideo "to make up for the London fiasco" was not due to vanity—though he had his share of that—but to his realization that he could not put over with his own compatriots his idea of freeing trade unless he could show that it had substantial support abroad. His success in getting general agreement on it at Montevideo was gratifying and important.

Indeed, I am inclined to think that if Hull had succeeded in having freer trade endorsed by the London Conference, World War II might have been deferred long enough for further steps toward peace to be taken. A general easing of the world's economic tensions would have meant a quicker recovery from the depression and prevented—to mention only one possible result—Mussolini from going to such extremes as invading Ethiopia and later joining with Hitler to form the Axis. Hull could have achieved agreement on it at London—as indeed he almost did, for the British and other European delegations were more sophisticated and experienced than his own publicity-obsessed colleagues—if Roosevelt had backed him up.

Hull's singleness of purpose in furthering his program accounted for his deal with Saavedra Lamas, who at first was disposed to be troublesome. Hull quickly got to him, and in return for Saavedra's support of his program agreed to endorse Saavedra's famous anti-war pact—the pact that, with United States help, eventually brought him the Nobel Prize.

This pact had been submitted to many countries separately, as the Kellogg Pact had been, and also to the League of Nations. It won few signatures; not because the various countries were against peace but because the pact already, in fact, existed. Saavedra Lamas had it drawn up by Daniel Antokoletz, an Argentine of Serbian parentage who was one of his specialists in international law (and a member of the Argentine delegation at Montevideo). It contained nothing that was not in the Gondra Treaty, adopted at the Inter-American Conference at Santiago, Chile, in 1923, or in other inter-American agreements and the Kellogg Pact. It was a rehash with Saavedra Lamas' name attached. The Brazilians and Chileans didn't want to sign; they thought it was a silly and meaningless duplication. Neither did we want to sign. But Hull, seeing no harm in the thing, played up to Saavedra Lamas' vanity by agreeing to support it. And his endorsement brought a number of other signatures.

The Agreement on the Rights and Duties of States, better known as the Non-Intervention Treaty, was another important achievement at Montevideo. Intervention was a charge our Latin-American neighbors, especially the smaller among them, felt fitted the United States. Cuba was especially resentful of the Platt Amendment to its constitution and the subsequent so-called "Permanent Treaty." These recognized a special United States interest in Cuban affairs, and had been forced upon it after its liberation from Spain as the price of withdrawal of United States military forces from the island. Hull not only assured the conference that the policy of the Roosevelt Administration was one of scrupulous respect for the sovereignty of other nations, as the public statements of the President had already shown; he was also able to cite a recent statement of willingness to open negotiations with the Cuban government on the hated amendment and treaty. This made a most favorable impression on the Latin Americans. The promise, of course, was kept and the offending amendment, with its implementing treaty, abolished much to the annoyance, as I found out later, of many Cubans. The wisdom of this course since has been brought into doubt by a long series of events, culminating in the Communist seizure of this island under Castro.

There was a great deal of excitement at the time over what everyone hoped would be a permanent cessation of the war in the Chaco. The League of Nations had sent a commission headed by Julio Alvarez del Vayo, the Spanish writer who later became foreign minister in the Communist-dominated Negrin government of Republican Spain, to ascertain on what terms peace could be made between the belligerents, Bolivia and Paraguay. This commission was in South America when the Conference took place. After some discussion the First Committee, on the Organization of Peace, decided the Conference would not be interfering with the work of the League Commission if it also offered its services in bringing about peace in the Chaco.

When the resolution to that effect was about to come up before the Conference in plenary session, the two belligerents attempted blackmail. They threatened that if the amendment were brought up and adopted they would withdraw from the Conference. So terrified were the other Latin-American delegations by the threats that one plenary session was actually cancelled. At a four o'clock meeting that day Hull put up a determined fight to keep the frightened *Latinos* from postponing the next day's session. The meeting dragged on into the evening, with Hull eloquently maintaining that nineteen sovereign states should not permit two little nations to dictate whether they were to meet in plenary session. He had apparently lost, and the delegates had actually risen to leave, when he made a final, and this time successful, plea.

The next day the Bolivians and Paraguayans—being largely Indian they are great bluffers—turned up for the plenary session.

The combined efforts of the conference and the League of Nations commission established a two weeks truce. At its final plenary session, on December 26, the conference was addressed by Alvarez del Vayo and we heard many flowery speeches celebrating the armistice, with much cheering. All it came to in the end, unfortunately, was the extension of the truce for two more weeks. Then the fighting resumed.

Our engagement with the Haitians had prevented Maria and me from going with the Secretary and Mrs. Hull to Buenos Aires. We did, however, arrive in Buenos Aires in time to see the Hulls before they left for a train tour through the lake district and then to Santiago de Chile. We visited friends in Buenos Aires, then flew to Santiago for New Year's Eve. Two or three days later Secretary and Mrs. Hull arrived. The American Society entertained them at a reception, and President Alessandri at a dinner that same night.

The Secretary asked me to meet him at the Embassy the next morning at eight. Our ambassador was Hal Sevier, who had unknowingly done me such a great favor when he demanded, and was given the Chilean post.

As I entered the hall of the Embassy the next morning I came face to face with Hugh Cumming. He was looking perfectly aghast.

"My God, Spruille!" he exclaimed, "the Ambassador's all lit up already!"

The Seviers, it will be remembered, were soon recalled from Chile a second time.

Chapter XVIII

THE timing of the Pan American Commercial Conference demanded by Saavedra Lamas became a matter of protracted negotiation in which Hull's objective was to fix a time when Alec Weddell would be on leave. Since Weddell knew little about Spanish and less about commerce, and most certainly could not handle Saavedra, the Secretary did not want him in the delegation. But after the date had been set, Weddell changed the time of his leave. Therefore, as the United States Ambassador to Argentina, he had to be named as chairman of our delegation. He was glad to leave the de facto leadership to me.

Our third delegate was Julius G. Leahy, an old consular official who had become Minister to Honduras when the consular service was merged with the diplomatic service. He served there for seven or eight years, and finished his career as Minister to Uruguay. Once again, we travelled on the *American Legion.*

On board with us was another old friend, José Manuel Puig Casauranc. He was no longer foreign minister, but was on his way to his new post as Mexican ambassador to Argentina. He was of course chairman of his country's delegation to the Commercial Conference. With him were his wife and four children.

Mary Elena Puig Casauranc at that time was one of the most beautiful women I have ever seen; and in her qualities, too, she was extraordinary. She told many amusing stories about the life of Mexican officialdom. The leading Mexican politicians used to resort to a house outside Mexico City and there gamble for high stakes and long periods, drinking heavily the while. When Mary Elena, as a young bride, discovered that José Manuel was going out there she just went with him. There were assorted hussies around the place, but they did not daunt Mary Elena. She would settle down on a sofa and sleep while her husband played poker. She never let him out of her sight; and it was a good way to handle Puig Casauranc.

Stopping off at Montevideo I found I had been scheduled to speak at three luncheons on the one day we were to be there. I took soup at one, and made my speech. At the next I had the meat course, and made my speech. At the third I ate dessert, and made my speech. It was a bit harrowing. Especially since I was worried about Maria. We had gone to the country club during our stop in Rio, and there some bug or other had bitten her. By the time we reached Montevideo she had chills and fever. I left her in the stewardess' care while I went through the day's formalities, but with a trepidation that the event justified. When I returned to the ship I found that during the day her heart had three times nearly failed.

We arrived in Buenos Aires in the midst of a state visit from President Vargas of Brazil and his wife to President and Mrs. Justo. There was much festivity. We were invited to a big reception given by President and Mrs. Justo in honor of their guests—at the Argentine executive mansion, the Casa Rosada. Fortunately someone had warned us not to check our wraps as we entered, but to leave them in the car. As we were leaving we saw pandemonium in the coatrooms, where women, having found that the checking system had completely broken down, were helping themselves on the principle of "first come, best served." Many valuable furs were lost that night.

The crowded reception consisted chiefly of President Justo, with his cane of office and his Presidential ribbon, accompanying Mrs. Vargas through serried ranks of politely applauding guests, followed by President Vargas accompanying Mrs. Justo. Since they were all dumpy little people, the spectacle was less than majestic. It was more exciting to get into one of the dining rooms at last, where supper was being served, with champagne. We needed it. The affair lasted until two in the morning.

2

In the midst of the usual incessant social activity the conference opened on May 6, 1935, and ran until June 29. We divided into seven committees in addition to the steering committee on which I had to act. Since both Weddell and Leahy were weak in Spanish despite years in Latin America, I was obliged to keep a watchful eye on all the committees in addition to those on which I chose to sit; the conference, therefore, was very strenuous for me.

A great many questions were considered, and a remarkable number of agreements reached. Some of the proposals, like that concerning pan-American passports, required considerable finesse. The question had come up at Montevideo. There the United States had offered to facilitate inter-American travel through an Executive Order waiving passport and visa formalities for properly identified persons coming to this country from Latin American nations. The general question of passports was put over to the Commerical Conference.

In Buenos Aires another idea was brought forward with strong backing. This proposed a pan-American passport allowing any resident of any of the twenty-one republics to travel freely throughout the hemisphere.

Although three of the republics were proposing resolutions in favor of the pan-American passport, our instructions from the State Department were not to take part in any discussion of the subject. Reluctant to have the United States be the one country refusing even to debate the question, I telegraphed the Department and suggested we offer to agree, as we had indicated at Montevideo, to do away with passports entirely, and visas too, under a bilateral treaty with any American republic that would undertake to screen its citizens before they left the country.

I persuaded the Department to accept my idea. Therefore, instead of refusing to discuss a pan-American passport, I was able to say in a plenary session, "You see, we want to go even further than you do. You are too conservative on this matter."

To the best of my knowledge, no such bilateral treaty was ever signed; but the formula got us neatly off the hook.

Another quandary, from which we escaped in a rather amusing way, was created by those same three republics in submitting proposals for the definition of an immigrant. Here again the Department's instructions were categorical. As chairman of the delegation, I was to say, when the subject came up, "This word is defined by law in the United States, and we will accept no other definition. We will not even discuss it."

As in the case of passports, I felt that refusal to discuss the proposals would put us in an unfortunate position. I had a Spanish translation made of our law defining an immigrant. Curiously, it begins with a series of paragraphs on what an immigrant is not. I sent this translation to the Department in time for it to be studied before the debate began, and I asked the Department for authority to try for agreement on a definition identical with our law, but in Spanish. It was granted.

At the conference, I appointed myself to the subcommittee that would handle the question. The proposals of the three sponsoring delegations differed enough for me to keep the members fighting with one another right up to the day before the final plenary session. My pride was now involved. I wanted more than a mere report of inability to agree. Having become very friendly with the Mexican delegate on the committee I took him into my confidence. He went along with my plan, and I gave him a copy of my translation.

Once more the members appeared about to agree; once more I tossed in a monkey wrench. At last they threw up their hands in despair: "It's no use. We just can't get a meeting of minds."

"Wait a minute," I said. "We've worked hard here, and it would be a great pity to have to report to the main committee and finally to the plenary session that we couldn't solve our problem. Of course a definition is the most difficult thing in the world."

I turned to the Argentinian.

"How, for instance, would you define a hat?"

"It's a head covering," he answered.

"Sure, it's a head covering, but so is a mantilla; so is a helmet. There are lots of head coverings. So you haven't defined a hat."

They all shook their heads. "Those are pearls of wisdom. What would you suggest?"

"Since we can't define what an immigrant is," said I, "let's try to define what he is not."

"That's fine. That's very good. How would you do it?"

My Mexican colleague popped right in with, "Yes, that's a stroke of genius. For instance an immigrant is not [paragraph *a*]."

I came back with, "An immigrant is not [paragraph *b*]."

We carefully concealed the translation in front of us, mixed in with other papers. My co-conspirator gave *c* and *d:* I gave *e;* he gave *f, g, h;* I gave *i*. These were promptly written down and applauded.

"Why," said the other delegates, "this is marvelous."

We made up our report in five minutes—a literal translation of the United States law. It went right on up from the full committee to the plenary session and was adopted. It still stands.

One amusing incident was caused by the Bolivians who had, for some reason, co-opted the Argentine poet Jorge Erana Urioste as a member of their delegation. He proceeded to introduce a resolution that was practically a grandiloquent guide to Bolivia. All about the crystal waters of Lake Titicaca and the glorious snowcapped Mt. Illimani looking up at the sunrise and the sunset; and much more of same. In view of all these extraordinary natural phenomena, ended the proposed resolution, the pan-American Commercial Conference offered a vote of applause to Bolivia. It was terrible.

I didn't want to appear to be looking down my nose at the beauty of Lake Titicaca and Mt. Illimani; nevertheless I persuaded the

Mexican and Argentine delegates to join me in taking issue with their encomiast. Fortunately he lost his temper and insulted them in committee, so we had no trouble getting rid of his resolution.

That kind of frivolity was not the only irritating distraction at these international conferences. Another was the introduction of last-minute resolutions. At the Commercial Conference, after the steering committee had agreed that no new projects might be presented, I arrived at my office early one morning to find two new and extremely distasteful resolutions awaiting me. They were projects we could not possibly agree to; yet I knew that Saavedra Lamas, anti-American and generally cantankerous as he was, might be provoked by my opposition into leading an acrimonious debate that could result in defeat for us. I had to find a "front," and quickly, for the steering committee was to meet at nine and it would take me fifteen minutes to reach the meeting.

I telephoned José Carlos de Macedo Soares, the Brazilian foreign minister, and asked him to oppose the resolutions. He agreed they were undesirable, but he could not attend the meeting because President Vargas was taking leave of President Justo that morning and he must go with him to the final interview. Gilberto Amado, his legal adviser, also had to be there, as well as the Brazilian ambassador, José Bonifacio de Andrada e Silva. That left Sebastian Sampaio to represent Brazil at the meeting of the steering committee. Could I get support for Sampaio? he asked. I promised to line up other Latin American delegates, and he said he would instruct Sampaio to oppose the resolutions very positively.

I called Puig Casauranc, who agreed to support the Brazilian opposition, although as a new ambassador he was unwilling to take any initiative against Saavedra. I also persuaded a Nicaraguan, a Chilean, and one or two others to go along. But they also had their reasons for hesitating to take any initiative. Everything depended on Sampaio.

He was a weak reed, as I knew from acquaintance with him in New York, where for years he was consul general. He was a timid little man with a big inferiority complex; in short, a rarity among Brazilian diplomats. I was disappointed to learn that he would represent Brazil, but felt certain that in spite of his timidity he would certainly obey his foreign minister.

By the time I arrived the meeting had started. In drawing lots for precedence the United States had come out second to Brazil. My place was on Saavedra's left. Sampaio, as representative of the Brazilian foreign minister, was at his right.

When the two critical resolutions came up, Saavedra made quite a speech. These, he said, were "must" propositions, they had to go through. I watched Sampaio. The harder Saavedra pounded the table the more frightened he became until, when it was over, he was literally more afraid of the Argentine foreign minister than of his own. He moistened his lips and opened his mouth to speak, but the words just wouldn't come out. The Mexican looked at me. If something was not said at once, Saavedra Lamas had only to bang his gavel and say, *"Aprobado,"* and that would be that. I asked for recognition.

"Mr. Minister," I began, "just before this meeting I had a very interesting conversation with the Brazilian delegate about these proposals, in which he said the following." And I proceeded to give the whole argument against them.

Poor Sampaio! He paled, flushed, and turned green. He was totally flustered. Saavedra knew of course that I was lying; he had seen how late I arrived for the meeting. He was furious but there was nothing he could say. I glared at Sampaio.

"I believe I have interpreted your remarks accurately, haven't I, Mr. Ambassador?" I asked him.

He knew I would go straight back to Macedo Soares. He gasped, swallowed, stuttered, and finally managed to articulate, "Y-y-yes. You have."

I turned to the Mexican, who backed me up and was in turn backed by the others. We killed the resolutions right there, without even allowing them to be assigned to committees.

3

The history of pan-American conferences is a history of agreements reached at great expense of time, energy, and money, and later ignored or forgotten. The Commercial Conference adopted resolutions or reached understandings on more than 50 matters of greater or less importance: facilities for entry and unloading of ships or planes, modification of port dues; simplification of customs procedures; exchange of sanitary information; quarantine of agricultural products, all of which were subsequently disregarded. It was not unique in that respect. Frequently during my diplomatic service some one on my staff or in the State Department would come to me with a problem on which he thought it important to reach agreement with the other American republics. And my answer would be, "What do you mean? We agreed on that at Montevideo." Or at Buenos Aires, or some other inter-American conference.

One reason for all this waste of effort is the failure of the various republics to ratify agreements. Before I left the State Department, the United States was in the lead on ratification of 103 conventions, agreements, and protocols on which no dissent had been registered. Argentina brought up the rear with two; and I learned from Dr. John Lord, who was head of the Pan-American Health Bureau, how it had come to ratify those.

They were sanitary agreements; and after most of the other republics had ratified them, Dr. Lord made a special trip to Argentina in the hope of getting ratification by Hipolito Irigoyen's regime. He could get nowhere and was about to give up when, in a final conversation with the President, he happened to mention the connection between rats and bubonic plague. Irigoyen shuddered.

"Do you mean to say," he asked, "that rats carry the plague?"

When Dr. Lord assured him they did, he said, "All right, we'll ratify the agreements."

Irigoyen explained that some thirty years earlier he had been sent as a political prisoner to Usuahia, a southern Argentine prison camp, bleak, windy, and filthy. He retained an indelible memory of living in a miserable hut, and of being awakened at night by rats gnawing his toes. Thanks to that unpleasant experience Argentina, by accident as it were, ratified the sanitary agreements.

So impressed had I become by the record of futile agreements from previous conferences that when I was elected by the Commercial Conference to make the closing speech in reply to Saavedra Lamas' speech for the host country, I decided to put on an act—corny though it was. I said I thought it imperative that we put a stop to the making of important international agreements and then going home and forgetting them. I asked all the delegates to stand for one minute and silently pledge themselves to see to it that the agreements reached at this conference were ratified and carried out by their respective governments.

They loved it. It was something nobody had ever thought of before. It gave them a chance for a sort of seventh-inning stretch. They crowded around to congratulate me on my inspiration. But when they went home they forgot the agreements as usual.

The day on which I made this closing speech was momentous, because Bolivia and Paraguay had finally agreed on the June Twelfth Protocol which led to the Chaco Peace Conference and the end of the war. Everyone was cheering as wildly as if the protocol were the final peace. When the Conference met, the band played the national anthems of Paraguay and Bolivia and of all six mediatory powers while we bobbed up and down like corks on the waves. I had no idea as I went through the ordeal that this day was the prelude to one of my longest and most difficult diplomatic assignments.

Chapter XIX

UPON my return from the Commercial Conference I went to see Sumner Welles, the Under Secretary of State. He was effusively grateful. From the way he talked, one might have thought I had been risking my life for my country under shot and shell. I took this excess of praise to be a measure of the concern he and Hull had felt about what Saavedra Lamas might have done to the conference.

Welles went on to say that the President and Secretary of State had authorized him to ask me whether I would accept the embassy in Peru. I said I would.

"All right," said he. "You'll be hearing from me in due course. There may be a few weeks delay, but I'll be getting in touch with you."

Several weeks later, perhaps in early September, I was in Washington and went to call on Hull late in the afternoon. As I entered the office Harry McBride, an old career man who was acting as principal assistant, said, "Where on earth have you been? We phoned New York and were told you were in Washington. We've been hunting desperately for you. The Secretary wants to see you. He's left now; but the first thing tomorrow morning."

"What's it all about?"

"I don't know whether I should tell you. Maybe Ed Wilson can."

Edwin C. Wilson was in charge of Latin American affairs. I went up to his office at once. He told me they were in a jam on the Chaco Peace Conference.

The first article of the June 12 protocol, on the day I made my closing speech at the Commercial Conference, had called upon the President of Argentina to convoke a peace conference. This conference, composed of representatives of the two belligerents and of the six mediatory powers whose efforts had brought about the truce—Argentina, Brazil, Chile, Peru, Uruguay, and the United States—had convened in Buenos Aires on July 1, 1935. Our representative was Hugh Gibson, at that time Ambassador to Brazil. Gibson was now insisting he had to get back to his post, and Hull had decided

I should succeed him. Wilson believed the conference soon would dissolve in a disastrous failure. Secretary Hull thought it might last another six months and even perhaps get a peace treaty.

I remarked, "When you say six months, I know it will take much longer. It always does in Latin America."

Hull strongly urged me the next morning to accept the assignment. I promised to think it over. After I left him I went in to see Sumner Welles.

Sumner discussed with me in confidence Roosevelt's fear of an impending war in Europe. From a safe he removed the draft of a letter from the President to the presidents of the other American Republics. The draft said that in view of the danger of European conflict it was necessary to isolate this hemisphere from possible involvement. Therefore he proposed that the American Republics hold a conference for the maintenance of peace; and that it take place in Buenos Aires, assuming President Justo to be willing. Sumner explained that Buenos Aires had been chosen because of Saavedra Lamas' virtual certainty to create obstacles if any other capital were designated.

However, said Welles, desirable though a maintenance of peace conference was, Roosevelt would look pretty silly if the war between Paraguay and Bolivia were resumed after he had issued this letter. The Chaco Peace Conference was going badly, and it was imperative that the situation be stabilized before the letter went out. That, it appeared, was the main reason for my being asked to succeed Gibson.

Before I left Washington I looked up my friends in the Department and the press. They frankly told me that the conference was a complete mess; that it was going from bad to worse; that it was obviously impossible to bring about a treaty; that it looked as if the war would start again at any minute; and that if I went as the U.S. delegate I would be stepping into a situation that would probably blow up in my face soon after my arrival.

Maria, however, urged me to go.

"You know Latin America and you know the Latins," she said. "If anybody can save the situation, you can save it."

When, at Sumner Welles' request, I met him in New York some days later, he took the same line as Maria. He admitted that the situation was desperate. The belligerents had been unable to reach agreement on a single point since the conference had convened. I was the only person who could bring them together. I knew the Latin Americans and I had shown at the Commercial Conference that I could handle Saavedra Lamas. The financial arrangements Hull had been able to make were excellent. Indeed, during those three years at the Chaco Peace Conference I was the second highest paid employee of the United States government. Even so, those years cost me the millions I would have made on the real estate development of my Stonehurst property. As related, I was obliged to abandon it because I could not get back to the United States to contend with my interfering neighbors.

While Maria was packing and arranging to leave the children at Stonehurst with her sister, I went to Washington to study the history of the Chaco dispute. Hull and Welles were all for my getting away immediately, but I refused to leave without a thorough briefing. I put in long hours at the Department, taking notes and getting copies of such documents as I felt I might need. On the trip down I had time for further study. By the time I arrived in Buenos Aires I was fairly well informed.

I was lucky. Gibson whose sole idea was to get out of the job, gave me almost no help. We reached Buenos Aires late on a Wednesday evening. Gibson met the ship, but had to rush off at once to a dinner engagement. We arranged to meet the next morning at the chancellery, where the Chaco delegation had a couple of rooms. When I arrived, Hugh told me he was leaving for Rio on Saturday, two days later. I protested emphatically.

"After all," I told him, "I'm coming into this thing brand new. I haven't even had any diplomatic experience beyond a couple of short conferences that were pretty sketchy preparation for negotiating a treaty of peace. I think you ought to stay a week or ten days until I become thoroughly familiar with the situation."

There was no holding him. I couldn't even get much out of him in the 48 hours before he sailed, for he and Mrs. Gibson had to pack and make the many farewell calls demanded by protocol. He gave me thumbnail sketches of the men who would be my principal colleagues, that was all.

Saavedra Lamas, who as foreign minister of the convoking power was chairman of the conference, Gibson loathed and despised; and from all accounts those sentiments were mutual. Gibson was a polished diplomat. He had been trained in Europe. His French was excellent. Saavedra Lamas hated him for all that he was, because that was what Saavedra himself wanted to be. It was intolerable to a man of his colossal vanity, who liked to think of himself as a great world statesman and peacemaker, to find himself confronted by an old-school, accomplished diplomat whose fluent French he not only could not equal but could barely understand.

Gibson rightly told me that Rodrigues Alves, the chief Brazilian delegate, would be a tower of strength to me. Felix Nieto del Rio of the Chilean delegation I thought Hugh underestimated; probably because of an incident involving the second ranking Paraguayan delegate (Geronimo Zubizaretta was first) and minister in Buenos Aires, Vicente Rivarola.

Hugh, who spoke almost no Spanish, had asked Nieto to go with him to speak to Rivarola about some agreement he wanted to reach with the Paraguayans; Rivarola had been Paraguayan minister in Chile when Nieto was under secretary of foreign relations. Rivarola promised to do what Hugh asked, and then did exactly the opposite. Shocked and enraged, Hugh demanded that Felix go with him to demand an explanation. Felix was amused, and possibly offended Gibson by showing it. Back they went to Riverola, who was quite casual about his breach of faith. Nieto, putting on a bit of a show, said, "Vicente, how could you do such a thing to an old friend? You deceived me. You broke your word to me."

Vicente's retort was, "Well, what are friends for? Whom are you going to deceive and doublecross if not your old friends?"

Hugh Gibson never got over that. Perhaps he was confused by Rivarola's unfamiliar Indian ways. Neither did the Basque stubbornness of a Zubizaretta (mixed with the characteristics of the Guaraní Indians of Paraguay) nor the grotesque vanity of a Saavedra Lamas fit into his diplomatic frame of reference. He was wholly out of his element; and that is probably why he was so fearful for the fate of the conference. I say this even though he was able to get along with Rodrigues Alves, Nieto, and Podesta Costa, diplomats who were experienced in European diplomacy and understood Gibson's way of thinking, as will be described later. Podesta Costa was the really working delegate for Argentina, and a very valuable one.

I would be leaving a most unfair impression of a great gentleman if I failed to say that when, on January 21, 1936, we signed the Protocolized Act extending the truce indefinitely and arranging for the exchange of prisoners, Hugh Gibson sent me an effusive cablegram of congratulation and followed it with a letter that read, in part:

> I suppose I know perhaps as well as anybody what a whale of a job that has been and what a predominant share of the credit should go to you. Nobody who knew when he was licked could have seen that thing through to a successful conclusion, and I take off my hat to you. In fact I couldn't resist taking it off to you via the Department, as

> you will see from the enclosed blurb which I have sent off on receipt of the news. I hope you are going to have something of a lull now. Don't work those fellows to death.

His "blurb" to the Department was couched in the same language.

Gibson also sent me another telegram, this one heaping encomiums upon Saavedra Lamas, which he asked me to convey to Saavedra. All of this praise was in quotation marks. The wire concluded, "End quote Horsefeathers."

2

The Chaco Boreal is a region in the center of South America about the size of Montana (almost 150,000 square miles). Its northeastern swamps have been aptly described as "a green hell." To the south, along the Paraguay River and its hinterland, are fertile agricultural regions. Far to the west, along the foothills of the Andes, are oil deposits concerning whose value opinions differ. Most of the rest of the Chaco is arid, tropical, and unproductive, with swamps in the Southeast, where the Pilcomayo flows into the Paraguay.

The Spanish colonial governments, interested in richer and more accessible areas, failed to define clearly the limits of this uninviting territory or to assign it to a definite jurisdiction. Consequently, after the Latin American republics became independent states and their settlements gradually extended towards the Chaco, its ownership became a matter of rivalry between Paraguay and Bolivia.

The pretensions of the two claimants were complicated, and were based on different interpretations of the principle of *uti possidetis*—that is, the extent of the territory possessed, at the time of liberation, by the Spanish colonial divisions from which their sovereignty derived. Paraguay held that the question was one of boundaries; Bolivia that it was territorial; and each, with increasing vehemence, laid claim to the entire Chaco. The issue was further complicated by Bolivia's desire for an outlet on the Paraguay River, which Paraguay opposed.

For fifty years the dispute dragged on while the disputants, with the help of other American republics, made repeated efforts to reach a settlement. Several treaties were signed, but only two of them were ratified by even one of the two nations. Meanwhile both of them maintained military outposts in the area, and clashes between armed patrols took place with increasing frequency until, in 1932, these led to full-scale war. The conflict lasted, with the exception of the two weeks truce of December 1933, until the signing of the protocol of June 12, 1935. This war was fought with the most modern equipment, by two small countries willing to sacrifice over 130,000 of their youth and to maim countless others in efforts to gain possession of an area of hypothetical value.

The war had its unique tortures of heat, harassing insects, and thirst. An example—extreme, to be sure—is the death from thirst of some 10,000 Bolivian soldiers cut off from their water supply by a Paraguayan contingent that had made a two-day trek around the Bolivian lines. In 1938, officers of our military mission, flying over the area, were impressed by concentric white formations, like the spokes of a wheel without the rim, scattered all about. After they landed, they found that the "spokes" were skeletons of those tortured men, lying with heads burrowed into the sand in spots where obviously they had hoped there was water.

While the war raged, the other American powers made continuous efforts to bring it to an end. On August 3, 1932, our government and the representatives in Washington of other American republics telegraphed a joint appeal to Bolivia and Paraguay urging them to settle their dispute by peaceful means and closing with the following paragraph:

> The nations of America likewise declare that they will not recognize any territorial arrangement of this controversy which has not been obtained by peaceful means, nor the validity of territorial acquisitions which may be obtained through occupation or conquest by force of arms.

A commission of neutral powers, with the consent of the belligerents, strove unsuccessfully to achieve a settlement. Then the League of Nations sent over the commission of which I have already spoken, which, with the cooperation of the Montevideo Conference, effected the brief truce of December 1933.

At last, on January 30, 1935, President Arturo Alessandri of Chile wrote a letter to President Augustin P. Justo of Argentina, who answered on February 8. I have copies of these two letters, which have never to my knowledge been published. They were procured for me by my good friend Félix Nieto of Chile, with whom I worked very closely while he was a delegate to the Chaco Conference. They contain the preliminary exchange of ideas for stopping hostilities that led to the formation of the conference.

President Alessandri was convinced that unless peace was established the adjoining powers might become involved in the war; and at that time he made several very violent, menacing statements calculated to alarm the Argentines and convince them that the war threatened to become general. The menace was real enough, as I became convinced after my arrival in Buenos Aires.

Argentina was backing Paraguay; indeed, Paraguay was so dependent on Argentina for access to the sea and as a market for its important orange crop that I am convinced it would never have gone to war without Argentine consent.

Unquestionably Argentina supplied arms to the Paraguayans. I had positive assurance of this during the Conference from the Paraguayan commanding general, José Felix Estigarribia. Moreover, Vicente Rivarola, Paraguayan Minister to Buenos Aires before and early in the war, admitted to me that on one single occasion he had obtained $10,000,000 worth of arms from Argentina. The Argentines did more; from the southern Chaco, which is in Argentina, and from Salta and other provinces just south of the Bolivian border, they had excellent opportunities to observe military movements. Estigarribia also admitted to me that the location of Bolivian forces was radioed to him by the Argentines.

To some extent the discovery of oil deposits in Bolivia had complicated the picture. But the influence of oil was greatly exaggerated by the Communists and others who represented the war as a fight between Standard Oil of New Jersey (to which I had sold its Bolivian holdings) backing Bolivia, and Shell backing Paraguay. Senator Gerald P. Nye, investigator of the munitions industry, telephoned me from Washington one night after my return from the Montevideo Conference and asked me to lunch with him. He had among his advisers John Kenneth Galbraith, the left-wing economist who has since gone on to glory. We met at the Biltmore, and Nye tried very hard to get me to say that the Chaco war had been provoked by the oil companies. Since that was nonsense, I was unable to oblige.

Still, the potentialities of Bolivian oil were not precisely ignored. Argentina had ambitions in that direction, and Brazil did not want Argentina to get the oil. Brazil, moreover, would have liked to tap the Paraguayan exports, and talked about building a railroad from Sao Paulo to the Corumbá area on the Paraguay River; but railway transportation would have cost so much more than river shipments that nothing ever came of it until years later.

There was continuous military rivalry between Brazil and Argentina, each trying to get its military mission into Paraguay. On one occasion the Argentines succeeded in persuading the Paraguayans to send down some 25 or 30 cadets for training by the Argentine air corps, at that time one of the world's worst. My friend Rodrigues Alves was Brazilian Minister to Paraguay at the time, and he told me of pointing out to the Paraguayans that there had been 100 per cent mortality among those cadets.

Chile, at the outbreak of war, was very pro-Paraguay. But the Paraguayan government had the misfortune to transfer to Chile as Minister one J. Isidoro Ramirez, who had made himself *persona non grata* in Peru. This stupid and venal man, who will figure in this story later as a delegate to the Chaco Conference, was caught red-handed in such undiplomatic activities as hiring agents to spy on the Chilean Army. Chile broke relations with Paraguay and transferred its support to Bolivia.

President Alessandri had good reason to fear that with Argentina helping Paraguay and Chile sympathizing with Bolivia some untoward incident could bring the two nations into the war, and that Brazil would subsequently join in on the basis of the *Diagonal*—the old concept of a Brazil, Bolivia, and Chile alliance against the aggressive ambitions of Argentina. Evidently he was able to convince President Justo. Argentina, I may say, although of course much stronger than Chile, has always been a little fearful of the Chileans, who are a nation of fighters.

Consequently, the Argentine and Chilean governments invited the United States, Brazil and Peru to join them in an effort to mediate in the Chaco dispute. Uruguay was later invited, and the mediatory group met in the Argentine Foreign Office in May 1935 and invited the foreign ministers of the belligerents to come to Buenos Aires and discuss peace. They came; and out of the ensuing discussions came the Protocol of June 12, followed by the Peace Conference.

3

The reason the President of Argentina was requested to convene the Peace Conference in Buenos Aires was precisely the same as prompted President Roosevelt to suggest that the Maintenance of Peace Conference be held there: the egomania of the Argentine Foreign Minister, Saavedra Lamas. Not a statesman in all the Americas had the slightest doubt that Saavedra would permit any peace unless he could appear before the world as the leading peacemaker. Every attempt to bring about a cessation of hostilities had failed because at one point or another he had disrupted it. So long as he was the

Argentine Foreign Minister the only way to get a peace treaty was to have the negotiations in Buenos Aires where he would be the chairman and get the credit, the glory, and as it turned out, the Nobel Prize.

That is a harsh indictment, in view of the hideous alternative, but I say it advisedly. Remember that Argentina was aiding Paraguay with arms and military intelligence. When the Nobel Prize was awarded to Saavedra, Rodrigues Alves said jokingly (nevertheless he meant it) that the prize was actually an incentive to war: people were encouraged to promote hostilities in order to win the prize by making peace. In Saavedra's case that was no great exaggeration.

He was a vain, pathologically ambitious, essentially a stupid and wicked man. His nickname was "Juan Cuello" (John Collar), inspired by his practice of wearing stiffly starched collars at least three inches high; also a stiffly starched red moustache and red hair (both dyed). He smoked cigarettes nervously, lighting one after another and tossing them over his shoulder after a few puffs, regardless of damage to floors or carpets. He respected no one. He sneered at his cabinet colleagues, and I have heard him refer repeatedly to President Justo in our conference meetings as "the little fatty upstairs." After the Maintenance of Peace Conference he began in one of our meetings to deride President Roosevelt because of his tragic disability, and had his ears vehemently pinned back by me. He was tricky and shrewd and not to be trusted.

During our sessions he was intolerably garrulous, interrupting anyone and running on interminably. At last I told my colleagues that for my part I was going to put a stop to it. They declared it could not be done; no one had ever been able to shut him up. At the next meeting I got the floor and began a speech that I made as tedious as possible. Saavedra Lamas interrupted and held the floor for an hour.

When at last he subsided I said, "Mr. Minister, I have the floor. You interrupted me with your interesting discussion, which I was very happy to hear. But unfortunately, due to my limited knowledge of Spanish (my colleagues almost laughed openly) when I'm interrupted I lose my chain of thought, so I shall have to start all over again at the beginning."

Back to the beginning I went, and managed to be even more tedious than before. Again he interrupted. Again, when he had finished I said, "As I told you, Mr. Minister, when interrupted I lose my chain of thought and have to start over."

And I started. A third time he interrupted, and a third time I began all over again, after smiling pleasantly and saying that I deeply appreciated his illuminating words but unfortunately I just could not remember what I had said. Never again did he interrupt me during the three years he remained foreign minister.

The more intelligent and decent Argentines, including his colleagues in the regime, disliked the man, disagreed with many of his policies, and detested his methods. Among them were my colleagues Podestá Costa and Isidoro Ruiz Moreno. And Vice President Julito Roca, son of the former President, General Julio A. Roca, told me frankly that when they were both out of office he would never speak to Saavedra Lamas again. When I remarked that at least Saavedra believed in democracy and liberty, he answered, "No, he doesn't. You've been listening to his speeches. When the central government intervened in the province of Sante Fe I refused as Vice President to preside over the Senate when the measure was passed. I objected to it in the Cabinet and I left the city to avoid presiding when it was passed because I considered it thoroughly undemocratic. But Saavedra Lamas drafted the law and all the documents in connection with that intervention. That will give you some idea of his devotion to democracy."

Still, Saavedra had a considerable popular following. He gave eloquent lip service to the democratic principles embodied in the electoral law put through by his father-in-law Saenz Peña, one of Argentina's great presidents (whose widow, left almost wholly dependent on her son-in-law, was treated by him like an undeserving poor relation). He had succeeded in getting his anti-war pact endorsed by the Montevideo Conference (I have told how); and he had brought to Argentina various international conferences and important visitors. Besides, he had held prominent posts and was greatly admired for his oratory. And just as the Maintenance of Peace Conference was about to convene late in 1936 he was awarded the Nobel Peace Prize.

The award of the Nobel prize to Saavedra Lamas is the source of a distasteful memory to me, in which the United States was an accomplice in satisfying Saavedra's overpowering ambition.

To fix a starting point, I became implicated in Saavedra Lamas' plans just after we had agreed to the Protocolized Act that extended the truce indefinitely and arranged for the exchange of prisoners. The Argentine Ambassador in Mexico had called on me in my suite. His message was that his Foreign Minister had the support of many countries, including all of the Baltic and Balkan states, for him to receive the Nobel Peace Prize. Saavedra, his agent declared, knew that all he lacked to be assured the award was the backing of President Roosevelt and Secretary Hull. Would I petition them on his behalf?

I was astonished at the presumption of this request, and explained to my visitor that my government had never done this in the past and therefore all precedent was against our intervening in the present instance. I added that if we were to back anyone it would have to be the recently retired Brazilian Foreign Minister Melo Franco, who had been largely responsible for bringing about the settlement of the Leticia dispute between Colombia and Peru. I was, in short, totally discouraging.

A few days later, Saavedra Lamas summoned me to his office where, putting on all his charm, he said that he had understood fully what I had told his ambassador but nevertheless he begged me, as a personal favor, please to communicate his ambitions to Roosevelt and Hull. He would be forever grateful, he assured me, even if they were unable to support him in his quest for the Nobel Peace Prize.

Of course, I had to accede to his request. I cabled to Washington giving a full account of the affair and including the "out" I had prepared for the President and Secretary so that they could gracefully decline the request.

You can imagine my perplexed surprise when my cabled instructions arrived. Washington said the support sought by Saavedra would be forthcoming. It was, and the Prize ultimately went to Saavedra Lamas. And from that moment on, Saavedra, even during Roosevelt's and Hull's presence in Buenos Aires for the Maintenance of Peace Conference, went out of his way to be nasty and insulting.

I have never felt the same since about the Nobel Peace Prize. I am in accord with my Brazilian colleague who remarked, at the time, that apparently the best way to win this world-famous prize was to start a war and then help settle it.

It is probable that in his intrigues to get the Nobel Prize for himself instead of President Justo, Saavedra cheated himself out of the presidency of Argentina. He avoided giving the slightest credit for inspiring and organizing the Peace Conference to either President Justo or President Alessandri. Any candidate chosen by President Justo to succeed himself was sure of election. Saavedra's great reputation might have appeared to merit the office, but the President could hardly overlook his behavior in connection with the prize. Roberto M. Ortiz became his successor.

As the conference dragged on it became increasingly evident that holding it in Buenos Aires with Saavedra Lamas in the stellar role had been no guarantee of his cooperation. Repeatedly he accused

Chile and Brazil of wanting to disrupt the conference for the purpose of moving it to Santiago or Rio de Janeiro. That, of course, was the kind of thing he himself would have done. I was able to reassure him first hand so far as Brazil was concerned, for I had the personal assurances of the Brazilian Foreign Minister, José Carlos de Macedo Soares, on the point. Nieto also assured him that Chile had no such ambition. But he could never be convinced for long at a time. He kept reverting to this egomaniacal obsession, and also to an obsessive fear of the *Diagonal.*

Meanwhile his policies were calculated to stir up suspicion and distrust responding to his own. He used the conference for purposes of intrigue with the ex-belligerents, directed to the end of extending Argentine control to the whole Chaco and even to Bolivia. He even signed an agreement with Bolivia during the conference providing for an Argentine-financed railway from Yacuiba in Argentina through southeastern Bolivia to Santa Cruz, the second largest Bolivian city. This project the chief Bolivian delegate to the Chaco Conference, David Alvéstegui, regarded, he told me, as a first step toward Argentine dismemberment of his country, leading certainly to a general war against Argentine aggression.

Rodrigues Alves became convinced that Saavedra Lamas intended to postpone a territorial settlement in the Chaco until he had first insured maximum Argentine influence in both Paraguay and Bolivia, and especially Argentine control over Santa Cruz and the oil fields; and he urged his government to counter the Yacuiba-Santa Cruz railway project by building a railway from Corumbá to Santa Cruz. Felix Nieto suspected Saavedra Lamas of having designs on the Magellanes area of Southern Chile. And both Chile and Brazil, concerned over Argentine military expansion, began to increase their own military establishments.

While the ex-belligerents intrigued with Saavedra Lamas to obtain such advantages as they might, they feared and distrusted him. Above all, they came increasingly to suspect that peace between them was not their adjoining neighbors' primary concern at the Peace Conference.

Here, then, in its main features, is the picture of the most obstructive difficulty that tormented the Chaco Peace Conference; that threatened it repeatedly with failure and the prospect of renewed and widened hostilities and protracted it through three anxious years until the retirement of Saavedra Lamas from office made possible an enduring settlement of the Chaco dispute. It is one of the ironies of history that the man who managed to get the Nobel Peace Prize by hashing together an "anti-war pact" and attaching his name to it, and by robbing Presidents Alessandri and Justo of the credit for bringing about the Peace Conference; this man, the powerful chairman of the conference, was entirely indifferent to the humanitarian purpose for which it was convened. The "great peacemaker" was the one insurmountable obstacle to peace.

Later I shall describe the other difficulties which plagued the Conference.

For example, on December 31, 1935, some optimism was beginning to be felt amongst the mediatory delegates. Accordingly, Rodrigues Alves was encouraged enough to give a New Year's Eve party with champagne and dancing until 4 A.M. One can imagine with what distaste I was awakened by the Bolivian Foreign Minister at 7:30 A.M. He was enraged by an insulting and threatening radio speech made the previous evening by President Ayala of Paraguay. As a result, Elio declared he had called a press conference for 11 A.M., in which he would give Ayala a thorough dressing down; after which he and his delegation would depart for home leaving the responsibility for the prisoners up to the Conference. The Paraguayans, of course, would respond with equal rudeness and violence, blowing the Peace Conference sky high. I dashed over to Elio's suite at the Plaza Hotel sending word to Nieto to join me there (it was no use trying to get Rodrigues Alves as he never would stir until nearly noon). By emphatic arguments we got the press conference delayed until afternoon, then to the next day, and afterwards for 48 hours. Finally, we calmed the parties so that negotiations could proceed.

Chapter XX

THE ninety-day truce agreed upon in the June 12 Protocol was inspired by an extravagant optimism. During those ninety days the question of frontiers was to be settled, the prisoners were to be exchanged, and a peace treaty negotiated. In fact, when the truce expired Bolivia and Paraguay had not been brought to agree on a single point. They had, however, demobilized under the supervision of a neutral military commission set up under the Protocol, and the Conference had thereupon declared the war at an end as the Protocol prescribed. But there was no peace and no longer even a formal truce to prevent a resumption of hostilities.

The protocol, partly by design, partly because of haste in the drafting, lent itself to conflicting claims; and the ex-belligerents took full advantage of its ambiguities. One, which caused much delay and was never actually clarified, lay in an apparently random use of singular or plural in speaking of the line(s) separating the two armies. Paraguay insisted that the intention had been to draw an intermediary *line* between their farthest advanced positions at the time the firing ceased. Bolivia, on the other hand, contended that the armies should be kept apart by a neutral zone lying between two distinct *lines* of separation.

If Paraguay's view were accepted, then its army could properly control traffic on the only road connecting Argentina with the rich Bolivian province of Santa Cruz. If Bolivia's prevailed, the road would lie in the neutral zone and would be policed by officers of the mediatory powers who logically were in command of that zone. Months were consumed in bitter contention over these opposing views. And after the truce expired the two armies were left no further than 150 meters apart in some places and the Paraguayans controlled the road under a rather shaky "de facto" supervision of two neutral military observers who daily risked being fired upon by one side or the other, who then could claim the opposite side had done it. The confusion—and danger—with the two opposing forces facing each other across the undefined line or *lines,* was apparent. I warned my officers to be extremely alert, as their lives were in danger.

The Protocol had called for the exchange and repatriation of prisoners; and on this subject also the ex-belligerents were far from being in agreement. Bolivia, holding only 2500 Paraguayans, contended that all prisoners should be exchanged at once. Paraguay, imprisoning some 17,000 Bolivians, argued that only an equal number should be exchanged, rank for rank, and the repatriation of the rest should await the final treaty; otherwise it would be restoring to its enemy a whole army trained in Chaco warfare.

By the time I succeeded Hugh Gibson and automatically inherited from him the chairmanship of the committee on exchange and repatriation of prisoners, every chancellery in the Western Hemisphere, as well as the Peace Conference, was receiving irate letters and telegrams from individuals and organizations, demanding to know why the prisoners had not been repatriated. The question of prisoners had become involved in the public mind with that of the extension of the truce.

The Protocolized Act was designed to take care of both. But there were serious difficulties involved, quite apart from the intransigence of the ex-belligerents and the disruptive tactics of Saavedra Lamas. This document and the negotiations leading to it will be detailed later.

One obstacle was the number of delegations. In addition to those of Bolivia and Paraguay there were the delegations of six mediatory powers. This was too many delegates for intelligent negotiation even if every one of them had been a model of reasonableness. And they were not. Considering the interminable, and pointless, wrangling in the United Nations and the Organization of American States, the value of limiting participants in negotiations has still to be appreciated.

The leading Peruvian delegate, Felipe Barreda Laos, Ambassador to Argentina, was almost as vain as Saavedra Lamas. He dyed his hair black instead of red, and later nearly died of poisoning from it. No discussion was possible with him and he would agree to nothing that he had not himself proposed or could not be made to think he had proposed. If one got him aside and suggested he propose that black was black he would do so, with verbal fanfares of self-congratulation. He could even be induced to allege that black was white. The second Peruvian delegate, Luis Fernán Cisneros, was a fine and able man, but unfortunately participated very little in our negotiations because it meant coming up the river from Montevideo, where he was Minister.

Eugenio Martinez Thédy, the Uruguayan delegate we had to put up with most of the time, was a speaker of great volubility but otherwise contributed nothing to the Conference. He was the Uruguayan ambassador on post, but was outranked in the Conference by Pedro Manini Rios, leader of a small political party that was part of the government and a man of presidential calibre. However, just a few weeks before we signed the Protocolized Act extending the truce indefinitely Manini Rios gave up hope and went home. Curiously enough, in 1938, after we had enticed him back to Buenos Aires, he repeated this performance just a couple of weeks before we reached final agreement on the peace treaty itself.

Another difficulty was having ambassadors on post serving as delegates. The Bolivian government had wisely demanded that special ambassadors be sent to the Peace Conference, for the reason that ambassadors accredited to the Argentine government would be subject to pressures from that government. Unfortunately, only Brazil and the United States really complied with the Bolivian demand. My Brazilian colleague José de Paula Rodrigues Alves and I were the only ambassadors accredited exclusively to the Conference who served right through to the signing of the treaty of peace.

Rodrigues Alves was the ablest diplomat I ever knew—brilliantly intelligent, witty, suave, flexible, and on occasion unbendingly severe. He began his career as an aide to his father, a former president of Brazil; went into the diplomatic service, and followed that career ever since. He was in Buenos Aires on his way from Chile to his new post in Rome when his government delegated him to the Chaco Conference. He never reached Rome, as I never made it to Peru. After the Conference he was reappointed Ambassador to Argentina, which was considered the most important post in the Brazilian foreign service.

His wife, Dona Cotinha, although old enough to be Maria's mother (she was much older than her husband) took a great liking to Maria, and being in her sphere as able a diplomat as her husband became an infallible and much appreciated guide through the labyrinth of diplomatic society. The two of them became almost as close as Rodrigues Alves and I; and that was close indeed, for in fact we became the unofficial steering committee of the Conference.

It was inevitable, with as many as twenty delegates at one time from the eight powers, that the actual work of the Conference would come to be done by a few delegates. But the secrecy to which those few had to resort was hardly according to protocol. We dared not confide in Saavedra Lamas, for he would have spoiled everything, either through vanity or stupidity. The same thing was true of Barreda Laos. Martinez Thédy was not only utterly incompetent; like all other ambassadors accredited to Argentina he lived in awe of Saavedra Lamas. And so did Barreda Laos.

So also did the Chilean Ambassador to Argentina, Luis Alberto Cariola, who was also a delegate and whom we had to steer around. But Chile had sent a special ambassador in the person of my good friend Felix Nieto del Rio, of whom I have already spoken. He was there until July 1936 when he was sent as Ambassador to Brazil, and was an invaluable member of our informal negotiating committee.

I had known Felix since 1915, and we had been good friends since 1920, when he was attached to the Chilean Embassy in Washington but worked in New York and lived in Kew Gardens, just outside the city. When Maria and I took a house there, Maria saw a great deal of his wife and I of Felix. They lived by a tight budget on his low salary from the Chilean government, and Maria would send his wife baby clothes and other things to help them out. When I made my business trip to Chile in 1931, Felix was Under Secretary of Foreign Affairs, and I saw quite a lot of him. By the time we became colleagues at the Chaco Conference, we were intimate enough to speak our minds to one another with perfect frankness.

Another close associate was the third ranking Argentine delegate, Luis A. Podesta Costa. As I have noted, he had no use whatever for Saavedra Lamas, never kowtowed to him, and understood perfectly that he had to be kept in the dark as much as possible. Until he left in March 1938 to return to the League of Nations where he had worked before, he was secretary general of the Conference. His knowledge of shorthand was very useful. If we were discussing the drafting of a particular clause, he could note everything said and, often by the time we had finished, would have prepared a most satisfactory formulation. Until he left, he was our valued collaborator. When he and Nieto were no longer there, Rodrigues Alves and I for the most part did the planning and worked out the strategy by ourselves.

2

The Protocol of June 12 stated that the Conference would promote the exchange and repatriation of prisoners "bearing in mind the practices and principles of international law." Under international law each belligerent is obliged to support the prisoners it takes, and to accord them the same treatment as its own soldiers of corresponding rank. The Paraguayans, who held the most prisoners and were convinced they had won the war, were in desperate financial straits. My idea was to have each side engage to pay the other an agreed sum for its men held prisoners. The Paraguayans would collect from the Bolivians several times as much as they would pay. It seemed to me the idea might appeal to them, though it by-passed international law.

Rodrigues Alves, Podesta Costa, and I talked it over and became convinced it was a possible solution. The Paraguayans were interested. But when we approached the Bolivians they balked. Their financial situation was also desperate. We were at an impasse with the way out perfectly clear and no means to avail ourselves of it. It was before the days when Uncle Sam would pick up such tabs indirectly through pretended loans or even gifts to such indigent countries.

Just when we needed it, our luck turned. Mauricio Hochschild happened to come through Buenos Aires on his way to Bolivia.

I had known Mauricio since 1922. He was an Austrian by birth, an Argentine by citizenship, and a Bolivian businessman by vocation. With European financial backing he had organized companies in Bolivia and gone into mining, principally tin, of which he was the second largest producer by 1935. Patiño was first, Aramayo third.

Maria and I invited Mauricio and his wife (his first, whom he had remarried as number three) to lunch. He wept on my shoulder about his business affairs. The situation, he said, was disastrous. The war had sent Bolivian taxes sky-high and depressed the Bolivian currency. As only tin exports could bring in dollars and sterling the government was forcing a ruinous rate of exchange upon the tin companies. Half of everything they took in went right into the government treasury. He desperately hoped the peace treaty would bring some relief.

That was my cue.

"That's a dismal picture, Mauricio. I can see what a bind you're in. But that is peanuts compared to what's going to happen to you if they start fighting again?"

He shook his head. "Oi! Oi! Oi! That would be terrible."

"Yes," I agreed. "But that's what's going to happen, unless. . . . There's only one way out."

He jumped like a fish at a big, juicy worm.

"What's that?"

"We've got to get some money." And I told him our proposal that each ex-belligerent should reimburse the other for the upkeep of its men held prisoners. Bolivia, I explained, would have to pay a very large balance to the Paraguayans. We had even worked it out at so much a day per prisoner.

"I've got to have 150,000 pounds sterling," I said. The pound had not yet been depreciated. "If we can pay the Paraguayans I'm sure they will agree to extend the truce so we can negotiate a peace."

"How would you want it?"

"In the Banco de la Nacion of Argentina, to the order of Foreign Minister Elio of Bolivia. But I must know that it's there, and the exact amount, so that he can't say he's got any less or commit any other evasion. And if we need more, I'll let you know."

Mauricio left that very night for La Paz. Within ten days he was back and the money was in the bank. He and the Patiños and Aramayos had divided the amount among them.

"If you need more, I can get it," he said. "We've got to have this peace treaty."

The Bolivians, as I had known they would, tried to tell me they had received only £100,000.

Right at the start of these deadly earnest discussions, the Paraguayans began haggling about the amount of payment per day per man. We bargained over those prisoners as if they were so many cattle, with the mediatory delegates, especially myself as chairman of the prisoners' committee, dealing first with one side, then with the other, for the ex-belligerents had not yet been brought to speak to one another except through intermediaries. We kept Saavedra Lamas in ignorance of the whole thing, especially of the money Mauricio had raised. He would have wrecked the negotiations.

The final bargaining was done in Asuncion. It was clear to me that we would never get the truce extended without direct discussion with President Eusebio Ayala of Paraguay. The chairman of the Paraguayan delegation, Geronimo Zubizaretta, had all the stubbornness of his nation's Basque and Guaraní Indian forebears. Besides, he had presidential ambitions, and that made him timid. He was too hard to pin down.

I persuaded Rodrigues Alves, Nieto, and Podesta Costa that we should send a mission to Asuncion—except that they wanted me to do it. The State Department was scandalized by such an unprecedented proposal but at last consented, with the proviso that other delegations, especially the Argentine, be represented. I went as ranking member of the mission, taking with me my assistant Allan Dawson. The other members were Rodrigues Alves, Nieto and Podesta Costa.

We left Buenos Aires on December 21 and returned on December 23. On December 22 the Foreign Minister, Gerónimo Riart, gave a dinner for us in the house where Sarmiento, the Argentine patriot, died. The whole Cabinet was there and the commanding general, José Felix Estigarribia, with the officers of his staff, all the top officials of Paraguay except the President. The dinner was served in a long open gallery, and while we ate we were eaten, for December is midsummer in South America and Asuncion is very hot and humid. Insects of every size, shape, and color crawled over us or swarmed about us and drowned in our wine. I had never seen or felt so many in my life.

After the dinner and the speeches, I undertook to close the deal on the prisoners. The garden on the other side of the house, away from the lights of the terrace and most of the bugs, was quiet and dark. And there I stood, barely able to see their faces, with the Foreign Minister, the second Paraguayan delegate, Vicente Rivarola—whose duplicity had so shocked Hugh Gibson—and General Estigarribia, haggling over shillings and pence for all the world as if we were in an Oriental bazaar.

The Bolivians were reluctant to pay the £150,000 they had. The Paraguayans demanded near £200,000; the Bolivians offered £100,000. I knew, of course, that I could go higher than £150,000 if need be, but that would be reckoning without the Bolivians. We stood there in pitch darkness and traded for an hour or more. At last we settled for £132,000. That plus a few odd shillings, and pence, as finally stipulated in the Protocolized Act, was the amount the Paraguayans were paid.

To those who may think it was disgraceful to haggle over human lives, my answer is that not only the lives of 20,000 prisoners were involved, but thousands of others that would be sacrificed if the deal fell through. We were not just bargaining for prisoners; we were bargaining for peace.

3

President Ayala proved to be a man of great character and intelligence. The marvelous showing Paraguay made in the war is attributed, by those who know, to the commanding Colonel (later General) Estigarribia, President Ayala as the organizer, and a young Paraguayan graduate of Boston Tech who did wonders with the few river gunboats that constituted the Paraguayan Navy. The President was quite an orator; and when I had a private interview with him after the mission had made its formal call, he opened it with an eloquent discourse on Paraguay's territorial rights in the Chaco. When he had finished he sat back, obviously impressed with his own persuasiveness and awaiting my applause.

I said, "Mr. President, I'm deeply impressed with everything you have said. It confirms all that I have read and heard about the Paraguayan case."

He was visibly delighted to have convinced the American Ambassador. After a brief resume of his argument and the corresponding arguments I had read and heard, I continued, "You make a most convincing case; a case that would be extremely difficult to knock down. However, Mr. President, just as I'm acquainted with your arguments, I'm acquainted with the Bolivian ones. And after studying both sides, and listening to you and to Bolivian Foreign Minister Elio as I have, I come up with the conclusion that you are both absolutely right; no question about it. And therefore, since you're both right you must both be wrong."

He took it beautifully. After a hearty laugh, he answered, "Well, you know, Mr. Ambassador, you're right. I'll be perfectly frank with you. Our arguments really aren't worth anything. But let me say, on the other hand, that if the Bolivian arguments are correct, then Bolivia, by law and by title and by every other reason, should own everything in Argentina right down to and including the Rio de la Plata and Buenos Aires. If the Bolivians had any reason on their side, that would be the answer. On the other hand, as I tell you, our arguments aren't worth anything."

"Well," I said, "that's fine. Now we can settle down to negotiations and perhaps get somewhere."

And we did. By the time our mission had finished talking to the President, singly and together, we had reached with him what we thought was a promising agreement on the crucial problems involved in the extension of the truce. We paid for it with great discomfort.

The Argentine government had courteously offered to send us to Asuncion in a military transport or bomber. Even the Argentine Podesta Costa blanched, for, as I have said, Argentine military aviation at that time was wholly unreliable. We easily persuaded Podesta Costa that a civilian plane would be much more comfortable, and he in turn persuaded his government to charter for us a Panagra trimotor Ford. We were scheduled to take off in the cool of the dawn on January 23 for our return to Buenos Aires. Our plane was standing on the field awaiting us when President Ayala summoned us.

It was past noon when we were free to take off, and all those hours the metal plane had been standing in the burning tropical sun. When the doors were closed and the pilot started warming up his engines, I was spared passing out from the heat only by the fascination of watching Felix Nieto, seated in front of me. The sweat was pouring off of Felix as if a spigot had been turned on over his head. It was a fantastic sight.

Damp but triumphant, we arrived in Buenos Aires, only to meet with Zubizaretta's flat refusal to accept Ayala's agreement.

What a farcical situation! Instead of mediating between the Paraguayans and the Bolivians we now found we had to mediate between the President of Paraguay and the chairman of the Paraguayan delegation. Zubizaretta wanted to succeed Ayala in office and was irritated by his support of the candidacy of Foreign Minister Riart. Zubizaretta threatened to resign as chairman of the delegation if we went ahead on the basis of our agreement with Ayala. He knew that Ayala did not have enough influence with the Paraguayan Congress and people to win ratification of an agreement that the chairman of the delegation had rejected. We knew it too. We could do nothing until we had worked out a compromise agreement acceptable to both. It was at this point that Manini Rios lost heart and went home.

4

Less than a month later the Protocolized Act was signed. The inflammatory question of "line" vs "lines," which had been the crux of the negotiations over extending the truce and the cause of continuous bitterness between the ex-belligerents, was simply postponed by the expedient of repeating what was in the original protocol. I say "simply," but before we got to that we went through a period of almost constant negotiation that was so delicate we did not dare let Saavedra Lamas know what we were about. We held secret meetings and even arranged street-corner rendezvous with other delegates to avoid observation. We knew that our offices were watched.

We adopted some curious stratagems. On one occasion, Rodrigues Alves, Nieto, Podesta Costa, and I were meeting in my drawing room at the Alvear Palace Hotel. Neither Saavedra Lamas nor Barreda Laos had been told of the meeting. But Martinez Thédy knew about it and showed up, and some way had to be found to get rid of him.

Among other proposals received from the Bolivians that morning was a paragraph drafted as a possible clause in the Protocolized Act by Tomas Manuel Elio, the Bolivian Foreign Minister, who was still in Buenos Aires heading their delegation. Martinez Thédy came in and began his usual incessant and meaningless talk. Some one said, "Now, wait a minute, Mr. Ambassador. It seems to me you have a really brilliant idea there. Let's see if we can express your thought a bit more sharply."

And he ran off a version of what the Bolivian Foreign Minister had written.

"Isn't that what you had in mind?" he asked.

It wasn't remotely what Martinez Thédy had in mind; Thédy had nothing in mind. But he was so delighted to have an idea attributed to him that he answered, "Yes, yes! That's it."

Podesta Costa had piles of paper before him; it was easy to hide the draft of Elio's paragraph. "Let me see if I can get that down on paper," he said. "What did you say, now?" And as Martinez Thédy talked, he just copied word for word what the Bolivian Foreign Minister had written. Martinez Thédy was ecstatic. Here was a well drafted clause that could go right into the Protocolized Act.

"As chairman of the prisoners' committee," I said, "I think this is so delicate that you ought to go alone and talk to the Bolivian Foreign Minister. If you can get him to accept this clause it will really be a great victory."

So off went Martinez Thédy. It took him almost three days to sell the Foreign Minister his own idea; for when, after a long introductory harangue, he laid before Elio the paragraph he had himself written, Elio suspected a trick. We never tipped him off and so we won three days to work in peace while he and Martinez Thédy argued it out. Later, of course, we confessed to Elio and all had a good laugh over the incident.

As we reached the final stages of the negotiation we had, of course, to bring Saavedra Lamas in, and in such a way that he would think everything was his doing. I may say that just as we did not want him in the picture, he did not want us, and in particular he did not want Rodrigues Alves and Felix Nieto. I was chairman of the prisoners' committee, therefore he couldn't very well sidestep me; and Podesta Costa was useful to him—after all, he did need someone to keep the records.

Saavedra Lamas had, back of his palatial town house, a pretty garden overlooked by a wide terrace that opened off his dining room. He liked to hold our meetings back there, not only because it was so pleasant but also to keep away from the Foreign Office so that—as he thought—Rodrigues Alves, Felix Nieto, and the other delegates would not know we were meeting. Of course, as soon as we left Saavedra and his terrace, Podesta Costa and I would go straight to the hotel where the others were waiting to receive word of what had happened.

The Bolivians were being a little troublesome. Saavedra Lamas, Podesta Costa, and I met with them on the terrace one morning and then recessed for lunch. Instead of lunching I went over to the Chancellery and drafted a clause I thought would satisfy them. I appended it to a one page memorandum in which I had roughly outlined the argument we should present to the Bolivians that afternoon. Briefly, it was that they had broken their word and misinformed us. But it had to be said politely; we couldn't tell the Bolivian Foreign Minister and the ranking Bolivian Ambassador that they were doublecrossers.

I showed my crude memo to Saavedra Lamas and read it to him; then, by the grace of God or instinct, put it in my pocket. Podesta Costa agreed with me, and said to his chief, "Of course you must say this politely; don't use this language."

We had hardly got under way after the Bolivians returned, when Saavedra Lamas suddenly turned to me and said, "Where is that memorandum you showed me? That's fine. I want to give a copy to Dr. Elio."

I said, "You have it." He looked through his papers.

"No, I haven't got it; I gave it back."

"No. You've got it."

Podesta Costa backed me up. At last Saavedra gave up the search, and asked me, "What did you say?"

I told them politely. And so we were able to make progress with the Bolivians, even though Saavedra Lamas prolonged the meeting with his interminable speeches until he had to break it up because of a dinner engagement.

The other delegates were awaiting us in Rodrigues Alves' suite. Podesta Costa and I went over at once and reviewed the afternoon's work with them, including the clause I had drafted. Having heard the Bolivian views, we made some minor changes in the clause, then asked Zubizaretta to join us. He made one change, then gave us a draft of another proposed clause. The Paraguayans, he assured us, would accept these two clauses.

Then we called up the Bolivians once more. They were still in their office coding messages to their government. Rodrigues Alves, Podesta Costa, and I hurried over there and were lucky enough to find Foreign Minister Elio and Carlos Calvo, the second ranking Bolivian delegate, a distinguished lawyer and a very fine man, as

Spanish as Elio was Indian. By ten o'clock we had the Bolivian acceptance of the clauses the Paraguayans had earlier approved.

We now had complete agreement between the ex-belligerents; and later that night our unofficial steering committee got together to discuss strategy. We had to inform Saavedra Lamas. Podesta Costa telephoned and asked him to call a meeting the next morning on his terrace. This would make him think he was doing the whole thing.

We met on the terrace at eight o'clock the next morning. Behind a low wicker coffee table, on a wicker sofa, sat our host. Podesta Costa and I took low wicker chairs across from him. Orange juice and good black, hot coffee were served.

We finished with the Bolivians Elio and Calvo quickly; Saavedra Lamas was always blatantly pro-Paraguayan (during the Peace Conference he even proposed an elaborate scheme for the dismemberment of Bolivia). Then Podesta called Zubizaretta. In the few minutes before he arrived we coached Saavedra Lamas:

"All you have to say is, 'Ambassador Zubizaretta, this is your own draft of this clause. You completely agreed with the other when we went over it with you yesterday. I'm happy to tell you that we have secured the Bolivians' acquiescence. They agreed under some protest; nevertheless they have agreed. Therefore, when shall we sign the Protocolized Act? Monday afternoon? Tuesday morning? When?' "

We dinned it into his head. We needed Saavedra as spokesman, first because the Paraguayans were so completely under Argentine control; and second, because he was, after all, the Chairman of the Conference.

Zubizaretta arrived, and Saavedra Lamas, after helping him to orange juice and coffee, started to read those paragraphs and to make a speech. You will recall, we had postponed the question of "line" *vs* "lines" by repeating the original Protocol. But Saavedra Lamas began to discourse on that dangerous subject. Zubizaretta was getting nervous. I vainly tried to interrupt. Podesta Costa tried. We tried to divert Zubizaretta's attention, without success.

At last he remarked, "I don't know. I want to think this over. Maybe I've made a mistake. Maybe there's a catch somewhere. I'm not sure I want to sign."

Felix Nieto had once observed, "When the Foreign Minister uses his voice, he loses the use of his head." The truth of the remark was being demonstrated and it pointed to disaster. I put my toe under the wicker table and upset everything—hot coffee, orange juice, ice water, everything—into Saavedra Lamas' lap. He jumped up with a cry of pain. I gave Podesta the high sign. We grabbed Zubizaretta, who had been sitting in the corner of the sofa and was untouched.

"So it's all right? You agree to have the signing on Monday or Tuesday afternoon at five?"

"Yes, that's all right," he said dubiously.

Podesta Costa seized his arm and literally propelled him out to his car, got him into it, and sent him on his way.

Our troubles were not over; our action had to be ratified by the entire Peace Conference. We arranged for a plenary session. Then I cabled the State Department, giving the full story of our successful negotiation and announcing that we were about to sign the Protocolized Act. I warned them that my cable was "strictly confidential;" the term "top secret" had not yet been invented. But on Monday morning, to my profound embarrassment, for I had been especially insistent on secrecy, all the Buenos Aires papers carried huge headlines and lead articles datelined Washington, announcing the agreement and outlining its terms in considerable detail. Someone in the Department had given out the story. Fortunately for me, there were also some leaks from the Argentine Foreign Office, probably when the newspapermen rushed over there with the Washington story, demanding confirmation.

When the delegates met that morning in Saavedra Lamas' office, everyone had read the news. Saavedra began to pin the usual bouquets on his swelling chest, and of course I seconded him; at that moment it was the only way to handle him. But the flower-tossing was a bit premature.

In our excitement we had forgotten to break the news to Barreda Laos and Martinez Thédy. In Thédy's case it did not greatly matter; he was not prone to become obstreperous about anything if he was allowed to make a speech now and then. But Barreda Laos was different. He was as vain as Saavedra Lamas, and opposed everything on principle that he had not sponsored or received the credit for sponsoring. And here he was, confronted with a *fait accompli* of which he had had no inkling until he had read about it in the papers. He was fit to be tied, and I must say with some reason.

When Saavedra had finished congratulating himself several of us asked for the floor. He recognized Barreda Laos, who launched into a blistering attack on the State Department and the Argentine Foreign Office. He then said—what was certainly true—that as an ambassador and chairman of the Peruvian delegation he had a right to know what was going on. His country had been insulted. In his rage he almost reached the point of announcing Peru's withdrawal from the Conference, which of course would have wrecked it and would almost certainly have meant trouble between Peru and the ex-belligerents.

When he concluded I asked for recognition, but Saavedra Lamas said, "No, as Chairman of the Conference it is my right to speak first."

And he proceeded to go after Barreda Laos with the one weapon he knew how to use brilliantly: sarcasm. In effect he likened the Peruvian Ambassador to a stupid, ignorant little boy in a primary school, and in the most witty, ironical, biting, injurious words. I watched the Peruvian's face, and I knew he was ready to announce his own withdrawal and that of his country from the Conference.

Barreda Laos was preparing to reply, but I quickly interrupted, claiming the floor.

I had no idea what I was going to say. I only knew that somehow I must hold the floor until the tension was relieved. I began to talk about American football. None of my audience had ever seen it played. I described the running and passing plays, the kicking, the calling of signals, the scoring of points. I droned on and on, and I could feel the tension lessening as they wondered what I was driving at.

Finally I said, "As in all sports, you have to have team play. After all, we mediators are a team." Having elaborated on that theme for a while I continued, "I've seen many a game where the difference between victory and defeat depended on kicking a field goal. We've scored a touchdown, but we've got to make that extra point because it may make the difference between victory and defeat. Of course the Foreign Minister Saavedra Lamas is our quarterback. He calls the plays; he thinks up the strategy. And he's the man who can make this field goal. We've got to have that extra point, and we've got to have Dr. Saavedra Lamas *dar la Patada* (slang for kick the ball)."

For some reason the expression struck them as funny. They broke into laughter, including Barreda Laos. My rambling, incoherent, and wholly unfunny disquisition had saved the situation.

The next day, January 21, 1936, the Protocolized Act was signed. In the seven months since the signing of the June 12 Protocol the ex-belligerents had rejected 65 proposals of the mediatory powers. The Act extended the truce indefinitely and fixed the terms for the release and repatriation of the prisoners of war. The Conference could now direct its efforts to the treaty of peace. Little did we dream that it was two years and four revolutions away.

Chapter XXI

THE first revolution took place in Paraguay in the autumn of 1936 (spring in North America). President Ayala along with the Liberal Party that had been in power for more than 30 years were thrown out by the Colorado Party, which put forward Rafael Franco. Franco was a former colonel and a thoroughly bad character. He was brave enough, but during the war, in flat disobedience of orders, he had twice endangered his troops in spectacular attempts to make himself a hero. General Estigarribia had to rescue him, and severely reprimanded Franco, thereby winning his implacable hatred. While Franco was President, the Paraguayan hero of the Chaco War was in exile.

The revolutionary government sent to the Conference two new delegates, Manuel Angel Soler, a perfectly decent chap who knew nothing of diplomacy or of the world outside Paraguay, and Isidoro Ramirez, the measure of whose diplomatic ability was that he had managed, as I reported earlier, to lose his country the sympathy of Chile in the war by causing a break in diplomatic relations. The new foreign minister, Riart's successor, was an incompetent firebrand by the name of Juan Stefanich. He frankly did not want peace, and his wife was even more bellicose than he. She told me at a dinner in our home in Buenos Aires that she would rather see her husband, her sons, and all her male relatives dead than to see her country make peace.

About the time the new Paraguayan delegates arrived in Buenos Aires, a revolution in Bolivia brought in as President another bad character, Colonel David Toro, who had been the commander of Bolivian troops in the field. In a previous chapter I have told how 10,000 Bolivian soldiers died of thirst after the Paraguayans had cut off their water supply. Toro at the time was engaged, with some of his officers and a clutch of Indian wenches, in a drunken orgy during which this field commander of the Bolivian Army was "married" to his little Indian playmate in a riotous mock wedding.

Drunkenness was the outstanding characteristic of President Toro, as it had been of Colonel Toro.

The Bolivian Foreign Minister, Tomas Manuel Elío, had left for La Paz immediately after the signing of the Protocolized Act. Toro supplanted him with the former Bolivian Minister to Washington, Enrique Finot, another firebrand who, even before I left for the Chaco Conference, had said my mission was futile. Elío was reassigned to the Conference as ambassador and chairman of the delegation. His return to Buenos Aires provided Saavedra Lamas the occasion for one of his more outrageous displays of irresponsibility.

Elío had accepted a formal invitation from Félix Nieto to visit Chile after he was named ambassador to the Conference. Nieto asked Rodrigues Alves and myself to go with him when he explained this visit to Saavedra Lamas. I thought the visit a serious mistake, but Rodrigues Alves saw no danger in it. There was no excuse for Saavedra's having the slightest suspicion.

But Saavedra Lamas didn't need excuses. He buttonholded me on a Monday afternoon at a reception and declared the visit meant that Chile was trying to steal the Peace Conference. I assured him he was mistaken. The next day he was ranting again, and we realized the situation was serious, knowing of what extremes he was capable. Other efforts to calm him failed. Within 24 hours his temperature was so high that I telephoned Félix in Santiago, demanding his immediate return.

On Friday afternoon the Conference met for the first time with the new Paraguayan delegates. To the consternation of all present, Saavedra Lamas opened the session with the words, "If I were a Paraguayan, I would be very much worried. I have reason to believe—in fact I have documentary evidence to prove—that Chile and Bolivia, the only two delegations not present, are planning a secret attack on Paraguay."

Rodrigues Alves and I immediately protested that no such thing was going on. But Saavedra Lamas, Foreign Minister of Argentina, Chairman of the Peace Conference, and virtual suzerain of Paraguay, was an authority the Paraguayans could not take lightly. We could do no more than have the meeting adjourned after, finally, silencing Saavedra.

The effect on the Paraguayans of that vindictive and totally baseless accusation took more than two weeks of constant persuasion to overcome. It threatened to disrupt the Conference and wreck all chances for a peace treaty.

An unusual diplomatic incident developed out of Saavedra's obsession. He continued to repeat his charges of conspiracy after Nieto returned from Santiago, becoming increasingly objectionable. Having run across Julito Roca, the Argentine vice president, at an exclusive club one day, Félix complained that Saavedra's base suspicions and intrigues were endangering the Conference. He suggested that President Justo, as one of its moving spirits, had a responsibility to take his Foreign Minister in hand.

"I know you're telling me the truth," said Julito. "What about your colleagues? How do they feel?"

"Naturally," answered Nieto, "the Argentines can say nothing. The Peruvian and the Uruguayan are ambassadors on post and wholly subservient to the Foreign Minister. But Rodrigues Alves and Braden will confirm everything I have told you."

And of course we did. Julito agreed that President Justo should most certainly be informed, and arranged to bring us together with him at dinner a week later. After a couple of days he told us he thought it would be only fair to have Saavedra Lamas present. We agreed.

Nieto, Rodrigues Alves, and I decided in advance, as we always did in the Chaco maneuverings, our plan of attack and just who was to say what. We followed it pretty closely. The three of us denounced Saavedra Lamas with complete candor and detail while the President and Vice President of Argentina sat there and listened. He tried to defend himself and we knocked the props out from under him; for once he was unable to talk on interminably. He was livid. At one point I thought he was going to have apoplexy.

The evening ended with President Justo rising and thanking us for our frankness. He was vitally interested in the success of the Conference, he said, and therefore instructed his Foreign Minister to *get on* with the business of peacemaking and not to let anything else interfere.

"In other words" he concluded, "You've got to give it the kick forward."

With that he kicked out his foot and made a forward movement with his hands, unconsciously reminiscent of my comparison between Saavedra Lamas and a quarterback kicking a field goal.

For a while thereafter, Saavedra behaved comparatively well. But he was too vain and ambitious to restrain himself for long—especially when such an opportunity for misbehavior as the Maintenance of Peace Conference offered.

2

When the Protocolized Act had been signed, President Roosevelt sent to all American Presidents the letter of which Sumner Welles had shown me a draft, suggesting a conference on the maintenance of peace in this hemisphere, to be held in Buenos Aires in order (though it remained unsaid) to appease Saavedra Lamas. It was not the first attempt at appeasement, nor the last failure. The Conference met in December 1936.

Late in November it was decided that not only would Secretary Hull head our delegations, but Sumner Welles would be second delegate. Adolf Berle, one of three assistant secretaries, was also named. Incidentally, I believe that was the only inter-American conference ever attended by the President of the United States and both the Secretary and Under Secretary of State.

The Administration attached such importance to the conference and was so eager to make our delegation representative of the country that it kept adding delegates for one reason or another until one day somebody in the State Department woke up to the fact that there were far too many. Thereupon the Department wired and asked me to serve as principal advisor to the delegation. I answered that I must be a delegate or nothing; otherwise I would lose face with my colleagues, all of whom were to be delegates; but I would be glad to help in any way I could. In fact, no sooner had Hull arrived in Buenos Aires than he began to consult with me. So did Welles; and throughout the conference I walked a tightrope, trying to be as helpful to each of them as I could without antagonizing the other.

President Roosevelt traveled to Buenos Aires by cruiser. He was welcomed at the pier by President Justo and his Cabinet. Then came the usual procession of open cars. As we started up the wide street that led from the pier I had one of the worst scares of my life. Suddenly the thousands of people lined up behind ropes on either side broke through the ropes and police lines, surged into the street and completely surrounded the Presidential car. I doubt whether anyone in that procession was less petrified by fear than I was, seeing the Presidents of the United States and Argentina helplessly exposed to assassination. Fortunately it was a friendly crowd, just overeager to show its admiration for Roosevelt.

The rest of the route was equally jammed with spectators. Every roof, window, terrace, even every tree was filled with cheering people.

It was an unforgettable outpouring of enthusiasm by a people that had never been especially friendly to the United States.

While Roosevelt was in Buenos Aires, Saavedra Lamas, aside from minor discourtesies, gave little offense. Thereafter he was intolerable. Unfortunately he had received his Nobel Prize just before the conference began; otherwise he might have been afraid of losing Hull's support. Now he didn't care what Hull thought, and he acted accordingly. He ridiculed, obstructed, and insulted the United States at every opportunity; and since he was chairman of the Conference as Foreign Minister of the host country, the opportunities were plentiful.

At last Welles appealed to me for help. I arranged a meeting in my apartment between him and Leopoldo Melo, who as Minister of the Interior was head of the Justo Cabinet. Melo, a man of great wisdom and integrity, had been my attorney years before when I was briefly interested in the possibility of floating an Argentine loan in the United States; we had remained good friends. From our meeting he went to President Justo and demanded that Saavedra be restrained.

The Foreign Minister's behavior improved for a few days, as it had after Julito Roca's dinner. But by the time the conference ended he was out of hand again. His closing speech was so insulting to the United States that the delegates from the other countries were embarrassed and outraged.

Hull was violently angry. Maria and I spent a couple of hours with him and Mrs. Hull the day before our delegation sailed. I told him I had been tipped off by someone in the Foreign Office that Saavedra Lamas did not intend to see him off—a deliberate affront. He answered that he was damn glad and that he would refuse to shake hands with Saavedra if he did show up.

We should let President Justo know, said Hull, that so long as Saavedra Lamas was his Foreign Minister it would be impossible for us to get along with that blankety blank (here he used his best cuss words). And he proposed that formal representations be made either by himself before he left, or Weddell or me afterward, to the effect that Justo had better ged rid of Saavedra Lamas.

I argued against the idea, and I have never been sure that I was right. Welles, when he heard of it, opposed it vehemently. I don't think Sumner alone could have dissuaded Hull, and I have often speculated on what might have happened if I had encouraged him. I knew Justo well enough to have made the protest to him informally without giving offense. On the other hand, a formal protest by Hull or Weddell would have been taken as an attempt at intervention and in the end probably have helped Saavedra and embarrassed the United States.

3

As the Maintenance of Peace Conference got under way, Saavedra Lamas began trying to eliminate the Brazilian and Chilean Foreign Ministers, Macedo Soares and Cruchaga Tocornal, from the concurrent daily meetings of the Chaco Conference. He was vastly irritated that they would neglect the Maintenance of Peace sessions in order to attend ours, and expressed his irritation in extremely unpleasant remarks. Indeed, so bitter did his exchanges with Macedo and Cruchaga become one day that the Bolivian Foreign Minister turned to the Bolivian Ambassador and said, "Perhaps we should offer our mediatory services to the mediatory Foreign Ministers."

One day Saavedra advanced a startling proposal. In a rambling, incoherent speech he suggested that he appoint a committee of three to carry on the work of the Chaco Conference on the side, as it were, and thus leave the other delegates and the Foreign Ministers free to concentrate on the Maintenance of Peace Conference.

It was obvious that he intended to appoint Barreda Laos, Martinez Thédy, and probably an Argentine. Thus he would have a committee wholly subservient to himself and could forget the Chaco, and with it his fears and suspicions of the other Foreign Ministers. From his point of view it was a brilliant idea.

But the Foreign Ministers were as bright as he was. The minute he finished his speech Macedo Soares spoke up. "That was a stroke of genius! I've never heard a more brilliant idea! I consider it so vitally important that as Foreign Minister of Brazil I gladly volunteer to serve on the committee."

Cruchago Tocornal immediately stepped in. He said, "I agree completely with my colleague. My country would never forgive me if I failed to follow his example. I, too, gladly volunteer to serve."

Then, before the embarrassed and frustrated chairman could appoint himself, Cruchaga observed that it was self-evident that the third member should be the United States Secretary of State, Cordell Hull.

Of course those present had to agree. Asked whether Hull would serve, I expressed doubt.

"If he won't," they said, "then you are to serve as his alternate."

Thus the Committee of Three came into being. We held meetings, calling in the ex-belligerents alternately, and made some progress in spite of the fact that the Paraguayan Ramirez was extremely difficult, lying and reversing himself and in general behaving in a shocking manner. Nevertheless we did make progress, largely due to the interest and prestige of the two Foreign Ministers, and to my being able to speak for Hull.

The next afternoon we met again in Saavedra's office. The Bolivian Foreign Minister, Enrique Finot, and Ambassador David Alvestéqui, who had succeeded Elío in October, had arrived and we were making more progress than in months when the Paraguayan Foreign Minister, Stefanich, was announced. We recessed for 15 minutes to receive him and Ambassadors Soler and Ramirez. As we stood around, chatting, I noticed that Saavedra Lamas, Stefanich and Finot were not in the room.

A sure instinct propelled me through the little anteroom to the front door. There, entering the Brazilian Foreign Minister's car, were the missing Ministers.

"Where are you going?" I asked. "We only took a recess. We were making great progress."

Saavedra Lamas waved me aside, jumped into the car, and slammed the door; and off they drove. The session was disrupted, those attending outraged, and Macedo Soares was infuriated by the appropriation of his car. That evening we learned from the kidnapped Ministers that Saavedra had taken them to his garden, where in short order he had them practically at one another's throats. The excuse he gave later was that he had thought only a skillful hand was needed to bring about complete accord, but he had found them unreasonable. He had not only been unpardonably rude; what was far worse, he had destroyed all progress we had made and left us worse off than before the Maintenance of Peace Conference.

4

Saavedra Lamas had tried to undermine Félix Nieto; he had tried to undermine Rodrigues Alves; he had tried to undermine David Alvestéqui. At last he turned his attention to me. Rumors began to circulate in Paraguay about my one-time interest in Bolivian oil, with the implication that the Paraguayans should protest my participation in the Chaco Conference.* They were traced to a new Argentine

* When Finot was Foreign Minister of Bolivia, his government seized the Standard Oil properties. I had reason to suspect that Saavedra was behind this move but in any case Hull sent two messages to Finot protesting this action. Finot later admitted to me that if Hull had persisted, the properties would have been returned forthwith, particularly as the alleged reason for the seizure was, to say the least, specious.

When the second change in government came in Bolivia, the Bolivian military adviser to their Argentine delegation was ordered back to La Paz to become Minister of Mines and Petroleum. I, therefore, arranged with the Bolivian Chief of Delegation, and Ambassador, to give a luncheon for me with the new Minister of Mines and Petroleum; the new Vice President of Bolivia, who was then in Buenos Aires, would also be present. In order to have support for my arguments, I arranged for my Brazilian colleague, having posted him in advance, also to be at the luncheon. We spent all afternoon, until close to five o'clock, discussing the matter and both the new Vice President and the Minister agreed to see that Standard Oil got back its properties. I reported this to Washington, and to the two representatives in Buenos Aires of the Standard Oil Company, requesting them to inform their executives in New York. When, a little later I inquired from them what had developed, they said the man in charge in New York was in Europe and they had heard nothing. In fact, they heard nothing until one day an old friend of mine, Ham Metzger, showed up in Buenos Aires on his way to La Paz to represent the company.

I asked him whether he was going in his capacity as Vice President of S.O. of N.J. or S.O. of Bolivia. He said neither, that he was going without any title or, for that matter, any powers. I objected to this as a perfectly futile procedure: he must have position and power if he were to get anywhere. I explained to him fully my arrangement with the Minister of Mines and Petroleum and the Vice President, telling Ham that there was no doubt but that the properties could be returned and S.O. put back in the place it had formerly occupied without any further expense or trouble. He said he would immediately communicate this to his principals in New York.

During the following eight or nine months, I was thoroughly occupied with the Chaco Peace Conference and I assumed that S.O. through Metzger was working out something with the Bolivian government.

In April I again urged that delegates visit the ex-belligerent countries. Later on I will describe our Chaco negotiations in La Paz but while I was in that city, after the all-day meeting with the military junta, the Chilean Minister gave a cocktail reception in his home. The Minister of Mines and Petroleum approached me and said, "Mr. Ambassador, I have endeavored several times to get the Standard Oil matter fixed, and have even agreed on the terms which would return Standard Oil to its previous status quo. But each time I had everything arranged with the Cabinet and the Congress to approve the suggested deal, always Mr. Metzger had to consult with New York and the weeks would go by until the program I had suggested could no longer be carried through. I am distressed not to have kept my agreement with you, but military attaché. Fortunately they caused no trouble because I had the confidence of the Paraguayan delegation. Having failed there, Saavedra inspired attacks on me in various scurrilous publications. One attack, in an oil magazine devoted to traducing foreign companies, was so outrageous that the Chilean and Brazilian ambassadors formally protested, and Saavedra was obliged to back down. At their request, Ramon Castillo, who had succeeded Leopoldo Melo as Minister of the Interior, suppressed the offending issue.

But the Foreign Minister did not give up. He began intrigues against me in Washington, but got nowhere with Hull and Welles. At last he sent Dr. Federico M. Quintana, Argentine Ambassador on leave from Chile, to warn Rodrigues Alves and me jointly that our failure to cooperate with him might force him to declare us *personae non gratae*. We answered that we were accredited not to the Argentine government but to the Chaco Peace Conference. Morover, as we were both ambassadors and chairmen of our delegations, he as chairman of the Argentine delegation, but of the conference only through courtesy, was our co-equal with no more power to make such a declaration of us than we of him. That was the last of that.

---

it is not my fault. It is due to the delays and the backing and filling by Standard Oil."

That evening I had Metzger come down to the legation where I was staying. He explained that his company was willing to make certain substantial payments to the Bolivian government in order to get the matter adjusted. I told him there was no question but the whole business could be readily settled on any such basis. I, of course, informed Washington of all of my conversations. But, again, months went by, nothing being done by S.O. All of this was in April.

Finally, after we obtained the Peace Treaty and the Arbitral Award had been obtained, I returned to the United States. During this interim period, Sumner Welles and some of our other officials in Washington intervened and forced an unsatisfactory settlement on S.O.

In due course, the Chairman of the Board of S.O of N.J. invited me to lunch with him and his directors. I accepted. After some general conversation my host, with considerable profanity, cut loose against the "blankety-blank crooked Bolivians who had stolen their properties." I replied that he was entirely mistaken and that it was Standard Oil itself who had been at fault through the whole business. He rather belligerently asked me to explain. I gave him all of the facts, and when I had fininshed with, to say the least, scant courtesy, he turned to the S.O. attorney who was present and said, "Is this true?" The attorney's confirmation of my story resulted in more profanity, this time directed at his own staff. But, so far as I was concerned, the matter had been terminated.

This was one more example of trying to run such matters from a New York office instead of having a competent and fully authorized representative on the ground to deal with them firsthand.

As the situation worsened I tried a little intrigue of my own. The tabloid *El Mundo,* edited by Carlos M. Saenz Peña, was liberal, reforming, courageous, and had a much bigger circulation than either *La Prensa* or *La Nacion*. If *El Mundo* could tell the Argentine public how their government's foreign minister was obstructing the work of the Chaco Peace Conference, he might be forced to resign. I communicated this idea in a personal letter to Sumner Welles, and received a panicky telegram demanding that I keep hands off. Being still rather new to diplomacy I had not yet learned when not to agitate the Department.

Meanwhile I had asked Saenz Peña to lunch and told him the story of Saavedra's behavior. He was shocked. "If you will give me the facts," he said, "I'll blast him out of office."

I did so, keeping discreetly in the shadows myself, and dealing with him through our secretary of delegation, Allen Haden, who was Saenz Peña's friend. Saenz published two editorials that rocked the country and the Cabinet. Saavedra Lamas twice offered his resignation to President Justo, who was at last ready to accept it when the Chilean Ambassador, doddering old Barros Borgoño, and the Uruguayan cipher Martinez Thédy insisted on a special meeting of the Chaco Conference to vote confidence in its chairman. I was able to get their flowery superlatives eliminated; even so the watered down statement finally voted was enough to save the day for Saavedra. I am convinced that if my plan had succeeded we would have saved a year.

The future looked dark. In September 1937 I reported to the State Department that if Saavedra remained chairman of the Conference, it must inevitably fail. As the inauguration of January 1938 approached, it became evident that the new President, Roberto Ortiz, had been induced to retain him as Foreign Minister. Fortunately, however, Saavedra himself unintentionally saved the situation by antagonizing the Minister of Public Works, Manuel R. Alvarado, who happened to be a powerful politician. Alvarado refused to remain in the Cabinet with Saavedra. Also, Rodrigues Alves and I, at Ortiz' invitation, told the President-elect about our troubles with the Foreign Minister. Two weeks before the inauguration President-elect Ortiz named Jose Luis Cantilo, then Argentine Ambassador in Rome, Foreign Minister replacing Saavedra Lamas.

Saavedra let it be known to the Peruvian Ambassador that he expected the Peace Conference to hold a *sesion solemne de homenaje* (solemn session of homage) in his honor. I arrived at a meeting late. Barreda already had gotten the assent of the other delegates—even

Rodrigues Alves—so he confronted me with this proposal. All the delegates, he said, were for it. "I take it you'll agree."

"No," I answered. "I don't agree."

But I must agree, he protested. Saavedra Lamas was chairman; he was leaving; he wanted this session.

With the second Argentine delegate, Dr. Isidoro Ruiz Moreno, listening to every word, I said that Saavedra's vanity and perverseness had prevented our having a treaty months, possibly years, earlier. Besides, he had insulted President Roosevelt and had intrigued against pretty nearly all the delegates including myself. And I warned Barreda Laos that if he brought up the subject at the impending session I would repeat in the Minister's presence every word I had just said. Rodrigues Alves beamed.

After an amusing session, full of awkward pauses, at which Saavedra was all charm and expectation and Barreda Laos dared not broach the subject the Chairman was waiting to discuss, the delegates got together again. Barreda, finding me adamant on the session of homage, suggested a dinner.

"No dinner," I said.

At that Ruiz Moreno, by then Number One man on the Argentine delegation, a distinguished lawyer and president of the Argentine Institute of International Law, spoke up.

"Whatever you agree on, you'll have to have while he is still Foreign Minister. Otherwise I will not attend. After he leaves office I will never speak to the man again as long as I live."

At last, after some urgent persuasion by an emissary of Saavedra's, I consented to a lunch, which the other delegates had thought he would never accept, on the condition that there would be only one speech, to be delivered by Rodrigues Alves as Vice Chairman of the Conference, after having been approved in advance by all the delegates.

On the day before the lunch, Rodrigues Alves decided he had to make a 12-hour round trip to Mar del Plata, leaving me to preside and make the speech, which I duly submitted to all the delegates, including the guest of honor.

I began with a long tribute to the great silent leader, which completely mystified the guests because Saavedra Lamas had never been known to be silent. At last I named him: President Justo. From there I went on to liken the Conference to a great liner beset by storms and calms, with Justo as captain and Saavedra as first mate. Now our first mate was leaving us, I said, and we wished him godspeed.

He was livid with rage; nevertheless I had his respect, as he proved when six years later I returned to Buenos Aires as Ambassador on post. Also the respect of his delighted compatriots, because I had refused to pay homage where no homage was due.

5

The revolutions of 1936 and 1937 brought complete changes of government in both Bolivia and Paraguay. And each new set of delegates to the Peace Conference wanted to repudiate everything its predecessors had agreed to. We were able to prevent that: fortunately all the American governments (except Mexico, where recognition is constitutionally automatic) had made recognition of the revolutionary regimes conditional upon approval by the mediatory delegations, who in turn made it conditional upon the observation of commitments made by preceding governments. Still, it was a great strain and a great handicap to have to educate and persuade new delegations, especially when we had to deal with Foreign Ministers like Finot in Bolivia and Stefanich in Paraguay, who had steadily opposed peace and were for fighting the war to a finish. I confess there were times when I felt that the only way to get an agreement between Bolivia and Paraguay would be for the mediatory powers to knock their heads together.

The mediatory powers had no such belligerent and impractical idea. Where they erred was in getting discouraged, and losing interest. As early as 1936 Chile withdrew Nieto del Rio, and in spite of my unremitting efforts no Chilean ambassador was accredited exclusively to the Peace Conference until April 1938, when at my urging Manuel Bianchi was appointed. Saavedra Lamas made motions toward withdrawing the Argentine representation, and we went over his head to President Justo. Brazil several times wanted to withdraw Rodrigues Alves; whereupon, with his consent, I would get the Bolivians, who had demanded ambassadors accredited only to the Conference, to insist that he stay. At last the State Department began to show impatience; and when the new Argentine administration was inaugurated I received a telegram saying that since Saavedra Lamas was out and Hull was finding it difficult to justify to Congress a special embassy at the Conference, I should now leave Buenos Aires for my new post as Ambassador to Colombia.

I answered that if I left, the Conference would certainly blow up and the war would resume. Moreover, I dared to predict that within four months from our first meeting with a new Argentine Foreign

Minister we would have a treaty. As it turned out, I was wrong; it took four months and five days. But at that moment the Department allowed me only two.

In May the Conference at my insistence once more sent committees of delegates to Bolivia and Paraguay. I wanted to recreate the psychological conditions that had prevailed in June, 1935. This time I went to La Paz, as chairman of the committee. With me were Manini Rios, head of the Uruguayan delegation, whom we had enticed back to the Conference, and young Orlando Leite Ribeiro, deputy for Rodrigues Alves who would not go to La Paz because of the altitude.

The only Bolivian hero of the Chaco war, Colonel Busch, was now President, and most of the Cabinet posts were held by members of the military junta that had thrown out the Toro government. The Foreign Minister, however, who had succeeded Enrique Finot was a civilian —an old diplomat, Diez de Medina, a namby pamby in terror of his military colleagues. We could get nowhere with him; so we had an all day meeting with the junta-Cabinet, whose two principal members were Colonel Felipe M. Rivera, Minister of Mines and Petroleum and former military adviser to the Bolivian delegation in Buenos Aires, and a Colonel Olmos, Minister of War, who had a reputation for being venal and tough.

The three mediators sat confronting a circle of stone-faced military men. We could get nowhere with them. At last I decided it was time to throw a bomb I thought I had.

From one source and another I had learned that between twelve and fifteen million dollars' worth of arms and military equipment had been bought by the Bolivians within the year, contrary to every implication if not the actual wording of the June 12 Protocol. I now taxed them with a breach of their solemn agreement.

My bomb was a dud. Colonel Olmos answered that my information was correct but incomplete; they had bought ten million dollars' more of which I appeared to have no record. He went on to make a speech.

Bolivia, he said, had allowed German generals to misdirect its opening maneuvers in the Chaco War. It had also been negligent in knowing too little about the Chaco; especially where water was to be found. Those mistakes had been rectified. They had put 1,600 junior and non-commissioned officers in the Chaco learning the terrain and the location of every water hole; these officers were ready to take over and instruct the troops to be sent in with the new arms and equipment. In other words, the Bolivians were ready to defeat the

Paraguayans, and wanted no part of any peace treaty. They were going back to war.

As soon as he had finished, Colonel Rivera began. He agreed with Olmos, he said, and he was speaking both as a member of the Cabinet and an officer of the Bolivian Army. All the other officers (there were 20 in the room) joined in the chorus.

Poor Manini Rios almost fainted. Having ambitions to become President of Uruguay, he saw his whole political career in ruins. He hadn't wanted to come here anyhow, and he had been ill with altitude sickness ever since he arrived—until that very morning, to be exact. He was positively green. In short, Manini Rios was pathetic.

Rodrigues Alves' young stand-in saw his whole diplomatic career ruined by this assignment to a post far beyond his years and experience.

I was none too happy myself. But I knew I must not show that I was awed or even impressed by Colonel Olmos. When the war whoops died down I turned to him and said, "I am shocked by what you say. You admit having broken your solemn agreement. You even boast of a worse breach than I knew of, although that is a matter of degree and the fundamental breach of faith is what concerns me.

"But when you tell me," I pushed on, "you don't want a peace treaty you are flagrantly violating your country's pledged word in the Protocol and the Protocolized Act. And before you continue such a policy I want you to know that my government will consider that an unfriendly act. And you know what I mean by an unfriendly act [a *casus belli*]. My government will proceed accordingly. And I turn to my two colleagues from Brazil and Uruguay, who will confirm to you that their governments will consider it an unfriendly act."

My two colleagues from Brazil and Uruguay were fortunately in such a panic, first because of Olmos and second because of me, that they were struck dumb. I went on: "Furthermore, I can assure you that the other mediatory powers will agree that it is an unfriendly act. And if the six mediatory powers take it as an unfriendly act, you may be sure that the rest of the American Republics will do the same.

"That, Colonel Olmos, is what you are facing," I concluded, "and you had better realize it. If we are to continue these conversations I want no such approach. You are not going back to war; you're going to abide by your commitments. You want a peace treaty. You'll negotiate, and make every possible effort to obtain it. And there will be no more breaches such as buying arms or training troops in the Chaco."

It was my great good luck that Olmos was too much of a bully to take it. For of course he could have called my bluff lying down. The State Department would no more have backed me up than it would have jumped seriatim off the Washington Monument. Neither would any other American chancellery. The most any of them—including State—would have done is break down and sob.

This the inexperienced Bolivians did not know. The junta caved in and consented to negotiate. We made some progress, and when the afternoon session was over it was agreed the committee should continue negotiations with the Foreign Minister.

After a wasted day I got in touch with Miguel Echenique, an American-educated Bolivian who had become the Patiño general representative in Bolivia. He arranged for me to see President Busch, secretly and alone.

We were leaving on Saturday. At midnight on Friday I took a taxi to Echenique's house. He, meanwhile, slowly drove through a street alongside the Presidential palace. As he passed a side entrance, the President stepped out and entered his car. We met in Echenique's library.

President Busch was said to be tough and—because of his German name—totalitarian. I found him unworldly and immature; a man of no political background or experience. But he had character and intelligence, and he kept faith with me. I had to persuade him that there was no great wealth of oil in the Chaco—I had obtained Standard Oil reports which disillusioned all of the adjacent powers on that point—and also that the schemes of the junta were illusory and threatened disaster to Bolivia. At the end of two and a half hours we had worked out a Bolivian-Paraguayan boundary in the Chaco that Busch agreed to accept and by which he stood when Diez de Medina and Finot (who had become head of the Bolivian delegation) tried to repudiate it.

During our discussion of boundaries I produced several maps of the Chaco—all inadequate. Finally I said, "Let's use the best map available," and drew out a numbered and secret Bolivian General Staff map. The President's eyes opened as wide as saucers. I smiled and said, "Mr. President, don't be surprised that I have this map. It was of course stolen from your General Staff, but not by me. I swiped it from the Argentines."

That was literally true. The map proved extremely useful to us that night.

Busch agreed to a plan I had formed two years earlier: to bring the Bolivian and Paraguayan foreign ministers to Buenos Aires, when the negotiations reached a sufficiently hopeful stage, to recreate the excitement and apprehension that had led to the June 12, 1935 Protocol. He also accepted an important face-saving device for both countries. We fixed two zones, one in the west and the other in the north, in which the boundary lines were to be determined by arbitration, with the mediatory delegates representing their respective Presidents as arbitrators. I may say here that in the north I got the exact line that he agreed to that night; and in the west a somewhat better one for Bolivia.

In making these agreements with no official witnesses I was taking what the State Department would have thought a foolhardy chance. But I knew that with official witnesses present—either Diez de Medina or my colleagues—a frank talk would be impossible and there would never be any agreement. If I had not taken the chance there would have been no treaty.

I had enough confidence in President Busch that as soon as the meeting was over I telegraphed the accomplishment to Rodrigues Alves and the State Department. I reminded the Department that the two months granted me were now up, and innocently inquired whether I was to leave for Colombia. I was told to stay right where I was.

6

The new Argentine Foreign Minister, Jose Luis Cantilo, was inclined to dismiss the Chaco problem as a tiresome chore. His interest was in Europe. At first he was difficult about the plan to bring the Bolivian and Paraguayan Foreign Ministers back to Buenos Aires. We appealed to President Ortiz, and the Foreign Ministers duly arrived just before the great Argentine national holiday, May 25.

The Paraguayan revolution of 1937 had brought to the Presidency the Chief Justice of the Supreme Court, Felix Paiva, who for reasons of prestige had chosen as Foreign Minister Cecilio Baez, an elder statesman in his eighties who back in 1907 had been President of Paraguay. Hardly had Baez arrived in Buenos Aires than he fell down stairs. Strangely enough, the accident did not kill him, but it shook him up badly and made it hard for him to control his bladder. During the interminable opening speeches of our first session with the two Ministers the poor old man had a humiliating accident. That afternoon at his first sign of restlessness, Cantilo on a pre-arranged signal from Rodrigues Alves or myself led him across the hall (crowded with newsmen) to the bathroom of the Foreign Minister's suite.

The session broke up too late for a communiqué to or interviews with the press to make that day's papers. But the press did well enough on its own. Under screamer headlines the evening editions declared that there had been a serious crisis in the Chaco Conference. The stories made much of the fact that at one point the Argentine and Paraguayan Foreign Ministers emerged from the Conference room and hurried across the hall; the Paraguayan in evident distress and Cantilo himself looking very much concerned. Fortunately (the reports went) the difficulty was speedily surmounted by some master stroke of diplomacy, for within minutes they returned, both smiling happily, to the Conference.

When the mediatory delegations made their proposals to the ex-belligerents after the ceremonial sessions, our expectations were fulfilled. The Paraguayans turned them down; the Bolivians accepted. Once more the negotiations were bogging down. There was danger that the Foreign Ministers would go home while we dickered drearily, first with one side, then with the other. How to keep up the tension became a serious problem.

My solution was probably undiplomatic; possibly unethical; but it worked. Only my Brazilian and Chilean colleagues knew about and approved it.

I called in the AP and UP and other American correspondents and got them to help me explain to the Argentine journalists what we considered off-the-record and background information and how to use it. In this Allen Haden, who had been a newspaperman, was invaluable. Gradually we brought in and instructed the Argentine press. Then, working through the American journalists, I held a daily press conference. On one occasion, I remember, we heard a rumor that the whole Bolivian Army had moved up and was facing the Paraguayans. I sneaked it out to the press, which gave it scare headlines and created great excitement and apprehension.

We were having hard going with the Paraguayans, as always. (Two years earlier Soler and Ramirez had made concessions that might have brought peace; then Ramirez repudiated them in a memorandum comparable only to the later Hitlerian and Communist diplomatic brutalities.) Zubizaretta had returned as chairman of the Paraguayan delegation after the 1937 revolution; and Zubizaretta, though a man of integrity, was as stubborn as ever.

We kept up a formidable pressure on him; and at last, on June 29, Efraim Cardozo, a young Paraguayan delegate, telephoned, asking me to see Zubizaretta and himself that afternoon with no other delegates present. After elaborate preliminaries they produced a memorandum I consider historic. Essentially it was the treaty of peace. I was elated.

Zubizaretta had taken the ideas we had been pushing so hard and combined them into the draft before me. Now he and Cardozo authorized me to negotiate on the basis of the draft, but insisted no one but myself must know about it. I protested; I would have to tell the State Department. I would have to deal with Diez de Medina, therefore he must know. And since Argentina was the host country and its Foreign Minister was chairman of the Conference, Cantilo must be told. They agreed I might tell the Department and Diez, but were adamant about Cantilo. At last they agreed on my notifying President Ortiz.

The President was at his summer palace. I raced out there at 60 miles an hour. After describing my interview with the Paraguayans, I handed him the sheet of paper. "There, in essence, is the peace treaty," I said.

He read it through, then turned to me, replying, "Mr. Ambassador, I wish I had your optimism. This won't make the peace."

"Yes it will. This will lead to the peace treaty."

"I hate to disagree with you," he said, "but it isn't good enough."

I answered that I was sure it was good enough.

"If you're so convinced of it," the President replied, "it is certainly worth a try. I don't think you'll succeed; but go ahead. And consider yourself my ambassador from this minute on. Any commitments or any statements you make for your own government I authorize you to make for me and my government. Consider yourself Argentine Ambassador as well as Ambassador of the United States."

Never have I been paid a higher compliment.

And never have I worked harder than during the next 48 hours, developing that Paraguayan document into the treaty of peace.

When at last the Peruvian and Uruguayan delegates had to be told, I hit on the idea of persuading Barreda Laos that the brilliant idea of two zones in which the frontier would be fixed by arbitration was his. It necessitated taking him to see Diez de Medina, with whom we went over and over the two zones. Seeing that Diez accepted them, he was finally persuaded of his own alleged genius; fortunately, because otherwise he would surely have opposed the treaty.

But the visit to Diez led to an unpleasant incident. That afternoon Enrique Finot, who had been chairman of the Bolivian delegation since May, came to see me, bringing Diez de Medina. He wanted me to tell him just what I had said to the Foreign Minister that morning. I did so; whereupon he turned to Diez and said, "You see, I told you what would happen to you in talking alone with a mediatory ambassador [he had been there when we arrived, and could have stayed]. You ought to have had me with you."

Maria was in the room knitting and started to leave as the voices rose. I motioned her to remain, and said, "What do you mean. You know that this agreement has been reached and that it is perfectly all right."

"How do I know it's all right? How do I know it will be carried out?"

"You know because the mediatory ambassadors have also agreed to it. We had a meeting this morning after we met with your Foreign Minister, and it was agreed to."

"How do I know they'll keep their agreement?"

"You know perfectly well that they will meet any obligation they have undertaken."

"No," he said. "I don't trust them. They're a bunch of women."

"We keep our word," I told him. "And I don't permit that kind of talk."

At that he thumped his chest and boasted, "I am the Ambassador of Bolivia."

"Well," I answered, "I am the representative of the United States."

"Poh!" he exclaimed. "I laugh at the United States."

Maria was in a panic. I was gripping the arms of my chair, and she thought I was going to pull myself up and hit him. Instead, I said, "The interview is over." I nodded toward the door, and allowed them to open it for themselves.

For two days the work of the Conference was suspended while Maria and I coldly cut the Bolivian delegate, Finot, but were most courteous to his wife; while the Bolivians tried hard to find an acceptable substitute for a formal apology; while my colleagues argued with them that Bolivia really could not take on a country as big as the United States—and one whose Ambassador had proved himself their good friend; and while I insisted on nothing less than an apology in the presence of all the delegates. At last the Bolivian capitulated, and work on the treaty was resumed.

Our troubles were not over. Zubizarreta, who had actually drafted the essence of the agreement everyone had accepted, began to raise difficulties. Knowing from previous experience how the Paraguayans act when they get cold feet—particularly Zubizarreta, with his visions of creating a political issue that would make him President of Paraguay—I realized that the situation was precarious. I had to force a showdown.

Therefore I deliberately provoked a violent quarrel, protesting vehemently that what he had said amounted to a violation of the June 13 Protocol. We became so heated that Cantilo arbitrarily closed the session.

Forty-eight hours later we met again. After Cantilo had timidly applied some soft soap, old Baez spoke up. Paraguay, he said, wanted it understood that she would never break her solemn pledges; she would never go back on any international agreement. And much more of the same, eloquently.

When he had finished, I said, "That was magnificent, Mr. Minister. I know you mean it; I know you are speaking for your President and your nation, and for your brave armies who fought the war. But it is the exact opposite of what Dr. Zubizaretta, Ambassador and chairman of your delegation, said 48 hours ago in this very room to these very same delegates."

I repeated what Zubizaretta had said.

"Now what I want to know is, who is speaking for Paraguay—Dr. Zubizaretta as Ambassador or yourself as Foreign Minister?"

It blew up the session. A recess had to be called, at the end of which Zubizaretta resigned as chairman and ambassador, because old Baez insisted that what he had said must prevail. If I had not pointed out the contradiction it would have been smoothed over and Zubizaretta would have won the argument. But that would have meant no treaty.

Politically the Paraguayans were left on a spot, for Zubizaretta was powerful (I have told how he successfully defied President Ayala). Fortunately the young delegate, Efraim Cardozo, had the courage to act; and even more fortunately, General Estigarribia was in Buenos Aires at the time. Cardozo pled with him to step into the situation. Between them they persuaded Baez to telegraph President Paiva and get him to appoint Estigarribia in Zubizaretta's place. From that time we had no trouble with the Paraguayan delegation.

During these last difficult negotiations, Cantilo lost heart. Manini Rios had already beaten his second retreat. On the afternoon of July 3, Cantilo pronounced the situation hopeless and declared there was nothing to do but to admit defeat and close the Conference. I was able to get the session adjourned before he could take the threatened action.

That night the American Society of the River Plate was giving its annual Fourth of July dinner. I knew Cantilo would be seated beside Maria. I impressed the seriousness of the situation upon her, told her just what I thought about it, and in short briefed her so thoroughly that, as always, I could depend on her to save the day.

That she did. She got Cantilo into a discussion after he had said that the negotiations were a waste of time; and at last she said, "My husband has told me that it was only a question of a few more days."

"Yes," he answered, "but your husband is always very optimistic."

She reminded him that admission of failure would mean a black eye for everyone, himself included, and suggested that if he would just let the thing go on for a week or two longer, he might find that peace was not impossible. He promised to do so.

That was near midnight on July 3. On July 9 the treaty was signed in the midst of tremendous rejoicing, with the heads of the mediatory states exchanging congratulatory telegrams with the ex-belligerents and the Argentine Congress and Senate holding a solemn joint session (their second in history) of homage in honor of the delegates to the Conference. It was immediately ratified; in Bolivia by a constituent assembly that had been convened to write a new constitution, in Paraguay by plebiscite.

Little remained to be done. The matter of the arbitration was already settled, although only those at the top knew it. Before the treaty was signed, the boundaries had been fixed, and President Ortiz had wisely insisted they be drawn on a map. All the delegates, including those of Bolivia and Paraguay, knew exactly where the Presidents of the six mediatory powers, acting as arbitrators through their ambassadors, would place the frontiers. Only the press and the public were deceived; but the deception was vital to the peace settlement.

When the results of the arbitration were made public, our military missions would place stone markers along the frontier and report to the Conference. For that I was not needed in Buenos Aires. I could now, I wired the State Department, go to Washington and from there to my new post, leaving Ambassador Weddell to represent the United States until the Conference ended. The Department approved. Not so my colleagues. Cantilo at once made representations to Washington through Ambassador Felipe Espil for my departure to be delayed, lest some unforeseen emergency arise that no one but myself could handle. The other mediatory powers did likewise. At a farewell dinner tendered me by all the delegations, Cantilo announced that the dinner was somewhat premature, since the State Department had that very afternoon granted his insistent request that I be allowed to remain in Buenos Aires. It was very complimentary.

The next two months were pleasant. For the first time in three years I was under no pressure. At our scheduled one or two meetings a week we drank coffee and chatted. Meanwhile I was reading up on Colombia, doing a little work on my final report, and finishing up the work of the delegation.

It had been a hard assignment. For three years I had not dared leave Buenos Aires, even during the periods of terrible summer heat. Always there were unexpected difficulties—some trouble of our military observers in the Chaco; or the Bolivian President or Paraguayan Foreign Minister sounding off with a belligerent speech. Someone had to be there to handle such things immediately if the Conference was not to be destroyed. There was one period when I used to spend sleepless nights thinking of the war that would certainly follow the failure of the Conference—a war that I knew must inevitably coincide with the one brewing in Europe.

On a wall in my home hangs a photograph of Efraim Cardozo, the young Paraguayan delegate who risked his political future during the final negotiation of the treaty. I am proud of the inscription, which is in Spanish. It reads:

"To Ambassador Braden—to whom many mothers owe the lives of their sons."

Chapter XXII

IN April 1937 Sumner Welles wrote me that the President wanted me to go to Colombia, which he said would be raised to an embassy. He also emphasized that it was no run-of-the-mill post, but a tough assignment.

That I hardly needed to be told. With war in Europe imminent, the German airline SCADTA in Colombia was a potential menace to the Panama Canal. I had seen enough of the Condor and Lufthansa companies and their operations in South America, and knew enough of German intrigue there, and of German hopes of renewed war in the Chaco, to consider the SCADTA situation as serious as any an ambassador could face. Events proved that I was right.

Other problems included the Colombian debts, national and local, to American bondholders, all in default, and those relating to American oil and power interests. When I reached Washington late in 1938 I did as I had done before leaving for the Chaco Conference: I called for all of the State Department files on every important topic I could think of in connection with Colombia. I was assigned a room with a long table on which I frequently had several piles of documents as much as two feet high, to the discomfiture of the personnel, who had never seen anything like it. It was customary for an ambassador, career or non-career, assigned to a new post to come back to Washington, call on the President and Secretary of State, be entertained by the chief of mission of the country to which he was going, and make a superficial review of any matter he was asked to look into by some Cabinet officer or business firm. In short, his life between posts was pretty exclusively social.

When I became Assistant Secretary of State I changed that. Every single official going to one of the American republics, whether as ambassador or in a lesser capacity, was thoroughly briefed on problems and policy, first by a desk-man, then by the deputy director and director of the office. After that I had one or more sessions with him, going over everything item by item and emphasizing policy. Only then did I permit him to go into the field. I made them work. That seemed to me the obvious preparation for a new post; but it largely was unheard of in the Department, and the other sections did not adopt the plan while I was there. My system now has been generalized.

Besides studying the files on Colombia I talked with representatives of the American companies that had investments or trade there. I did not have to look them up; they came flocking to see me. And the Colombian-American Chamber of Commerce, representing all business firms in this country with trade or interests in Colombia, gave a big luncheon for me at the Bankers' Club in New York.

The Pan-American Society honored me with a big dinner, for which they took the whole Biltmore Roof. At that dinner I first met the famous Captain ("Cap") Torkild Rieber (R.I.P.), chairman of the board of the Texas Oil Company, who was later forced to resign because of his alleged close association with Hitler's agent, Dr. Gerhard Westrick. Rieber went on to make a huge fortune building ships for the United States during the war. While we were at dinner, G. Butler Sherwell, who had just come back from Spain, congratulated Rieber on having supplied Franco with $5,000,000 worth of gasoline. Rieber was delighted and proud of himself, and told me in some detail how he had extended this substantial credit to Franco.

It shocked me that a man would deal so freely with his company's assets. As it turned out, the Texas stockholders did not lose, because Franco won his war. Actually, Rieber had gambled on one totalitarian world power against the other: the Falangists supported by Hitler against the Loyalists supported by Stalin. My own attitude toward these two forces was "a plague on both your houses."

Rieber's title was real. He had been captain of a Texas Company tanker and from that had worked up to become chairman of the board. When Gulf Oil decided to sell the famous Barco Concession in Colombia, Rieber bought it, and took over the South American Gulf Oil Co. He then persuaded Socony Vacuum to take a half interest in it. A few days before I sailed for Colombia he embarked on a chartered United Fruit passenger ship with all the Texas Company and Socony Vacuum directors and a few other business friends and associates, for a luxury cruise to the Barco Concession. He invited me, as the new Ambassador, to go along; and he never was able to understand why I refused.

I shall have more to say later about Cap Rieber and his Colombian operations. W. R. Grace and Co. consulted me about their coffee interests, factories, and shipping in the person of their vice president in Washington, Robert H. Patchin. American and Foreign Power was in a real mess in Colombia, and I talked with Curtis Calder, then its

President and later chairman of its board and that of Electric Bond and Share.

I first met Calder back in the '20s at a big party given by Ed Kilburn, vice president of Westinghouse, who became my firm friend during the Chilean electrification. He was a Texan, and had been brought North by Sidney Z. Mitchell, then president of Electric Bond and Share, the biggest of all the big holding companies. Mitchell, a graduate of Annapolis—at the foot of his class, had built up this pyramid of power companies. He put Calder into American and Foreign Power, a subsidiary formed by Floyd B. Odlum, later president of the Atlas Corporation. Having made holding companies pay off so profitably in the United States, Mitchell and Odlum decided they should do the same in Latin America. Odlum made a sort of Grand Tour, buying up properties in 11 countries, including Colombia.

Curtis and I became good friends. He and his wife, Maria and I, often went dancing together. In Chile in 1931 I was impressed by the bad situation of American and Foreign Power subsidiaries there, and upon my return I warned Curtis that trouble was threatening and his manager was not the right man for the job. He was unconcerned.

Going to Chile again in 1933, I learned the subsidiaries were having exchange difficulties and Calder's manager was going into the black market.

I warned Curtis: "That's all right for a Chilean company, but an American company should not risk it. They will find out some day, and you'll be in trouble."

Once more he didn't believe me. After my return from the Commercial Conference, I again warned him that he could expect trouble any day. He asked what I would suggest, and I said, "You've got to send somebody down there to put things in order, and that quickly."

He had no one to send. My going was mooted, and I indicated my willingness if the terms were satisfactory. Nothing happened.

That was in July 1935. In September, just after I had agreed to go to the Chaco Conference, he called me. "Spruille," he said, "I'm in hell's hole in Chile."

"I'm not surprised," I answered, "in view of what I've been trying for several years to tell you, and particularly in view of our last conversation."

"Yes, I know. I need you desperately. I want to see you tomorrow. You fix the terms—whatever you want—to go down to Chile for us."

"Curtis," I said, "you're just 24 hours too late. Only this morning I accepted the ambassadorship at the Chaco Peace Conference, and

I'm leaving for Washington at 8:30 tomorrow morning to be sworn in."

I consented to think over his situation and advise him. Thurman Lee was with me at Stonehurst, and agreed to go the next morning to Calder's office and convey my recommendations.

I knew that the Chilean Minister of Finance was the critical or sinister figure at that point. My advice to Curtis was to retain as his attorney my friend Ernesto Barros Jarpa, and to do so as quickly as possible. He sent word how grateful he was for my advice.

About six months later Curtis came through Buenos Aires. When I asked whether he had retained Barros Jarpa he said he had not; that his vice president in Chile had advised against it.

Not more than three months after that, the Chilean government forced his company into a deal that involved sharing the directorships and accepting a Chilean governmental nominee as president. The nominee was Ernesto Barros Jarpa.

Before I left for Bogota I had a long talk with Calder. He admitted his company's investment in Colombia was about 30 per cent water; they had paid too much for their properties. Even so, they were entitled to a return on the remaining 70 per cent, but they had never made a penny on their common stock and not more than one per cent on their senior securities.

"The Colombians are yelling to high heaven," said Curtis, "that we don't give them enough power. How can we on the rates they fix? I can't go out and borrow money here at five or six per cent and put it in down there where we get only one per cent on our senior securities and nothing at all for our management or other expenses."

And of course he was right.

I went to Colombia well informed about the troubles of American and Foreign Power. Other business concerns interested in Colombia came to me: the National City Bank, South American Gold & Platinum, the various oil companies, and others, whether they were in trouble or not. But there was one exception: Pan American Airways.

Meanwhile I was going over the SCADTA—a German Airline—files very carefully, learning as much as I could. There were a very few vague hints of a possible tie-in between Pan American Airways and SCADTA. So few were they, and so vague, that recognizing them at all might almost be likened to clairvoyance. I began asking in the State Department for information on the relationship between Pan American Airways and SCADTA.

No one could answer. Some alleged there was none. I asked for a check with the War and Navy Department. Neither knew of any tie-in. At last, a week before I sailed, I asked Larry Duggan, at that time head of the American Republics Division, to make an appointment for me with Juan Trippe, President of Pan American Airways. Larry telephoned in Sumner Welles' name, and the request for an interview was practically a command from the State Department. Yet the best Mr. Trippe could do was to give me an appointment at his office the day before I sailed. I was too much concerned to stand on ceremony; I accepted the appointment. But when the day came, Mr. Trippe found he just could not see me; he was called out of town—so sorry.

Mr. Trippe may have really regretted that "urgent out-of-town business" later. For at that point I blew my top. I called Duggan and told him to raise hell with Pan American, and to demand that I be received that very day by someone in authority. The result was an appointment with Evan Young, a vice president whom Juan Trippe had hired away from the Foreign Service. I walked into Mr. Young's office very much annoyed by the cavalier treatment I had received. And when he tried to evade the issue and to give me the impression that Pan American had no interest in SCADTA, I pounded the table and said, "Mr. Young, Pan American Airways *has* an interest in SCADTA, and I propose to know what that interest is!"

Whereupon he broke down and confessed that Pan American's interest was 84 per cent. If the smooth and diplomatic Mr. Trippe had kept his appointment I might not have learned that all-important fact until too late, and future events might have taken a different turn.

2

Besides being frequently and most generously entertained during this interval between posts, I was honored by one invitation which added considerably to the burden of work I had undertaken. Johns Hopkins University invited me to deliver the Meier Katz Lecture and at the same time to receive the honorary doctor of laws degree at a special convocation. Maria and I went to Baltimore and spent a couple days as guests of President Isaiah Bowman. The convocation was held on January 4, 1939, with Dr. Stephen Duggan, head of the Carnegie Endowment and father of Larry Duggan, reading the citation; after which I delivered my lecture, a resume and general discussion of the Chaco peace negotiations with some conclusions on the subject of war. It was the second time in its history that Johns Hopkins had had a special convocation; and since the first had been held for Marshal Ferdinand Foch, I felt almost as much honored by the convocation as by the degree.

In 1937 I sold Stonehurst, and Thurman Lee rented a house for us on East 81st Street. Our children were living there, with Maria's sister Laura superintending the household. After Maria and I returned the house was completely full, for Maria's sister Anna was there, as were my eldest daughter Maruja, who had been married in Buenos Aires, and her husband, William Lyons. The house was also full of dogs, and the room of my younger son, Spruillito, was lined with glass tanks containing little tropical fish.

Those fish caused me some mystification upon our arrival in New York. The reporters, who were at the ship to interview me, wanted to know when I had become interested in breeding fish. I didn't know what they were talking about until I learned that Spruillito had won a prize offered by the Natural History Museum for the production of a new breed of fish. Instead of entering the contest as Spruille Braden, Jr., he had entered as Spruille Braden.

The fish story did not end there. Spruillito was extremely proud of his fish, and had electric lights behind the tanks to show them off. His brother and sisters did not share his enthusiasm; they had to maintain a running fight to make him change the water in the tanks often enough to prevent an unpleasant smell from permeating the upper floors. They were not sorry when I told Spruillito he could not take his treasured fish with us to Colombia.

Neither Maria nor I was able to get around to packing until the night before we sailed. I was moving luggage downstairs around three in the morning when, coming upstairs, I found on the landing a suitcase standing in a pool. I began loudly airing my opinion of all three dogs. But the water was coming from the suitcase and the suitcase was Spruillito's; he had dismantled his tanks and placed them in it, water, pebbly sand, fish, and all. I had done the dogs a grave injustice.

We sailed on one of the large Grace Line passenger ships. Spruillito and our daughter Laurita sailed with us, as did Maria's sisters, who, with the dogs, went on down to Chile. The usual way to go to Bogota was to get off the ship at Baranquilla, on the Caribbean side of the Isthmus, and continue from there by plane. But I had decided even before leaving Buenos Aires that I would go through the Canal and leave the ship at Buenaventura on the Pacific side. I wanted to consult the commanding officer in the Canal Zone, General David L. Stone, about the Canal defenses and about SCADTA. I found him and his staff pretty nervous about what SCADTA's German pilots might do to the Canal in case of war. They were not especially alert to other dangers.

Buenaventura was then one of the most unlovely towns in the world. It was tropical, malarial, sopping wet, and very muddy. It was also primitive. We spent a night in its one hotel, uncomfortable and none too clean, and left by train the next morning at dawn, which was none too soon. Captain John C. (Toby) Munn, my Naval attaché who was to become invaluable to me, met us in Buenaventura and shared the discomfort of our night's lodging.

On the train to Cali we had a private car, with guards stationed at each door. In Cali we were met by the mayor and various officials of the Colombian Foreign Office, and were entertained by the American colony at a big reception and dinner. We spent the night in a rather better hotel than that at Buenaventura, and in the morning reentered our private car for the journey to the end of the railway line. There the two automobiles I had brought along were offloaded—a Packard limousine for formal official use and a Plymouth for general utility. (I bought these cars myself, for as Ambassador I was not entitled even to one, although my Naval attaché rated a car and driver.) The Embassy had sent down two men who could drive, one of them the so-called messenger who was really the official chauffeur.

We piled our luggage into the Plymouth and drove the Packard over the 11,000 foot Quindio. On that lap of our journey we were unguarded, although holdups and murders were not uncommon there. From those heights we descended into the Magdalena River valley, to Apulo, 500 feet above sea level, the favorite watering place of the *Bogotanos*. We were never tempted to return. The place is very hot, and infested with venomous snakes and insects.

There the President's luxurious private railway car awaited us for the final climb up to Bogota, about 8,500 feet above sea level. We arrived after dark and our private car at the end of the long train was practically out in the yards when we stopped. We walked what seemed to us half-way across Bogota before we finally espied the official red carpet, the armed guard, and the chief of protocol waiting to receive us.

Having been told it would be unwise to count on living in a hotel until we could find a house, I had rented one through the Embassy from a wealthy Colombian who lived most of the time abroad. It was beautiful but flimsy. Before we had lived in it very long, a six-inch hunk of the wall in the impressive main hallway fell out for no apparent reason, letting in unexpected light and air. When it rained, as it does constantly at certain times of the year, we had to have a large supply of pans and buckets to take care of the leaks. Just before our first big reception, as I walked through one of the living rooms I felt the floor heave under me. It even heaved under Maria's slight weight. We had it tested, and found that if a crowd should occupy that room at the reception they would certainly go through the floor—a drop of not more than four feet but enough to break some arms and legs. The boards had to be taken up and the beams reinforced before we could entertain.

The whole staff was waiting in this house to receive us, with champagne; and the wives had had dinner prepared for us. Presently the butler entered and announced, *"Quando les provoca"* (When you are provoked).

In Chile the verb *provocar* in that sense has a sexual connotation. Maria and I were a bit taken aback and he had to repeat the expression before we realized that it meant, "Dinner is ready when you are." It is the usual Colombia way of announcing a meal.

We never had a better servant than that butler. He took charge of the household and ran it with great intelligence and efficiency. We had inherited him from our landlord, and when we left I bequeathed him to the embassy, to take the place of our chief messenger, who was retiring.

We had no such luck with cooks. There wasn't a good cook to be had in all of Bogota. Even having the best restaurants cater for our luncheons and dinners was unsatisfactory. A cook known as a *banquetera* (a banquet cook) was recommended to us. She was so nervous that she went to pieces every time we gave a luncheon or dinner; that is to say, a couple of times a week. So Maria, during most of our three years in Columbia, would have to supervise and even cook the meal, dash upstairs and dress, dash downstairs again for a final look at what the so-called cook was doing, then receive her guests and hope for the best.

Such crises are not unusual in an embassy, to judge by our experience. I remember a particular one when I was Ambassador to Cuba. We were giving a large formal luncheon for Cardinal Denis J. Dougherty, who was quite a gourmet. At 11:00 A.M. the cook, the assistant cook, and the dishwasher all walked out; 46 people were due to arrive at one. Maria went down to the kitchen with her personal maid and the laundress, took 46 partridges out of the deep freeze, prepared the meal, then dressed and came down to receive.

During lunch, the Marquesa Piñar Del Rio turned to her and said, "I see you have a new chef."

"Yes," said Maria, "I have."

"He's much better than the one you had," the Marquesa assured her.

Having to live like Gilbert's "working monarch" in Bogota was especially hard on Maria, for she was never well during the three years we were in Bogota. For some unknown reason—it may be the combination of high altitude with humidity—the climate of Bogota often is extremely trying for foreigners, especially for women. Maria would become depressed and start to cry without having the slightest idea what she was crying about. Or she would become so irritable that occasionally I actually departed the house in order to leave her alone, knowing it was just a case of nerves.

After we had been there about a year the senior secretary of the embassy, Gerald Keith, spoke to me confidentially of his concern about Helen, his wife.

I interrupted. "You mean she starts to cry without knowing why," I said and went on to describe Maria's symptoms.

"How did you know? Has she told Mrs. Braden?"

"No. I'm describing Mrs. Braden's own behavior; and it seems to happen to most of the women members of our staff, unless they're young girls like my daughters."

Even the *Bogotanos* were affected; and as there is a streak of despondency in the Indian character, there were many suicides. The *Bogotanos* attributed them to the hot winds from the *llanos* (the plains of the Orinoco, to the South) and to speak of "suicide weather," just as the Chileans would speak of "earthquake weather." There were several favorite suicide methods, of which the most popular was jumping over the Tequendama Falls, about 25 kilometers from the city. Another, which became popular during our last year there, was to put a stick of dynamite in the mouth and ignite it. That was especially unpleasant for the Embassy—the city square invariably chosen for this was only a couple of blocks from the chancellery. Also cutting the wrist arteries was quite popular.

Whatever the method chosen, the suicide invariably left behind a poem, and the poems were invariably published. Many suicides, for reasons unknown, were committed on Sunday. On Tuesday the poem, often several of them, and more often terrible drivel, were published in the leading newspapers.

3

A day or two after our arrival in Bogota I called a meeting of the Embassy staff to give a positive statement of my policies. I noticed that Jim (James H.) Wright, a junior secretary (his official rank was third secretary) appeared enthusiastic. I later learned of his efforts to persuade the charge d'affaires to seek action by the State Department on several problems I mentioned, but without success. William Dawson, the minister preceding me, was gentle, affable, likable, but without drive. Thus the Colombia mission had no chief of any particular strength or decisiveness since Jefferson Caffery left in 1932.

Jim Wright proved to be the one man I could really depend on. He had a brilliant mind, and it was not beyond his remarkable memory to know practically all of Shakespeare. He had served nine years in Germany, spoke German fluently, and was without illusions about the Nazis. Nor did he have illusions about the Communists; he was sure Alger Hiss was a Communist years before Hiss was exposed.

Jim soon became my right hand. He learned how my mind worked and the way I expressed myself; he could draft a dispatch I would sign with almost no revising. I put him through hell, though, to teach him. I once asked him to reduce a 30-page statement he had drafted to one page. On his first effort he brought it down to 15; on the second, to two. I then compressed it to the required single page, adding another thought. Jim went off fuming, but he learned the lesson.

When Jim was recalled to Washington I submitted a highly laudatory report on him. He served in the Department for some time, in jobs far beyond his age and rank. I wanted to take him with me when I went to Argentina as Ambassador. But Harry Norweb was succeeding me in Cuba, and as Norweb was more interested in talking to his brokers in New York by telephone and in his numismatic collection, Jim was sent along as counselor to do his job. When I became Assistant Secretary of State, I made Jim a special assistant to me. He and his wife Midge also became our close personal friends; we had them stay with us for a time after we returned to Washington from Argentina.

Jim was stricken with leukemia while working with me in the Department and at first was given three months to live. But he made such a remarkable comeback that it was decided the diagnosis might have been wrong. When I was leaving the Department I urged on Secretary Marshall and my successor as Assistant Secretary, Norman

Armour, the appointment of Jim Wright as Ambassador to Nicaragua, where his work would not be strenuous and he could get plenty of sunshine. Instead, they made him Director of the Office of American Republics, a gruelling job whose incumbent is obliged to work days, nights, Sundays, and holidays.

From that time Jim's health steadily failed. He died a little more than a year after I left. I have always regarded his death as one of the great personal losses of my life.

After a short time in Colombia I acquired an extremely able and hard-working commercial attaché, Merwin Bohan, who had served both in Chile and Bolivia. As soon as he arrived I told him I wanted to be ready with a "blacklist" of those dealing with the enemy so that we would not have to rush one out when we came to need it, as I was sure we would. We went to work on it at once, and Bohan was tremendously helpful. After Pearl Harbor, when all missions were ordered to prepare blacklists, I merely sent ours to the Department.

My naval attaché, Captain John C. (Toby) Munn was a flying officer in the Marine Corps. He had under him two tough Marine sergeants who were really tops. Munn lived in Bogota, but was also naval attaché in Ecuador, Venezuela, Panama, and Costa Rica. He had a single-motored Grumman amphibian. On flights to Cali, a frequent run, he would fill the tank before taking off. Then, when he reached the point where he had to begin the climb over the mountains (he had to rise up to 21,000 feet) he would circle until the plane was light enough, make the climb, cross over, and drop quickly down to Cali, arriving with hardly a drop of fuel left. I protested vehemently through State to the Navy Department against risking the lives of an officer and a sergeant in such an inadequate plane.

The military attaché was a colonel who had his headquarters in Costa Rica and unless summoned for some special reason dropped by for a few weeks about every 18 months. That was in the beginning. By the time I left Colombia we had a permanent military attaché, a colonel whose staff consisted of a lieutenant colonel, a major, a captain, and I don't know how many sergeants. Our naval attaché's office grew in about the same proportions, but by that time the invaluable Toby Munn had been transferred.

After we entered the war, the economic and political work greatly increased, and my staff was increased correspondingly. But before that we never seemed to have sufficient stenographic and clerical help. My efforts to persuade the Department to send more clerks and stenographers failed repeatedly. They did send down one man, an excellent stenographer, but he had to work not only for me but for my two top secretaries. After working three months and losing 25 pounds, he quit. I bombarded the Department with demands for adequate help, and all the other chiefs of mission were doing likewise. It was no use. Cordell Hull had decided that the budget, which as late as 1938 was about $15 million a year, was exorbitant and had to be decreased. It looked like a pretty hopeless impasse. And it lasted more than a year.

At last I achieved a breakthrough, not because I planned it but because luck was with me. In April 1941 I came to Washington alone. One night, after spending some time with friends at my hotel, the Carlton, I saw Frances Nash Watson, daughter of Father's friend E. W. Nash with whom he started the Braden Copper Company, having supper with her husband General Edwin ("Pa") Watson, Missy Le Hand, and Harry Hopkins. I stopped at their table to greet them and they invited me to have a drink. I had never before met Hopkins, but of course I knew how close he was to the President.

They asked me about the situation in Colombia, and I took the opportunity to air my grievance to Hopkins.

"Do you mean to tell me," he asked, "that the Department doesn't give you adequate stenographic help?"

"Exactly, as I've told you," I answered.

"All they've got to do," said Hopkins, "is move their little finger. They can have $500,000 before ten o'clock tomorrow morning for that if they want it—whatever they need. You tell them I said so."

And that was all I needed. I went over to the State Department the next morning and told the top administrative people, including Sumner Welles, what Hopkins had said. Within a few weeks I had all the help I had asked for.

During that same encounter with Harry Hopkins, he happened to bring up the subject of hotels, and I mentioned the inadequacy of those in Bogota. The principal one was the Granada, which people liked to call the *Gran Nada* (the great nothing). Hopkins asked whether that was true of other Latin American cities.

"There are some good hotels in Buenos Aires," I told him, "and some in Rio; but in general the South American hotels are none too good."

"That we can easily fix," said he. "How much will it take to put up a good hotel in Bogota? Ten million d 'lars?"

"You can build a perfectly adequate hotel for far less than that."

"Well, it doesn't matter," he said. "Whatever it is. In these other cities, whatever they need—we'll just go down there and put up hotels and go ahead and run them."

"Mr. Hopkins," said I, "I've never been in the hotel business, but I have been in real estate, and I know that one of the most difficult problems in the hotel business is to get management. And without adequate management you just lose your shirt."

His answer was that they would get young men just out of college to run the hotels. They wouldn't expect a return of more than three or four per cent; that would be quite sufficient.

"You can't get that return," I told him, "without competent management. You ought to plan on making 20 or 25 per cent and then maybe you'll be able to make six or seven."

"No, no. We don't want that. We only want two or three or four. As a matter of fact, we ought to do that in a whole series of businesses; just take some college boys and send them down there and let them go to it. We can pay them twenty or twenty-five thousand dollars a year."

Obviously Harry Hopkins had no idea of the value of money, or of the nature of business. But he did get me the stenographers I needed.

4

President Eduardo Santos of Colombia became my very good friend. He was an honest and patient man, an advocate of representative republican government but politically timid. When I first arrived he was a bit fearful. The last two Presidents had been accused of allowing themselves to be dominated by the United States, and he had no wish to incur the same criticism. It was not long, however, before he gave me his confidence to the point of entrusting me with his private telephone number, so that I could bypass the Foreign Minister, Lopez de Mesa, a fantastic character who lived in the stratosphere, as the *Bogotanos* liked to say, and was almost impossible to bring down to mundane affairs. Santos and I did a lot of business over that private wire. If I had to use him, he would invite me to come at once to the palace, or pick me up for a drive while we talked. Or I would meet him at his house. I found him always approachable, understanding and reasonable, though often indecisive.

Apropos of this relationship, in 1954 we were both luncheon guests of Dean Carl Ackerman at Columbia University, and during lunch Eduardo said he had always felt that the ideal relationship between a big power and a weaker country was demonstrated while I was Ambassador to Colombia.

I said, "Of course that was largely your doing."

"No," he answered, "it was due to both of us. We worked together on it."

"Well," I said, "I have an argument against that. I followed the identical policies and procedures in my other posts and didn't have the same happy results. Witness, Peron. I tried to do exactly the same thing with him. It is the president not the ambassador who does it."

The Foreign Minister, Lopez de Mesa, except that he was blond and beardless, looked like Don Quixote and was just about as down to earth. His literary style was one of the most difficult I have ever encountered. Several of his books are gifts from him to me. I have never found the courage to read them. On one occasion I had to cope with a translation of two pages from his pen. We had received a circular instruction from the Department to ask the Foreign Minister for his views on the nature of the post-War world, and to request that he be brief. Those two pages were the result.

I gave the statement for translation to an American who had lived in Latin America all his life, enough of it in Bogota that he knew its excellent Spanish. He worked on that document three or four days. Then I turned it over to Gerry Keith and Jim Wright, and when they were through I had a go at it myself. It took me two hours, dictionary at hand, to revise it into what I considered a faithful rendition of the original but in intelligible English.

Even though Lopez de Mesa was notorious for having his head in the clouds, he was capable of being quite practical and painstaking when the spirit moved him. Moreover, he could be a charming conversationalist. And in his official position he strove to be fair to the United States.

He was a bachelor, but by no means an ascetic. At the time I was there he was rumored to be among the lovers of a German woman who was known to be a Nazi spy. By another German woman he had had an illegitimate son who, under his mother's name, was a Captain in the Colombian Army and very pro-Nazi, like a great many of his comrades. One day my daughters Laurita and Pat were out riding with some young friends when they were joined by a group of Army officers. Later they all decided to stop for an aperitif. My daughters spoke Spanish without accent, and the young officers did not trouble to dissemble their political sentiments. Their pro-Nazi remarks got the restaurant-keeper so enthusiastic that he led the whole party into a back room and proudly showed them a bullet-making machine. Of course the two girls at once reported to me, and

I informed the Minister of War. The place was raided and the machine confiscated. One of the young officers was Lopez de Mesa's son.

I genuinely liked the Foreign Minister; but as the pressure of work and worry increased with the War, I found it exasperating to be instructed on his theory of the evil of mining in general when I tried to discuss the specific evil of the smuggling of platinum out of Colombia for the German war machine. I had to appeal to Santos, who arranged that on any problem I had to discuss I should deal directly with the Minister concerned. Thus I was enabled to settle specific questions without having to go through the Foreign Minister, although I was careful to keep him informed in a general way, lest I antagonize him.

President Santos led a wing of the Liberal Party. The other was led by Alfonso Lopez, whom I had met at the Montevideo Conference and to whose brilliant "fronting" for me in a meeting of his committee I paid tribute in a previous chapter. The two men thoroughly disliked one another, and Santos was always nervous about Lopez' reaction to his conduct of Colombian-American relations. Lopez was not too good a friend to the United States, although he had been educated in this country and had many American business associations. Ironically, many Colombians during his presidency assumed that this background naturally predisposed him to accept American domination. They were mistaken.

In their youth, Lopez and the dictator of the Conservative Party, Laureano Gomez, had been great friends in spite of their political differences. Later they became ardent enemies, and during my stay in Colombia there was great bitterness between them. Some years afterward, Lopez' wife died and Gomez wrote him a letter of sympathy that revived their old friendship.

Laureano Gomez, a senator and the owner of the newspaper *El Siglo,* made Lopez' anti-Americanism look like warm friendship. For that matter, although he became President of Colombia, he was anti-Colombian to the point that he actually published a violently insulting book on the thesis that all equatorial peoples were worthless, including his own. He seemed to prefer the Germans, with whom he had various business connections. Politically he was strongly pro-Nazi.

After I had been in Colombia a while I suggested to Santos that if he had no objection I thought it might be well for me to meet Gomez, who had been whooping it up against the United States on the Senate floor and in *El Siglo* even before my arrival. Santos thought it a good idea, so I arranged the meeting. It lasted four hours.

I lost no time in broaching the subject of his grievances against the United States—"Yankee imperialism" and all that, and especially our "steal" of the Canal Zone. To my astonishment after half an hour he interrupted what I thought quite an eloquent and persuasive dissertation on the "steal" to say that he thought the separation of Panama had been the best thing that ever happened politically to Colombia because the Panamanians were a hopelessly inferior lot.

No, he continued, his principal grievance was the attempts of our Protestant missionaries to convert the Latin Americans. I was able to set him right on that, partly from my own experience in Chile. We always had Catholic priests at our mines, I told him, and permitted no Protestant missionaries to work among our employees, having observed that what conversion did was to deprive the convert of the consolations of the Catholic faith without really winning him over to Protestantism, thereby leaving him vulnerable to Communist infection.

We discussed his criticisms point by point, and at the end of our interview Laureano declared that there was absolutely no reason why our two countries should not be the best of friends. In the glow of this sentiment we bade one another an affectionate farewell, and for six months there were no attacks, while his every reference to me personally was couched in terms of high esteem. I entertained him at the Embassy and saw him on other social occasions. We were the friendliest of enemies.

Then suddenly and for no apparent reason he returned to the attack. Once more I got together with him for a long talk, after which everything was fine again. And so it went, right up to Pearl Harbor.

Among my genuine friends in the Conservative Party was Augusto Ramirez Moreno, a man somewhat younger than Laureano Gomez, and a remarkable orator; the only man who had ever defeated Gomez in debate, and who on that occasion would certainly have taken over the Conservative leadership if the chairman had not adjourned the meeting. I met Ramirez soon after I arrived, and for some reason he took a liking to me. He was friendly to the United States and especially admired Roosevelt. Therefore I relied on him and on Roberto Urdaneta Arbelaez, later President of Colombia, when I needed cooperation from the Conservatives.

I had it on Pearl Harbor Day. When the news broke, they voluntarily came to the Embassy residence. From there they telephoned prominent Conservative leaders all over the country, and within a couple of hours had some 20 important commitments to petition

President Santos to break relations with the Axis. Incidentally, that same night I myself persuaded Alfonso Lopez to telephone the President recommending the break. The President therefore, with the backing of his Liberal opposition and of twenty important leaders of Gomez' party, broke off relations the next morning—an action he would hardly have dared initiate.

5

There was strong anti-American sentiment among the Colombian clergy; and in the Aruba area some of the Spanish priests were tied in with the Nazis and engaging in actual espionage—a situation that was not unusual in Latin-American countries having a Spanish priesthood. I made it a point to meet as many as I could of the clergy, including some anti-American Jesuits. Some strong anti-American propaganda was being generated by a Spanish religious order near the Gulf of Aruba.

But the main Catholic attack came from much higher up—from the Archbishop of Colombia, in a pastoral letter after the pattern of Laureano Gomez' onslaughts, but with some additions. One of these was the so-called "Moreno story," which has been a favorite all over Latin America among anti-American Catholics.

It was attributed to my good friend Dr. Isidoro Ruiz Moreno; to the effect he had asked Theodore Roosevelt, during Roosevelt's tour of the South American countries, "When does the United States expect to take over Latin America?"

The former President was supposed to have answered, "As soon as our Protestant missionaries have converted all your Catholics to Protestantism."

I have always considered the story apocryphal. But even if it was true, the obvious meaning of Roosevelt's reply was, "Never."

So viciously anti-American was the Archbishop's letter that when it was read at mass Maria nearly left the church and some of her friends were embarrassed and expressed their regret to her after the service. Once more I went to the President, this time to ask whether he had any objection to my talking to the Archbishop. He thought it was a fine idea.

His Excellency received me in a peculiar way that of course I understood, although never before or since has any Catholic prelate done just that. He sat enthroned on a dais two or three steps high, while I looked up at him from a cane bottom chair below. I began to repeat the explanations which had satisfied Laureano Gomez, but I had not gone far when the Archbishop interrupted me:

"You don't know the whole story, Mr. Ambassador. I had two other paragraphs that my advisers persuaded me to leave out. They were on the Panama Canal."

It was not his fault that he had failed to shoot the works. Nevertheless, what I suppose I should call the audience ended on a fairly friendly note.

When I came to the United States in the spring of 1940, I made a point of seeing Cardinal Spellman, to whom I described this whole situation. He at once offered to take it up with the Vatican and ask that proper instructions be sent to the Papal Nuncio and to the Archbishop. I told him I thought it would perhaps be better for me to handle the situation on the diplomatic level, rather than have orders come from the Vatican and possibly antagonize the recipients and do more harm than good. I would appeal to him if I found I was failing. One thing, however, I did want, if he could arrange it: to have an American bishop visit Bogota. There had never been an American bishop in Bogota, and very few American priests.

A few days later his Eminence invited Maria and me to lunch on the following Saturday to meet Bishop (later Archbishop and Cardinal) John F. O'Hara. Bishop O'Hara had been brought up in Montevideo, which meant he spoke perfect Spanish, and was in the Consular service before he entered the Church. At the luncheon, as arranged, I invited him to visit us at the Embassy in Bogota; and he accepted.

He came. And he did a magnificent job. Just by being the first American bishop to visit Bogota, as well as being a guest in the Embassy and having me accompany him on his protocolar calls made a deep impression. The Papal Nuncio entertained him at lunch, and we invited the leading priests, prelates, officials, and citizens to meet him at luncheons and dinners.

When I took him to call on Lopez de Mesa, the Foreign Minister opened the conversation with the words, "Excellency, I want to express my opinion to you. I have given a great deal of thought and study to it, and in my opinion the entire policy of the Catholic Church is totally mistaken."

I had warned the Bishop that he was about to meet an eccentric; so he took this in stride. And there they sat for half an hour, arguing the Vatican's attitude toward Hitler and Mussolini and what Lopez de Mesa declared to be its lack of Liberal principles.

When that was over, Lopez said, "Now, I have another bone to pick with you, and that is that I think the Catholic Church in the United States is all wrong."

And they went at it hammer and tongs for another half hour.

On the morning of his last day with us, the Bishop went to say mass at a nearby convent, and asked me to wait until he returned so that we might share breakfast. He brought with him a little Monsignor who, he told me, was the author of the Archbishop's anti-American pastoral letter. In my presence he turned to the Monsignor and said, "Now, in anything else you ever write, whether it is for the Archbishop or anyone else, if you touch on the United States you are to submit what you have written to the Ambassador for his review and approval before it is made public in any manner."

And the Monsignor meekly acquiesced.

We had no more trouble with the Colombian hierarchy. Later, indeed, when I supported the idea of founding a school in Colombia by the American Catholic clergy, I won their enthusiastic friendship. Bishop O'Hara's visit, exhausting as it may have been to him, contributed greatly to the improvement of Colombian-American relations.

Chapter XXIII

THE American business firms in Colombia were, as I have said, almost all in one or another kind of trouble; some of their own making and some due to government controls and government failure to meet obligations even under concessions. This, of course, was by no means peculiar to Colombia.

When I reached Cali on my way to Bogota, I learned that the American-owned telephone system of Bogota had been expropriated, and that the Baranquilla Light & Power Company, a subsidiary of Curtis Calder's American & Foreign Power, was about to be taken over. This news, coming immediately after the Mexican expropriation of American oil properties, was extremely disturbing. My ambassadorship seemed to be beginning inauspiciously.

Curtis Calder's general manager for Colombia, an Irishman by the name of Foley, had got his start in Mexico. He was one of the type I used to call "the old-time Americans from Mexico"; they called the Latin Americans "natives," although the people who thus by implication became colored—and therefore to be ridden over roughshod—might be just as white as themselves. They did much to give Americans a bad name throughout the Southern Hemisphere.

I found the company and the Minister of Industry exchanging sour notes in an evident attempt to see which could outdo the other. Meanwhile the company had eleven lawsuits pending. One morning Foley came to see me. He had just lost one of the suits. I asked what he proposed to do about it.

"Well," he answered. "I've talked to my attorneys, and they advise me to split it into 10 different pleadings in addition to the original one, then to renew that and go ahead with the 10 new ones and the other 10 original suits." (The local attorneys in Colombia, Chile, and elsewhere often turned out to be tougher than company representatives.)

"Now, look here," I said, "you can't expect to get anywhere by multiplying lawsuits. Public opinion is swinging very much against you; and you can't blame the public. They don't know why you can't give them more power. All they know is that they can't get enough for their own homes, let alone for the development of new industries. You've got to go to the very top with this matter, and I am ready to offer my services as Ambassador. I am willing to go to President Santos and tell him exactly what they will be up against if they insist on nationalizing."

I told him what I had learned from Sidney Z. Mitchell: As power expands, the curve of investment grows in almost geometrical progression. It doesn't increase by the same amount yearly. If it begins with $50,000, the next year it will have to be $100,000, then $200,000; and so on as long as power is increased.

"I'll explain that to the President," I said, "and ask him how they are going to get the money, first to pay for your properties, then to make the new investment that will be necessary each year. They will be under strong pressure not to increase rates, and without higher rates they can't make a profit or even break even. On the contrary they'll have a deficit, and that will mean falling back on the taxpayers. But when they go to Congress asking for funds in geometrical progression they will very probably be turned down. So the service will continue to be poor, and public criticism will no longer be directed at a foreign company, but at the Colombian government.

"Then I will suggest that we get in touch with Curtis Calder, and that the government name representatives to sit down with him and work out a solution, with myself when necessary sitting in as mediator."

Oh! said Foley. That would get them nowhere. The Minister had declared emphatically that the trend all over the world was to government ownership of public utilities; and that was where Colombia was headed, and no argument about it.

I decided to act on my own. The next day I saw President Santos and gave him the argument I had outlined to Foley. I suggested that a new concession be negotiated with the company enabling it to charge high enough rates to cover costs, pay something on all securities including common stock, and raise money for expansion.

"If you agree that I am right," I said, "I am willing to go over the local manager's head and cable my friend Curtis Calder, president of the company, asking him to send someone down to work this out with you."

"I think you're right," said Santos.

Calder sent down a fine, distinguished old man of the "elder statesman" type, who had at one time been Foreign Minister of Nicaragua. Being himself a *Latino,* he knew how to deal with the Colombians;

he also knew the company's side of the dispute. An operating vice president came with him, who remained just long enough to be sure we had the right information on the company's needs. Foley, I need hardly say, was furious.

The agreement, which took 18 months to work out because of several Cabinet changes, was advantageous to both sides. Both Calder and Wm. S. Robertson (he had rejected my advice to retain Barros Jarpa in Chile), as well as several other company officers, told me it was the most satisfactory agreement American & Foreign Power had ever had.

Before I leave the subject I should point out that my argument to President Santos was proved wrong. I never guessed that the United States government would ever put the American people as taxpayers in direct competition with themselves as stockholders and bondholders. The following story will illustrate my meaning:

At a National Association of Manufacturers luncheon in the early 50s I was seated on the dais next to Robert L. Garner, vice president of the International Bank for Reconstruction and Development. He asked me what I thought of the power loan just made to the Philippines.

"I can't discuss that with you," I answered, "because I don't know conditions in the Philippines. But I do criticize you for the loan you've just made for power in Chile."

"But why?" he asked, evidently astonished.

"Because you know perfectly well that American & Foreign Power has millions invested in Chile, which came from the American people. And you know that the Chilean government has broken its agreements, imposed impossibly low rates, and made all kinds of unfair exactions. Now you come along with financing for a new development to enable the Chilean government to sell power to American & Foreign Power for resale. The government has actually increased its own rates, but won't permit the company to charge any more for the power it has to purchase at the higher rate. The company is caught between the upper and nether millstones.

"You should never have loaned the Chileans one penny," I went on, "without insisting that the American security holder be protected. Indeed, you might much better have supported American & Foreign Power. They can finance the development of all the power Chile needs if the company will only be permitted to charge fair rates."

Bob admitted I was talking sense. The story typifies the double fleecing of the American taxpayer that has characterized our bureaucratic government-to-government foreign investments since World

War Two. These days matters have become more complicated. With one hand the U.S. government finances an organization to encourage private enterprise and investment in Latin America and with the other it prohibits sending of U.S. capital abroad.

The American telephone company, which Bogota was expropriating, had been in continual trouble over rates and service. It was owned by the Associated Telephone and Telegraph Company, with headquarters in Chicago, and dictatorially controlled by the head of the company, one Arthur F. Adams. Besides those in Bogota, the company had interests in Venezuela and Ecuador; and Adams was known to operate his Latin American properties with the advice of a dancing team whose male member had perhaps at some time or other come from Mexico. Adams and his girl friend would go to the night spot where the dancers were employed, and take a table beside the dance floor. There, over champagne, he would consult the dancers about what to do in Colombia or Ecuador. I once tried to consult him by telephone from Bogota, and found that he had wasted his champagne.

He had as his technical manager in Colombia a big, husky American, very decent and honest, but hardly up to dealing with the *Bogotanos*. For that job he retained the services of an Italian who boasted of having been with Mussolini in the March on Rome. This questionable character was trying to negotiate the sale of the company to the municipality.

I had trouble getting the company's accounts, as submitted to the authorities, and when I finally did, I found they had been seriously falsified. Meanwhile Mussolini's buddy made his sale: the municipality was to take over the telephone system and the company was to receive municipal bonds in payment. The expropriation had been averted. Everything looked just fine.

The *Bogotanos* are too shrewd to fall for such subterfuges. It would not take them long to discover that they had been had; and then they quite properly would stop payment on the bonds. The Associated would cry "Robbers"; the whole story would be misrepresented in this country; the fraudulent sale would reflect on all Americans in the eyes of the Colombians; in short, there would be a mess involving Colombian-American relations.

There was nothing to do but unmake the deal. That was risky for me. If the Associated's stockholders lost out, the company could say, "We made a good bargain, but the Ambassador prevented it from going through." I would have found myself involved in an unpleasant controversy.

Nevertheless, I persuaded the municipal authorities and the governor of the department to cancel the deal. Then I was able to help put through an honest sale. But not until I had forced the company to fire its Italian negotiator. Adams had fired his honest American manager, knowing he was partly responsible for my getting the true picture, and had replaced him with a perfect nonentity. The Italian was in complete charge. Through the Department I made it clear to Mr. Adams that I knew all about his agent's deceptions; and I stressed the Italian's boasts about being an original Fascist. At last he was replaced by Spencer Phoenix, an honest, fine man who had been connected with New York banking firms; and the vexatious negotiation was brought to a successful end.

2

The South American Gulf Oil development was so important I had decided even before leaving for Colombia to see it for myself as soon as practicable. In June, therefore, I flew to Baranquilla and from there to the point on the Magdalena River where the pipeline was to emerge. Then we followed the pipeline by automobile into the Catatumbo jungle forest, one of the thickest jungles I have ever seen. It was almost pitch dark along the trails that had been cut through, and the area swarmed with jejenes.

My first experience of this insect had come on our way to Cali, when Maria and I got off our private car at one of the stations. Maria looked down and saw what looked like a gray mist on her stockings. When she started to brush it off it proved to be a cloud of jejenes. They infest the tropics, and their bite makes a mosquito bite seem positively soothing. Not only do they cover one's arms and legs with bites; the bites itch agonizingly and go on itching for weeks and months.

Another hazard of the jungle was the Motoloni Indians, a tribe so primitive they did not use feathers on their arrows—a fact, fortunately, that detracted from their aim. They would lie in ambush and attack the white men, then disappear into the jungle. Or they would attack boats from the banks of the little stream where the refinery stood; so that all boats had to be surrounded by wire mesh. The men guarding the camps at night were protected by the same mesh. While I was in Colombia about a dozen men were killed each year by the arrows of the Motolonis.

In spite of these hazards and the incredible heat, Rieber and his manager and his crews were doing a magnificent job; a demonstration of superb engineering skill. The pipeline started in the jungle where the oil wells were, went up some 2,000 feet, and then down again almost to sea level. It crossed the Magdalena River and ran on out to the coast. Every foot of it had to be buried, which meant miles and miles of trenches.

After seeing that and going over the refinery and the wells and the campsite for the employees—in the steaming jungle three degrees north of the Equator and near sea level—it was a relief to enter the plane of Rieber's manager for the flight back to Baranquilla. It was a sudden transition to the utmost in luxury—comfortable armchairs, drinks, and a steward dancing attendance. On our way out we occasionally flew low over Indian settlements whose residents hopefully shot their primitive arrows toward the plane.

Before I leave the Catatumbo, I cannot forbear to mention one of its most extraordinary features: its famous lights. Every night what looks like an electrical display appears over the jungle—lights shooting up through a general glow. The inhabitants believe they are the souls of the departed. So far as I know their cause has never been determined, but everyone has seen them who has been near the jungle.

Back in Baranquilla, I attended a dinner in my honor, the last of a series of social affairs that had started before my trip into the jungle. It was my first visit there as Ambassador, and our Consul General, Nelson Parks, and his staff, as well as the Colombian authorities, had really put themselves out to entertain me.

The next morning my son Bill, who was attending Columbia University, and my youngest daughter Patty, who was in Bryn Mawr, arrived in Baranquilla by Grace Line ship. With the representative of the Tropical Oil Co. and the Andean Pipe Line Corporation, the three of us flew from Baranquilla to Cartagena, from where I was to visit the Tropical Oil Co. installations and the pipeline operated by the Andean Corporation.

The only skyscraper in the magnificent old Colonial town of Cartagena was the office building of the Tropical Oil Company, and that was a skyscraper only by contrast, being no more than four or five storeys. It looked incongruous, but I was grateful for it because of the penthouse apartment of James W. Flanagan, organizer and head of the Andean National Corporation.

Flanagan was another of the old type of American-Mexican-Irishman. He had started in Mexico as a railroad fireman and engineer. He made a fortune out of the Andean pipeline, and set himself up near Toronto in what looked like a modest country house but proved upon entering to be an Arabian Nights palace. Maria and I visited him there when we came to the States early in 1940. He entertained lavishly and was very popular with the people of Toronto. His collection of pre-Colonial Central American gold and jewels was one of the most superb I have ever seen.

The Cartagena penthouse contrasted most favorably with my tent in the jungle. It was spacious, luxuriously furnished, high enough to get what breeze there was, and presided over by two Filipino servants who attended to our every want as diligently and efficiently as if their employer had been present. We were once more entertained day and night and all night. After a couple of days of this I had a silly experience.

The United States had a Naval mission in Colombia, headed by a very fine officer, Captain Lawrence F. Reifsnider. All the inspections and the social affairs had left me no opportunity for a talk with him until our last night there, when the representative of Tropical Oil gave a dinner with no more than 30 or 40 guests at his home on the shore outside Cartagena. After dinner I suggested to Captain Reifsnider that we go out on the porch and have a talk. As we sat there in our big rocking chairs, the waves broke soothingly on the rocks below and I went sound asleep listening to myself. I have occasionally gone to sleep listening to someone else, but never before or since have I put myself to sleep. I woke up still talking and with a vague idea that I had been saying something about the PWA. I never knew, for Captain Reifsnider was too diplomatic to tell me what I had said.

Finally we left Cartagena to visit the Tropical oil fields and refinery located up the Magdalena River at Barraca-Bermeja. We flew in a Junker plane so decrepit that I expected it to crash momentarily.

3

The Tropical Oil Co. was the first to go into Colombia, where it developed the Barranca-Bermeja fields. The concession was to run "from the date of initiation of operations" for a given number of years, at the end of which period the fields would revert to the government. The date of initiation was in dispute between the Colombian government and the company. The government contended that operations had begun when the company began to sink its first exploratory well; the company that they had begun when oil was first produced commercially. The difference of three or four years in the date of expiration which the dispute involved was of course extremely important to the company.

I was sorry to see this difference growing up between Tropical Oil —i.e. Standard Oil of N.J.—and the government; therefore I took the matter up with President Santos and the Minister of Mines and Petroleum. Our discussions finally reached the point where the Minister said:

"If you could get the company to do some relatively simple things —things they should do anyway—I would make a deal. I have to have a reasonable basis on which to announce publicly that we have made a deal, because there has been so much press agitation on the question of the date when this concession is to end."

The question was already in the courts and going up to the Supreme Court, so the Minister's problem was very real. He stated his demands, which were relatively insignificant, and said, "On that basis I am ready to make an agreement extending this concession 15, 20 years. I don't care how long—25 if they want it."

Elated by the offer, I called in the Tropical Oil representative and put it to him. He flatly refused it.

"Well, for heaven's sake," I said, "consult your people back home about the proposition."

He duly reported that they had turned it down. I learned subsequently that they had done no such thing; he had simply not consulted them. When I came to the United States some months later I talked to Flanagan and was told the company would have been delighted to accept the offer. In the meantime the Colombian Cabinet had changed and the Minister was out. That meant an entirely new start.

Again in 1941 I was able to arrange a deal. I saw Flanagan in Panama and explained it to him; but he handled it awkwardly. In the end they had to give up the concession. It was a repetition of the experience I had had in Bolivia during the Chaco Conference, when the Bolivian government had availed itself of my good offices to offer terms that would have secured the Standard Oil of New Jersey concessions in that country. Stupidity in the United States and lack of authority or incompetence in the field had resulted in unnecessary expropriation.

4

The other major problem in the oil industry involved all the numerous companies in Colombia. The main companies were the

Tropical-Standard Oil group; the Texas Company and Socony Vacuum (now Mobil Oil), apart from South America, Gulf controlled both of them; Richmond Oil, a subsidiary of Standard Oil of California; and Royal Dutch Shell. The subsidiaries, however, were legion; and the reason lay in the Colombia oil law.

It must be said in fairness to the Colombians that they had tried to adopt a sensible oil law. Some years earlier they had brought down George Rublee of Dean Acheson's law firm to help them draft it. And it was as good a law as one could wish except for seven items, two of them insignificant, three important, two vital. Of these last two, one was an impracticable restriction of the number of acres that could be conceded to any one company—100,000 acres in the Magadalena Valley and 200,000 in the Llanos, the southeastern plains, close by and at the same altitude as the Venezuela lowlands. Reasonable limits in the U.S. but not in the wilds of Colombia.

Wildcatting for oil is a notoriously expensive and speculative undertaking. A company taking a concession in Colombia had first to bring in geophysicists and geologists to go over the area and decide where the first wildcat well should be drilled. It had to bring in the drilling apparatus. By the time a company drilled its first well it would have spent a minimum of half a million dollars in the Magdalena Valley, a million in the Llanos. But to wildcat a property requires not one but many wells, and a company could spend millions just to find out whether a concession was worth anything or not. If it did strike oil, it had to invest tremendous sums in development before it could take out a barrel commercially.

From the Llanos oil could have been taken out much more cheaply through Venezuela, to avoid pumping it up over the Andes; but that the Colombian government would not permit. A company, therefore, having found oil in the Llanos would have to spend a minimum of one hundred million for its pipe line, refinery, and other necessary equipment.

No company could afford to put such amounts of money into the number of acres allowed it under the law. Hence the companies without exception had formed numerous subsidiaries, each taking the maximum acreage permitted. Of course, the practice was a glaring evasion, of which any crooked or socialistic government could easily take advantage if it wished to cause trouble.

I was gravely concerned about this situation—for one thing because of the attitude of Alfonso Lopez, who used to make disturbing remarks about it when in his cups. And he was in his cups with a fair degree of frequency; indeed, while he was President there was a saying that Venezuela had as President Lopez Contreras and Colombia had Lopez *con tragos* (with drinks). At that he was an abler and more intelligent man than most so-called statesmen.

In his cups Alfonso Lopez would say, "This is just fine. Let the Yankees come in with all the money they can bring. Then, when they've found the oil and put in the refineries, we'll take over." It is a theory that has spread far in recent years.

The second vitally important flaw in the oil law was a provision giving any inspector for the Bureau of Mines and Petroleum, regardless of his technical knowledge, the absolute right to decide where a company should drill. He could make the holders of a concession drill holes a foot apart all over it if he saw fit. That item meant a serious hazard for the companies.

Another difficulty that could not be cleared up in the legislation at the time derived from a change made about 1865 in the law governing landownership. Before 1865, private surface ownership included subsoil rights; thereafter subsoil rights belonged to the government. A company wanting to explore could therefore negotiate for both surface and subsoil rights with an owner whose title predated the change. If the title postdated the change, a concession must be had from the government. The government, in its eagerness to profit from concessions, was putting pressure on the courts and doing some other pretty questionable things to make difficulty for any company that took over a privately owned property.

The American Minister at the time the oil law was drawn, Wm. Dawson, had evidently understood nothing of what went on, for his dispatches wholly ignored its bad features. My experience as an engineer told me just how bad they were. The State Department had never questioned the law, having the impression from Dawson that it was excellent. It was this attitude the oil companies encountered when they tried to talk to the Department. They were used to it; they had met such complete lack of sympathy with or understanding of their difficulties in Venezuela, Mexico, and other countries that their attitude might be summed up thus:

"It's like our wildcatting risks: we go in and do the best we can and hope that by forming subsidiaries and affiliates we can fight it through."

Their situation in Colombia was not helped by the fact that they were all more or less at swords' points. Tropical Oil, the pioneer company, wasn't sure it did not prefer a bad law; that might discourage other companies from coming in and taking concessions Tropical might want to exploit.

Socony Vacuum was particularly vulnerable on the matter of drilling exactions. Its representative was a younger son of a noble English house. I called him in to discuss these hazards, and he brought with him his lawyers, one of whom, a Colombian, also represented the National City Bank. He and a New York lawyer had assured Socony that its concessions were perfect in every particular, and when I mentioned its precarious position he lost his temper and told me I didn't know what I was talking about. At a meeting in New York at the National City Bank he severely criticized me as a poor Ambassador who interfered with things which were none of his business.

Before I left Colombia Socony found itself in exactly the kind of trouble I had predicted, with the government going after it hammer and tongs. Whereupon the Englishman came and wept on my shoulder and wailed about how right I had been and why, oh why! hadn't they listened to me? The Colombian lawyer, when he saw me, looked very chagrined, and the New York lawyer who had backed him up admitted his error. I must admit that I had enough malice in me to get a certain satisfaction out of their discomfiture.

The difficulties of those oil companies were typical of the worst problems I encountered in every diplomatic post I held: invariably if they had been taken in hand at their inception they could have been quickly and easily settled. If our Minister and the State Department when the oil law was drafted had known something about the petroleum business and had studied the draft intelligently, no trouble need have arisen. But as the companies proliferated so did the potentialities for woe. And to worsen matters, several of the companies retained local attorneys, a few of whom wanted to avoid trouble and therefore misled them, as had happened to Socony Vacuum.

In a previous chapter I quoted President Roosevelt's rules for a successful civil service career—which, added up, to one: Be on time, don't be drunk on the job, and live long enough. Our diplomats tend to let troublesome problems alone, on the theory that 80 per cent of them will solve themselves and the other 20 per cent, being insoluble, had better be dropped. They can always excuse inaction, resorting to the argument, "This is what might have happened; so you see the situation could have been much worse." That attitude is a great evil of American diplomacy.

The U.S. oil companies because of their fear of prosecution under the Clayton Act and the anti-trust laws dared not have meetings, even under my auspices. I got around this hurdle by asking them to act as advisors to me and therefore to meet in a group with me. I asumed all the responsibility for these gatherings. After they left, the Shell representative, Max Burns, an extraordinarily able, experienced and intelligent man would join me alone. Thus we made a most useful working arrangement with President Santos and the Colombian authorities.

Slowly, I got the various oil companies together. I was helped by my engineering experience, and by conversations with the heads of the companies on my trips to the United States. The time came when I was able to call their representatives into my office, jot down the points on which they should reach agreement among themselves, and advise them to draft a joint memorandum to the Colombian government. To my stupefaction, I found they didn't know how or could not agree.

The incompetence of many American businessmen in dealing with governments is something that has to be experienced to be believed. Either they will fail to state their case convincingly or they will include statements they have no right to make to a government. In extreme cases they will even assume the attitude taken by the Standard Oil Co. of New Jersey in the Bolivian case I spoke of: That it would not be "dignified" for the company to approach the government; the government should come to the company.

Those companies in Colombia were in the end unable, even with the help of whole batteries of attorneys, to draft a satisfactory memorandum. I finally had to draft it myself, then bring them together and get them to agree to it.

Royal Dutch Shell—the only non-American company in Colombia, however, raised no difficulties. The British had had the sense to put an able representative, Max Burns, in the field; and as proof of Max's ability, he later became President and Chairman of the Board of Shell for the whole United States.

Having brought the companies together as my advisors, I pointed out to President Santos the advantages that would accrue to his country from the changes in the oil law requested in the memorandum. If investments were thus safeguarded, I argued, millions of dollars would flow into Colombia for exploratory operations. Richmond Oil, for example, was planning to invest four or five million dollars a year; the other companies a little more or less than that. And if they struck oil, that meant enormous investments in development.

Santos had his own problems. There was the attitude of Alfonso Lopez; anything Santos wanted Lopez automatically opposed. And the Conservatives, under Laureano Gomez, were always ready to make trouble. It was not until I was about to leave Colombia that I got a complete agreement, including Santos' promise to push through the necessary legislation and assurances from both Lopez and Gomez that they would support it. The agreement would have been achieved a year earlier if some of the companies had not delayed it by vacillation and timidity.

If I had remained in Bogota I would have got action on the agreement. But after I left there was no one in the Embassy to hold the companies in line and keep up pressure on the government. Jim Wright had been transferred and the Chargé d'Affaires lacked the necessary energy. Arthur Bliss Lane, who succeeded me as Ambassador, had no understanding of the problem. I urged the Department to push it through. The Department—Lawrence Duggan and Philip Bonsal—did nothing. For want of energetic action the legislation was allowed to lapse; whereupon the companies for a considerable period abandoned their explorations, to the accompaniment of protests from the Colombians.

This was one reason why I took up the matter again after I became Assistant Secretary of State. During a visit to Washington by President Mariano Ospina of Colombia, I had a meeting at Blair House with him, Roberto Urdaneta Arbalaez, later President, and Eduardo Zuleta, subsequently Foreign Minister and twice Colombian Ambassador in Washington. Once more I stressed the millions that would flow into Colombia for exploration if the investments of the oil companies were properly safeguarded. They promised to revive the legislation and get it through their Congress. While I remained in the Department I did all I could to push it, but our Ambassador at the time, John C. Wiley, understood it no better than Lane had. At last, however, changes were made in the law which Ambassador Zuleta Angel—another uniquely competent man—assured me were what I had been urging.

I have always considered that negotiation a good illustration of the assistance an ambassador can give in the creation of friendly economic cooperation between two countries, and in avoiding such misunderstandings and mutual recriminations as would have followed if Alfonso Lopez' irresponsible idea—"let them put in their money; then we'll take over"—had been allowed to prevail. I am bound to admit, however, that my view seems old-fashioned. Not only has it become the rule for foreign governments to expropriate American investors; the State Department actually seems to approve—and worse still, even lend indirect financial aid.

An amusing incident in Bogota illustrates the stupidity of which Washington officials are capable. One Ruth Sheldon Knowles, sent by Secretary of the Interior Ickes on a Grand Tour of Latin America, was commended to my good offices by the State Department, which described her as a geologist who had written for various petroleum magazines and the *Saturday Evening Post.* Her father Heinie Sheldon, had been my classmate at Yale, and she was the fifth wife of Carroll Knowles, another Yale friend who was—to put it mildly—erratic. Carroll had turned promoter after graduation, and on one promotion stuck my father for some $1,500. Every few years he turned up with a new wife. Now he wrote me, also introducing Ruth Sheldon Knowles—"Ruthie to you." I turned Ruthie over to Jim Wright, who fed her the information we thought she should have. She wrote a report on Colombian oil—actually the Embassy wrote it for her—and we sent her on her way.

She made the rounds of the Latin American countries, living in the best hotels and entertaining at the expense of the American taxpayers. And from each country she visited she wrote a report on petroleum. The one we had taken the trouble to write for her because of her husband's letter of introduction seems to have been the only one that made much sense. I saw some of her stuff from Venezuela, and it was terrible. But following her trip, all responses to inquiries about Latin American oil, and all decisions of the United States Department of Interior on the subject, were based on Ruthie's analysis of petroleum.

5

Shortly before I arrived in Bogota the United Fruit representative in charge of operations was released from jail. He had been imprisoned for using unbecoming language over the telephone to President Alfonso Lopez. (The situation was aggravated because the call had been traced to the home of our commercial attaché.) After investigating, I felt that although the representative—another old Mexican hand—was certainly in the wrong, the outgoing President had perhaps been unduly harsh. One of my first problems was to quiet the *affaire* down.

United Fruit had been in Colombia for some years. Its own large plantations were surrounded by those of small producers whose fruit was bought by the company and shipped out on its private railway. There had been no trouble until about four years before I arrived. Then the banana trees were hit by the sigatoka disease—a mold for which the company developed the only cure: spraying with copper sulfate.

That meant piping every row of trees—an expense at which the smaller growers balked. They wanted the company to pipe their farms and at the same time to pay them more for their fruit. The dispute over these demands exacerbated feelings already aroused by agitators who were constantly whipping up feeling against the company among the growers.

The company was stubborn; the growers, resentful. It became necessary for me to act as mediator. With a young United Fruit representative who spoke Spanish beautifully and knew how to get along with the *Latinos,* I began discussions with the Minister of Agriculture. Progress was slow; Ministers succeeded one another with surprising frequency, and with each one we had to begin negotiation anew. I left Colombia for my new post just as agreement was in sight. It was completed after I left.

Then there were the Colombian loans—national, provincial, municipal—all in default, with the American bondholders angry because they could not collect, the Colombians because the default had impaired their credit. The Colombians had an added grievance; they felt, as all Latin Americans did—and with some reason—that those loans had been practically forced upon them through high-pressure salesmanship by American investment houses, without consideration for their ability to pay.

There was also what was known as the bankers' short-term credit of some $14 million, advanced by a group of New York bankers after the 1929 crash under pressure from Secretary of State Henry L. Stimson. Why the Secertary or the bankers thought that at that date the loan could be passed on to American investors is unclear. In any case the bankers soon found that they had made a long-term loan, and even though the Colombian government continued to pay interest at something like 3½ per cent they were angry at both the Colombians and the State Department.

They were not wholly reasonable. I remember a luncheon at the National City Bank during one of my trips North, at which Gordon Rentchler, chairman of the board and a good friend of mine, held forth on the outrage of that low interest rate. As we were returning to his office a vice president drew him aside for a brief conversation. It ended with Gordon clapping him on the back and saying, "Attaboy! Fine! That's just great."

Turning to me he said, "That makes the day worth while. We've just loaned a Pittsburgh company $10 million for ten years at 3 per cent."

On that same trip I met with the chairman of the bondholders' protective association, John C. Traphagen, who was then president of the Bank of New York and Trust Co. I found him, as well as the executive vice president and manager of the bondholders' committee, surprisingly lethargic. On the strength of discussions I had had with President Santos and his Minister of Finance, Carlos Lleras Restrepo (years later to become president), I was able to tell them that if they acted at once they could get a settlement at 4½ per cent, more or less. They were afraid to go to the bondholders with the proposal, and by the time they had overcome their fears it was too late. Sumner Welles, Henry L. Morgenthau, and Jesse Jones had stepped into the negotiation and made a settlement at 3 per cent.

In the end the banking group came off as well as the bondholders, and the debts were pretty well cleaned up. Then President Santos made his only demand for a *quid pro quo* during my ambassadorship.

The Colombians needed financing for several perfectly sound projects, and had applied for a loan from the Export-Import Bank. When I went to take leave of President Santos before a trip to the United States in 1941, he said, "After all, I've shown my desire to cooperate with the United States. Now I think the least you can do is to help us with an Export-Import Bank loan."

He was right. Never had an ambassador had better cooperation from the government to which he was accredited. The support given me by President Santos in the SCADTA case alone was of incalculable value to the United States, as the next chapter will show. I readily promised him my help.

In Washington I encountered opposition. I worked with the Colombian desk officer and with the economic specialist in the Office of American Republics Affairs. We could get nowhere.

At last one day the three of us had lunch with the Colombian Ambassador, before going to see W. L. Pierson, President of the Export-Import Bank. I had devised a way of getting around our difficulties, which I explained to my companions during lunch. They were pleased. They said it was a stroke of genius. Indeed, one of them was so impressed that he later claimed credit for the idea.

Pierson was also impressed.

"I agree with you," he said, "and I'll recommend the loan—$10 million for eight years. But it has to be approved by Jesse Jones, and I warn you he is adamant against it."

The Colombian Ambassador had also discussed the proposal with Jones; he knew Pierson was right. There was nothing for it but to try my luck.

Jones was not in Washington. Thanks to Sumner Welles I learned that he was in New York visiting one of the Fisher brothers of General Motors, somewhere on Park Avenue.

There was no time to lose. I was about to return to Colombia. I caught the next train to New York, found out which Fisher brother lived on Park Avenue, and telephoned. Mr. Jones could not talk to me. He was in bed, very ill with influenza.

Nevertheless Sunday morning I went to Mr. Fisher's apartment and, in a way, bullied my way past the maid who admitted me. Jesse Jones received me in his bedroom in pajamas and dressing gown. I don't know whether it was weakness or boredom that weakened his resistance; but it was weak. He gave his approval, and Colombia got its loan.

By the time I reached Bogota the Colombians, in their enthusiasm, had prepared $20 million worth of further projects. Some of those I did not think sound, and I refused, politely but firmly, to support another loan. They understood, and appeared perfectly satisfied. After I had left Colombia they finally did get their $20 million, and much more later—several hundreds of millions. The original loan was paid off in three years instead of eight.

Chapter XXIV

COLOMBIA in 1939 swarmed with Nazi spies. Hitler was fully aware of its potential importance as a base of operations against the adjacent Panama Canal in his projected war. If the United States government had been half as aware of the obvious, my difficulties would have been greatly diminished.

There were many open Nazi sympathizers, not only among the five or six thousand Germans in Colombia but among the Colombians themselves. The situation was favorable for Nazi propaganda and subversion. The Germans were genuine settlers who expected to spend the rest of their lives there. They were chiefly engaged in small business, which brought them into close contact with the Colombians. Many of them had married Colombian nationals. In short they were part of Colombian life. This contrasted with the "Yanquis," who mostly were connected with large corporations.

My very good friend Eddie Rickenbacker gives testimony in his autobiography that bears on Germany's determination to regain her position as a world power after World War I. Eddie cites a conversation he had with Hermann Goering in October 1922, who said to him:

"Our whole future is in the air. It is by air power that we are going to recapture the German Empire. To accomplish this we will do three things. First we will teach gliding as a sport to all our young men. Then we will build up a fleet of commercial planes, each easily converted to military operation. Finally we will create the skeleton of a military air force. When the time comes, we will put all three together—and the German Empire will be reborn. We must win through the air."

The German prestige was greatly enhanced by SCADTA.

This wonderful airline, one of the first—possibly the first—in this hemisphere, was developed right after World War I by Peter Paul von Bauer. From Bauer down to the least mechanic the personnel was German. It may have been one of the ingenious devices for circircumventing the Treaty of Versailles. Certainly its pilots were German flying officers; and except for the chief pilot, Hans Siegstadt, and a Colonel Boye, they were rotated from one Latin American German line to another—SCADTA, SERTA, Condor, Lufthansa—to learn the terrain and flying conditions of the continent before returning to the Luftwaffe.

The Colombians did not know this. They regarded SCADTA as their own airline and its personnel as wholly loyal to Colombia. The line had been a godsend to a country broken up by the Magdalena torrid plains, equatorial jungle and three high mountain ranges that made overland communication painfully slow and laborious. For example, the flight from Bogota to Baranquilla took two-and-a-half hours. The trip by river could take 30 days if one happened to get hung up on a bar. The Colombians had good reason to be grateful to SCADTA. Besides, during a territorial dispute with Peru, Colonel Boye had delighted them by flying all over the disputed territory in a gleaming silver painted plane, in an impressive show of Colombian patriotism.

The Colombian government was no more aware of Pan American's 84 per cent interest in "their" airline than I had found our own government departments, though the ownership dated back 10 years or more. The line even employed a few Colombian pilots, in response to public demand. While I was there one of the planes in command of a Colombian pilot and co-pilot crashed in the mountains killing seven people. We intercepted a message from the Germans to Berlin reporting the incident and observing that perhaps the disaster would put an end to the attempted infiltration of Colombian pilots.

Pan Am operated to Colombia and down the eastern coast of South America. On the western coast it shared with the Grace Line a 50-50 ownership of Panagra. (Curiously, Pan Am and Panagra were constantly having disgraceful fights with each other in Colombia, which I told them to stop forthwith because of the bad image for American companies they were creating in Colombia.) But Pan Am's ownership of the famous Colombian line was apparently a close secret until I pried the information out of a disconcerted Evan Young.

Juan Trippe, founder and president of Pan American, graduated from Yale around 1919. He began his career in aviation by operating a little airline between Florida and Cuba, and went on to develop the great network that today extends all over the world. He ran Pan Am as he saw fit, in spite of some resentment among the board members, who, on one occasion, wrested absolute control from his hands, as I was told by the executive vice president, George Rihl. But the revolt failed. The company records were in Trippe's head instead of the company files. He came back as undisputed czar.

Trippe is suave and soft-voiced, and I found him a past master at side-stepping subjects he preferred not to discuss—such as SCADTA. My first real contact with him came at a meeting in the Department, arranged by the head of the Office of Transportation and Communications. We started to discuss SCADTA, and before I knew it Trippe was describing his problems in Asia.

"Now, Mr. Ambassador," he asked, as sweet as molasses, "what do you think we should do in this situation?"

"Mr. Trippe," I answered, "I'm not here to consider what you should do in Asia. We're discussing SCADTA, and that's the only subject I'm going to talk about."

"Oh, yes, of course, Mr. Ambassador. Forgive me."

2

When Evan Young admitted Pan Am's 84 per cent interest in SCADTA, I vigorously expressed my view of a policy that permitted Germans, with a world war imminent, to control an American-owned airline right next to the Panama Canal. I insisted that Pan American exercise the responsibility of ownership and put in American personnel. He assured me that he would himself go to Colombia in May with one of his associates to do this and to work out, in cooperation with the Embassy, a new agreement with the Colombian government. He insisted that the situation would be handled to my complete satisfaction.

He went on to assure me that Peter Paul von Bauer was absolutely reliable, trustworthy, and loyal to the United States.

"He's Austrian not German," said Young. "And he is anti-Nazi. In fact he has some Jewish blood, and that makes him all the more so. He's really terrifically anti-Nazi. Besides, he realizes that in aviation the United States must dominate in this hemisphere, and that no one can presume to oppose American policy.

"You can talk to him as frankly as you would to me," he went on, "and you can count on him to be as patriotic an American as I am in this matter."

He would of course let Bauer know of my impending arrival, he promised, and tell him to call on me at once. I said that was one of the most important things on my docket; I wanted to see Bauer immediately.

I reached Bogota in January 1939. Bauer reached my office in April. He was another of those sweet people; his tongue fairly dripped treacle. He was mine to command, he cooed; I had only to tell him what I wanted; his role was to obey.

What I wanted, I told Mr. von Bauer, was a long talk with him. And I gave him an appointment for 10 o'clock the next morning.

I did not keep it immediately. Instead I had Jim Wright tell him I was unexpectedly tied up on an urgent official matter, talk to him in German about Germany and how happy the Wrights had been there, and casually drop into the conversation a number of questions I had listed. The ruse worked; Jim caught him off guard. When I asked him the same questions, in different order but officially, demanding serious answers, he contradicted himself several times—not importantly, but enough to convince me he was not to be trusted no matter what Mr. Evan Young thought.

As for that gentleman, he did not show up in May. He never did show up or even acknowledge my repeated demands to know when he was coming. I had Jim Wright, who went North during the summer, see him and give him a piece of my mind—Jim knew my mind well on that subject. Mr. Young apologized and solemnly promised to keep his promise forthwith.

He did not. At last, early in September, Pan Am's staff attorney, David Grant, showed up in Bogota with a list of 10 of the leading German SCADTA personnel who, he said, had already been discharged, and seven more who were to be let out immediately.

"Well," I said, "that's not satisfactory, but at least it's a beginning."

He was going to Medellin, to make sure that the other seven were discharged. By the time he got back, in early October, I learned that nobody had been let out, and there was no apparent intention to let out anybody, although by that time the war had begun. I gave Grant a dressing down that must have impressed him, for he described it afterward to several of my friends, as he said "coming from a Dutch uncle."

He was determined to tell yet another fabrication; this one to President Santos. He intended to see the President and tell him that Peter Paul von Bauer personally owned 51 per cent of SCADTA. I insisted he could not do that, since Pan Am owned 84 per cent. He tried to argue that I was wrong. During the conversation he said, "Trippe is the only one who knows what's going on."

I did not let him go to Santos, who would have known he was lying.

As soon as the war began, I felt it was my duty to tell Santos and his Minister of War the truth about the SCADTA ownership. They both refused to believe it.

"That can't be true, Mr. Ambassador," Santos protested, "Only two weeks ago Bauer sat just where you're sitting now and gave me his solemn word of honor that he owned 51 per cent."

And he repeated what the Minister of War had already told me: they had Bauer's affidavit that he owned 51 per cent of SCADTA.

By that time I had sufficiently won their confidence to convince them without producing documentary proof, as I offered to do. Now, with Grant so insistent on repeating Bauer's lie to Santos, I became pretty well convinced myself that Bauer and Pan American connived to put over the deception on the President.

I was able to persuade Santos to agree to let out the top SCADTA officials—Bauer, Tietchen, Colonel Boye, and a few others. Beyond that he was reluctant to approve a change in the personnel, whose loyalty to Colombia he could not bring himself to doubt. He was personally devoted to the chief pilot, Hans Siegstadt, who always flew the Presidential plane.

He did, however, agree to put armed co-pilots on all planes. He called them co-pilots, but they were really Colombian military flying officers. They were to see that the German pilots and co-pilots kept their planes on course.

Santos phrased his order in such a way that Pan Am and Panagra, flying through Colombia, were not required to have military co-pilots. On the other hand he could not, without making it discriminative, apply it to SCADTA flights within the country while exempting privately owned planes. Tropical and South American Gulf Oil each had several planes, and Gulf had a Swedish Nazi chief pilot who regularly joined other Nazis at the end of a long pier in the old port of Baranquilla, where they exchanged signals with submarines off shore. It was not a bad thing, I felt, to have Colombian military co-pilots on private planes.

A South American Gulf Oil plane, in fact, caused the only untoward incident during the months that the order remained in force. Cap Rieber and his Nazi manager actually had their pilot take off without the military co-pilot, who was beside the plane signalling to be taken aboard. And that in a place so isolated that it could be reached only by plane—or by boat if one were lucky enough to have a private launch. Rieber's manager, the chief culprit, tried to tell me he had thought the co-pilot was merely waving good-bye. I pinned his ears back and when he had the effrontery to return to the subject as I was leaving Colombia, and try again to excuse himself, I pinned them back once more. The action was a deliberate and outrageous insult for which, as Ambassador, I apologized to President Santos.

It had not taken the Germans long to learn that I was demanding their elimination from SCADTA, and to attempt an extremely clever counter-measure. They persuaded the Ecuadorian government to back them in a proposal to extend the operations of their Ecuadorian line, SEDTA, into Colombia and on north. If the Colombian government had consented, I would have got them out of SCADTA only to be confronted with exactly the same menace to the Canal from SEDTA planes.

I learned of this proposal from the Colombian Minister of War, Castro Martinez, and went at once to Santos. It was not easy for the Colombians to refuse. Colombia and Ecuador were both neutral, as we were, and very friendly. Fortunately, we were able to work out a formula enabling Colombia to reject the SEDTA application without offense to the Ecuadorian government.

3

After having been misinformed by David Grant, I burnt up the wires again, urging the Department to insist that a fully authorized executive be sent to Bogota. On October 16 he arrived in the person of the executive vice president, George Rihl.

Rihl was another old Mexican hand, but a superior man. He had started in the oil industry, and got into aviation by developing a little airline to transport oil company payrolls, above the reach of bandits. Pan Am later took over the line, and Rihl with it. I met him in Pan Am circles in New York and was casually friendly with him at the Montevideo Conference, where he was an observer and lobbyist for Pan Am.

Like Trippe, whose attitude he was bound to reflect, Rihl was evasive and obstinate. It took until October 25 to get him to agree on the number and categories of Germans to be replaced in the beginning, and to work out a long-range program for their total elimination. To dismiss them all at once, he insisted, would be impossible; a sudden changeover would disrupt operations and bring tremendous protest from a public dependent on SCADTA for transportation.

The agreement concluded, Rihl took off for New York with a promise to put it through within three to four weeks. A couple of weeks later, he returned and to my astonishment told me Trippe had vetoed everything. I was understandably enraged. He had with him J. Maxwell Rice, a junior Pan Am executive, who drew Gerry Keith aside and asked him to tell me that Rihl had had one heart attack and to get me to go easy on him lest he have another. I answered that I would "go easy" on Mr. Rihl when he lived up to his agreements, but not before.

Once more we worked out a plan even more detailed than the first, which Rihl assured me would be carried out. I was disposed to believe him, since I knew him to be in daily consultation with his New York office. Nevertheless I called in my stenographer and in Rihl's presence dictated a telegram to the State Department giving the details of the agreement and ending, "I have dictated this in the presence of Mr. Rihl, who agrees to everything here stated."

He tried to squirm out of it. I said, "You heard it. Where is there any change to be made? You agreed to everything I have said."

Again nothing happened. Again I began heating up the wires to Washington, concluding with a telephone call to the Department on New Year's Eve. That brought Rihl back to Bogota, accompanied by a number of Americans who, he alleged, were to take over as administrative officers, executives, and chiefs of division in SCADTA.

When he brought two of them to my office, an amusing thing happened. It was possible for someone to be in a little office off of a gallery extending from my waiting room, without being seen. Toby Munn and Gerry Keith were there when Rihl came in, and heard him warn his companions, "Now don't forget what I told you. This Ambassador is a clever bastard. You look out for him."

Having learned by now to question Pan Am's word, we checked on Mr. Rihl and his entourage for the next few weeks. Not a single one of those Americans ever went near the SCADTA offices, hangars, or planes. On Thursday, February 15, I summoned Rihl and Rice to my office and told them that unless the few Nazis they had agreed to discharge were out by 6 P.M. the following Monday and the Americans in full authority I would cable the Department that I could no longer accept responsibility in connection with the Panama Canal. Moreover, I would denounce Pan Am to the President, to Congress, and to the American people. They writhed and protested. Trippe tore down to Washington and warned the State Department of dire results if I carried out my threat. The Department cabled expressing concern but leaving the decision to me.

I sent Toby Munn down to Baranquilla to check up on Rihl, and told him to take Parks, the U.S. Consul, with him in order to have a witness. He returned Saturday night with the report that Rihl would not allow Parks to be present at their meeting, and had flatly refused to let out the Nazis. On Sunday I wired Parks to see Rihl and tell him I demanded a personal apology to Parks for his rudeness and one to me as Ambassador for his outrageous behavior to myself and to the American consul; moreover I was sending Captain Munn back to Baranquilla that day, and if by 6 P.M. the next day he could not report that the principal Nazi executives and administrators were out, I would take the steps I had threatened.

Toby saw Rihl that night. He was still obstreperous; he was not going to comply.

"Well," Toby advised him, "you'd better look out. This Ambassador doesn't fool. When he says he's going to do a thing, he does it. So watch your step."

Rihl bluffed up to the last minute, but at 6 P.M. on Monday Toby telephoned me that this first preliminary stage in clearing out the top Nazis was completed.

After the American administrators took over we began to learn just how dangerous the SCADTA operation was. One night some of them happened to enter the office in Baranquilla long after the closing hour. They found the SCADTA chief of communications, Hans Hasendorf, communicating with Berlin over a radio set that was supposedly just strong enough for use between the office and the airport.

At about the same time we intercepted a letter from one of two SCADTA pilots who had left Colombia right after the war began, and had reached Berlin by way of Japan and Russia. He wrote a fellow pilot of SCADTA how, elated to be back in time to take his place as a fighter pilot, he had gone to see Hermann Goering, head of the Luftwaffe. Goering stormed at him for having left Colombia, where he was needed, for Germany where there was no shortage of fighter pilots.

4

One important agreement I worked out with George Rihl included a provision, of crucial importance to the safety of the Panama Canal, for the immediate installation of three Adcock Direction Finders.

During the consultative Panama Conference, immediately after the war began, I went to Panama to confer with Sumner Welles, who headed our delegation. While I was there, the commanding officer had me flown over the installations, which were woefully inadequate from the viewpoint of defense. The anti-aircraft emplacements were clearly visible from the air. The emergency locks being started on the Atlantic side were so near the original ones that a single bombing raid could have destroyed them both at the same time.

Worst of all, the only listening device in the Zone could detect a plane coming from one direction—and then only when it was no more than fifteen miles away. If two squadrons of planes came in from two different directions and, worse, at different altitudes, we might detect one of them—too late for our fighter planes to take off—and possibly damage some of its planes with anti-aircraft fire. The other could meanwhile come in undetected and bomb the locks.

I insisted on the installation of the Adcock Direction Finders. One was to be installed in the Gulf of Aruba, one in Cali, and one in Baranquilla; and the three would make it possible to locate any plane in the air by triangulation. The planes were to be triangulated every fifteen minutes. Since no more than a dozen would be flying over Colombia at one time, it would be easy to trace them; and if any plane was not where it should be or could not be found the Canal Zone could be alerted.

Nothing was done to provide the Canal with a measure of protection from SCADTA pilots. I cabled the Department. Still the direction finders did not come. I sent a scorching telegram demanding that the Secretary or Under Secretary find out why Pan American had failed to send those finders and when it proposed to do so.

In due course, I received a message from the Department. An officer of Pan Am, I was told, had seen Under Secretary Welles and had been most apologetic. He reassured Sumner Welles by telling him that the first direction finder, "complete with pole," was being shipped the following Saturday by air freight; and that the others would be sent the same way within a couple of weeks.

Welles was a very busy man and knew nothing about the Adcock Direction Finder.

I wired back suggesting sarcastically that the Department convey my congratulations to Pan Am on the astonishing advance in air freight. The Department, I said, would understand my admiration when it realized that the machinery for one Adcock Direction Finder weighed many hundreds of tons and would fill a room 14x14x10 feet; also that the pole had to be of kiln cured cedar from sixty to eighty feet long and from ten to fourteen feet in diameter at the base. (Presumably Welles had thought it was some kind of magnetic pole.)

5

When the February changeover was completed, President Santos urged me to go slow on further changes. I wanted to ease out some of the pilots (one had endangered my life and those of six other passengers by flying straight up and down the mountains between Bogota and Medellin and ending with a power dive through a forest into the Medellin airport—an exhibition of skillful and wholly reckless flying obviously intended to give me the scare of my life, as it did). But Santos said, "Let's wait a little."

And he had been so cooperative that I had not the heart to be exigent.

But when Hitler began his blitzkrieg on May 10, 1940, the problem took on a new aspect. I was in Washington that day, in the Department. With some difficulty I got Sumner Welles on the telephone and told him it was imperative that I see him at once.

"What is it?" he asked.

"You know about my promise to go slow in getting the rest of the Nazis out of SCADTA. But this invasion means that the war is really on. I've got to act now, and I need your authority. I want to tell you what I propose to do."

Later Sumner Welles and I came to a parting of the ways, but I shall always be grateful for what he said then. "I'm sorry, Spruille, I'm tied up in a meeting," he stated. "I can't even talk to you on the phone any longer. You go ahead; and whatever you do, I'll support you."

I called Gerry Keith in Bogota and told him to ask Santos for an interview in my name. He was to tell the President that with Hitler on the offensive we could no longer take the time for a gradual housecleaning in SCADTA; those pilots had to go at once.

Late that afternoon he called me back with Santos' answer—a very courageous answer, for it meant braving the wrath of Laureano Gomez and the whole Conservative opposition, and even some disaffection among the Liberals. Santos had said, "Whatever you want to do, go to it."

At once I telephoned Rihl and told him I was taking a late train to New York, and would expect him at 1:00 A.M. in my suite at the Plaza. He sputtered a bit; but he came.

"This invasion," I told him, "means that we've got to make a complete changeover in SCADTA, and we've got to do it right now."

It was a large order. Of 134 Nazi personnel, 84 were still in their jobs, and most of them were highly skilled—pilots, co-pilots, mechanics. Under Colombian law they were entitled to severance pay based on their length of service. There would also be the expense of transporting American replacements to Colombia.

"What'll we use for money?" asked Rihl.

"You'll have to put it up."

"How do we get repaid?"

"I don't know how you get repaid. But you've got yourselves into this jam. You say you didn't realize war was coming in Europe. Everybody else in the world realized it, and that we couldn't help getting involved. You knew we weren't going to stand for Nazi military pilots flying around the Canal Zone; on that score alone you're responsible. However, I will undertake—without any obligation—as Ambassador, to do my best to see that you are reimbursed for any out-of-pocket expenses."

Rihl heard me through. "This is so vitally important," he said, "that I'd like to come back early tomorrow morning with Trippe and the others."

"Very well," I answered, "but when you come with Trippe, remember that the question will not be whether the thing is to be done, but how it can be done most quickly."

The next morning I insisted on talking about what had to be done and how to do it. When the question of financing the changeover came up again I repeated that I would try to see that they were repaid, but that right now they would have to spend the necessary money.

A year after I had transferred to Cuba Pan Am presented the government with a bill in excess of the cost of the changeover. They had had Avianca, SCADTA's successor, borrow the money. Default would have ruined Avianca and left the Colombians feeling, justifiably, that the Yankees had swindled them. I was obliged to recommend payment of Pan Am.

They had been outrageous; they would be outrageous later; but I have only praise for the way George Rihl and Pan Am handled the change. Somehow they managed to find the necessary pilots, co-pilots, mechanics, and other personnel. They brought them into Baranquilla one or two or three at a time and kept them dispersed so that no one noticed what was happening. Finally, on June 10, 1940, eighteen months before Pearl Harbor, they went into action.

That night, when all the planes were in the hangars and all the personnel out of the hangars and the offices, the Germans were given their notices that they were no longer employed, and the Americans came in and took over.

The next six months were nerve-racking. The opposition was screaming with rage, and one accident would have created such a political inferno that it might have been impossible to keep the Germans out. They were doing their best to cause it. For six months every plane out of Bogota—or most of the other cities—was tampered with. How the Nazis got at them no one knew; but get at them they did, and tampered with the engines, the fuel, the water, the oil—everything. Thanks to the extreme care exercised by Pan Am, the worst effect was delay. An attempted bombing was thwarted by the pilot, who was able to open the door and toss out a small package, one of several providentially placed on a seat in the hurry to take off. The hot, smoking package burst into flames in mid air.

During that anxious time it was a great satisfaction to have my judgment vindicated. When the Americans took over the SCADTA planes they and Toby Munn found the borings for bomb racks and machine guns. They also found—fortunately without mishap—that on the SCADTA maps the Colombian peaks were charted 1,500 to 2,000 feet lower than their actual heights. The intention evidently was to cause accidents in case the line was taken over and those maps got into the hands of American pilots.

Another vindication, which luckily involved less risk, was that three shortwave broadcasts from Berlin threatened Santos' life and mine for having eliminated the Germans from SCADTA.

I was reporting fully all this time to the Department on the whole situation. Apart from the danger to the Canal, there was the possibility of a Nazi attack on the Aruba and Curacao refineries, source of 80 per cent of the gasoline for the British Air Force. Whether or not my reports were 100 per cent accurate I would not know; most of them were. It did not help my delicate situation with regard to SCADTA when President Roosevelt declared one night over short wave that the Nazis had hidden airfields in Colombia.

I realized I would have to take the responsibility. If we couldn't prove the charge I could not pass the buck to the President. We had had some indications of hidden airfields, but without positive proof. I called my staff together and said, "Boys, the President has gone out on a limb with this statement. Now it's up to us to get the proof that he is right."

The announcement created a sensation in Colombia precisely at a time when I needed no sensations. Laureano Gomez was very unpleasant about it. However, we did pull together some persuasive evidence in support of the President's ill-timed and unnecessary claim. Indeed, Edgar Hoover sent me a most interesting large folder (it was stolen as my books were being packed when I left the State Department) showing with maps where the supposedly hidden airfields were, where there was gasoline storage, oil storage, water storage, spare parts, and so on.

6

In order to give the Colombians a bigger stake in SCADTA, I suggested that Pan Am take over and merge with it a small Colombian company, putting a Colombian national in as President to succeed Bauer. They were glad to do that. The company was reorganized as Avianca, with the Colombian I proposed as president. Soon, the sabotage decreased rapidly and I began to breathe more easily. After Pearl Harbor I was able to persuade Santos to isolate the 134 Nazis from SCADTA. He didn't have to build a concentration camp; he just marooned them in one of the deep valleys from which there was no egress except up the mountains to Bogota. I was particularly concerned about the pilots, who might have been able to cause real trouble.

After the reorganization the new company Avianca began to make money. Under Bauer it had never made a dime.

George Rihl and I, in spite of our knock-down-drag-out fights, ended up as being good friends. I have a letter that I value from Tony Satterthwaite, a Foreign Service officer who specialized in aviation, dated November 25, 1943:

> Dear Mr. Ambassador:
>
> I had dinner with George Rihl last night. He said (I will try to quote), 'Braden is the best goddamned ambassador we ever had in Colombia or anywhere else. I fought worse with him than with any man I ever knew. He put me in the hospital. But he really did Pan American Airways a great service. He kept us from getting so deep in the doghouse with the Army that we never would have gotten out. The United States got what it wanted when he was there.'

I never blamed George for what he did. But I had to get extremely tough with him, and it is quite true that when the fight was finished he did go to the hospital because of exhaustion. It is true, too, that Pan

Am was heading for real trouble with the Army. Before the Nazis were let out the Canal Zone's commanding general was so anxious about the potential danger to the Canal, and so outraged by Pan Am's inaction, that I had difficulty in persuading him not to exclude its planes from France and Dubruk Fields in the Zone.

Some years later, at a dinner party in New York, Juan Trippe finally acknowledged to me that I had been right. Pan Am, he said, should be grateful to me for what I had done for them in Colombia. I did not tell Mr. Trippe that in the SCADTA affair I had not been so interested in the welfare of Pan American Airways as in the security of my country.

Chapter XXV

THE attitude of our government departments toward the nation's security has often—I might even say more often than not—been extremely frivolous. Most recently we have witnessed the inexcusable blundering, or worse, with respect to Cuba.

It was 1939. I was Ambassador to Colombia. Colombia was adjacent to the Panama Canal. It swarmed with Nazis. World War II was clearly imminent. The Ambassador to a country of great strategic importance to the United States had not one penny from his government to finance the gathering of intelligence, nor any agreement that intelligence was important. If this situation were not so common it might be called fantastic.

My Naval attaché, Toby Munn, was allowed a munificent $1500 a year by the Navy Department to pay informants. It was paid in monthly installments for six months, then suddenly discontinued. From there on, where intelligence was concerned, I was strictly on my own.

A refugee Catholic priest who had been beaten up by the Nazis in Germany, had set up a little church reading room in Bogota, and was beaten up again with impunity by local Nazis. Through him I found some very helpful anti-Nazi Germans. One of these, Erich Rath, also a refugee from Hitler performed in a manner I can only characterize as worthy of a skilled professional intelligence agent. Perhaps that is what he was, I never tried to find out. It was enough for me that he perfectly fulfilled my requirements.

One valuable service he rendered was to classify all SCADTA employees according to degree of Nazism. There were 154, whose classifications ranged from "violently anti-Nazi," "anti-Nazi," "neutral," to "Nazi," "strongly Nazi," "violently Nazi." When we were able to verify, we found his only errors had been on the side of understatement. He contributed significantly to the location of the hidden airports mentioned in the preceding chapter.

I also enlisted the services of a former chief of Colombian national police, who worked for me effectively with a Colombian assistant. He had acquired quite a lot of experience earlier in running down Peruvian espionage and subversion in Colombia; he was extremely useful.

Richmond Oil, a subsidiary of Standard Oil of California, at my request put the two Colombians on its payroll—salaries, traveling expenses—everything. And W. V. Vietti, manager, consultant, and representative of Texas Oil in Bogota placed Erich Rath on his payroll with the understanding that when I did not need him the company might use his very considerable abilities.

Before leaving Colombia I suggested to Secretary Hull that he write the presidents of the two companies, thanking them for this patriotic service. I drafted the letters, and the Secretary, approving the idea, sent them. By that time Wm. S. S. Rodgers was president of the Texas Oil Company. He later told me with some amusement that in the same mail with Hull's letter thanking his company for its patriotism he had received one from someone else in the State Department roundly berating Texas Oil as pro-Nazi and unpatriotic.

This combination of Colombians and anti-Nazi Germans made up my intelligence organization until toward the end of my stay in Colombia, when one FBI agent was added. I don't think we had another embassy with anything comparable. Of course I was getting information in other ways, too; and it was vitally important to get everything I could.

We had, for example, the complete record of the meetings of the wife of one of the Allied ministers with the German, Italian and Spanish envoys. She was a Fascist.

This lady, by the way, hated and resented Maria because of her ambassadorial rank; also because of her youth and her instant acceptance in Colombian society. On one occasion when Maria entertained her at luncheon she commented on some little ashtrays that she said were exactly like some of her own that had been stolen; and she wondered whether they could be the same. This in the United States Embassy!

"That's interesting," answered Maria sweetly. "We've lost some, too; so maybe the ones you had were ours."

I was in the process of organizing my amateur intelligence service when I came up to the United States in the spring of 1940. And since neither I nor Toby Munn had had experience in that field, and we had to depend on trial and error, I stormed around Washington for a month about the importance of having adequate intelligence in Colombia, of all places, and how I must get the low-down on Nazi fifth column activities and how to set up an efficient counter intelligence.

Spruille Braden and friend John Mulcahy toast the day's salmon catch at the American industrialist's Waterville, Ireland, estate.

The Bradens as guests of Elizabeth Arden, during the running of the 1965 Kentucky Derby.

Paul E. Magloire, President of Haiti, presents the Haitian Honneur et Merite Grand Cross to Spruille Braden.

TIME

THE WEEKLY NEWSMAGAZINE

SPRUILLE BRADEN

Sometimes sovereignty is more precious than liberty.

(Latin America)

At conclusion of his Ambassadorship to Argentina, Spruille Braden makes the cover. Reprinted by permission from TIME, The Weekly Newsmagazine: Copyright TIME Inc., 1945.

Former Colombian President Alfonso Lopez speaks at a formal dinner honoring Spruille Braden. Next to the latter is President Santos, and next to him future President Urdaneta Arbelaez.

Spruille Braden is second in line behind the Papal Nuncio as the procession of diplomats leaves a traditional *Te Deum* ceremony at t Bogota cathedral.

William Braden, around 35, in the field at the Braden Copper Company in Chile.

Always stately in her style, Mary Kimball Braden at the age of 37.

Elkhorn, Montana, where Mary Braden, having no confidence in her Helena doctor, went in 1894 to give birth to Spruille.

ille Braden, at about one year.

At three, according to one mother's fashion of the time, in yards and yards of lace.

Great-great-grandfather Braden, bottom center, with Grandmother Braden in the fourth row up, over his left shoulder.

Grandmother Braden, in her mid 30s.

.leras Restrepo, now President of Colombia, was Minister of Finance when Spruille Braden was Ambassador.

Presenting the Spruille Braden Award to a champion military equestrian team. Maria Braden watches.

An English cartoonist accurately characterizes the policies of the U.S. Ambassador to Argentina.

Spruille Braden is seated between Cordell Hull, left, and Alec Weddell, listening to Manini Rios at the VII International Conference of American States.

The swimming pool is there but the photographer missed his aim. The result: This exceptional view of an estate outside Buenos Aires.

The Chaco peace negotiators, with the chief participants in the front row, from the left: Cisneros, Martinez, Thedy, Manini Rios, Rodrigues Alves, Elio, Saavedra Lamas, Zubizarreta, Spruille Braden, Cariola, Nieto del Rio, Podesta Costa.

Another President receives the Pan American Society's Gold Insigne from Spruille Braden.

Verbena and Spruille Braden, following their wedding ceremony, with Rev. Dr. Paul Wolfe of the Brick Presbyterian Church in New York City.

Granddaughters Kimi and Alina, and little great-granddaughter Maria with Spruille and Verbena Braden.

At the Beverly Hills home of another dear friend, former movie actress Irene Dunne.

The late Cardinal Spellman, Spruille Braden, and Ciro Freitas Valle, Brazil's Ambassador to the United Nations.

At the inauguration of President Somosa of Nicaragua, who stands at Verbena Braden's right.

Caras y Caretas, an Argentine magazine, and many others used this cover for the Chaco Peace Conference. Saavedra Lamas is saying, "Cut so that no roots will remain."

The marketplace in Coro Coro, in whose hotel Maria Braden frightened off an intrusive man.

CARAS Y CARETAS

PARAGUAY

ARBOL DE LA DISCORDIA

BOLIVIA

Saavedra Lamas. — Corten de manera que no eche más raíces.

The Chaco Peace Treaty is signed. As the document, having been passed around the table, reached Spruille Braden, the dignitaries assembled, led by President Ortiz, saluted his contribution with spontaneous applause, an honor accorded no other present.

The termination of the bloody Chaco War brought the first joint session of the Argentine Senate and House to pay respects to the peacemakers.

The handsome U.S. Embassy building in Havana, Cuba, first occupied by Spruille Braden.

Cuban President Fulgencio Batista, finger on lip, on a New York tour. Fiorella LaGuardia was host.

Cuba was one of the many nations visited by Eleanor Roosevelt on her good-will tours.

Sailing for South America during the period of the Chilean Railway electrification: Tom Hamilton, top left, Spruille Braden in white trousers, Maria Braden, and, next to her, William Braden.

Spruille Braden presents the Gold Insigne of the Pan American Society to Franklin Roosevelt in 1934.

A formal portrait of Spruille Braden at the time of the Chilean Railway electrification project.

The cabin in Elkhorn, where Spruille Braden was born, is separated by more than years from the magnificent Stonehurst, which in 1921 required a staff of 10 to run it.

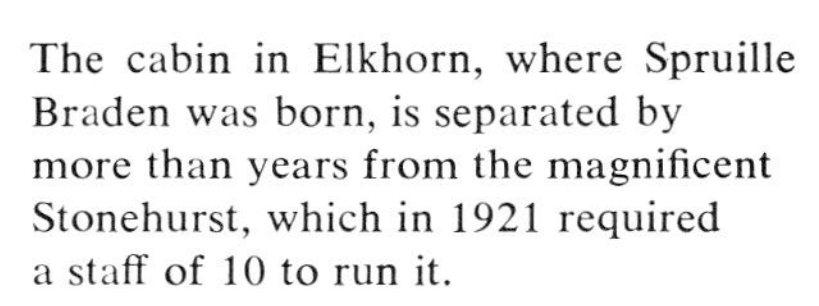

A gallery of Spruille Braden growing up: From top left, in New York at 5 and in Chile at 12; then, at 14 and flanked by teammates on the Yale water polo team.

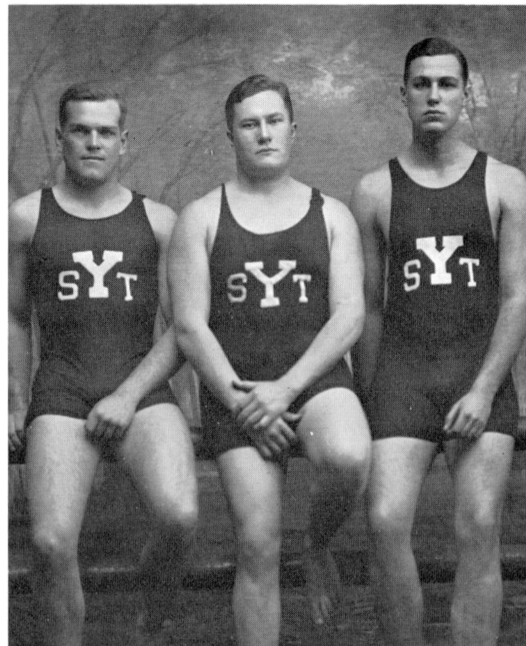

Secretary of State James Byrnes discusses with the new Assistant Secretary his area of responsibility.

Maria Braden, President Miguel Aleman of Mexico, Mrs. Peter Rathbone, and Spruille Braden at a New York party for the visiting head of state.

On behalf of President Truman, Dean Acheson pins on the coveted Medal of Freedom, the highest decoration given to U.S. civilians.

The retired public servant with a few honors and awards he could not receive or wear so long as he was in government service.

Three good friends meet to discuss the future: At Spruille Braden's left, John Lodge, Ambassador to Argentina, and Ambassador to Spain Robert Hill.

Spruille Braden and Richard West during the presentation of Mr. West's portrait at the Metropolitan Club.

True to form, Washington was inclined to pooh-pooh my anxiety. But immediately after the Germans invaded Holland and Belgium, I did perceive a feeble gesture of cooperation. General Sherman Miles, I was told, then head of Army Intelligence (G-2), would give me the whole story on intelligence work.

General Miles, son of the famous Civil War General and Indian fighter Nelson A. Miles, came over to the State Department the day before I left for Bogota, accompanied by a young major. When I told him what I wanted, he said, "Oh, we can certainly give you all of that."

And he told me about Leland Stowe's recent articles on what the Nazi fifth column had done in Norway. They were excellent and informative pieces and had created a sensation; and of course I had already read them. In my naivete I assumed that the United States intelligence services had agents among the top Nazis in Germany; I was expecting to get real information. But the only information General Miles could give me in addition to that published by Leland Stowe was a resolution of the Los Angeles Chamber of Commerce stating its intention to look into any Nazi activities there might be in this country. The General thought it would be a good idea if all the other chambers of commerce would do likewise. That was all the War Department had to offer in May 1940.

The young major with him was going to follow me to Bogota in a few days, General Miles said, in order to negotiate a preliminary military agreement with the Colombians. He duly arrived, and he did a fine job. Unlike most of the officers who were soon coming down in swarms he realized that the United States Embassy was likely to know the country and the people better than he and therefore could be very helpful. He asked for my cooperation and I was glad to give it unreservedly. The name of the young major was Matthew B. Ridgway.

2

Again in 1941 I came to the United States in the spring. And again I could do nothing in Washington. On the train to New York I ran into Ulric Bell, former correspondent for the Louisville *Courier,* who had been our press officer at the Montevideo Conference. As we talked, I began to air the subject uppermost in my mind: the desperate straits I was in for lack of adequate intelligence.

"You've probably read something about General Donovan [the

famous "Wild Bill" Donovan, of World War I fame] and what he's been doing," said Bell.

I told him what I knew about Donovan—that he had made a trip to northern Europe on his own, and had reported to the President, who had sent him to southern Europe from where he had just returned. Why he had made those two trips I had no idea.

"As a matter of fact," said Ulric, "he went over to study this fifth column that you're so worried about. And if you'd like to meet him, I'm working with him."

I said I did, and Ulric arranged for Donovan to breakfast with me two days later. We sat at the breakfast table from eight o'clock till noon while he told me about the first-hand accounts he had had of Nazi fifth-column activity all over Europe, even from German officers he had known during and after the First World War.

As he recited the sequence of subversive activities, through propaganda into sabotage and espionage, I recognized them as having already happened in Colombia. The result was that before I returned to Bogota on May 15 I sent down word that I wanted to see President Santos at once. By this time the Berlin radio had three times threatened Santos' and my life; therefore Pan American provided a special stratosphere plane that flew Maria and myself and our son Bill from Panama to Bogota to avoid possible sabotage.

I saw the President within two hours after my arrival, told him who Bill Donovan was and what I had learned from him, item by item, just as Bill had given it to me.

"Mr. President," I said, "that's what is happening here. You've had the first phases. Now, there's one thing Bill Donovan told me that's part of the routine—to instigate revolution. So that's next on the schedule."

"Wait a moment, Mr. Ambassador," said the President. "I've gone along with you. You've given me proof; I can't deny that all of these things have happened. But that—no! There you're wrong. There will be no attempted revolution. That you can bank on."

On June 2, just two weeks later, the revolution was attempted; and to the President's chagrin it involved officers and men in the Colombian Army of whose loyalty he had been unshakably confident.

Toward the end of my long session with General Donovan, he had asked if I wanted to meet the head of British Intelligence. I assented and Donovan said, "All right, Mr. So-and-So will call you."

I later learned that Mr. So-and-So had a quite different name; and since the publication of H. Montgomery Hyde's book on British Intelligence, *Room 3603,* his real name, William (later Sir William) Stephenson, is well known.

Mr. Stephenson called up, and we met at the Metropolitan Club in New York. After we had gone over the whole picture in Colombia he said, "It may interest you to know that I'm reorganizing my intelligence service in Colombia. I'm sending a man down there whose real name is Stagg."

"Yes," I said. "I met him years ago. He's Ecuadorian."

"No, he's not Ecuadorian; he's a British citizen. He's using his fictitious name up here; but in Colombia, where he might be recognized, he will have to use his real name. I'll have him come around and see you. I'll put him under your orders. He will report to you, and you may use him as if he were your own man."

Of course Stephenson knew that the British Minister and his legation staff were phlegmatic. They didn't even know that his organization existed.

Stagg had agreed with Stephenson to assume the role of playboy. He and his attractive wife would drift in from Ecuador and play around in Bogota. He played polo; he played tennis; he was a free drinker and splurger; he loved to dance, to go to parties, to entertain. It was perfectly obvious that he was just a frolicsome dilettante.

He played the part so well that some members of my staff became pretty much annoyed with me for giving him so much time. When he showed up at the chancellery I would have him sent in at once, and see him alone. Off of my big office was a little cubbyhole office I could shut off entirely. Here Stagg and I talked without being overheard. I would abruptly terminate a staff meeting to see Stagg in this office. I also had him at the Embassy. My staff just couldn't understand what had gotten into me.

Stagg did a fine job. His organization was tops. As an example, one Saturday afternoon Jim Wright came to the Embassy residence and said he had just passed the German Legation and found the whole street full of cars. I was expecting a call from Stagg. When it came I told him what was happening. "How can we check on it?" I asked.

"I can get that for you easily," he said. "Meanwhile I'm coming out on another matter."

Not more than ten minutes after he arrived an agent of his, with his wife, came in. They had walked at a normal pace down that block past the German Legation and memorized the license number of every car—at least twenty-five in all. Thanks to this phenomenal feat of memory we were able to learn that every owner was tied in with the Nazi movement.

3

One evening Stagg called up and said he had to see me urgently. I told him to come to the Embassy residence. He brought with him a copy of a letter that purported to be from Major Elias Belmonte Pabon, Bolivian military attaché in Berlin, to the German Minister in La Paz. It spelled out in considerable detail a revolutionary plot to overthrow the government of President Peñaranda, whom I mentioned in my story of the Chaco Conference as having been the Bolivian commander in the Chaco War. Of course I found it tremendously interesting. But I asked, "Well, what's the story? What are you seeing me about?"

"We've been able to get this transcript of the letter," said he, "but we want the original. It is coming to Bolivia by diplomatic pouch, and we felt that somewhere along the Brazilian coast or between there and La Paz your government could intercept the plane and get hold of it. That, of course, will blow the lid right off in Bolivia; for here is the Bolivian military attaché plotting with the German Minister to overthrow his own government."

"I fully realize that," I said. "But how do you propose to interfere with a diplomatic pouch?"

"That's what we want you to do. The United States can do that."

"That I very much doubt," I answered. "We're still technically neutral, and I hardly think Washington will agree to intercept that pouch, take out the letter, and either photostat it and send it on or keep it—either way. That's pretty serious business, interfering with diplomatic correspondence. However, I'll cable Washington and give them the gist of the thing."

That very night I sent a message in our most secret code, giving the sense of the letter and conveying Stagg's request that the United States intercept the original. As I expected, the Department answered at once that it would have nothing to do with raiding diplomatic pouches.

Some time later, over the radio one morning came the sensational news that a letter had been placed in the hands of the Bolivian government proving that the German Minister in La Paz was in the thick of a plot to bring about a Nazi coup in Bolivia; and that he was engaged in this conspiracy with Major Belmonte Pabon, the Bolivian Military Attaché in Berlin. The text of the letter I had read some weeks earlier was given over the radio, word for word. The Bolivian government, the broadcast continued, had immediately shipped the German Minister out of the country, and broken off diplomatic relations with Germany.

I was delighted, and more than ever impressed by the resourcefulness and efficiency of the British intelligence. By the time Stagg showed up at my office later that morning, I had the newspapers with the story. To the usual incomprehension of my staff, I had him admitted at once. We went into my little inside office and I closed both doors.

"Well, you certainly pulled a beautiful one that time," I said. "I do indeed congratulate you. But how on earth did you get at that pouch?"

"Oh," he said, "we didn't."

"What do you mean, you didn't? The letter is published, word for word, just as you wanted it to be."

"Yes," said Stagg, "but we never got it."

I was too dumbfounded to catch on. I could only repeat: "What do you mean, you never got it? Here it is. It's published. It's news."

"Oh, no," he said. "We forged the letter."

When I recovered from my astonishment, I realized that the United States was going to be blamed for the break between Bolivia and Germany, as indeed it was. I cabled Sumner Welles at once:

"You'll be interested to know there is no such letter."

And Sumner was floored. Like me, he had believed that the British had somehow got hold of the original of the letter whose contents I had cabled.

Meanwhile both the ousted German Minister and Major Belmonte were also protesting that there was no such letter. But their protests were not convincing and they didn't insist upon them as innocent people would. And indeed they were far from innocent. After the war we learned from documents found in Germany and testimony taken there that Major Belmonte connived with the Nazis throughout the war against his own country, and though still in Germany was implicated in the overthrow of the Peñaranda government in December 1943.*

But we never discovered any trace of the famous letter of 1941.

For twenty-two years, when I recalled that incident (I have never made it public) it was with a strong doubt in my mind. I was pretty

* *Consultation Among the American Republics With Respect to the Argentine Situation. Memorandum of the United States Government.* ("The Blue Book"), Washington, D.C., February 1946, pp. 30-33.

well convinced that the text of the British forgery never had been taken from the copy of a genuine letter, as Stagg had given me to understand it was. In other words, the whole thing—the "copy" shown me as well as the "original" sent to the Bolivian government—was, I believed, fabricated.

My doubt was resolved in 1963 by the appearance of *Room 3603,* in which is told what I assume is the official British version of the story.

Early in May 1941, says Hyde, Wm. Stephenson received from J. Edgar Hoover a message saying that Major Belmonte, in Berlin, was understood to be in touch with Nazi elements in Bolivia and planning a coup to supplant the Peñaranda government with a pro-Nazi dictatorship. President Roosevelt was eager to get evidence confirming this report.

Stephenson thereupon sent to Bolivia one of his agents, Montgomery Hyde himself. In La Paz Hyde learned that Belmonte had been corresponding from Berlin with the Bolivian Chief of Staff and hinting at a possible coup; also that the government had wind of this correspondence and was seriously concerned. Hyde further learned, he tells us, that the plans for the revolution were expected to be sent from Berlin by courier to the German Legation in La Paz in a German diplomatic pouch. Chance, he says, put him in touch with a Bolivian having some knowledge of Belmonte's project; and "having collected all the information he could from this source and made certain other arrangements," he returned to New York.

Stephenson meanwhile, as a precaution, cabled an agent in Brazil to be on the lookout for any courier carrying a German diplomatic bag believed to contain "incriminating documents of the highest importance"; the courier was arriving in Recife by the Italian Line LATI and going on to La Paz. If the agent was unable to possess himself of the documents, his instructions are said to have been to report the courier's movements "so that appropriate action could be taken elsewhere."

At this point and in the middle of a paragraph the diplomatic courier with pouch fades out of the British story, to be supplanted by one Fritz Fenthol with a sealed letter addressed to the German Minister in La Paz. Stephenson's agent is said to have reported Fenthol's arrival in Recife, ostensibly representing the German Potash Syndicate, and his departure by air for Buenos Aires whence he was said to be going on to Bolivia. Contact was made with Fenthol's secretary, says Hyde (where she was he does not say), who sold Stephenson's agent the information about the sealed letter. Shortly thereafter the local FBI representative (in Buenos Aires?) reported to his headquarters (in Washington?) that he understood Fenthol to have been deprived of a letter by a British agent standing next to him in an overcrowded lift in the German Bank Building in Buenos Aires.

At the beginning of July, according to Hyde, Stephenson informed London that American officials knew some document had been intercepted and were impatiently eager to get hold of it; whereupon London further cabled that the Bolivian government must be informed without delay so that it might suppress the coup, and suggested that the matter "be discussed frankly with the Americans who should be left to take action if they so wished."

Stephenson thereupon turned the Belmonte letter over to Hoover, and a surprised and delighted Hoover passed it on to Hull, who "lost no time in sending a photostat copy to the Bolivian Government, after he had shown it to President Roosevelt." The letter, says Hyde, was typewriten in Spanish, dated June 9, 1941, addressed to Dr. Ernst Wendler, German Minister to Bolivia, and bore what appeared to be Belmonte's signature. The Bolivian Chief of Staff pronounced the signature genuine.

I need hardly say with what keen interest I read Mr. Hyde's version of an intelligence operation in which I had been briefly involved (although he does not mention my part in it). And it seemed to me obvious that he does not want to *tell* his readers that the Belmonte letter never existed but wants them to *believe* that it never existed. Certainly he set at rest what little doubt was left in my own mind.

I had, of course, an advantage over other readers of the book: I knew, what Hyde never says, that no Belmonte letter was ever taken from Fenthol or anybody else, and that the "original" of which a photostat reached the Bolivian government was a forgery. What I was not sure of was *who wrote* the original of the forged letter. If Hyde had mentioned the "copy" Stagg brought me I might still be wondering.

Hyde's account is the classic "amalgam," the combination of truth with falsehood that is of all snarls the hardest to unravel. I shall not seriously try to unravel it. My comments are those of an amateur who by reason of official involvement is interested in a satisfactory explanation of a rather conventional "cloak and dagger" story.

The story about Stephenson's receiving a message from J. Edgar Hoover concerning a Nazi menace to the Bolivian government is possibly true. Bolivia was important to the United States as a source of wolfram, as Hyde remarks. For that reason President Roosevelt would have been concerned about a possible Bolivian Nazi dictatorship, quite apart from his antipathy to Nazism and open sympathy with the British.

That Hyde was sent to Bolivia I do not doubt and I venture to assume that the "other arrangements" he mentions having made there included assembling authentic Belmonte letters for use by Stephenson's incredibly skilled forging establishment, "Station M," of whose "nefarious activities" (in my opinion truly if necessarily nefarious) Hyde reveals a tiny sector.

Provided with the latest political information brought by Hyde direct from Bolivia, Stephenson obligingly wrote the "letter" that would—when "Station M" got through with it—constitute exactly the kind of evidence President Roosevelt had asked for. Incidentally, addressing this "Belmonte letter" to the German Minister was a stroke of genius, as the result proved.

Having forged the letter, Stephenson had to devise the appearance of authenticity. One step in this process—possibly the first—was Stagg's visit to me. My cable giving the gist of the letter and conveying the request that it be intercepted (Stephenson knew as well as I did that the request would be refused) was an excellent way to make Hull and Welles believe there was such a letter somewhere on its way to Bolivia.

Following my exchange of cables with the Department, Stephenson had his agents tell the "local FBI representative" about the alleged theft in Buenos Aires of the non-existent letter. With Hoover thus alerted, and Hull and Welles prepared to believe the story, they would all have been ready to accept the forgery as genuine. Stephenson's exchange of messages with London, if it ever took place, was just so much hocus pocus designed to set fires under Hull.

I think the Bolivian government might indeed have learned of the supposed letter from a photostat sent by Hull. Both he and Roosevelt would certainly have wanted the Bolivians to know about an impending Nazi coup and would have considered it perfectly proper to warn them.

Hyde, I believe intentionally, gives his show away by saying. "That the Germans were engaged in subversive activities in Bolivia at this time there can be no doubt, although the precise extent to which Major Belmonte was involved in them must remain a matter of conjecture."

He would hardly have said that if the "Belmonte letter" had been genuine.

There is a contemporary parallel that needs to be drawn to that

Nazi interest in Bolivia. The Germans felt that whoever controlled Bolivia, the "heartland" of South America, was in a position to control all of the southern hemisphere. The same geopolitical thinking surely led the Communists to send Che Guevara into Bolivia, where he was subsequently killed in the jungles along the foothills on the eastern slopes of the Andes.

4

Having told about my more successful ventures into the unfamiliar world of intelligence, I must now confess one complete fiasco.

While I was setting up my amateur organization, Toby Munn and I decided it would help our intelligence work if the Colombians set up an intelligence service of their own; and we hit upon the idea of persuading them to ask the United States for an Army officer to organize and direct one for the Colombian Army. This was before my "briefing" by General Miles, when I still entertained a sort of E. Philips Oppenheim illusion about our magnificent Army Intelligence. I was able to brief Santos so fully on the importance of an expert intelligence service that he made the request. At the same time the Colombians said they'd like to have somebody to help on their materiel and quartermaster division.

The quartermaster officer our Army sent down was Major Brisbane Brown. He had been so severely wounded in World War I that he was hospitalized for three years after the war; and he had just about every military decoration there was. He was able to stay in the Army, but had transferred to quartermaster work, at which he was excellent. He did a fine job in Colombia.

The Army was curiously reluctant to send down an intelligence officer, but at last sent our highest ranking Colonel. He was one of the finest figures of a man I've ever laid eyes on; about six feet two and perfectly built, with graying hair and mustache—a most distinguished looking officer. He brought along a nice wife, and a charming daughter as tall as himself. What he could not do, no one could. I was delighted.

But as time went on it became apparent that this paragon was falling flat on his face. At last, in desperation, I called him in.

"Now, Colonel," I said, "this is what I'd like you to do. You know we've found that the Germans have their people employed in all the roadhouses and other public places on every road leading to Bogota. I'd like you to put yourself in the position of a German and work out a plan for moving in and taking the city. You know what military measures are necessary. If you'll draw up a plan we'll study it and learn what counter measures we should have in mind."

He went off and labored, and came back with a brief and wholly inadequate document that didn't begin to cover the subject. I tried again:

"I must have been at fault; evidently I didn't adequately describe the problem. Let's boil it down. In the last analysis you've got to get the President and to do that the Presidential guard, and then the Presidential palace and the Ministry of War [the three buildings were grouped quite closely together]. Most of the Colombian presidents lived in the palace, but Santos lives out at his private home; a special contingent would be required to seize him. How would you handle all that?"

He handled it in a plan for a "B-day," on which the Presidential guard would be overcome.

The guard building was a two-story structure as solid as an armory, with thick, nail-studded doors opening into a patio around which were sleeping quarters for officers and men. Just inside the entrance was a room with bunks for the guard members on duty; opposite that the room for the officer of the day or night.

My strategist consulted Major Brown: could Major Brown make a car backfire? Sure, Major Brown could, whenever he wanted to. On this skill of Major Brown was built the plan for B-day.

Every night for a month a car was to be brought into the square fronting guard headquarters and made to backfire. At first people would think there was shooting in the square; then they would grow accustomed to the sound; then indifferent. And every night during the same month one of the few guards allowed leave each day would be plied with liquor until he passed out, and delivered that night by a party of drunks who would roll up to the guard building and announce through a little window in the big doors that they were bringing home an incapacitated guardsman. Whereupon the big doors would of course be opened to receive him. Perfectly silly.

After a month of these goings-on came B-day, when the drunks leading the drunk would step inside and shoot the officer of the day and the eight guardsmen on duty. The sound of shooting would alarm no one, because of Major Brown's talent for making a car backfire; therefore, proceeding to overcome all the officers and men in the place would be a cinch.

One day the Minister of War asked me for an interview—not at the

Ministry; not at the chancellery nor the Embassy; somewhere else, but secret. We met after dark at the house of my senior secretary, Gerry Keith.

"Mr. Ambassador," asked the Minister, "what do you think of your Intelligence colonel?"

What could I say except, "I don't think very much of him."

It was at that moment that I had the inspiration to suggest bringing in the FBI. It was vital to maintain this intelligence liaison with the Colombians. I told the Minister I was deeply sorry to have been so mistaken about our Army intelligence, but that the FBI was really wonderful. And I proceeded to convince him that the qualifications and training of an FBI man were just what the situation called for. That time I was right. Having convinced the Minister, I had great difficulty convincing the Department, which then had to convince J. Edgar Hoover. At last the FBI sent down an excellent man who did such an exemplary job that before long the FBI had men in many of our embassies all around the hemisphere; although my predecessor in Cuba, Ambassador Messersmith, refused to have even one.

As for the colonel, I was obliged to report to Washington that the Minister of War had requested his removal. Of course he blamed me and never forgave me. I would have been sorry for this if he had not been harsh and overbearing toward officers who had the misfortune to serve under him. His withdrawal did not hurt his career; he was promoted to brigadier general and later became military attaché in Argentina, where he served until I became Ambassador and refused to have him.

5

The Colonel, our quartermaster major, and another officer made up a sort of military mission. A naval mission had been sent down at the time I became Ambassador. It was headed by Capt. Lawrence F. Reifsnider, in whose company, it will be remembered, I talked myself to sleep at Cartegena. He was one of the finest officers I have ever known in any service.

The British for years had maintained a naval mission in Colombia, headed by a retired admiral who daily competed with his own drinking record of the day before and invariably won. The Colombian navy consisted of two English-built destroyers and some gunboats. The crews were drunk and disorderly; the ships were filthy; and there was no discipline whatever. The Colombians badly needed help with their navy.

When I met Capt. Reifsnider in Washington while I was Ambassador-designate, he told me frankly that he did not want to take the job. He was in command of one of our big battle cruisers and didn't want to give it up. But his chief reason for reluctance was the feeling in the Navy that any officer who accepts detached service will be looked down upon thereafter, and that it will hurt his chances for promotion. At last, under great pressure from the Navy Department, he accepted out of loyal obedience, and not expressing anxiety over his future career.

He was in Colombia three years, and during most of that time he was ill. But in a matter of months he had transformed that slovenly, dirty, miserable little navy into a disciplined, well organized, efficient force with clean ships and clean men. He won great esteem for the United States and its Navy, and his reward was exactly what he had feared.

Instead of promoting him to rear admiral, as his seniority and record warranted, the Navy revived the forgotten rank of commodore for him and two other captains, and sent them to transport duty in the Pacific. Eventually he was promoted to rear admiral, but first he had to be punished for what his superiors had done to him and he had done for them.

When I arrived in Colombia my military and naval attachés were, as I said, also accredited to other republics. But as things got tough in Europe a military attaché was accredited exclusively to Colombia, and before long his assistants were falling all over themselves. The same mushroom growth took place in the naval attaché's office. We had no need at all for so many men, and their being sent was one of the military establishment's minor impositions on the American taxpayers.

In the beginning my military attaché, Col. Carl H. Strong, was very decent and simple, but before I left Colombia he had become the exact opposite of Toby Munn: so uncooperative and insubordinate that I had to demand his recall, over which the War Department quibbled—although he had disobeyed its orders as well as mine—so long that all I got was a final apology for its behavior in the matter after I had left Colombia for Cuba.

I assume that what got into Strong was what happened in the Army itself. It became so full of its own importance that General Miles' assistant, a Colonel (later General) Head, went around the hemisphere telling the military attachés that we were going to get into the war; that the military had taken over in Washington; and that they, as representing the military, were to go ahead and do as they thought best and pay the ambassadors no attention. It was all rather mystifying until I learned from a confession or two what was going on. The military did not take over in Colombia while I was there; nor later in Cuba or Argentina. Soon the military attachés' office was expanded by adding a lieutenant colonel, a captain, and a lieutenant.

A little less of that "do as you please" spirit would have meant a lot less embarrassment for two officers sent down in 1941 to follow up Major Ridgway's excellent work of the year before by negotiating a military agreement with Colombia. A Colonel Reynolds came representing the Army and a Captain Riefcole the Navy. Reynolds, as the ranking one of the pair, brought out a document giving the procedure to be followed to get the agreement they wanted, which was contained in a second document.

"I'm sorry," I told them, "but you can't use either of these here under any circumstances."

He had used them in Venezuela, the Colonel told me rather uppishly.

"Sure you can use them in Venezuela," I answered. "You're dealing with the President, General Isaias Medina Angarita, a military man who knows your language."

And I explained that Venezuela had had a long series of military dictatorships, and that what could be done there was no criterion of what could be done in Colombia, which was a representative republic.

He stubbornly insisted that they were going to follow their own procedure in Colombia as they had in Venezuela, and the Colombians would have to take it and like it. I finally had to give him direct orders as Ambassador that under no circumstances was he to follow that procedure, or to show the Colombians the proposed agreement.

"You can get everything in this document," I assured him, "but with a different approach and in different language." And I told him what his procedure should be.

The Colombians were so concerned about the situation that President Santos asked me to have the meetings at Gerry Keith's house instead of the chancellery or the Ministry of War. The Colombians present were the Chief of Staff, his deputy, and the chiefs of the air corps and navy. Gerry Keith went along with Col. Reynolds and Capt. Riefcole, to help on any questions that might come up.

After the first meeting they were walking on air; everything had gone beautifully, with no trouble whatever. I was a little surprised.

"I'm glad you followed my procedure," I said; and immediately read in the Colonel's face that possibly they had not followed it so very exactly. Anyhow they couldn't have been more pleased.

The next day, about fifteen minutes after the hour for the second meeting, I received a phone call from them. Could they see me at once?

"Yes; what's the matter?"

"We can't tell you on the phone."

They came tearing into the chancellery, and told me that the only Colombian who had shown up was an aide of the chief of staff. He informed them that the conversations were terminated on orders of the President. On being questioned they admitted they hadn't stuck to the procedure I had prescribed.

At once I asked to see President Santos. He was very much disturbed. He handed me a copy of the agreement I had ordered them not to show, and described the proceedings that had led up to its presentation, and that I had known would shock the Colombians.

The approach was authoritarian: "The United States wants this and this; and we will do thus and so; and you've got to do thus and so."

I suggested to the President that he leave the matter to the Minister of War, with whom I had become quite friendly. I said I would ship the Colonel and the Captain back to the Canal Zone to wait until Martinez and I had worked out an agreement satisfactory to everybody, when I would recall them for the signing.

And that is what was done. Before they left the next morning for the Canal Zone I showed them a draft agreement Jim Wright and I had prepared. It was about half as long as theirs and included everything they were demanding, plus some things they were not, but wanted.

Then I dictated in their presence my report to the State Department, stating that Colonel Reynolds had acted in flat disobedience of my orders. Colonel Reynolds was deeply distressed; and though I got the military a broader and better agreement than the one they had so peremptorily demanded, my handling of the matter did not endear me to the War Department.

6

Colombia has a great deal of alluvial platinum, most of it in the Chocó Territory and the adjoining provinces along the Pacific Coast. Shortly after the war started in 1939, I began talking to the Colombians and appealing to Washington about the steps to be taken to ensure that this platinum would come to us and the Allies instead of the Axis powers. Typical of Washington, from then until we were actually in the war I was unable to get anything in the way of assistance or constructive ideas. From the Colombian government I was able to get such aid as a neutral country could give; this was not too much.

The platinum became so valuable that it actually caused shootings in the remote districts where it was produced. There was bootlegging, there was hijacking, and there were some most unsavory characters mixed up in both. The metal was shipped by plane to Buenos Aires, where it got into the hands of the Germans and Italians—mostly the Germans—and was flown on to Europe for use in the German war machine.

I kept struggling on the matter, and through my friendship with Santos was able to get the government to take steps that brought a protest from the Argentine government. About that time we got into the war and Washington suddenly woke up. I was deluged with cables demanding that I stop the outflow of platinum at once.

In spite of the difficulties, the Colombian government was able to take effective steps to stop the illicit trade and divert the metal to legitimate channels. Then I persuaded President Santos to issue a decree that no platinum could be sold or imported except against an irrevocable letter of credit in a New York bank. The Argentines, spurred on by the Nazis, were furious at the top of their lungs; nevertheless the decree was issued, which of course gave us complete control over Colombian platinum. It may be imagined with what satisfaction I reported my success to Washington.

At that time, the man in the State Department on this job called me long distance from Washington to say that my arrangement was not satisfactory.

"What more can you want?" I asked him. "You've got it absolutely in control, with the New York banks."

"Well, there are too many banks in New York."

I said, "There are not too many banks. You know very well that the National City, Guaranty Trust, and a few others are the only ones that are going to have anything to do with it anyway. But you can certainly notify every bank in New York City that it is to give no irrevocable letters of credit for platinum without your first being informed. That's how simple it is."

But he gave me a long argument about how the thing had to be done all over; it couldn't possibly be done that way. That was one of the occasions I blew my top.

"I am not going back to Santos," was my parting shot. "I'm not going to ask him for another thing on platinum. We've worked it out in a way that gives the United States complete control, and you can damn well handle it there by notifying all the New York banks, for you're not going to get anything better."

And that was that. Santos could not have been more cooperative than he was throughout. If I had been fool enough to run back to him saying the State Department wasn't satisfied and the decree must be changed to designate one or two banks *by name* to make the control so much easier, Santos would have had every right to throw me out unceremoniously for demanding something that for him would have been impolitic and probably illegal. Then the State Department would have been offended and the Colombians would have cried "Intervention!" In short, there would have been an unpleasant and wholly unnecessary "diplomatic incident."

As I tell this story I am reminded of the editorials that called me "a bull in a china shop" in diplomatic affairs because I got tough with Peron, State Department appeasement of dictators having already become the official fashion. Santos was our friend and an honorable man; a man with whom the representative of a friendly power could reach a friendly agreement. The agreement on Colombian platinum was just one of many proofs of this. It was the attitude of the State Department that would have had the effect of a bull in a china shop.

Chapter XXVI

FOR some time I had been reminding the State Department that Maria's health made it imperative for us to leave Bogota. There was talk of transferring me to Mexico; but Mexico City, although lower in altitude than Bogota, is pretty high up, and I was doubtful whether the move would help her much. At last the matter was satisfactorily adjusted by the transfer of George Messersmith from Cuba to Mexico and my assignment to the Cuban post.

We left Colombia in early April 1942. Our daughter Patricia and our son Spruillito were with us. Our eldest daughter Maruja, who had been visiting us in Bogota with her husband Bill Lyons, had come back to the States. Our eldest son Bill had graduated from Columbia University and was an ensign in the Navy, and our daughter Laurita was working in censorship in New York.

The old Pan American clipper on which we left Colombia was supposed to stop in Cienfuegoes. Instead, after touching at Jamaica, it flew right on over Cuba to Miami. There we were met by Ellis O. Briggs, the chargé in Cuba. He had flown from Havana with the Naval attaché, a Marine colonel who had survived several bad smashups and was as nervous as a jumping jack except when he was at the controls of a plane, when he would lovingly pat the instrument board like a mother her baby. From Miami to New York we traveled most uncomfortably by train—the wartime demoralization of railway passenger traffic had already set in.

As I had done before going to the Chaco Peace Conference and to Colombia, I insisted on going through the files that would help me in handling the problems I would meet in my new post. Then it had been a relatively simple matter: the files on one subject would contain references to others, and I was able to follow through, so that when I left I was prepared on all of them (the only exception had been Pan American's interest in SCADTA). However, on my last trip up from Colombia I discovered to my consternation that many of the telegrams and memos I wanted to examine in discussing the questions on my agenda, and whose numbers I had listed, were unavailable. After a month's search a few were turned up, but most of them had just disappeared. The mushroom expansion of the Department had utterly disorganized its filing system. Preparation for my Cuban post was much more difficult than for the Chaco Conference or Colombia. One important document I wanted was found finally behind a filing case.

2

One problem I was determined I would not carry over from Colombia to Cuba was the Coordinator of Inter-American Affairs, Nelson Rockefeller. I was not in Washington when his agency was created; but the story I heard was so characteristic of President Roosevelt that I never doubted it. Like so many outside agencies, it originated in the mind of Harry Hopkins, who knew and catered to the President's love of the novel and the grandiose. In this case Hopkins also played up to Roosevelt's inexplicable animosity toward the State Department.

The Department, in a way, had asked for it by failing to assert that foreign affairs were its exclusive concern and that no United States Department or Agency was to do anything in a foreign country without its knowledge and consent. It even carried its namby-pamby attitude to the point of permitting representatives of Agriculture and Commerce to sit on its personnel board. (When I became Assistant Secretary I proposed to make this privilege reciprocal, but was not there long enough to get beyond irritating some of the officials in those two Departments.) In the field I always laid down the rule—and enforced it—that as Ambassador I was in charge of United States affairs and no official American activities were to be initiated without my knowledge and approval. But the Department was in no very strong position to combat the Hopkins proposal for a coordinator of all United States activities in the American Republics; it had shirked its responsibility to coordinate them itself.

Having persuaded Roosevelt, Hopkins, who was by that time enjoying a luxurious social life among people of great wealth, had met Nelson Rockefeller somewhere, and recommended him for the job. I was never able to learn what qualifications Nelson had.

Nevertheless Nelson had a fine family example to follow. The Rockefeller Foundation had the practice of putting up funds for a constructive project—health, education, agriculture—provided they were matched by the government of the country to be helped. Then, as the project was developed the Foundation would gradually diminish its participation until the local government was financing the work entirely. To the extent this procedure was followed by the Coordinator's Office it was sound. Although its projects could hardly be classified as coordination of United States activities abroad.

Most of the schemes dreamed up by the Coordinator's staff—a number of whom, if not communist fellow-travellers, were do-gooders and one-worlders like so many in federal agencies at the time—had scant relation to any kind of coordination. They shot off on the tangent of promoting "cultural relations" between this country and the other American republics by sending out art shows (they shipped one to Colombia for which I arranged a distinguished official opening, only to be embarrassed by finding it worse than mediocre); motion pictures; ballet companies; "Ambassadors of Good Will" of whom many were so inept that they created exactly the opposite sentiment. On my last trip north from Colombia I was able to avert the visit of one such "Ambassador," a divorced Hollywood male star, whom Nelson was bent on sending the rounds despite the improbability of a divorced man being able to create any great amount of good will among Catholic peoples.

I was always completely frank with Nelson about my opinion of his activities and his personnel. During that same trip to Washington, after I had dwelt on the incompetence of his division chiefs, he finally said I would have to admit at least that their work on the newly instigated Proclaimed, or Black List, especially the filing, was good. I went upstairs with the men in charge and looked over the files. Honesty compelled me to tell Nelson they were not.

Perhaps I sound cantankerous. I may say that when the first mission was sent around to ask that coordinator's committees be formed in all Latin American countries, I gave a big dinner for them and arranged a number of smaller meetings. Afterward I saw the report of John McClintock, one of Nelson's right hand men, to the effect that of all the ambassadors they had met, I had given them the best cooperation. But as time went on I lost confidence in them so that one of the last things I did before leaving Colombia was to write a memorandum recounting in detail the mistakes that had been made.

This memorandum I took to Washington with me, and gave a copy to Larry Duggan, at that time Special Advisor to the Secretary on Latin American Affairs. Larry arranged a meeting in his office with

Nelson and some of his top assistants and turned it over to me, with the remark that I had some criticisms to make. I handed Nelson a copy of the memorandum, then read some of the salient points. He said, "Let us take this and study it; then we'll have another meeting."

Some ten days later he invited me to lunch at the Metropolitan Club to discuss their answer. I accepted on the condition that Duggan be present.

The luncheon was a culinary triumph. It matched the mood of our host. Before we had even attacked the oysters he announced that his staff had gone over my criticism very carefully and that Harry W. Franz would read their rebuttal. Franz was a hardboiled, skilled newspaperman who seemed to work alternately for the United Press and Nelson. As we ate our way from the oysters through the filet mignon to baked Alaska he read to us. At the end—he must have read for more than an hour—he sat back with a look of triumph.

"Well," said his expression, "we've put you on a spot. What are you going to do about it?"

"Mr. Franz," I said, "has made a very interesting exposition. It's well reasoned and logical; really quite impressive. My only criticism is that all of his basic premises are 100 per cent wrong. Excepting for that, it's fine."

I don't think it took more than five minutes to knock down the whole elaborate argument. Then, since they could not rebut cold facts, we turned to Cuba.

"Now," Nelson asked, "what would you like us to do in regard to Cuba?"

"Nelson," I answered, "there's just one thing I insist on, and that is that *I* am the Ambassador. I want your solemn promise that nothing—and I mean nothing—will be done there by your office without my prior approval. I'll form a coordinating committee there and I'll cooperate with you. But absolutely nothing is to be done—no one is to be employed, no contract is to be signed—without my knowledge and approval. If that's understood I think we can work together very well."

Nelson agreed with alacrity.

Obviously I had averted a great peril by obtaining Nelson's agreement to keep hands off in Cuba. And he kept his word scrupulously, even to the point of asking my approval before sending down representatives to carry out an order from the President himself.

3

The incident began during a Cuban visit of Secretary Henry Morgenthau of the Treasury. The Secretary was enjoying the beach at Varadero, about three hours from Havana by car. I had given him my number, although the telephone service was poor, and had also put his aide in touch with one of my secretaries (Bob McBride—now ambassador in Mexico). Preparing for his return to Havana, we arranged a big luncheon to introduce him to the top Cuban Cabinet officers before he took off for Washington in the afternoon.

Morgenthau arrived in a towering rage. It took some time to calm him sufficiently to get an explanation.

He had talked to some boat builders at Cardenas, near Varadero, and they persuaded him they could produce a whole fleet of wooden steamers in short order, to help replace the tonnage being lost to submarines. Excited by the prospect, the Secretary had his aide telephone Bob McBride, who took the matter to my economic counselor, Al Nufer, in order not to trouble me with it. Al had looked into the matter for me much earlier, and told Morgenthau's aide of our memorandum report.

Before I left Washington President Roosevelt had talked to me about the possibility of a great fleet of wooden boats in the Caribbean. I therefore had investigated, making several critical discoveries: the Cubans couldn't build a wooden steamer; there was insufficient timber available and insufficient time to get it kiln dried in any event; supposing the wooden hulls could be produced, obtaining the hardware and the engines would have placed severe demands on our industrial resources. Our memorandum report stated that we felt the whole idea was a pipe dream.

But the Secretary wanted to read no memoranda: he wanted to begin building ships. And he was much incensed at the delay.

"Well," I remarked, "if you felt so strongly about this, it was something to take up with me and not to be left to subordinates."

That calmed him a bit. He decided to telegraph the President. When he had finished dictating, I said, "Of course you realize, Mr. Secretary, that I disagree with everything you've said in that message, and I shall have to send a telegram too."

I followed his message with one stating my complete disagreement with him and giving my reasons. He sputtered a little, but there was nothing he could do.

I was waiting with some interest for the next development when Nelson Rockefeller one day telephoned me from Washington.

Morgenthau, he said, had brought up the project in a Cabinet meeting, whence at the President's suggestion it had been dumped in Nelson's lap. He was obliged to make a report on it because that was what the President had ordered. Would I please get him off the hook by permitting him to send a couple of experts down to investigate? I would; they came; and after two weeks (the Cuban beaches are delightful) they went back with a report that backed up my own on every point.

I have always appreciated Nelson's behavior on that occasion.

The National and Columbia Broadcasting Companies had arrangements with the Coordinator's Office for broadcasts throughout Latin America, about which the less said the better. I wrote Nelson that we—my coordinating committee and I—would prefer the money to the broadcasts. It enabled us to put on our own program by Herminio Portell Vila, professor and historian; one a news commentary and the other a weekly program called *Buenos Amigos,* in which stories were recounted of friendships between Cubans and Americans to point up the close historical relationship between the two countries.

There were objections to Portell Vila from both Cubans and Americans—not to mention the British. He was a natural born oppositionist; therefore all Cuban governments hated him and so did some of their supporters. In the early days he had been very critical of the United States because of our interventions and our "dollar diplomacy." I always defended him, for he was a man of absolute honesty and great courage; and if he was occasionally critical of the United States, that only made his favorable remarks the more impressive. In later years when he was spoken of as a presidential candidate, the standard joke was that as an inveterate oppositionist he would overthrow his own government.

Throughout my Cuban embassy I had no real trouble with the Coordinator's Office in Washington, although I was obliged to call them down occasionally for their extravagant use of the telegraph. Their greatest offense was a pile of telegrams five or six inches high describing the Allied invasion of North Africa, which the press was not exactly neglecting. Not only did the Coordinator's Office repeat what the press was telling us; it interspersed its repetitions with long-winded messages telling how Washington thought the local press should handle the news—as if the local press were likely to accept instruction on how to handle one of the most spectacular events of modern history. The cost of this officious stupidity for Cuba alone was thousands of dollars; but they were circular telegrams sent to every U.S. embassy or legation in Latin America. Any criticism of such wanton extravagance was of course countered by the standard bureaucratic answer: "Don't you know there's a war on?"

4

On one occasion I had to follow up after one of Nelson's more exuberant attempts to promote "cultural relations" with Latin America. It involved the Mexican painter David Alfaro Siquieros, who had painted for the library in Concepcion, Chile, a powerful mural that aroused the enthusiasm of someone in the Coordinator's Office.

In no time it was decided to arrange an exhibition of Siquieros' work at the Museum of Modern Art in New York, and to bring the painter, with his wife and child, from Chile to the United States for the occasion. The Coordinator's Office telegraphed the invitation, with an offer of all expenses plus a stipend. Naturally it was accepted; arrangements were soon made; and Siquieros and his family were on their way.

Only a few years before—in 1940 to be exact—Siquieros had been front-page news in the United States as one of a Stalinist gang that on the night of May 23–24 tried to murder Leon Trotsky in his home outside Mexico City, and did kidnap and murder his American secretary, Sheldon Harte. That, indeed, was the reason why Siquieros found it healthier to live outside his native land. Yet he was in full flight to the United States to be the honored guest of its government. And then someone in the Bureau of Immigration told the Coordinator's Office that the government could not legally permit him to enter the country, first because he was a Communist and second because he was an accused murderer.

The Coordinator tried to head him off at Lima, too late. He tried to stop him in Ecuador, too late, then wired Colombia and missed him. At the same time I was asked to get him off the plane. I had no right to remove him, but the Cubans obligingly did so at my request. Once he was off the plane, protesting vociferously to the secretary I had sent to make sure he was removed, I could refuse him priority for any flight, thus marooning him in Cuba. Emitting loud wails of anguish, he repaired to the Sevilla Biltmore Hotel where he lived in luxury with caviar and plenty of champagne to weep into.

In due course the manager of the Sevilla Biltmore demanded that his bill be paid. Siquieros had no money; he was the guest of the U.S. government. He sailed along on that tack for a few days; then the manager suggested that he paint a mural over the bar in payment of his bill; a proposal loftily rejected as beneath so great a painter. My secretaries finally got him out of the hotel and into a house. One day they told me he insisted on seeing me. When he came in, he wept; the tears rolled down his cheeks in chagrin over his exclusion from the United States and the exhibition of his paintings. Naturally there was nothing I could or wanted to do to assuage his grief.

Meanwhile Nelson was imploring me to get the fellow off his neck. He asked whether I thought $10,000 would suffice to pay his bills and get him from Cuba to Mexico—if Mexico would have him. I said I thought so. If not, Nelson said, he would ask for more.

Some Cuban and American friends had founded the Cuban-American Cultural Institute. Not wanting this Communist to collect money from the Embassy or even from the Coordinator's Office, I conceived the idea of having the Institute contract with Siquieros for a painting. I figured that $2500 should be enough to pay his bills and get him over to Mexico; therefore I arranged with these friends to negotiate with him for a mural at that price. He demanded much more, but finally settled for that. He was overpaid. The picture, a thing with Lincoln portrayed on one side and the Cuban Liberator, José Martí, on the other, was an untalented daub. Nevertheless, Nelson sent down the money, we passed it under the table to the Institute, the Institute paid for the picture, and the Siquieros episode was ended.

5

Wherever they could get away with it some Washington officials, from Wallace on down, went in and took over embassy jurisdiction, completely bypassing local ambassadors. Of course it was the fault of the ambassadors who permitted themselves to be bypassed.

One who did not was Ellis O. Briggs, who in 1944 was promoted from Counselor in Cuba to Ambassador in the Dominican Republic. Ellis was a man of great ability and courage, and made an outstanding record. He had entered the Foreign Service shortly after the Rogers Act, and was the first to be made a chief of mission.

Unlike his predecessor, Avra Warren, who had been palsy walsy with Rafael Leonidas Trujillo, self-styled "Benefactor" of Santo Domingo, Briggs treated the monster with chilly correctness and soon won his venomous hate by interfering with his schemes for stealing a large share of the American funds being spent in Santo Domingo for one purpose or another.

During the same period Ellis occasionally had reason to level at the Coordinator's office the satirical wit that makes his books frequently hilarious reading. By the time Nelson came winging his way into Ciudad Trujillo on an official tour of the Caribbean late in 1944, both the Benefactor and the Coordinator were taking a jaundiced view of the American Ambassador.

The delighted Benefactor decided he could insult the American Ambassador with impunity, and at the dinner for the Coordinator he placed Nelson in the seat of honor on the dais and Briggs off at a floor table. Now it just happens that an Ambassador is always the ranking American official in the country to which he is accredited and Briggs quite correctly refused to permit the President of the United States to be insulted in the person of his representative. This did not endear him further to the dictator or the dictator's guest of honor.

Precisely at that juncture Hull stepped out and Stettinius stepped in as Secretary of State. At once the new Secretary summoned Nelson back from Ciudad Trujillo to become Assistant Secretary of State for Latin American affairs. The Coordinator did not even stop off in Cuba. And a few days later Ellis Briggs' resignation, submitted along with the pro-forma resignations of all other chiefs of mission after Roosevelt's reelection in 1944, was accepted. His was the only one.

Nothing could have been more gratifying to Trujillo. For Briggs it meant that he was completely out of the Foreign Service—at that time a career officer had to resign when he became a chief of mission.

Ellis Briggs and I had been friends before he went into the Foreign Service. I returned to Washington. Fortunately the late John G. Erhart, one of the finest career men the Service ever had, was in charge of personnel. With his help and that of Briggs' other friends I was able to get Ellis made a special appointee to Chungking as minister-counselor and ultimately reinstated in the Foreign Service. Later in that same year (1945) when I became Assistant Secretary of State, one of my first acts was to have Ellis ordered back to the State Department, and to make him Director of the Office of American Republics Affairs. Thus was prevented the destruction of a distinguished diplomatic career.

6

The Board of Economic Warfare had just been formed when I was transferred to Cuba. The power behind Henry Wallace in its organization was Milo Perkins, formerly a small but able businessman who had latched on to Henry and who remained a man to be reckoned with in Washington as long as Henry himself was. Perkins not only conceived and put over the idea of the BEW; he also put over, in Hull's absence, an Executive Order that came near putting the BEW over the Department of State. When Hull returned, he promptly had this order followed by a second returning to the Department those broad economic controls the first had transferred to the BEW.

Having learned from Jim Wright how important Perkins had made himself and the BEW, I had a talk with him. It was soon clear to me that his brilliant mind and soaring ambition for power would make operations complicated and difficult for the Department and our embassies. I then went to the Senate to see Henry, who talked a lot without seeming to know much about anything. My argument seemed to convert him to the sensible views of Secretary Hull. Indeed, he came around surprisingly as I explained how different BEW projects thrown to me could not be carried out because of conditions in the field.

He had an appointment at the Navy Department; I was going to the White House. As we were leaving, I said, "You agree that the State Department must have absolute control. Then let me tell Secretary Hull of our conversation, and that that is your opinion."

He agreed. But I made the mistake of accepting his offer to drop me at the White House. Although we talked of other things on the way, as I left him he said, "Wait a minute, Spruille. I told you it was all right to tell Hull about this conversation and that I agreed with him. But don't."

That commitment on which Henry reneged might possibly have averted much confusion and a gigantic waste of money.

Soon the State Department began pressuring me to let the BEW send down a mission; they were sending missions everywhere. I kept answering that the Embassy could get anything in Cuba required by any branch of the government. I needed no mission from the BEW.

I was able to hold out until Sumner Welles brought President Fulgencio Batista to this country on an official visit in December 1942. As Ambassador I accompanied Batista and was with him or on call most of the time.

He left for Cuba from New York a few days before me. When I got back to Washington, Jim Wright said, "They've pulled a fast one while you were away. The BEW has named a special assistant to the Ambassador who's to be the special representative of the BEW in Cuba, and he's taking with him two special assistants. They've practically signed a treaty on it."

Jim was sympathetic, but I detected considerable glee elsewhere, especially in the attitude of Philip Bonsal and Larry Duggan. I was the only ambassador to hold out against the BEW; and at last I had gone down to defeat.

There was nothing I could do in Washington. The Department had capitulated; the BEW men, with assorted clerical assistants, were about to leave for Cuba and would arrive at about the same time I did. I located the second Executive Order Hull had had the President sign, which as it were restored to the Secretary of State authority over his own Department, and culled from it what I needed.

Back in Havana, I wrote a memorandum of instructions that I signed as Ambassador. I then called in my economic counselor Albert F. Nufer, along with my commercial and agricultural attachés. Going over the instructions with them, I said, "You're going to be present when I receive this Chester Davis who has arrived as the special assistant to the Ambassador and chief of the BEW mission to Cuba. I'm going to tell him and his special assistants that they are to do nothing without first getting your approval. And if any questions arise they must be resolved by me."

I impressed most emphatically upon them my order to be tough. This was necessary because they were all just too sweet and gentle for the work I had in mind. Indeed, I frequently had to remind them thereafter that they were not mean enough carrying out my order.

When my special assistant and his special assistants were shown in I was ready for them. "I don't want any misunderstandings," I told them. "Here are my instructions."

I read the memorandum aloud and presented each of them with a signed copy. They were flabbergasted. Instructions from an ambassador were something they had never heard of. But they couldn't take issue with me because the memo repeatedly stated, "Pursuant to the President's order . . ." When they started to object to any provision, I answered, "Oh, no, no. We're going to follow the Presidential order."

"But our regulations . . ."

"I'm sorry. Your regulations don't hold here. I'm the United States government here. I'm the Ambassador, and what I say goes."

"But not only our regulations; our instructions . . ."

"I can't help it. You'll just have to write back that I said you couldn't cary out your instructions."

Before long I heard that they were looking for office space. I called in Chester Davis and asked him about it.

"Yes," he said, "we've got to get office space."

"Oh, no," I answered. "You've been appointed as special assistant to me. I'm not going to have you off in another building. You've got to be right here where you're available any time I want you. That's why we've given you a room on this same floor. We'll put your two other men downstairs where they'll be available to Nufer and my other aides. You won't need any more space."

"But what about room for expansion?" he asked.

"No room. Why?"

"Well, we have such and such jobs to do."

"Any jobs that have to be done," I told him, "we'll do right here in the Embassy. If I need more help, I'll make that decision. You'll not be expanding, so you won't need more space."

But, he insisted, we must have a manager for the BEW mission.

"Manager," said I. "What for?"

"For the accounting. For the purchasing."

"What do you have to purchase?"

"Well, we might want to purchase some furniture."

"What furniture? You've got desks, haven't you? You've got filing cabinets. I can't see that you need furniture."

He thought they might need stationery, or a typewriter. I assured him the Embassy would take care of any such need. But, he suggested, they must have someone to keep their accounts. I answered that the Embassy's accountant could easily handle that.

That stopped them for a while. Then they came in and said they had to have a lawyer. I asked what for.

"To handle any legal problems that may come up."

"Nothing is easier," I said. "Here is a list of the leading Cuban law firms. Each of them collects thousands of dollars yearly in retainers from American firms. They're all delighted to be called into the Embassy and asked for advice, or to do any legal work for us without fee. I don't permit them to serve without fee; but I can get a lawyer whenever one is needed, from the best legal talent in Cuba."

Before long Chester Davis went back to Washington to consult with Milo Perkins; and the State Department began asking me if I wasn't being a little too rough and whether I wouldn't relent just a little bit. I was adamant.

At last the BEW pulled out the two Special Assistants to the Special Assistant. Not long after that I asked someone in the Department during a telephone conversation, "When are you going to have Chester Davis recalled?"

"For heaven's sake, Mr. Ambassador," he answered, "do you realize that you have only one BEW man in all of Cuba, and the lowest number we have anywhere else is 200 in Mexico? Can't you please put up with *one?*"

"Well," I answered, "he's drawing a salary and allowances. However, if you want to throw away the taxpayers' money, that's your lookout."

"But the BEW is making things so disagreeable for us," he said plaintively. "Every time the subject of Cuba comes up the Vice President flies into a rage and Milo Perkins storms. You'd make things a lot easier for us if you'd just keep Davis there."

I finally agreed. "But I'm going to put him to work," I said. "I think my agricultural attaché is a little overworked, so Chester Davis can help out on that end of things."

"O.K. Only take the heat off of us."

So Chester Davis was at last put to work. What was more, he became interested. And when I was about to transfer to Argentina where there was a BEW office (by that time it was the FEA), Davis came to me and said he could arrange to be transferred to Buenos Aires if I would take him. I took him. Later he became agricultural attaché in Cuba. He also became a competent, high-class officer, and incidentally a great booster of mine.

Some time after I had put BEW firmly in its place, I was approached during a trip to Washington by someone in the State Department with a request that I permit two BEW officials to call on me. One was Hector Lazo, who was in charge of acquisitions; the other Morris S. Rosenthal, in charge of distributions. They came for the purpose of defending what they considered their just prerogatives in Cuba.

Having disposed of their arguments, I remarked, "The trouble with you people in BEW is that you have an inferiority complex."

I had quite a little fun developing this idea until Lazo had to leave. Thereupon Rosenthal said to me, "You know, Mr. Ambassador, you're perfectly right. The great trouble with Lazo is that he and his whole division have an inferiority complex because they know that my office is so much more efficient."

On a few rare occasions I consented to have a special BEW mission in Cuba, but I was careful to see to it that they stuck to what they came for and got out when they were through with that. Once, when the head of a mission tangled with the Prime Minister and was about to return to Washington defeated, I was able to save the situation for him; whereupon he, too, became my friend.

A visit I did not permit was threatened by BEW's "Big Boss"; I had heard too much about Vice President Wallace's antics on a grand tour of the west coast of South America.

For example, on his way to the Lima airport to emplane for Chile, followed by a motorcade of Peruvian officials in high hats and cutaways and military officers in full dress uniforms with long sabres, Henry decided he needed some exercise. He stopped his car and got out. The members of his official escort had to follow suit. Henry started walking, then broke into a jog. The perspiring officials did likewise. There was a tumbling of silk hats and a tripping over ceremonial swords, ending in general pandemonium. On his return through Lima, Henry's reception was icy.

As he was finishing this tour I received word from the Department that he and Larry Duggan, who accompanied him, would touch down briefly in their Panagra flying boat at Cienfuegos, and that I was to meet them there. My Naval attaché flew me over. During our conversation Henry suggested we go for a stroll—no jogging with me—up and down the steep street outside the Air Station. As we walked, he said, "Mr. Ambassador, as soon as I return to Washington I propose to ask the State Department to arrange an official visit for me to Cuba."

"Mr. Vice President," I replied, "from time to time you have expressed to me, if not antipathy at least a disinclination to deal with the State Department. Instead of asking the Department, why don't you leave it to me?"

This struck him as an excellent idea.

The next morning I had an appointment with the Minister of State (Foreign Minister), who opening the conversation with the words, "Mr. Ambassador, I saw the pictures of you and the Vice President in the morning papers. I propose to instruct our Ambassador in Washington to invite Mr. Wallace to pay Cuba an official visit."

"Mr. Minister," I replied, "don't bother your Ambassador. Just leave the whole matter to me."

This struck the Foreign Minister as an excellent idea.

And so an almost certainly disturbing official visit was averted. It may have been dirty ball on my part, but it was decidedly in the best interests of Cuban-American friendship.

Both the BEW and the CIAA were typical bureaucratic rackets.

Their extravagance and stupidity were boundless, and so, if ambassadors permitted, were their numbers. In Brazil, I was told, the BEW alone had over 2000 self-styled "ambassadors of good will." They made it impossible for Brazilians to get hotel reservations, plane reservations, sleeper accommodations, and they inspired Foreign Minister Oswaldo Aranha to remark that if we sent down any more "ambassadors of good will," Brazil would be obliged to declare war on the United States.

Chapter XXVII

MY running skirmish with the military continued during my Cuban mission. When I arrived I found General Wm. O. Ryan awaiting me. The Army had decided a few days earlier that it needed an air base in Cuba for the final training of our pilots and of those from Britain and other European countries being trained in this country. No one had thought to mention this in Washington, either to the State Department or to the Ambassador-designate.

General Ryan had to see me at once, to tell me how urgently necessary it was to get the land for this projected base. The Cuban government would have to expropriate it. Though I had not yet presented my credentials, I went at once to see the Prime Minister, my good friend Carlos Saladrigas. In three days the agreement was made, and the Army could proceed with what became the Batista Air Base.

The officer sent down to command the base was Col. Leigh Wade, one of our earliest flying officers, who had made the world tour with James H. Doolittle (now Lieutenant General) in the very early days of flying. He was a top notch officer and a fine man, and I never had better collaboration from anyone than from him. Indeed, he and his charming wife became fast friends with Maria and me.

Wade, however, had nothing to do with the construction. That was the responsibility of the Army Engineers' Office in New York, which had made the construction contract on a cost-plus basis.

It was not long before rumors were mounting of bribery and corruption at the air base. Large amounts of material had to be bought in Cuba. The purchasing agent for the construction company—one of its top men—was said to be accepting bribes from the Cubans, not only on purchasing but on employment.

I investigated and soon had convincing proof of a scandalous situation. I talked to people who admitted having paid bribes. The question was, what to do about it.

An attempt to get legal action would be useless. No witness would come out in a Cuban court and say he had bribed anybody. I demanded that the Engineering Corps force its contractors to put a stop to the corruption. By the time my demands reached New York and went through channels, nothing happened. My last resort was to almost certain illegality. In this case as in many I had to take action with no holds barred.

Fortunately the Cuban Chief of Police General Manuel Benitez was not involved in that particular graft. Fortunately also, at that time he was eager to do me a favor. He dispatched his police cars one afternoon at about five, when there were a maximum number of employees in the construction offices getting ready to leave, and arrested the bribe-taker in front of everybody, putting him in handcuffs. Then they took him to Rancho Boyeros, the commercial airport, and put him on a plane for Florida with admonitions not to return. The witnesses didn't know what had happened to him, but they saw the police cars, the arrest, the handcuffs; also that he was there no more. The action shocked the other grafters and would-be grafters into temporary honesty, as it was intended to do.

My protests against corruption and extravagance annoyed the Pentagon. And so did my subsequent criticism of its inability to decide what use to make of the base, which had cost the American taxpayers more than $16,000,000. Before the construction was completed the original intention was abandoned. For a while the base was used as a recuperation center. Then plans were to use it for long distance bomber flights, and we had to negotiate with the Cuban government to clear people out of the zones along the southwest coast. The pilots would presumably dump their bombs there harmlessly before coming in to land at Batista. A few bombs were dropped, and that was the end of that project. No real use was ever found for the base. At the end of the war it was turned over to the Cubans who turned it over to the termites. It became one of the hundreds of installations abroad forming an enormous burden of waste borne by the American people.

When it was proposed to build another, smaller base in Piñar del Rio, I kept a suspicious eye on the project. Pan American Airways had there something it called a landing field, which was really nothing at all; and its executives had cannily seen the value in arranging to put a real airfield on the site that would be convenient for Pan Am's use after the war.

Developing the site, I found, would involve large construction costs. Moreover, a knoll too big to be leveled hid the control tower from one end of the field. About a kilometer away was a practically ready made airport—level, with excellent drainage. About all it required to become an ideal landing field was a roller and some concrete.

I recommended that the Army, instead of spending millions on the Pan American site, acquire the natural airfield. The proposal agitated the Pentagon. A whole flock of colonels under a brigadier general flew in one evening about six o'clock, and argued the matter with me in the chancellery for a couple of hours. The Army Engineers, it seemed, had put in reports exactly contrary to my own recommendation; but thanks to Leigh Wade's knowledge of flying and grasp of the facts in the case, I was able to get the good location accepted. Nevertheless, I had once more tangled with the Pentagon and the Pentagon did not forget.

2

My first military attaché in Cuba was Col. Albert L. Loustalot. Neither he nor his assistant, Col. Wm. E. (Ned) Boone, a reserve officer, ever tried to throw any weight around. But Loustalot was soon retired. He was succeeded by Col. Egon R. Tausch, who had been serving as military attaché in the Dominican Republic. I had been tipped off that Tausch was arrogant and difficult to handle. When he arrived I called him in and made it quite clear, as my custom was, that I was running United States affairs in Cuba.

After a couple of days my new attaché hopped over to Florida for consultation with G-2. From there he was summoned to Washington. After his return a Colonel I had known at Yale arrived from G-2 in Miami and came with Tausch to the chancellery. In the course of a long talk he made it clear to Tausch that the Army understood I was the boss in Cuba. Later Tausch confessed that when he first arrived he had expected to act, as he had in the Dominican Republic, on the basis of his instructions that the Army had taken over foreign affairs. But G-2 in Washington had told him that tangling with me was like tangling with cactus, and that the Army wanted no more difficulties with Ambassador Braden. I had no further trouble with my military attaché's office during my Cuban mission, although the Pentagon and I continued to have frequent run-ins.

Officers not stationed in Cuba sometimes tried to presume. Lieut. Gen. George H. Brett was at that time stationed in Panama, in command of an area that included the whole Caribbean and extended as far as Chile and Argentina. Brett, a great ribbon-hunter, tried to horn in on Cuba. He thought he should be able to fly in, just as he did into other Caribbean countries, see the President, and make any arrangement that suited him. I gave him to understand that all agreements to be made in Cuba would be made by me or under my supervision. He kept out until I left for my post in Argentina. Almost at once he and Admiral Walter S. Anderson arrived to make an agreement with the Cubans and got pretty much what they wanted.

Brett was very friendly with the Dominican "Benefactor," Trujillo, and would pop into Ciudad Trujillo to go hunting with him. On one occasion he flew in with former Ambassador Avra Warren, who had not only buttered up Trujillo but had had the shocking taste to send his son to a school where pupils wore the Dominican uniform. Neither Brett nor Warren bothered to pay their respects to the incumbent Ambassador, Ellis O. Briggs, as was their obligation. Another time Brett and Trujillo agreed to exchange photographs; whereupon Brett sent his official plane all the way to Panama for the sole purpose of bringing back his picture to Ciudad Trujillo—a round trip of about 1600 miles.

Brett accompanied me when I was sent as special ambassador to the inaugural of President Teodoro Picado Michalski in Costa Rica. I was provided with a military plane from Havana to Panama, and from there was to fly on to San Jose with Brett. As Maria was not well enough to go with me, I took along my daughters Laurita and Patty, little dreaming of the discomfiture I was about to cause two of the General's aides.

On announcing that Ambassador Braden was arriving with two daughters, Brett said to one aide, Lt. Col. John Fitzpatric, "You take the elder daughter," and to another, Capt. Wm. Clark, "You take the younger." And he added, "You are to pay attention to them and to accompany them throughout their stay here and during the trip to Costa Rica. And those are orders."

Now it just happened that those two daughters of mine were (and are) not the wallflower type. On the contrary, they were about as attractive a pair of young women as ever deplaned before a waiting honor guard and an assembly of top brass. The two aides had no way of knowing, and were expecting the worst. However, as we scrambled down a small ladder with what dignity we could muster, it did not take the General's staff long to decide that his orders had not been unduly severe. Indeed, Bill Clark proposed to Patty that same night, and kept right on until he was accepted.

Never was a budding romance more assiduously encouraged. General Brett was rather disposed to strut during the inaugural and to try to pull his rank; a disposition with which I was entirely able to cope, to his patent displeasure. Even had he caused real embarrassment, I would have had to forgive him. For when he found out that Bill Clark was in love with Patty he became an elderly Cupid in uniform, sailing into Havana on great shining wings whenever he could find the flimsiest excuse—as for example, "on his way" to Ecuador or Peru—and always with Captain Clark in attendance.

The night Bill and Patty became engaged, she phoned Maria and me at a dinner in honor of President-elect Grau San Martin to say she had something to tell us. We guessed what it was. They were at an all-night cocktail party to which we were to go from the dinner. General Brett was also there; and after we arrived he and Maria connived to prevent me from talking to Bill alone and warning him of Patricia's faults as well as virtues—a practice I made with future sons-in-law, to the inexplicable distress of my daughters.

We were sitting on the terrace of the Embassy at about 5:00 A.M. drinking champagne. The General went inside, and returning he sat down beside Maria.

"I looked at myself in the mirror," he told her, "and I said to myself, 'General, you're tight.' "

He had thoroughly celebrated the success of his matchmaking.

3

With the Navy I had almost no trouble. They were more sophisticated and flexible than the Army officers—possibly because the Navy at that time had more knowledge of the world and its officers thus acquired more experience and savoir faire. The only slightly rigid Navy officer I ever encountered was Admiral John H. Hoover, who was then Vice Admiral with headquarters in Puerto Rico, and a fine man. One day I entertained him and his staff at a luncheon during which I told him I had learned that enemy submarines had just reappeared off the north coast of Cuba and I was much concerned.

"Oh, no," he said. "There can't be any submarines there."

"My source is excellent," I told him.

"I don't believe it," he insisted, "but we'll find out when they sink a ship."

That night they sank two. One of them was a great loss—a tanker that had been lined with glass to carry ammonia to the nickel plant at Nicaro.

My naval attaché was Col. Hayne Boyden, a Marine flyer who gave me no trouble. But he and my military attaché regularly received wild instructions from Washington, especially on how to get information. This caused me some concern. I knew that in intelligence work the employment of informers is dangerous. One has to know who they are, and how to evaluate the information they bring in. It is too tempting for an informer who has supplied valid information to earn his continued pay by fabrication.

Col. Mariano Faget, the head of Cuban Intelligence, was an experienced and excellent man, and I worked closely with him. Faget once assured me he would coach the worst stumblebum in Havana for fifteen minutes in my presence, send him to my Naval and Military attachés, and guarantee that he would come out with not less than twenty dollars. I did not risk a demonstration, but I was worried. I had the FBI, as in Colombia, and I did not want the military working at cross purposes with my legal attachés. I may say here that Faget's tireless, invaluable cooperation with our Intelligence during the war was very poorly rewarded, as has often been the case. When the influx of refugees from Cuba began after Castro seized power, Faget (I suspect at the instance of the FBI) was employed by our Immigration Service to screen refugees and prevent infiltration of Communists. He did such an excellent job that before long he was relegated to a back room and put to work on translation. The *New York Times,* in an article by Tad Szulc, characteristically misinterpreted this move. I urged Szulc, in fairness, to tell his readers how competent Faget was and how good a friend to the United States. I also protested to the State Department that Faget deserved better treatment at the hands of our government. Both Szulc and Assistant Secretary Richard Rubottom in the Department promised to bear my protests in mind. Neither ever vouchsafed the slightest sign of having done so.

One day the Naval attaché came in with some reports from an informant who was, he said, very close to Captain Vierra, a military officer in the Spanish Embassy (the Spanish and Cuban governments had withdrawn their ambassadors, but the Spanish maintained a Chargé d'Affaires with the rank of Minister-Counselor). Captain Vierra was supposed to be an important man and hand in glove with the Nazis and Fascists. I was extremely suspicious of the alleged information about this captain, and demanded proofs.

My attaché went away, and returned with some copies of a Spanish illustrated magazine. One had a picture of the alleged Captain Vierra, who, read the caption, was stationed in Cuba. In another issue was a photograph of an important meeting in which Franco sat on a dais surrounded by a cardinal and high government functionaries—and very near him Captain Vierra.

This same informant had earlier brought in a list of Nazi agents in the United States, and the cities in which they were operating. Our FBI men considered it sufficiently important to send to J. Edgar Hoover. The War and Navy Departments got it; there were meetings in Washington followed by investigations costing over $100,000 and arrests of unfortunate innocents whose names were the same as those of purported enemy agents on this list.

I was therefore more than usually skeptical of the reports on Captain Vierra. I called in my legal attaché Ray Leddy and said, "I just don't believe all this poppycock about this Spanish officer. I want it checked further."

Ray got hold of Faget, who finally located and arrested our "informant." Under interrogation he confessed he was getting so much money from the Naval attaché that he had had a printer fake pages with the photographs of Vierra and substitute them for the originals in the copies of the magazine he had brought in. It had not occurred to us to buy other copies of those issues or to send for them to Spain.

At that point I had had it. I issued written instructions to my Naval and military attachés to take on no informants without my approval. No ambassador had ever done such a thing before, and that order completely discomfited both Army and Navy Intelligence—particularly Gen. George V. Strong, the head of G-2, to whose agitation I ascribed much of the Navy's.

It went on until the State Department urgently requested me to come to Washington and try to quiet the rumpus I had caused. I could not leave at the moment, but sent a second secretary, Robert P. Joyce, my liaison with the FBI. After more ructions, he was able to pacify the Navy. But General Strong was implacable. He threatened to withdraw all military attachés from Cuba.

Nothing could have upset me less. I sent back word that he could withdraw them at any time so far as I was concerned. My answer must have shocked him speechless, for I never heard another word on the subject. Excepting for this confrontation Strong was an able and patriotic officer.

4

Before I left for Cuba J. Edgar Hoover said he would assign FBI men—so called "legal attachés"—to the Embassy there as he had in

Colombia. (My predecessor, George Messersmith, had absolutely refused to have the FBI.) While he was finding suitable men who knew both intelligence work and Spanish there was an interval when I had no intelligence aides except the military, air, and Naval attachés, who were hardly to be counted. Faget was doing a good job on the Germans and Italians; but the Prime Minister, Carlos Saladrigas, expressed concern about the 300,000 Spaniards on the Island, of whom he considered between fifteen and thirty thousand to be violent Falangists. At that time we were still fearful that Hitler might come West, and Carlos thought it important to know what those Spaniards were up to.

I thought so too; but what to do about it was a puzzle until I had one of my better brainwaves.

For some years Ernest Hemingway had been living at San Francisco de Paulo, just outside Havana. I met him through Ellis O. Briggs, then Counselor of Embassy, at the Floridita Bar shortly after my arrival. He was a big hulk of a man, a good boxer, and fast on his feet. He used to speak of boxing with me sometime. I always answered vaguely. He was several years younger than I; and besides his shoulders were tremendous. I had once felt his arms. They were as large as the average man's legs and hard as rock.

Hemingway was friendly with all kinds of people, from Spanish noblemen down to mere tramps. This gave me my idea. I asked him to come in and see me, and took him into my confidence.

"What I'd like you to do," I told him, "is to organize an intelligence service that will do a job for a few months until I get the FBI men down. These Spaniards have got to be watched."

He agreed, and immediately set about organizing in his house what he called his "crime shop." He enlisted a bizarre combination of Spaniards: some bartenders; a few wharf rats; some down-at-heel pelota players and former bullfighters; two Basque priests; assorted exiled counts and dukes; several Loyalists and Francistas. He knew them all well, and he managed to keep them all separate. He would go down one day and drink—and he could hold his liquor—with some of his barkeeps, and the next he would spend at an aristocratic shooting club, shooting and drinking champagne with the titled Spaniards. He built up an excellent organization and did an A-One job.

When finally the FBI men arrived, I wrote a letter of thanks to Hemingway for patriotic services. He came in to see me and said, "Now I want to be paid for all the work I've done."

I had no idea what was coming. I only knew it would be completely unexpected.

"What's on your mind, Ernest?" I asked.

"I have a fishing boat, the *Pilar*. It has a very high bridge but is old and dirty. I can hang canvas around the sides so nobody can see that the boat is armed. The subs are coming up all around Cuba, to surface alongside a Cuban fishing smack and buy all the water and food on board. I can really have myself a party provided you will get me a bazooka to punch holes in the side of a submarine, machine guns to mow down the people on the deck, and hand grenades to lob down the conning tower."

What he asked was against all regulations. But Ernest had done such an outstanding job that we scrapped the regulations, got him what he wanted, and sent him on his way. He did some very valuable work, locating submarines and getting the information to us.

He ran the boat with the same sort of motley crew as he had had in his "crime shop"—except that he also took along a marine sergeant and the ten-goal polo player Winston Guest, relative of Winston Churchill. Winston used to get pretty bored lying off Cuba, and—as Hemingway told it—decided to improve his mind by taking along some books. One of these was Renan's *Life of Christ,* and Hemingway insisted that after Winston had read about a hundred pages he could stand the suspense no longer and turned to the last page to see how it all came out.

That really was unfair to Winston, who was a very fine chap. Moreover, he made a sacrifice by working along with Hemingway, for he could easily have had a commission. Instead he eventually enlisted in the Marines, advanced quickly from private to captain, and when I left Cuba was, I believe, somewhere in the Pacific. After our return from Argentina he came to see Maria and me one evening at our Washington apartment. He was full of his Marine Corps comrades and what a fine lot they were; and he very seriously proposed (he'd had a couple of extra drinks, to be sure) that I permit him to take a few of them to Argentina to assassinate Peron for me.

I always hoped Ernest would get his submarine. It would have made a wonderful story. And he nearly did. He was lying off the coast about 100 miles west of Havana in a place where he was sure submarines would surface, when my Naval attaché, for some trivial reason, called him in. The next morning an aviator spotted a submarine in the exact place where Ernest had been lying in wait.

5

The first time we invited Ernest and his wife (his third, Martha Gellhorn) to dinner at the Embassy, he had no dinner clothes. He borrowed a dinner jacket from Winston Guest—no doubt the only man he knew with shoulders as big as his. His shirt he borrowed from someone else, and it couldn't be buttoned around his neck but he had partly hidden the gap with his black tie. Later he took the trouble to get his own dinner clothes.

On one occasion when he was a guest we were sitting on the terrace, and I happened to express my admiration for the old movie, *Birth of a Nation*. Ernest thereupon held forth about his grandfather, whom he characterized as an "old rummy," a member of the GAR. When *Birth of a Nation* came out Ernest was a boy. His grandfather, he said, would take him to see the movie every afternoon, except when the funeral of another GAR member took priority. On this simple theme he improvised for at least an hour, convulsing us all with Grandfather's remarks on the various aspects of the picture.

He could consume an astonishing amount of liquor—any kind of liquor—without appearing to feel it. I remember an evening when Maria and I had dinner with him and Martha Gellhorn at their home outside the city. I don't know how many cocktails we had before dinner; but Ernest didn't take cocktails, he took absinthe drip. During dinner we had white and red wine, followed by champagne. When Martha and Maria left the table, he ordered another bottle of champagne, just for the two of us. After we joined them I had highballs, but Ernest went back to his absinthe drip. And he remained cold sober.

Both Ernest and his wife went off thereafter to report the war. Ernest got himself into trouble now and then by forgetting he was a non-combatant—grabbing a gun and bringing in a few German prisoners for the fun of it. But the general to whose command he was attached took a liking to him, kept him near himself, and protected him from the consequences of his sudden enthusiasms.

The general began to suffer from shell-shock. He became very nervous and it was clear that the war was affecting him. Indeed, he realized it himself. Ernest finally decided to go up to the front lines to get away from the general.

One day a little doctor showed up; one of the psychoanalysts attached to the Army, along with psychiatrists and just plain psychologists, to treat personnel nervously upset by the fighting and in general to observe the mental effects of war on men under fire. The general had sent him, he said, to psychoanalyze Ernest because psychoanalysis was extremely important and the general was sure Ernest needed it. Ernest tried to brush him off, without success.

"Now, Mr. Hemingway," he said, "tell me about your dreams."

And Ernest answered profanely, "I don't dream. I've never had a blankety-blank-blank dream in my whole life."

"Oh, now, Mr. Hemingway, you must dream something. Just concentrate on remembering, and tell me what you dream."

This went on and on, with Ernest getting more exasperated and his little pest more insistent—he was afraid to go back to the general and admit that he hadn't psychoanalyzed Ernest. At last, in desperation, he said, "The trouble with you, Mr. Hemingway, is that you have no imagination."

The challenge, Ernest told me, was too much. Suddenly he clapped his hand to his forehead.

"It comes to me now!" he exclaimed. "I do have dreams."

"Of course, I knew you did. Now concentrate and tell me what they are."

"I'm concentrating," Ernest went on. "It's a lovely dream—they're all the same ecstatic dream. I wake up *so* refreshed!"

The doctor cheered him on. "Concentrate. Tell me. What do you dream about?"

"I can't quite get it yet, but it's marvelous—*so* refreshing! Yes—now it comes to me. Now it comes to me!"

"What is it? What *is* it?"

"It's wonderful—I dream I'm sleeping with a chartered public accountant."

The doctor was feverishly taking notes. He got it all down for the psychological annals of the war. Then, mechanically, he asked, "Who was the CPA?"

"My God!" exclaimed Ernest. "It was a man!"

After Ernest's splendid short novel *The Old Man and the Sea* was published he presented me with a copy in which he had inscribed:

> For Spruille Braden
>
> To my former commanding officer (in bad times) with old respect and permanent affection
>
> (signed) Ernest Hemingway
>
> La Vigia 1955

6

There were two major cases of espionage in Cuba. One involved the head of the Cuban radio, Major Juan Govea. He tried to interest me in setting up a radio station at Nicaro, the Nickel Company, on the north coast of Oriente province. I refused to endorse the proposal because I already had enough information on Govea to be suspicious of him.

At last I got enough discreditable information about him to justify requesting Prime Minister Ramon Zaydin, who had succeeded Saladrigas, to fire him. Zaydin took it up with President Batista, and to his chagrin met with an emphatic refusal—no doubt influenced by the fact that Govea's brother, a contractor, was involved with Batista's gangsters who were making millions through bribery, graft, and all kinds of shady deals.

Fortunately we had two sets of intercepts; one of broadcasts giving the locations of ships, which of course could be picked up by enemy submarines. The second really brought the showdown. We made a recording of a newscast by Govea himself. It gave the names, tonnages, and cargoes of a convoy that had come into Guantanamo, with descriptions and names of the convoying vessels, the convoy's point of departure, and the destination.

Once more I went to Zaydin, and this time I flatly demanded Govea's removal. Zaydin did not even inform the President, but at once summoned Govea to his office and told him he was through. Govea told the Prime Minister *he* was through. And he did have enough influence with Batista so that in spite of having been caught in the very act of aiding the enemy he retained his rank of major, although he was out of his strategic position. It was only much later, when Batista and I had made up after a serious clash, that the President, as a token of reconciliation, told me he had divested Govea of his military rank and fired him from the Army.

The second case was broken after a series of intercepts had been picked up by the FBI in this country. Clearly the broadcasts came from Cuba, probably from Havana. By that time we had our FBI men in the Embassy, who worked closely with Faget in ferreting out the enemy operator. They finally found him, mainly thanks to Faget's excellent work.

His name was Luening and he had his apartment filled with canaries whose chirping and singing drowned the sound of his radio. His apprehension could have been one of the war's major breaks in espionage. The FBI proposed to use him, keeping him under constant surveillance and feeding him fake information that would lead us to the other Latin American agents working with him.

Unfortunately we reckoned without the Cuban Chief of Police, Benitez, who saw a golden opportunity to take credit for a coup he had no part in. With his police sirens shrieking and the press in hot pursuit he arrested Luening, and boasted to the reporters that *he* had caught a dangerous spy.

It was Saturday afternoon. I was on my way from the chancellery to the Embassy in Country Club Park, and for that half hour I couldn't be reached on the telephone. That was ample time for Luening's discovery and arrest to become public knowledge and our plan to use him was ruined.

He was tried and convicted. The Cuban Constitution of 1940 had abolished the death penalty, but military law permitted a sentence of death even though he had not been court-martialed. Batista refused to make the decision, instead leaving it up to me. I decided Luening should be shot. That seemed to me the logical sentence, and I had no particular qualms about it, though I will confess I found his picture in the paper a bit disturbing. No doubt I would have felt much more discomfort if I had had to condemn a man actually before me.

7

Early in my Cuban mission I learned that a number of enemy agents—German, Fascist, Japanese—were being regularly locked up and were as regularly bribing their way out of jail. That is, every time we protested their being at large they would be rearrested. The Cuban officials responsible were profiting from each of our protests, each time releasing the prisoners, but meanwhile ships were being sunk daily off the Cuban coasts. To us these reappearing spies were a problem involving life and death.

At last Faget worked out a plan to remove them to one wing of the prison on the Isle of Pines. They could not be housed with ordinary criminals, but with a wing to themselves they could be kept in the same prison.

The scheme involved American maintenance of the prisoners and their guards and assumption of responsibility to the International Red Cross for their treatment in accordance with its rules. We calculated a cost—that the U.S.A. had to pay—of $184,000, for which I appealed to the State Department. To my embarrassment Sumner

Welles categorically refused it. Curiously, he offered less opposition to my request for funds from Byron Price's office to finance the proper organization of a Cuban censorship. But he would have nothing to do with any grant for incarcerating those enemy agents. I was stymied.

But not for long. Martha Gellhorn was preparing to visit Washington as a guest of Eleanor Roosevelt, and I felt her knowledge of how Mrs. Roosevelt won favors from the President could be turned to our advantage. The First Lady would wait until the President's attendants had moved him into bed, where he was immobilized, and then bring up any matter interesting her. He had to listen; he couldn't get away.

Before Martha left I had lunch with her and Bob Joyce, when I briefed her on the critical matter of the periodically reappearing enemy agents. She, then, briefed Mrs. Roosevelt and Harry Hopkins, who, at the time, was living in the White House. Mrs. Roosevelt went to the President and said, "Franklin, Martha has just told me a story about Spruille Braden's difficulty with enemy agents in Cuba," and described the situation and my desperate need of funds.

"Now, Franklin," she insisted, "you have got to get that money to him."

The next day Hopkins came in and said, "You have got to do that, Mr. President."

I have often wondered if Welles ever found out how I got through to the President and persuaded him to issue the order for the money we needed to lock up enemy agents on the Isle of Pines for the duration of the war.

A minor problem subsequently arose concerning a half-dozen German women subversives. One day Ray Leddy, my legal attaché, came to me and said, "Mr. Ambassador, I'm sorry, we'll have to rent a house, put electric wire around it, and provide special guards for those German women. We can't put them in the women's prison."

I was annoyed. "Why not?"

Ray explained that the matron of the women's prison had formerly run a brothel in Havana and had retained her professional habits. Every night she rented out all her charges. From her point of view she was doing all right, but our women prisoners, whatever their crimes, had to be presumed not to be prostitutes. There was nothing for it but to provide special accommodations for them that would meet the requirements of the International Red Cross and our own sense of human decency.

Chapter XXVIII

IN Cuba, from the early days of the Spanish conquest, corruption was endemic. If the burden of graft had been held to the U.S. norm of a mere five or ten per cent, Cuba could have become a world financial power. But the grafters' take was as high as 50 and 60 percent, and the Cuban officials had marvelous ingenuity in devising occasions for graft. The economy had to bear an appalling burden. Even so, the Cuban standard of living was one of the three highest in Latin America.

I knew about the corruption before I was Ambassador. Indeed, I had personally encountered it during my years in business. I had formed a syndicate with the Stewart Brothers (a leading construction firm) and the bankers Blair & Co. to go into the possibility of building the projected Central Highway. We gave up when some Cuban authorities demanded two million dollars in bribes, of which President Machado would take half and the rest would be divided among various senators and other officials. (The deal did go through, though not with us, and Machado got his million.)

Even knowing what I did, I was appalled by the extent and scale of the corruption, and the apparent apathy of the public. What looks like apathy, however, can be frustration; and many Cubans concealed under witty jibes at the corruptionists a dissatisfaction that provided excellent soil for Communist propaganda.

Naturally the Communists blamed the corruption on the "American imperialists." Americans were indeed involved in it. They were doing business in Cuba, and that had always meant paying bribes and making contributions to political parties. But the Americans generally were not responsible; it was a case of extortion. Nor were the Cubans fundamentally more immoral than other peoples. The corruption was traditional.

From the beginning of the occupation Spaniards flocked into Cuba to fill the official positions, from governor-general down to the humblest clerk. Often they were rewarded with the posts as political pay-offs or patronage. They came with one ambition: to get as rich as possible as fast as possible, and return to Spain with enough money to buy anything from titles and estates down to modest properties. Theft proved to be the quickest way to riches. The immigrant officials resorted to all kinds of corruption. They developed a devilish ingenuity in devising ways and means; and they undermined the theory of sound government.

Other immigrants remained, of course, from middle class merchants to humble workers. Their descendants formed the new Cuban population, and were ruthlessly exploited by the Spanish officials until they succeeded, with our help, in winning independence. Then Cubans took over the government where the Spaniards had left off—and with it the official acquisitive habits.

Only during the first four-year term of the first president, Estrada Palma, was the country honestly governed. To win a second term Estrada made compromises. All succeeding presidents enriched themselves while in office, some more discreetly than others. And the majority of the other administrative officials, the legislators, and the police emulated the presidents.

The Cubans drafted laws or decrees so cleverly that although they appeared to be generally applicable they would in reality affect only one particular case. Then the officials would collect blackmail for withholding enforcement. Or a person might be arrested and fined, say, a few thousand dollars for a dereliction plucked out of thin air by the police. When he had fought the case through the courts and of course won at an expense exceeding the fine, the officials would amiably consent to repay his few thousand dollars on condition that they retain a large percentage of it.

Cutting in on government payments was common official practice. Late one morning I was surprised to receive a visit from His Eminence Cardinal Artiaga. He had come to ask for help that unfortunately I had no way to give.

Some years earlier the Cardinal had agreed to provide to the Ministry of Defense three chaplains whose expenses—living, uniforms, travel—would be paid by the Church, which was to bill the Ministry every six months for half the amount. The Church had fulfilled its part of the agreement but the Ministry had never paid a cent. At last, that morning, the Cardinal had gone in person to plead with the Minister of Defense that the Church could not afford to sacrifice the thousands of dollars the government owed it.

The Minister of Defense couldn't have been more cordial. "Why, of course, Your Eminence," he said, "we'll be delighted to pay—but 50 per cent for me!"

In the early days corruption largely centered on such things as the lottery. The drawing was always arranged so that the people in power won the big prizes. When Alfredo Zayas was President, his wife notoriously always drew the first prize and his daughter the second—both without shame. Later, to spread the benefits over more people, the lottery tickets were sold only to a favored few, who resold them at a handsome profit.

Fantastic amounts of money were stolen through the distribution of sinecures, known as bottles—*botellas.* Some of these were real jobs that the holder was privileged to hand out; others were jobs created and paid for, but never filled. For example, a senator and leader of his party yearly received between two and four thousand *botellas,* from humble jobs paying $40 or $50 a month to important posts. Of these he distributed half to his followers and kept for himself the other half, including those which required no work. At one time it was revealed during an investigation that a dozen well-to-do women had *botellas* as night-watchmen on the piers. They never went near the piers; neither did they go near the pay offices; they received checks through the mail each month in payment for their non-existent services.

While Grau San Martin was President, he always invited Maria and me to lunch when I asked for an interview. After lunch he and I would repair to an inside balcony in the Palace, and there—he was extremely long-winded—I used to have to sit and listen for hours in order to get in fifteen minutes of what I had on my mind. Maria, in the meantime, would have to sit in the drawing room with the President's boring but ruthless sister-in-law, Doña Paulina Alsina, and any other members of his family who happened to be around.

On one such occasion Grau's son-in-law came in with a colonel of police bringing some eighteen police appointments—*botellas*—for Doña Paulina. As he started to present them, the son-in-law interfered. "What a minute," he said to her. "You got the last batch. I'm entitled to some of these."

They had a nasty quarrel about the *botellas,* wholly disregarding the presence of the American Ambassadress. Then the old Castilian courtesy asserted itself. Turning to Maria, Doña Paulina said, "Won't you take some of these?"

Maria in her innocence thought she was being offered the privilege of selecting the three policemen who guarded the Embassy. She answered, "Oh, thank you. We're very well satisfied with our policemen."

When she told me of the incident on the way home, I roared with laughter at her rage as I explained, "Why, Doña Paulina was just offering you a few *botellas,* that's all."

2

The economic development of the Island until well into the 20th Century was largely financed by American companies. Indeed, Cuban big business was American, and it provided a source of graft and extortion running into many millions yearly.

I have spoken of the Central Highway. A later deal on the government's indebtedness to the railways was handled in much the same way. United Railways, a British company, and the American-owned Consolidated Railways were unable to collect for transportation of government employees and freight, the debt rose to some eight million dollars. At last the two companies consented to a bargain that seemed to offer their only chance to collect. The congress authorized a bond issue of $10 million, fully secured by government credit. President Laredo Bru vetoed the bill, but it was passed by a two-thirds majority. The $10 million was delivered to the railway companies. They turned back two million to be divided among members of the government and the congress. The companies had to forgo interest on their eight million, except for the small amount paid on the bonds (if they chose to keep them.)

Batista at that time was a colonel at Camp Colombia, but already the strong man. He rated a fifth of the swag. After I became Ambassador, I attended a dinner party at which the President of the Senate held forth enthusiastically about President Batista's character.

"Such sentiment!" he said. "What a father! You know, I had charge of distributing the bonds in the railway deal. When I took Batista his share—$400,000 worth—at Camp Colombia, do you know what he did? Oh, the sentiment of the man! It was really beautiful. He took the bonds and patted them. And he said, 'These are for Papo. All for Papo.' What a father!"

Papo was Batista's nine-year-old son.

The President of the Senate—a charming man—later had to clear out of Cuba for a while. Before distributing the bonds he had had a bright idea. He clipped all coupons and kept them for himself. That did not prevent him from becoming Vice President eleven years later. Only eleven congressmen and senators refused to take any of the pay-off.

This incident gave rise to a typically Cuban story that started with the President of the Senate sailing on the Bremen for Europe. One day the First Officer reported that the anchor had been stolen.

"Did you look in the President of the Senate's cabin?" asked the Captain.

The corruption in the cases of the Central Highway and the railways differed from that in other cases only in scale. The government had threatened to take over property belonging to the American-owned tramway company, but the company, in spite of a Supreme Court decision ordering payment, could not collect without agreeing to surrender from 50 to 60 per cent of the price to government officials. The American Sugar Refining Co. was obliged to pay $113,000 in graft out of the $226,000 the government owed its mill at Jaranu. On that distribution I had the figures. Batista took $55,000; Gen. Benitez, the Chief of Police $25,000; and even a very rich Senator took $11,000.

One day when Ellis Briggs and I were discussing a debt to the tramway company at lunch with the Prime Minister and the Foreign Minister I remarked that the case was identical with that of the American Sugar Refining Co.

"They've been asked for a cut," I remarked, "and pretty much the same people are to participate in it. Moreover the amounts are almost identical."

"Now, Mr. Ambassador," protested the Prime Minister, "you can't really believe anybody got anything out of that Jaranu deal. I know it has been said that our friend the Senator got $11,000 but you know him and his complete integrity, and also how wealthy he is. He doesn't need $11,000. You can't believe such a thing."

I pulled a sheaf of papers from my pocket. "Would you like," I inquired, "to see just how the $113,000 was distributed?"

He scurried for cover. Not for anything would he even glance at that list. And he hurriedly promised to work for a fair settlement of the tramways.

The grafters were pitiless, sparing neither the poor, the young, the aged, or the ill. One victim I helped was an American veteran of the Spanish-American War for Cuban independence. He owned some land worth around $30,000. It was all he had, and when squatters settled on it he sought government help to remove them. The government decided instead to expropriate his land, and did. The old man was in actual want but he couldn't collect a penny. I was finally assured before I left that he would be reimbursed. But the final payment made to him was considerably lightened before reaching him by the officials involved.

3

Shortly after becoming ambassador, I formally announced I would receive no U.S. citizen, corporate or individual, who shared in any form of corruption. But I said I would go down the line 100 per cent in defense of their legitimate interests. At every opportunity thereafter I made it clear I would fight to prevent Americans being victimized by extortionists, but only if they kept their hands scrupulously clean.

It was hard at first for both the Cubans and Americans to take my policy seriously. The Cubans were incredulous. The chief of National Police, General Benitez, tried to put over a small bribe ($15,000 or $20,000) on a drydock. This occurred at an Embassy reception shortly after my first pronouncement, attended both by Benitez and the American company's lawyers. I stopped it, and the deal went through without extortion. As they realized I was deadly serious, Cuban officials, from Batista down, grew deeply resentful. They looked on it as taking bread from the mouths of babes.

One American who failed to take me seriously was a man I had known at Yale; he was boasting before my arrival that we had been college pals. He was vice president and general manager of one of the largest American companies in Cuba.

Rumor had it that his subsidiary company had sold a piece of property to the Ministry of Defense for $283,000, and had kicked back $183,000 to defense officials. I invited this executive to come to my office and explain. The property's real value was $70,000.

Fortunately I had a tile floor, for despite the day's cool temperature the perspiration rolled off his forehead and gathered in a pool on the floor as he sat on the sofa leaning forward during my questioning.

Having the facts secure, I telephoned the head of his company in New York. I knew him well, and didn't hesitate to say, "You know my ruling. Your representatives knew, for I told them myself. I expect you to fire this fellow."

He was fired within 24 hours. I saw him again when I returned to Cuba several years later. We were no longer old college pals.

Sosthenes Behn, head of the admirable and efficient International Telephone & Telegraph Corporation, also didn't take me seriously. Behn was as cosmopolitan as his company. He spoke French and Spanish fluently, and was a connoisseur of wines and food as well as a courteous and delightful host. I thought highly of his company and did it several good turns during my government service, but Behn was unfriendly to me and even went about Washington attacking me violently for standing up to Peron later in my diplomatic career.

Of that more later. Behn had a drawing room and dining room in the tower of the IT&T building on Broad Street. The luncheons he gave there were epicurean, and it was at one of these, when I was up from Cuba on consultation, that he took issue with me on my stand against corruption. Like many others, he insisted no company could do business in South America without paying graft.

I simply pointed to my father and the large scale operations he was able to carry on in South America without paying a penny of graft. I also reminded Behn that I had promoted the electrification of the Chilean railways and several other important businesses without bribing anyone.

"You simply don't have to do it," I said. "Moreover, in my experience when people start that sort of thing they soon find themselves stuck and unable to get away from it unless they have someone like myself to appeal to, who as Ambassador is willing to bear the brunt of official resentment."

Behn at last admitted I was right—except for utility companies, which, he insisted, couldn't get by even in this country without paying graft. I would not yield. Then he said he'd go along with me except for "a little graft."

"What do you mean by a little graft?" I asked.

"Up to $30,000 a year. I promise you I won't go over $30,000 a year in Cuba if you'll just give me that leeway."

"Not a penny. I'll fight for you if you stop, but I won't do a thing for you if you continue."

He stopped, because the alternative would have been going it alone against the ravening Cuban officials.

That my program worked is proved by the experience of the Consolidated Railways. The Chairman of its Board told me that up to the time of my pronouncement in 1942, his company had had to budget half a million dollars yearly for extortion. But from then on they paid nothing and after 1944 they were not even asked for any payments.

Later I extended the ban to political contributions, which saved the American companies millions of dollars. I remember Carlos Saladrigas, who was Batista's candidate to succeed him as president, saying to me one evening when he was dining with us, "If you'll lift your ban on political contributions, I'll undertake to show you $2,500,000 from American companies by tomorrow noon."

He could have done it easily.

4

Sumner Welles always regarded Cuba as his special bailiwick. Having intervened there three times, he had developed a feeling of proprietorship toward the island. Knowing this, I was surprised that he had not vetoed my being sent there, since he knew I was nobody's yes-man. But if he ever raised any objection I never knew it.

Cuba, when Roosevelt became President, was in deep trouble. Sugar had dropped to less than half a cent a pound, which meant there was actual want. Machado, who was president, had shown comparative honesty but aggravated the popular discontent by insisting that the public debt continue to be serviced. He was considered a terrorist and a corruptionist. Actually, if he had been able to content himself with one term he might have entered history as a very good president. During his first term he enriched himself by a couple of large-scale thefts (the Central Highway deal was one) but was otherwise fairly honest and forced those around him to be so. When it came to changing the constitution in order to run for a second term he had to compromise with the crooked politicians, and from there on his government was graft-ridden. A number of opposition movements were being secretly formed against him, one of which, the ABC, was headed by Joaquin Martinez Saenz and my friend Carlos Saladrigas. But nothing had got seriously under way when Roosevelt sent Sumner Welles down to straighten out Cuba before making him Assistant Secretary of State.

Sumner demanded that Machado sit down and deal with the opposition groups. What the United States decided with respect to sugar could make or break Cuba, so this demand had all the weight of the new Administration behind it. Machado yielded, and that show of weakness was his undoing. The opposition leaders, like so many sharks scenting blood, were on him in a flash and he was destroyed.

Sumner's stock was high with the Cubans. But instead of leaving succession to them, he put in his own hand-picked candidate, Carlos Manuel de Cespedes, whose father had been one of the Liberators. The son had inherited quite a fortune, had been educated abroad, and had lived abroad in diplomatic posts. He had a beautiful house in Paris, entertained lavishly, was a boulevardier and gourmet, and knew no more of his native land and how to cope with its politicians (they took some coping) than any other European. But Sumner liked him.

Not so the Cubans. When the new president went down the island to look over the damage in Sagua la Grande after a bad cyclone, Fulgencio Batista (at that time a mere sergeant) and his crowd rose up and took over. Sumner's president was out.

He tried to persuade Roosevelt and Hull to send in the armed forces. They denied him that satisfaction, but when Grau San Martin emerged as president from the ensuing pandemonium they permitted Welles to refuse recognition and to delay buying the Cuban sugar crop until he was out. That was short-sighted: Grau was so incompetent that the Cubans themselves would have thrown him out in half a year—for good. Instead he became a martyr and the idol of the Cuban people.

Batista was the strong man behind a succession of presidents. It was Batista who restored order, enriching himself as he did so. As president he piled up a huge fortune. He developed fascist ideas in the beginning. He was the first president in the hemisphere to appoint Communists to his Cabinet—two of the party's leaders. In this he was undoubtedly influenced by the growing strength of the Communists, who during the revolution had seized four sugar mills. This was an omen of things to come twenty-six years later under Castro.

When his term was about to expire, in 1944, Batista made Carlos Saladrigas his candidate for the succession. But by that time Grau was actually regarded in a supernatural light by the populace. I saw babies passed from hand to hand over their heads by 50 people for him to cure by his touch. People would get down on their knees in the dust of a country road to kiss his hand. The public was so wrought up that they regarded him as their savior. And, to make matters worse, so did he.

In this atmosphere it would almost certainly have been dangerous for Carlos to succeed Batista. He lost out in any case, partly because a large sum of money sent to purchase votes in one critical province was gambled away by the governor and partly because Batista, after realizing that the situation had been lost, forbade the use of force (what was called a *brava*) as a substitute for ballots. Grau was elected and the Cuban people went wild with joy.

That was on June 1, 1944. On June 3 Maria and I were at a dinner party in the home of some friends. Dinner was over and we were sitting on the terrace when suddenly the vice-president-elect and one of the senators-elect appeared, across the big lawn. They spoke to none of the guests and barely saluted our host, but excitedly demanded I speak with them at once. We went to the other end of the terrace.

They had just learned that a group of high army officers, including the chief of the national police, General Benitez, was meeting in a house in the outskirts of Havana, making plans to throw out Batista, cancel the election of Grau whom the army rabidly opposed, and take over power. I wondered how much Batista knew about it; he had certainly not wanted to give up the Presidency. (Benitez later said he was in the plot; but he was so unreliable that his statement meant nothing.)

"This is what's going to happen," insisted my informants. "And you've got to intervene."

"The United States can't intervene," I told them. "We have our international obligations."

"You've got to! They're going to cancel the elections, and there'll be bloody murder."

They were right; the cancellation would have meant a bloody revolution.

"I'll tell you what to do," I said. "Go to the Palace as quickly as you can get there. See Batista and give him the facts you've given me. Tell him I am at his orders; that I will go with him or with anyone he designates, or I will go alone to see these officers. I will tell them that so far as we are concerned Batista is President of Cuba until October 10 [Inauguration Day], and that after the inauguration ceremony Grau will be President of Cuba; and that my government will not recognize any other President or government. If we don't recognize any other President or government not a single ship will be allowed to enter or leave a Cuban harbor [we were controlling all shipping]. If they want to take over, we won't intervene at all. Our policy will be complete non-intervention."

Of course, no Cuban government could operate in such conditions. As soon as my statement reached the revolutionists, the revolution was over.

If the State Department had known what I said, it would have had kittens of 17 different colors. When I went to Washington I reported the incident orally. I never put it in writing.

A couple of days after the revolution that never was, Maria and I went to a cocktail party at the home of my Naval attaché, Col. John Hart. As we arrived I was told that General Benitez was in his cups in an adjoining room, and profanely abusing Batista. I took care not to enter that room, but presently he found me and continued the tirade. Hoping to silence him, I said just the wrong thing:

"Look, under the Cuban Constitution Batista can't be president for another eight years, but you can just put this down in the book now. I'm telling you that in another eight years, Batista will again be president of Cuba."

I over-estimated it by three months.

Thereupon he became so abusive of Batista that I said, "I can't have you talking this way about the President to whom I am accredited," and left him. I went at once to the telephone, called Carlos Saladrigas, and said, "Carlos, this is what has just happened at the home of my Naval attaché."

At ten that night, General Benitez was placed under house arrest, and three days later he was shipped out of Cuba.

5

Batista and I had some knock-down-drag-out fights, which I shall have occasion to mention later. But during several business trips I made to Cuba after I had left diplomacy, we became quite friendly. On one occasion he even broke all precedent by having me to lunch along with the Secretary of the Presidency and Carlos Saladrigas, this time Foreign Minister. I never ceased to give him what support I could in speeches and articles during the period when Fidel Castro was "getting his job through the *New York Times.*" This was nothing new on my part; I had been warning our government against Communism in Cuba from the time I became Ambassador; and I knew Castro and his gang to be Communists, no matter what the *Times* and its Mr. Herbert Matthews had to say.

On October 4, 1957, fifteen months before Castro came down from the hills, I sent an emphatic warning to Secretary Dulles through Terry Sanders, who had been a secretary of embassy under me in Colombia and by this time was in charge of the South America Division of the State Department. We had refused to ship a large order of arms to Batista that had been bought and paid for at the urging of our military, naval, and air missions, and a smaller order of anti-riot and police weapons Batista had bought and paid for on his own account. The Department knew I had had head-on collisions with Batista and entertained no personal bias in his favor, so I felt I could impartially disclose that our government's refusal to sell Batista any arms whatever would become public knowledge and undermine him.

For at the same time we were permitting clandestine shipments of arms to reach Castro in the hills. It was perfectly clear, I warned, that when these facts became known to the Cuban public they would be construed to mean we were backing Castro and working for Batista's defeat. Which is exactly what happened.

Terry Sanders later assured me he had delivered my message to Secretary of State John Foster Dulles. On November 8 I had Dulles' answer, by way of a press conference at which he triumphantly announced:

"There is no danger of Communism in Latin America!"

Chapter XXIX

WHEN Mr. Dulles announced there was no danger of Communism in Latin America, he was not trying to deceive either himself or the American people, whatever may have been the purposes of his advisers. Secretaries of State have to be informed; and for information they lean, especially if they are restless globetrotters like Mr. Dulles, on experts, or so-called ones in the Department. If the experts say, "No danger of Communism" the Secretary repeats, "No danger of Communism," and everybody is happy except those who know there is a very great danger of Communism. In Foggy Bottom there ought to be a sign: Don't question why we do it. Just assume it's our policy.

I began fully to realize the increasing danger of Communism, and its nature, during my mission to Colombia. The country was being flooded by anti-American Nazi propaganda brought in and distributed by the Communists, even though the Nazis had a strong organization in Colombia. When Hitler invaded Russia I was naive enough to think that the Communists would now work with the Western Powers. I told the members of my amateur intelligence organization to get in touch with them immediately and find out who our most dangerous enemies were. We never got even one name from them, or any other piece of information.

When I commented on this fact to J. Edgar Hoover, he laughed, and said, "That is exactly the experience we've had with them here in the States."

When I reached Cuba I was alarmed by the extent of Communist influence. In addition to having two Cabinet members, the Communists, through the party leaders, were firmly in control of the labor federation in Havana. To be sure, the Party still did not control some of the more important unions outside the Capital, such as the railway workers who were followers of Grau San Martin—like the Christian Democrats, sometimes nearly as dangerous. Nevertheless I found the situation so alarming that I sent the Department several dispatches on the subject and three times went to Washington myself, taking additional memoranda with me. To begin with, I was pretty innocent about Communism in the New Deal. During the years when the Federal departments and agencies were being successfully infiltrated (as Congressional Committees have since revealed) I was almost continuously out of the country. I simply could not imagine my warnings would be read by some officials in the Latin American Division with actual sympathy for the Communists. It took quite a time for me to believe it.

As the anniversary of the October Insurrection in Russia approached (November 7, new calendar) I learned it was customary in Havana to celebrate it with a meeting on the great steps of the Capitol, attended by Batista and his Cabinet, all prominent officials, the top military officers, and the diplomatic corps (except the representatives of Spain and the Axis Powers). These meetings were organized by the Communist-controlled "National Anti-Fascist Front," which actively participated in all so-called Allied meetings with its huge claque that tore the roof off with its applause at every mention of Stalin or the Red Army.

I had attended several similar smaller meetings and even they were too many. I decided I would not go to this Communist-organized celebration and sing the praises of Stalin and the USSR from the Capitol steps. So I took off for Cienfuegos—and ran plump into another celebration that was pretty much taken over by the Communist Party secretary there; a man by the name of Osvaldo Dorticos Torrado, who is now Castro's titular President of Cuba.

It was in the town's largest theater. All around the balcony ran a huge sign demanding "the second front," and throughout the meeting the Communist claque chanted the same demand. I had to speak. I reminded the audience that we had several fronts already. And I told about a man seeing some boys playing baseball who stopped and asked the score. It was 26–0 in the first inning.

"It looks," he said to a member of the team which hadn't scored, "as if you were going to be badly beaten."

"Oh, no" said the boy. "We haven't even gone to bat yet."

The Cubans love baseball, and my story swung the audience over to my side.

The second year I went to the meeting on the Capitol steps. Every mention of the Russians brought prolonged cheers; every mention of the other allies polite applause.

The third year (1944) I started my preparations early. At a certain point (I was now dean of the corps) I called in my diplomatic colleagues, the Russians excepted, took them into my confidence and got their complete support. Ten days before the scheduled celebration

I called in the Soviet Chargé d'Affaires (he had the coldest eye I've ever seen except that of his absentee chief, Gromyko).

"I've asked you to come," I said, "because I have to tell you that neither I nor any of my colleagues will be at your big show."

At first he couldn't believe his ears. Then he threw a tantrum. He actually turned purple. He pounded my desk and shouted that if the diplomatic corps, myself included, didn't show up, the consequences would be dire.

After this had gone on for some time I remarked, "You haven't asked me why we're not going."

That brought him up short. "Why not?" he said.

Opening a drawer of my desk I took out documents I had assembled, proving that the National Anti-Fascist Front had been blackmailing Cubans, Americans, and other nationals into contributing to the Front.

"This is blackmail and theft," I said, "and none of us will tolerate such dishonesty. Therefore we will not attend your meeting."

The Chargé d'Affaires went into complete reverse. He fairly groveled, begging that we come. At last he played his trump card, as it were.

"But, Mr. Ambassador, I'll go to any meeting in honor of the United States. I will speak. I will do anything, if only you will please, please come to our meeting."

"Don't you dare," I admonished him, "ever go to anything on behalf of the United States unless I personally ask you to."

That was the end of our interview and of the National Anti-Fascist Front, which dissolved and was heard of no more. The experience taught me once and for all a lesson that Foggy Bottom seems perennially unable to learn: There is just one language Communists understand, and that is a completely tough and uncompromising resistance to their policy of encroachment on the rights and dignities of free men plus the moral and, if need be, the physical force to carry through.

2

The first thing I did in Cuba was to defeat a Communist plot involving both our State and Treasury Departments. I can not point to this achievement as a proof of my sophistication about Communism. On the contrary, I was very slow to realize what I had contended with.

The story began with an experience reminiscent of my difficulty in learning about the ownership of SCADTA. Harry Dexter White, Henry Morgenthau's white-haired boy who by that time was Assistant Secretary of the Treasury, had headed a mission to Cuba not long before. It spent some time there and returned with recommendations that, as Ambassador-designate, I thought I should know about. In spite of my repeated and insistent demands, it was only at the last minute as I was leaving by train for Miami, to fly from there to Cuba, that I was able to get a copy of the mission's report.

On the train I read it, and was appalled. I am no economic or financial wizard but it took no expert to realize its implications. It recommended that Cuba have its own, independent currency, and a central bank empowered to lend up to 15 per cent of its capital to a whole series of subsidiary banks—an agricultural bank, an agricultural implement bank, a mining bank, and so on without limit.

There was no reason why Cuba should have a currency wholly independent of the dollar. It was doing perfectly well with its currency, which was interchangeable with the dollar. And I already knew enough of Cuban corruption to realize that if the crooked Cuban politicians ever got a central bank and a wholly separate currency they would steal just as fast as their printing presses could operate.

When I arrived in Havana the Cuban congress was already debating a bill to implement these dangerous recommendations; its importance was being discussed in the press. There was no time to lose. At my very first interview with Prime Minister Carlos Saladrigas I urged him to withdraw the measure at once. He was dumbfounded.

"Good heavens!" he exclaimed. "You're telling me we shouldn't pass this legislation! Your predecessor, Ambassador Messersmith, told us exactly the opposite. He insisted the United States considered it vitally necessary to its wartime collaboration with Cuba. And your State and Treasury Departments are daily summoning Concheso [the Cuban Ambassador in Washington] to interviews, to urge that the necessary legislation be put through at once."

When I had finished explaining why I thought it should not go through, Saladrigas was convinced.

"I'll put the brakes on that, and stop it," he said.

After the measure had been safely killed I wrote a long despatch to the State Department reporting what I had done, and why. I supposed the Department had not been alert to the iniquity of the proposals, and expected my action to meet with complete approval. The hornet's nest my despatch stirred up was the last thing I looked for.

It had barely had time to reach Washington when I received from the Department the meanest, nastiest message I have ever had except one that is also part of this story.

The gist of it was that I was to reverse my attitude immediately; that the Department considered the measure vital; that it had agreed upon it with the Treasury Department whose assistant secretary had headed the mission; that Cuba had a sovereign right to its own bank and currency; that I was apparently a tool of the American banking interests in Cuba and merely implementing their objections; that the matter was none of an ambassador's business, anyhow; and that the legislation was to go through and I had damn well better keep out of it.

I answered the Department that I resented being called a tool of the bankers; that I had not consulted them before sending my despatch but had since shown it to the representatives of the three big U.S. banks in Havana and they were delighted with it; that I was perfectly well aware of Cuba's sovereign rights; but that as a friend it was the duty of the United States to give the Cubans sound advice; that the implementation of the White Mission report would bring disaster to Cuba, and when that happened the United States would be blamed for having officially charted and urged the course that had led to it. That, I reminded them, would seriously impair our friendly relations with Cuba, which it was my job to promote. I did not, I concluded, so long as I remained Ambassador propose to allow any measure to be taken which would endanger those relations.

Although I did not then know what I was fighting, I realized that I was up against something very tough. (It was a few years before Harry Dexter White, who ran Secretary Morgenthau, and Lawrence Duggan, who ran our Latin American relations, were exposed as members of the Soviet spy apparatus.) I sent a copy of this despatch to Secretary Hull with a personal letter asking him to read it and suggesting that what was proposed for Cuba would seriously set back his efforts to free world trade. I reminded him of the tremendous volume of trade between Cuba and the United States, shackled by no blocked currencies, no controls—an ideal picture of the free exchange he envisaged for the whole world; a picture which would surely be destroyed if the White Mission's recommendations were adopted.

That letter won the fight. When Cordell Hull read it he hit the ceiling. My next communication from the Department was a snippy one-paragraph letter from Larry Duggan. After considering my reply, he said, they had come to the conclusion that while I was totally wrong, perhaps I had best say nothing more about the matter and neither would they. In other words: drop it. That was all I wanted.

3

The incident ended my friendship with Larry Duggan, which had become entirely cordial since our first meeting when I returned from the Chaco Peace Conference. At that time he was running the Office of American Republics Affairs. He was an attractive man who appeared to have great sweetness; and his wife, Helen, was equally attractive and sweet.

As I ran into trouble with American business firms in Colombia and had to crack down on them, Larry was always enthusiastic. I assumed he would be equally enthusiastic when I protected their rights. (One of my boasts was that no ambassador was tougher with American businessmen when they were in the wrong, and none more sturdily defended their legitimate interests.) However, I noticed that he showed satisfaction only when I was being tough with them.

Nevertheless, although he was clearly pretty far to the Left, we became sufficiently good friends so that when I returned to Washington to prepare for my Cuban mission Larry invited me to stay at his home. That I did not do, but we frequently lunched or dined together. I had a high opinion of his intelligence; moreover he lacked Sumner Welles' pomposity.

By that time Larry had been made special assistant to the Secretary of State; a position equivalent to the assistant secretaryship which I held later. He was in charge of all our Latin-American relations; and Philip W. Bonsal, who had been his assistant, was director of the Office of American Republics Affairs.

When I accompanied President Batista on his official visit to the United States in December of that year, I found a changed Larry Duggan. I vividly recall how, when I discussed the purchase of the Cuban sugar crop with him and Bonsal the morning I left, Larry's animosity was almost like an ugly living presence between us. It puzzled me greatly. This went on until, some time later, it led to one of the most disagreeable experiences of my diplomatic career.

President Batista and I had several times tangled rather unpleasantly. When I took the stand that no American company that paid bribes or contributed to Cuban political parties would be received at the Embassy or helped in any way, naturally his pocketbook and those of his gang were hard hit and Batista was resentful. Nor was my public announcement, made simultaneously, that I would go down the line 100 per cent in defense of the legitimate interests of U.S. nationals popular with these extortionists. Moreover, I discovered that Batista's payoff man was stealing lend-lease training planes for his private flying school and selling lend-lease jeeps down the island. I refused to accept the lame excuses offered me and ordered the stolen goods returned forthwith. I had to go to Batista to get it; but get it I did. This, I found out subsequently, was not the policy of our ambassadors elsewhere; and it certainly did not endear me to Batista and his entourage.

Neither did my refusing to give priority to three Pan American planes he had commandeered to carry a Cuban baseball team on a tour of the Caribbean countries at a time when more than a thousand Americans were stranded in Puerto Rico and Latin America unable to get plane passage home. On that occasion Batista sent me word he was going to shut down Pan American, and I sent him back word "go to it and I will take appropriate action."

These and other unpleasant incidents generated a good deal of heat between Batista and myself. Suddenly I received from Cordell Hull a letter whose first and last paragraphs the Secretary had written, but not those in between. (In the State Department one quickly learns to differentiate among the styles of various officials who have had a hand in writing a communication—a useful skill on occasion.)

The letter began with a reference to the personal friendship between Hull and myself and went on to express his appreciation of my help at the Montevideo Conference and of the important work I had done since. But (continued the second paragraph) in my present post I had done certain things (all enumerated) and said certain things (more numerous and all quoted) that had led Ambassador Aurelio F. Concheso to declare me *persona non grata* and ask for my removal as Ambassador. The last paragraph (Hull once more) said that in spite of this black mark, if I would resign as Ambassador to Cuba they would, because of my fine record, look around and find another post for me.

When I had recovered from my astonishment, I wired the Department requesting the source of its accusations. Back came a nasty telegram saying in effect that it was none of my business and that if I didn't hurry up and resign there would be no other post available. I replied that I intended to take my time both about replying and resigning; that I had been accused in great detail and intended to answer in detail, which would take two or three weeks.

It took two; and there was no further talk of my resigning. I pointed out that my statements Concheso had supposedly quoted had been made only in top secret despatches to the State Department and could have been seen only by the highest officials (*i.e.* Duggan,

Bonsal, and the Secretary and Under Secretary); and that no one else could possibly have had any knowledge of them. It was therefore apparent, I said, that whoever had drafted the Secretary's letter had taken those statements out of the despatches and put them in Concheso's mouth.

Recalling an ambassador is no mere routine matter; the conspirators had to get Hull's approval and his signature. That was their undoing. As the letter came from the Secretary of State, my answer had to go to him; they dared not withhold it. And when Hull read it and realized how Duggan and Bonsal had deceived him, he was furious. This he told me himself when I asked him about the incident later. Indeed, when Bonsal, who at that time was a State Department but not a Foreign Service officer, shortly afterward applied for admission to the Foreign Service Hull opposed him, and relented only under great pressure from Welles and other high Department officials.

As soon as an opportunity offered, I also discussed the matter with Ambassador Concheso, who was a friend of mine.

"Aurelio," I said, "I want to know just what happened."

"I'm glad to tell you," he answered. "We all knew, of course, about your differences with Batista. One day I got word from him that I ought to go to the State Department and say that you were too harsh. I answered that I didn't think I should do that, but that when an occasion arose I would put in a discreet word."

It is only fair to say that the Cubans had been so pampered by Sumner Welles and my other predecessors—Jefferson Caffery excepted—and by the State Department that I could perfectly understand their dismay over what must have seemed to them my odd and unreasonable behavior.

After this second instruction, Concheso told me, he had said one day in the course of a talk with Duggan, "Can't you get Braden to be a little easier on us? He's frequently pretty stiff in his attitude. Give him just a little hint not to be so tough."

"You mean he's *persona non grata?*" Duggan asked.

"I don't mean anything of the kind. Of course not."

But Duggan insisted on it. Bonsal was called in, and said, "All right. We'll get him out for you."

"I don't want anything of the kind," Aurelio insisted.

He gave me his solemn assurance that he had never consented to declare me *persona non grata.* But Duggan and Bonsal were not to be deterred.

4

Not long after that, Hull forced Sumner Welles to resign, and Duggan left the Department a few months later. Shortly after he resigned, he was appointed to assist my good friend former President Eduardo Santos of Colombia during a trip to the Latin American capitals to solicit contributions to the United Nations. Toward the end of their trip, as they were about to visit Cuba, Santos fell ill and was obliged to go on to New York, leaving Larry to visit Havana without him.

Larry was obliged to call on me—after all I was the American Ambassador. But he was frigid. I suggested he come to the Embassy for lunch or dinner; he would accept neither. At last I said, "Larry, bygones are bygones. As far as I'm concerned the incident of the Hull letter turned out all right and I hold no grudge against anyone. Still, I'd like to know the real story of the accusations against me and the allegation that the Cubans had asked for my removal."

He flushed, and refused to answer; and he was pretty snappy about it.

"Now, just a minute, Larry," I said. 'You were in charge of American Republics Affairs at the time, and you were supposed to be my friend. I've talked about this with Hull and with Concheso. And Concheso assures me he never said anything of the kind."

His embarrassment was acute. "Yes, he did! He did ask for it! He did ask for it!"

"He says he didn't," I answered, "and from what I've been able to learn, I don't believe he did."

Larry stood up and said, "I don't think there's anything to be gained by our discussing this further."

Out he stalked and I saw him no more. After I left the State Department in the middle of 1947, I had him to lunch and made another effort to overcome his baffling hostility, but without success. The next time I saw him was early in December 1948 at a meeting of a study group on Latin America in the Council of Foreign Relations. I remember that he went away off to the left on the question of American property interests abroad, and I answered him pretty sharply.

Less than two weeks later, on December 20, Larry Duggan jumped, or was thrown, from the window of his office in midtown Manhattan.

It was hard for me to believe that Larry had been a Communist agent, even after the appearance of Hede Massing's *This Deception*

(1951) in which she told in detail about bringing him into the Soviet spy apparatus (and how easily!).

Again I must say that if I had been more knowing about the Communist infiltration of the New Deal, I would have suspected Communism instead of the absurd extremes of Keynesism that I read into the White Mission report. White had proceeded on the classic Leninist principle that one way to destroy the enemy is to corrupt his currency and bankrupt his economy. And in that case bankruptcy would have been a wedge driven between Cuba and the United States, with a good chance of bringing about the Communist takeover years before (with plenty of help from Washington) Fidel Castro finally seized power. Duggan and White gambled for very high stakes indeed.

5

While Ernest Hemingway was running his "crime shop" he came to me and said, "There's a man I think you should get, and can get because he is now in Washington working for Nelson Rockefeller in the Coordinator's Office. I mentioned him twice in *For Whom the Bell Tolls*—Gustavo Duran—a Spaniard."

Duran, said Ernest, came of a fine family. He was highly cultivated, an excellent musician, and had been music critic for important Paris newspapers. But what caused Ernest to single him out for mention in *For Whom the Bell Tolls* was his military genius. He entered the Loyalist Army at the outbreak of the civil war and rose rapidly to the rank of lieutenant colonel. But in reality he exercised the command of a major general. Toward the end of the war, he and other Loyalists, under a General Martinez, fought the Communists. When the Loyalist cause collapsed Duran escaped to Barcelona, where he was rescued by a British destroyer and taken to London. There he met and married an American girl, Bonte Crompton, a sister of Mrs. Michael Straight, and then came to the United States. Ernest strongly urged me to bring Duran to Cuba.

It seemed an excellent suggestion, and I got in touch with the Department at once. By this time Larry Duggan was behaving pretty coldly; but he could not have been more eagerly cooperative than he was in this matter of Gustavo Duran, who was employed by Nelson Rockefeller's Coordinator's office but had been loaned temporarily to the Pan American Union. Larry would arrange to send him to Cuba at once, and did.

The Durans soon arrived in Havana, and Duran took over some

of Hemingway's intelligence work. When that ended with the arrival of the FBI operatives, he told me it was necessary for him to return to Washington in order to get his third papers. Ellis Briggs and other members of the staff were impressed by his enthusiasm about becoming an American citizen; it was almost like that of a religious convert. And once again, Larry Duggan was eagerly helpful.

I kept Gustavo on in Cuba as an attaché, and he was extremely useful. He translated my speeches into literary gems; he maintained cultural contacts helpful to Cuban-American relations; and he assisted other members of the staff in drafting despatches having to do with Nazi, Fascist, and Communist activities. He was especially useful where the Communists were concerned, for he knew the differences between Communists, Socialists, anarchists, syndicalists, and between Stalinist and Trotskyist Communists, as might have been expected of a Spanish Civil War veteran. Many of the despatches he helped draft were strongly anti-Communist.

So useful was he that when I became Ambassador to Argentina in May 1945 I requested his transfer to Buenos Aires. Before he left Havana he had a serious operation and when he arrived in Argentina, without his family, he was so unwell that Maria suggested we put him up at the Embassy. A long time afterward I learned that while there he never even attempted to pay for his own medicines. Also much later, our butler told Maria he had heard Duran criticizing me and my policies to a Spaniard who called on him several times.

In September of that same year I was suddenly called to Washington to become Assistant Secretary of State. I brought Gustavo with me and made him my third special assistant; his ability rated it and I thought in Washington his health might show more improvement than it had in Argentina. In November the first of a series of queries about his political affiliations came to me; they did not cease until long after I had left the diplomatic service.

It came from Senator Ellender, who asked Mr. Donald Russell, Assistant Secretary of State in charge of administration, whether Duran had any ties with Communism. I went at once to see Mr. Ellender and told him all I knew about Duran. Later I repeated my information to two members of the House Un-American Activities Committee.

They all seemed satisfied, but I was not. I asked Edgar Hoover to have a thorough and impartial investigation made of Duran—only to find I had run counter to Departmental procedure, under which Donald Russell should have made the request. I asked Russell to investigate, and he did so to a running accompaniment of criticism concerning Duran from a few Representatives on the Hill.

The reports accumulated. Indalecio Prieto, the Spanish Socialist leader who was a refugee in Mexico, had accused Duran of being a Communist. Our military attaché in Madrid sent in a statement calling him a Communist and a member of the Soviet secret police. Since it very evidently came from the Franco police, a considerable skepticism seemed in order. The FBI reports told everything and nothing. So many informants were quoted that the headings ran through the alphabet and into the aa's and bb's. Some were favorable, others not. No names were given, no evaluation of the comparative reliability of the sources. In short, the thing provided no basis whatever for judging the reliability of Gustavo Duran.

At last Mr. Russell's office telephoned me that Gustavo had been cleared. By that time he and his wife were hysterical with anxiety. Gustavo even went so far as to tell Jim Wright and me that he regretted having become an American citizen. And no sooner had he been cleared than he announced his resignation. He had, he told me, found another job.

I answered that I would have advised him to do just that as soon as he was cleared. Curiously, he refused to tell me what the job was until he came to take leave of me some ten days later. Then he said he was going to the United Nations.

I told him Maria and I were going to New York shortly for a few days and invited him and his wife to call on us. They did not come. Several weeks later he came into my office, but only to shake hands; he would not sit down. In the winter of 1947–48 the Guatemalan Ambassador, Dr. Jorge Garcia Granados, invited them to a party in my honor, on the occasion of my being presented with the Order of the Quetzal. They did not come. For several years we never saw him or his wife.

In 1949 Dr. Jose de Benito, a Loyalist and member of the Spanish Conservative Party, came through New York on a mission for UNESCO. I asked him to give me his opinion of Duran.

He had seen Gustavo in Paris during the summer, and had been surprised and displeased by the hostility in his criticism of me and my policies. De Benito upbraided him with disloyalty to a former chief who had been his good friend, going out on a limb to defend him. He told me he believed Duran had been a Communist when he joined the Loyalist Army but became so disgusted with Communist outrages that he left the Party before the end of the Civil War.

In early 1951 Senator Joseph R. McCarthy, addressing an American Legion meeting in New York, referred to Duran as a member of the Soviet secret police. The newsmen of course telephoned me to ask my opinion. I told them Gustavo had been cleared by the security office of the State Department, and that so far as I knew he was not a Communist. When the statement was published Mrs. Duran telephoned to express their thanks. Subsequently Gustavo invited me to lunch at a restaurant near the United Nations. At the end of the lunch, as we stood on the sidewalk, he said, "Well, now, I think it will be better if we don't see one another again."

I was startled, but all I said was, "If that's the way you want it, fine. It's all right with me."

Three years later the Civil Service Commission, which was investigating all American nationals employed by the United Nations, asked me to testify about Duran. The day before I was to appear, he telephoned to ask whether he might come to see me. I had prepared a memorandum, and when, that evening he came in I read it to him and discussed it with him in detail.

It mentioned certain things that had shaken my confidence in him —his having avoided me for years, certain incidents that had occurred, and above all his having said he preferred not to see me again. When I read that statement Duran said, "Oh, no, I never said anything like that."

"You most emphatically did," I answered. "It made such an impression on me that I told it to Mrs. Braden the minute I got home."

"I can't imagine my saying it," he insisted. "I never said it at all."

'Well," I said, "I cudgelled my brains trying to figure out why you said it, and the only thing I could come up with was that perhaps you felt you were protecting me, since you were being accused of Communist affiliations."

"Oh, yes," he said, without a second's hesitation, "that was it."

The next day, when I testified to his having said we'd better not meet again, I was surprised to hear Gustavo say to his lawyer, "I carefully timed that to protect Mr. Braden. That was the reason I said it. I thought it all out."

A couple of weeks after the hearing the lawyer came to see me, with a pompous brief on the legal aspects of "reasonable doubt"—he was an ostentatious man. Seeing that I was unimpressed, he said, "Well, I have one argument that will completely clinch the thing. It will prove that you were wrong in having a reasonable doubt about my client. That sidewalk conversation—Duran planned it all out, solely in order to protect you."

I let him go on a bit before I said, "Now, wait a minute. You're making things worse for Gustavo. You've raised still more doubt in my mind."

He looked startled. "Why?"

I told him about my conversation only sixteen hours before with his client.

"Gustavo insisted he hadn't said it at all—until I told him how I'd explained it to myself. Now he's taken over *my* explanation as his."

He had asked me to testify again, but I heard nothing more from him.

Chapter XXX

THE last commission signed by President Roosevelt was that naming me Ambassador to Argentina. The President died before it could be confirmed; therefore mine was the first commission signed by President Truman.

Throughout the war Argentina was consistently pro-Nazi. At the Rio Conference, six weeks after Pearl Harbor, Sumner Welles made the mistake of allowing the Argentines to water down the anti-Axis resolution to be adopted by the American Republics, as follows:

"The American Republics . . . *in conformity with the position and circumstances prevailing in each country in the existing continental conflict,* recommend breaking of their diplomatic relations with Japan, Germany, and Italy."

The words in italics were Argentina's carte blanche to maintain relations with the Axis Powers and to give them aid and comfort. President Ramon S. Castillo and his foreign minister, Enrique Ruiz Guinazu, were both notoriously pro-Nazi—a sentiment they shared with many people in influential, especially military, circles. The Argentines regarded themselves as our rivals for political leadership of Latin America. They also aspired to dominate the continent militarily. As early as September 23, 1937, in my despatch from the Chaco Peace Conference (Chapter XXI) warning that there could be no peace so long as Saavedra Lamas remained chairman, I commented on Argentine military expansionism, the nullification of democratic machinery, and the growth of an indigenous Fascism; and on the suspicions those developments were arousing among Argentina's neighbors.

Two days after the military coup that on June 4, 1943, overthrew the legally elected government of President Castillo, I arrived in Washington from Cuba for consultations. At that time Allan Dawson, who had been with me eight months at the Chaco Conference, was on the Argentine desk. He kept bringing me the cables Ambassador Norman Armour was sending from Buenos Aires. Allan was pleased. Larry Duggan, he said, would surely recognize the new government (headed briefly by Gen. Rawson, then by Gen. Ramirez, puppet of Col. Enrique Gonzales). This meant the end of that Nazi, Castillo. From now on Argentina would be with the Allies.

I looked at Armour's list of the new ministers. "Allan," I said, "you're crazy. This setup is going to be much more Nazi than the Castillo government; no question about it."

It soon proved to be so. Yet Larry Duggan, over Secretary Hull's opposition, got it recognized. (The Nazis and Commies were both authoritarian and often worked together. A similar and simultaneous enmity and collaboration exists between Peking and Moscow Communists. Sumner Welles was still in the Department, and Sumner certainly was aware how well I knew Argentina, how many friends I still had there, and how often in the years since I left there I had sent the Department information on Argentine developments. He disregarded my warnings against the new regime. Larry won him over easily, and the two of them built up so much pressure that poor, tired old Cordell Hull, who didn't know the inwardness of the situation, couldn't resist. Larry, of course, was following the Communist line of collaboration with Nazism that I had experienced in Colombia, but at the time I didn't suspect his motivation.

In September the Argentine foreign minister made a formal demand on Washington for arms to restore, as he said, "Argentina's position of equilibrium" with relation to the other Latin American countries. In answer Secretary Hull repeated a statement by Sumner Welles in October 1942 denouncing Argentina's failure to act against the Nazi agents whose activities were responsible for the loss of ships of the other American republics, with great loss of life. Hull added that under the Lend Lease Act we were supplying arms only for use against the common enemy.

During December 1943 and January 1944 our government received proofs 1) of Argentine complicity in the Bolivian revolution of December which made Villaroel president with Paz Estensoro as the real power; 2) of Argentine negotiation with the Nazis for deliveries of arms; 3) of Argentine designs against other Latin American nations. Secretary Hull notified the other American republics that we proposed to issue on January 25 a public statement of these facts and to freeze all Argentine assets in the United States. Two hours before the deadline President Ramirez asked Ambassador Armour to tell the State Department he would break relations with the Axis powers, Italy excepted, if we would cancel the announcement and the freezing order. The Secretary held his hand. Ramirez broke relations, but without informing Vice President Farrell, Col. Juan Domingo

Peron, and the other army leaders. They declared him a traitor, forced his resignation, and supplanted him with Gen. Farrell, Peron's puppet.

Hull refused to recognize the new government. He withdrew Norman Armour, and persuaded the Allies and the other American Republics, except Paraguay, to follow his lead. On September 29 President Roosevelt supported this policy of non-recognition in a strong statement excoriating Argentina for having "repudiated solemn inter-American obligations."

Cordell Hull resigned in November and was succeeded by Edward R. Stettinius, Jr. At the Mexico City Conference late in February 1945 (a sort of inter-American rehearsal for the United Nations Conference at San Francisco late in May) Stettinius appeased the absent Peron by accepting a formula that would permit Argentina to enter the United Nations along with the other American republics. Argentina was supposed to fulfill certain obligations stipulated in the Final Act of the Conference, known as the Chapultepec Agreement. He accepted the formula, moreover, after having learned that Argentine "adherence" to the Chapultepec Agreement would be an act of mere cynical opportunism.

On March 20 President Roosevelt approved a memorandum proposing that the Argentine government be recognized and invited to join the United Nations *after* having *complied* with the principles and declarations of the Chapultepec Agreement. Secretary Stettinius immediately waived the key condition of prior *compliance* demanded by his chief, as he himself conceded on May 28, the day before the opening of the San Francisco Conference.

"By voting to admit Argentina . . . the United States, however, has by no means changed its position that Argentina is expected to carry out effectively all of her commitments under the Mexico City Declaration. On the contrary, we consider that her admission to the San Francisco Conference increases her obligation to do so. We expect the Argentine nation to see that this obligation is fulfilled."

As I warned President Truman in a memorandum of July 12, 1946, the most serious continuing result of Stettinius' error in waiving compliance with the Chapultepec Agreement was "the conviction of Peron and his associates that if they persist in delay and obstruction they will once more gain their ends without real performance." Peron never missed an opportunity to take advantage of the moral flabbiness shown by Stettinius and Rockefeller, and by most of their successors right up to the time when Argentina succeeded in ridding itself of its oppressor.

2

The Americans were preparing to send ambassadors to Buenos Aires when Stettinius and Nelson Rockefeller made a trip to Cuba. As they were leaving they offered me the post of Ambassador to Argentina. I found this surprising. Although my knowledge of Argentine politics and personalities might seem to qualify me for the post, they knew I was far from being an appeaser. I could not help speculating on the possibility that the President himself had decided on my appointment and that they were offering me the post because he had ordered it. Later developments strengthened this suspicion.

I consented to undertake the mission on three conditions: 1) I would really be in charge; 2) a way had to be found to meet the enormous expense of maintaining our huge Buenos Aires Embassy; 3) I select my own staff, including the military attaché. My Colombia "strategist," General Lang, was attaché in Argentina and I would not keep him in the post.

My conditions were met. Shortly thereafter I received orders to represent the Department at ceremonies in New Orleans on April 14 celebrating Pan American Day, and from there to go to Washington to discuss my new appointment.

I took the Embassy plane to Miami, and from there hedge-hopped to Pensacola and on to New Orleans in a small commercial plane. In Pensacola I did not leave the plane during its five minute stop. The man across the aisle did so, and as he re-entered I thought I heard him say something about "the President's death." Not being sure, I asked no questions; but when I was met at New Orleans by a delegation of some twenty-five representatives of various organizations, my first question was whether or not there had been any important news since I left Miami early that morning.

"No," answered the chairman, "there is no news."

"No news whatsoever?"

"None."

I was relieved. But when we reached the exit of the air station there was a news vendor with his papers laid out on the steps. Even though they were upside down I could see the headlines were about the President. Turning to the chairman, I asked, "How is the President?"

"Oh, he's dead," answered the chairman.

The welcoming delegation and others ready to participate in the ceremonies were surprised and dismayed by my insistence that they be cancelled.

If Stettinius and Nelson had—as I suspected—been obliged to swallow my appointment as Ambassador to Argentina, the compulsion would explain a most peculiar action on their part. Without consulting me, they dispatched Avra Warren, Trujillo's friend who had placed his son in the "Benefactor's" military academy, and Lt. General Brett, Trujillo's friend and hunting companion, on a special mission to Argentina after my appointment but before I would arrive. Nelson had placed Warren in charge of the American Republics Division. He and Stettinius said his mission was intended to "size up the situation" and "to promote friendlier relations."

I objected because Brett and Warren might complicate my situation in Argentina. But it was too late. They had already left, and arrived in Buenos Aires a month before I could get there. Stettinius and Rockefeller appeared to be trying to establish a policy that—as they perhaps thought—I would have to follow after assuming authority.

Before I left Washington for Buenos Aires the results began to leak from the Pentagon. Warren and Brett had recommended we send a large Army mission to Argentina, headed by a brigadier general and including engineering and medical officers and a raft of other personnel. In addition, our Air mission composed of a lieutenant colonel and a couple of sergeants was to be greatly enlarged and placed under the command of a general. I made it clear to both the State Department and the Pentagon that no Army or Air mission was to be sent to Argentina unless I personally recommended it.

It had been arranged that Maria and I, with our daughter Laurita, would be flown to Buenos Aires in a military plane. General Brett sent his own plane to pick us up at La Guardia Field. When we arrived in Panama I had a long talk with the General, who had recently returned from his Argentine trip and was full of enthusiasm for Peron and the Argentine Army. "The best in South America," he said. He thought the two missions I had heard about in Washington should be sent at once.

"No," I said. "I've served notice that nothing is to be done about that until I get to Argentina and look over the situation."

As he continued to praise the Argentine Army, I remarked, "You surprise me. You once told me that the Chileans were by all odds the best fighters—that they could lick anybody else in the hemisphere. The Argentines have never been very belligerent. They haven't had a war since the Triple Alliance, and they've never distinguished themselves as military men."

"Oh," said Brett, "the Argentine Army is ten to one better than the Chilean. We've got to have the Argentines in our camp."

Peron had sold him a bill of goods; how large, I learned in Argentina.

Edward L. Reed, who had been serving as Chargé d'Affaires, told me Warren and Brett spent their time in Buenos Aires making ardent love to Peron. At last Warren drafted a cable to the Department praising him as a great man and great ally, declaring that henceforth relations between the two countries should be all milk-and-honey, and suggesting we consider sending the two missions and large quantities of materiel. It is customary for a chief of mission to sign all cables, but Reed flatly refused to sign Warren's because it misstated the facts. He had a violent scene with Warren and Brett before the cable was finally sent making perfectly clear that it expressed Warren's views, not Reed's.

3

Before I left Washington I learned that from 1,000 to 1,500 political prisoners were being held in Argentine prisons. Many of them I knew, and one, Enrique Gil, had been my close personal friend since 1917 or 1918.

When we reached Buenos Aires we were met at the airport by many friends of Argentine and other nationalities, by diplomatic representatives, by a general representing the President, General Farrell, a colonel representing the Vice President and real dictator, Colonel Peron, and by the Chief of Ceremonial and other Foreign Office representatives. As I greeted my friends I kept asking, in a deliberately loud voice so that all could hear me, "Where is Enrique Gil? I was sure he would be here to meet me."

Ed Reed, who headed the delegation, whispered, "Shush! He's in jail."

Whispering back, "I know it," I continued in a loud voice to ask about Enrique and to remark how strange his absence was. Reed and some of the others around me were embarrassed. But as we started toward the waiting cars I saw General Farrell's aide slip away and enter an office from which he quickly emerged.

We were staying at the Hotel Alvear while the Embassy residence was being cleaned. We had barely reached our suite when the telephone rang and I was asked if Drina Gil, Enrique's wife, could come up. As I hung up the phone I turned to Maria and said, "Our troubles are beginning. Drina will be in tears."

Instead, to our great surprise Drina practically danced into the room, wreathed in smiles, and announced that Enrique had just telephoned her. He had been released.

Thus ended my first encounter with Peron.

Since all the American and Allied representaives returned almost simultaneously there were four or five ambassadors presenting credentials daily. I made my protocolar call on the Foreign Minister the day I arrived, and the next afternoon presented my credentials to General Farrell. The traditional magnificent barouche was sent, with a company of the Guards, to convey me to the Casa Rosada. After the usual exchange of diplomatic clichés and a brief conversation with the President, the same stately equipage bore me back to my hotel.

The next morning I had a press conference with the American correspondents in Buenos Aires. During it Virginia Prewitt of the *Chicago Times* asked me what my policy would be with respect to democracy.

I answered that the United States, as a constitutional representative Republic, of course believed in its founding principles; that we had just concluded a costly global war in defense of representative government; and that anyone who doubted the sincerity of our convictions had only to consider what we had done during the war to know that we meant business. I added that we believed in the basic freedoms of speech, press, and assembly and hoped to see them practised widely, especially throughout the Americas.

The reporters present, who had interviewed Avra Warren only a few days earlier, were thunderstruck. Indeed, Virginia Prewitt a couple of times cried out, "Do you really mean what you say?"

I insisted that I meant every word of it. When word of my declaration got around Buenos Aires it created something of a sensation among the Argentines, who began to think that perhaps the United States was not, after all, indifferent to their plight.

That afternoon I met their oppressor for the first time, at a reception given by General Farrell to meet the returning diplomats and their staffs and introduce them to the members of his Cabinet. Peron, as Vice President, Minister of War as well as of Labor, and Secretary of Press and Public Information, stood next to Farrell in the receiving line.

When we had all filed by, the doors of an adjoining room were thrown open, revealing an elaborate buffet. As I entered, General

Farrell was standing behind the table and beckoned me to join him. There he regaled me with stories lampooning the regime that were going the rounds of Buenos Aires; many of them at his own expense, contrasting his alleged stupidity with Peron's intelligence, but more of them making fun of Evita's past in the oldest profession. One example typifies them all.

Evita, it ran, was in an elevator with a retired general. The operator kept mumbling under his breath, "La gran P," a frequent abbreviation of the word *puta* (whore). As they left the elevator the enraged Evita exclaimed, "That man must be punished! Did you hear what he said?"

"Think nothing of it, Excellency" the general replied. "I have been retired from the Army for five years, and people still call me 'General.' "

As this unedifying conversation continued I became increasingly embarrassed. The other ambassadors were waiting to talk to the President, and it looked as if I were monopolizing his attention. At last I managed to break away, only to be surrounded by Peron, the Minister of the Navy, Admiral Tessaire (almost the only high-ranking naval officer among the Peronistas), and a General who was Minister of Public Works.

Peron at once launched into a long, familiar speech describing those military and air missions just as I had heard them described in Washington and by General Brett in Panama. The vast quantities of materiel he demanded, Warren had already recommended in the cable Ed Reed refused to sign. But Warren left out one thing: the reason Peron gave for needing these tremendous amounts of military goods. It was the same as that of Ramirez. Argentina, he said, had received nothing of the kind during the war, and now required all that to bring its military establishment up to the necessary strength—especially vis-à-vis Brazil. Not a word about the reason for this dearth—that Argentina throughout the war had been on the side of the Axis.

I answered that first things must come first, and the first thing was Argentine compliance with the agreements entered into by the American republics at the Mexico Conference (the Chapultepec Agreement), to which Argentina had adhered as the price for resumption of diplomatic relations and its re-entry into full membership in the Pan-American Union.

Peron assured me all the obligations would be met, and tried to revert to the military missions and materiel. Once more I insisted I would be glad to discuss these demands as soon as Argentina complied with new Chapultepec obligations. The Minister of Public Works wanted us to help industrialize Argentina—especially by building a large steel mill. Economics, he said, was everything. Peron and Tessaire disagreed with that. But one thing was certain: All three were in a very receptive frame of mind.

Three protocolar calls by a new ambassador were *de rigueur:* on the Cardinal Archbishop; on the Chief Justice of the Supreme Court; and on the Vice President. I had told the Chief of Ceremonial that just before I left New York Cardinal Spellman gave me a personal letter to Cardinal Santiago Luis Copelo, written in his own hand. The Cardinal Archbishop was reputed to be pro-Nazi. I had met him during the Chaco Conference, but had never become friendly with him as I had with the Papal Nuncio, Msgr. Giuseppe Fietta. He was cold and austere, and Maria and the other Catholic women in the diplomatic corps, other than for the ceremonial kissing of his ring, always kept as far away from him as possible.

Significantly, Cardinal Copelo, even though I bore a letter from Cardinal Spellman, never made an appointment to receive me. The Chief Justice, on the other hand, was cordiality itself.

This may be an appropriate place to dispel any illusions about the idleness of diplomats. Regulations required that one keep a record of hours worked. Mine was meticulous and the samples that follow are typical.

One day in Buenos Aires I donned my full-dress suit with tails, white tie, but black vest, to attend a Te Deum at 10 A.M. From there I proceeded to a parade, interrupted my presence at the parade for an official luncheon, returned to the parade, and finally to four receptions (I have attended as many as five receptions in one day). I raced to my hotel to bathe and dress for a dinner party, white vest this time, given by the Argentine president for the president of Brazil. The opera followed, and a ball followed that. Maria and I returned home at 6 A.M., and I slept two hours, arose, dressed in my cutaway, and went to the formal opening of the Pan American Commercial Conference, where I headed our delegation.

In Cuba I would average about 84 hours a week on the job. It is only fair to say that in the late afternoon, travelling from the chancellery to the embassy residence, I often would take a twenty-minute snooze.

In the State Department I never finished the day without homework and the hours were similar to those in Cuba. The trouble in the State Department was that there literally was no time to think through any problem.

4

On June 1 the Chief of Ceremonial called for me in a luxurious limousine and accompanied me, with military and naval aides, to the Casa Rosada, where a guard of honor awaited me on the terrace. When I was ushered into Peron's private office he received me with a cordial abrazo. Our informal conversation of the President's reception was repeated like a stalled phonograph record. Then I enlarged on the subject of compliance with the Chapultepec Agreement.

There were four principal parts, I said. Two of these I would discuss as the United States Ambassador talking to the Vice President. These were Argentina's agreements:

a) to turn over to the United States and its allies all of the Nazi assets in Argentina;

b) to deliver to the United States and its allies all of the espionage, subversive, and other Nazi agents in Argentina.

Peron immediately acquiesced. He said he would appoint an officer as his representative to handle all of the details with any representative of my choosing. Any problem they could not solve, Peron and I would get together to discuss it. I agreed, but said I would prefer to have different representatives to discuss economic matters, and matters of politics, espionage, and subversion.

I may as well say right here that negotiation came to nothing. Foreign Minister Ameghino was succeeded by Juan Cook, a second rate politician who posed as a great friend of the United States, and who evidently expected to pull the wool over my eyes. Cook always promised with a great show of sincerity and failed to perform. He repeatedly agreed to turn over one Richard Staudt, who was high on our list of wanted Nazi agents, finally admitting that Staudt was a great friend of Peron's and could not be touched.

On the other hand, every effort was made to persaude me to ask for the former Austrian financier, Mandel, who escaped from Austria with a fortune and was now in luxurious confinement because of failure, it was said, to offer Peron a sufficient cut in his Argentine enterprises. Peron himself hinted that Mandel would be released or turned over to us if I asked it. I told him, as I later told Cook, that though we considered Mandel as an enemy agent, we were not particularly interested in him.

Returning to my conference with Peron, I said I would prefer to discuss two other parts of the Agreement not so much as the American ambassador but as Spruille Braden talking not to the Vice President but to his friend, Colonel Peron. I said on these two subjects the people of the United States, and therefore my government, felt so strongly they were a *sine qua non* for any understanding.

We knew, I told him, there were some 1203 political prisoners held in Argentine prisons, and that so long as there were any political prisoners the American people would not accept friendly relations with Argentina. Peron readily promised to have all political prisoners released forthwith. I then told him that so long as there was censorship of the Argentine press and radio our friendly feelings would be inhibited. I added what was practically a lecture on freedom of the press American style.

Presently he said he had something extremely important to ask of me. The American journalists in Argentina who were lying about his government must be silenced, as well as our editorial writers who were basing their comments on those lies.

Obviously my lecture on freedom of the press had made no impression. I repeated it, then cited an article in the *New York Times* that very morning. Arnaldo Cortesi had said that what he had seen in Argentina in a few short years was worse than anything he had seen during seventeen in Fascist Italy. If Cortesi's article was factual, I said, even the President of the United States could do nothing to silence him.

On the other hand I assured Peron that if any falsehood about Argentina should appear in any American publication I would, as Ambassador, personally request a retraction and correction, and if these were not forthcoming would publicly brand it false. But I repeatedly emphasized that so long as our correspondents adhered to facts and our editors based their opinions on those facts absolutely nothing could be done to stop them.

Our parting appeared to be as friendly as our greeting had been.

A couple of days later four or five political prisoners were released. I cabled this to the Department uncoded, but added the number of prisoners remaining, with names of their places of incarceration. I wanted Peron to be able to read my message without the handicap of decoding. Then a few hundred were released. I repeated the procedure. I used it three times; it was becoming hackneyed. On the next occasion I drafted a cable, took it to the Embassy residence and telephoned the chancellery, knowing that our calls were intercepted. I carefully explained that I wanted a cable sent to Washington (in a simple "grey" code that everyone knew), and read it two or three times, very slowly so that Peron's monitors could get every word. That brought the release of the remaining prisoners.

On June 15, by appointment, Peron sent a Mr. Lamuto, his Undersecretary of Press and Public Information, to see me. For the interview I called in Richard Howell Post, a second secretary who was handling our press relations. Lamuto announced his mission was extremely serious; he had come to protest against the continued defamation of the regime of Peron by the American press. Drawing a thick sheaf of copies of articles from his briefcase, he said here he had the facts. These stories from our press were provably scandalous lies.

I repeated what I had told Peron—that I stood ready to expose any lies that appeared in the American press—and asked, "What is the very worst case you have here? Let's take that first."

"The worst case," he replied, "is that of Arnaldo Cortesi of the *New York Times.*"

"You mean his recent report that Admiral Tessaire had threatened him with physical violence that might even prove mortal?"

"Oh, no. Admiral Tessaire was delighted with that article."

The worst article, it developed, was the one I had cited to Peron. Lamuto began to read from it. Among the first statements was a description of machine guns pointing up and down the street from parapets and windows along the Diagonal Norte, the avenue which the chancellery faced.

"That's a flat lie!" Lamuto exclaimed. "There was not a single machine gun along the Diagonal Norte."

Turning to Dick Post, I asked, "What about it?"

Drawing Lamuto to the window he pointed to a spot on the parapet of the adjacent building and to windows in other buildings where he had himself seen machine guns. Whereupon Lamuto admitted that Cortesi was right. We went through the article phrase by phrase and he acknowledged the truth of every statement.

When we were through I observed that he had himself called this the most lying of all the articles, yet he now admitted there were no lies in it. That was why we objected to the censorship: his government wished to suppress articles whether they told the truth or not.

Our visitor turned a double back somersault. Speaking for the Secretary of Press and Public Information (i.e. Peron), he announced he was authorized to say that anyone attempting censorship would be severely punished. Any attempt should be brought to the attention of the United States Embassy. I reminded him of such methods of censorship as delaying the transmission of a story until it was too late for publication, since nothing was deader than yesterday's news. Lamuto eloquently assured me that anyone would be severely punished who in any way interfered with the free exchange of news between Argentina and the United States, and that a simple complaint to the Embassy would bring about this punishment. I suggested that complaints instead be directed to the Argentine authorities but said we would gladly pass on to them any coming to our attention.

Lamuto assured me as he left that there would be complete freedom of the press for all journalists whether of American or other nationality. I immediately summoned the American reporters and repeated the conversation as well as my previous interview with Peron. They were jubilant.

A curious development ensued. The news stories sent by our reporters, and frequently editorial comment based on them, would be cabled back to Buenos Aires where the Argentine papers were emboldened to quote them. This virtual return to a free press began to undermine the entire government. Evidently Peron would not dare permit it to continue.

5

On June 29 he sent an emissary to request I call on him the next morning. On this visit there was no pomp, no guard of honor, not even the courtesy of a guide from the door of the Casa Rosada to Peron's office. Fortunately during my years at the Chaco Conference I had learned my way about the huge building so that I needed no guide. The only friendly face I saw belonged to the elevator operator, who remembered me from that period. Peron's aides were surly, but announced me. Their chief received me frigidly—no smiles, no *abrazo,* not even a handshake, only a rude, "Sit down."

He began the conversation, "There is a movement and movements."

I said, "What?"

"There is a movement and movements and we will not tolerate them."

"Mr. Vice President," I said, "frankly I don't understand what you are saying. What do you mean?"

"There is a movement and movements to overthrow me and this government and, as I have said, we will not stand for it."

"What has this to do with Argentine-United States relations?" I inquired.

"It has to do with them because your journalists form a part of these movements."

"You are quite mistaken, I can assure you. They do not form a part of any such movement."

"Yes they do!"

"No they don't!"

"Yes they do!"

"No they don't!"

We were going at it like a couple of small boys shouting "You're another!" Finally he broke off and said, "Mr. Ambassador, you should know that there are thousands of fanatics who adore me. They think your journalists form a part of these movements, and anyone they think belongs to these movements they will assassinate."

"Wait a moment!" I said. "I assume you mean what you are saying. In other words, you are threatening American citizens with assassination, and that I formally protest. It is the obligation of your government to protect the lives of these American citizens under all circumstances and against fanatics or others. I believe what you say because of the threats already made against certain American journalists and the fact that one or two of them, including Kluckhohn, have been severely beaten without any protection from the police or any arrests being made."

"I do mean exactly what I said," he answered, "and I cannot give any protection because, as I told you, they are fanatics."

I said, "Irrespective of that, the lives of American citizens must be protected by your government. You know who the fanatics are, and you must control them."

"I tell you I cannot. There are thousands of them."

"I don't care how many or how few there are, I still insist that the lives of our citizens be protected. Moreover, you know who they are."

"I know the ones in Buenos Aires; but I do not know those who come in from all over the country."

Again we argued back and forth like two small boys.

"You must protect them!"

"I can't and won't!"

"You must!"

"I won't!"

Once more he broke away from this childish exchange and said, "Mr. Ambassador, you should know that since your arrival in Buenos Aires you have been seen with Gainza Paz [publisher of the famous daily *La Prensa*], Mendez del Fino [President of the Stock Exchange], Bishop Andrea"—and so on through a long list of my old friends.

"Of course I have seen these people," I replied. "They are outstanding citizens and for the most part non-political. I have seen them as friends and propose to continue seeing them. But I don't see what that has to do with our present conversation."

"It has to do with it, Mr. Ambassador, because the fanatics to whom I have referred believe that all of these people form a part of the movement or movements and so will assassinate anybody who associates with them."

"Mr. Vice President," I replied, "you are merely adding one more U.S. citizen to the list of Americans to be assassinated by these fanatics. Whether it be journalist or ambassador, I demand that your government protect every United States citizen against assassination or even threats thereof."

"I tell you I can't and I won't!"

"You must!"

On this silly exchange the interview ended. Unaccompanied I found my way to my waiting car. It took perhaps ten minutes to reach the chancellery. Within five of the time I reached my desk, our journalists began telephoning members of my staff that they were being threatened. Cortesi thought it wise to sleep at a different friend's home each night. Joe Newman of the *Herald Tribune* took refuge at the Embassy. Each one took whatever precautionary measures he thought best. Some of them definitely were followed.

For a couple of weeks our intelligence people had been picking up stories to the effect that an attempt would be made on my life. The Chilean Ambassador had also run across such rumors. Therefore the members of my staff insisted that one of our legal (F.B.I.) attachés, who was built along the lines of Gibraltar and could shoot accurately with either hand the revolvers he carried in both side pockets, sit beside my chauffeur whenever I traveled in the Embassy car. Although I was skeptical of any attempt being made on my life, I consented to take this precaution largely because it was reassuring to Maria, who was badly frightened.

As soon as I returned from my unpleasant interview with Peron I wired the State Department asking for instructions to register a formal protest with the Foreign Minister demanding protection for all American citizens in Argentina, and that the Argentine Ambassador be summoned to the Department and handed a similar protest. It was not until July 5 that the Foreign Minister called me to his office and in the presence of a Colonel from Peron's office, assured me of safety for all Americans. Our Fourth of July ceremonies, however, including the reception of 2000 guests at the Embassy, took place without untoward incidents.

Then Peron made a first move toward a return to diplomatic amenities, by inviting me to inspect a motion picture studio. Evita, I was given to understand, would be there, and Peron himself would just happen to be present at the same time. Being quite sure that press photographers would also just happen to be there, and that the Peronista press would interpret pictures of me with Peron and Evita as proof of friendship between them and the United States Ambassador, I regretted on the invitation. I have always been rather sorry, for I never had another opportunity to meet Evita. She may have been a mediocre success in the two professions she tried before she met Peron; but her involvement in his career gave full scope to her real and formidable talents as a demagogue. I wish I could have formed a personal firsthand impression of her.

6

When I met Peron again he was once more extremely affable. The occasion was a luncheon in honor of my new military attaché, Gen. Arthur R. Harris. I may say that General Harris was not the first member of my military staff to be entertained by the Argentine government after my arrival. I was not long in Buenos Aires before being asked to attend a cocktail party planned in honor of my Air attaché, a nice non-political young chap whose idea of his job was to make as many friends as possible among high Argentine officers. He had ingratiated himself with Peron.

I agreed to go. Other military attachés were invited, as was the British Ambassador Sir David V. Kelly. When the event was announced in the press the list of guests was headed by the military—generals, colonels and others. Then came the civilians. At the very end were appended my name and that of the British Ambassador.

I realized at once the meaning of this unsubtle manoeuver. It was one of those typical tricks whose purpose is to test an ambassador's tolerance of indignities. I called in the guest of honor and said, "I'm terribly sorry. I would very much like to go to this party for you. But since they have announced it in this way, I cannot and will not go."

When Sir David telephoned to ask what I intended to do, I said I wouldn't think of going, and explained why. So neither of the two ambassadors showed up.

Peron had momentarily learned his lesson. The luncheon for General Harris was handled according to protocol. The chief of staff of the Argentine Army called at the Embassy and told me that if I approved and would consent to be present, they wished to give a luncheon in honor of General Harris, and hoped to honor the Chilean military attaché at the same time. I said I would be delighted.

The luncheon took place at the Circulo Militar, in the old palace of the Paz family, which the government had bought for a military club. As I entered the great circular main hall, Peron was standing in the middle of a horseshoe-shaped mass of officers. Once more he greeted me with a cordial *abrazo;* the violence of our last meeting appeared to be forgotten.

While speaking to some of the officers around him, I caught sight of General Ernesto Florit, who as a colonel had been the ablest military advisor to the Chaco Peace Conference, a fine looking, intelligent officer who had done an outstanding job. For a moment I wondered whether a cordial greeting from me would not be the kiss of death for him, then decided that since it was known that we were friends complete frankness was best. I went over to him and we greeted one another with *abrazos*. He was just as cordial to me as I to him.

After a brief conversation I returned to Peron, to whom I remarked on the splendid work General Florit had done for the Peace Conference. Of the military men of the two ex-belligerents and the six mediatory nations, I said, there was none whom I considered a finer or more intelligent officer. A year later I heard that Florit had been retired. I never knew whether or not my display of friendship had anything to do with it, but I have always felt it was bound to happen in any case. He had always been anti-Peronista; and besides, it was Peron's policy to eliminate all decent and patriotic officers.

There were only two civilians at the luncheon besides myself—the Foreign Minister, Cesar Ameghino, and the Chilean Ambassador, Alfonso Quintana Burgos. I sat at Peron's right; my Chilean colleague at his left. The conversation was perfectly friendly. The only time Peron seemed displeased was when, at the instance of the Foreign Minister, I told how President Ortiz had made me his ambassador for 46 hours during the Chaco Conference. At the end of the meal Peron completely ignored the Chilean Ambassador in order to take my arm and escort me to the door.

7

On July 20, having accepted an invitation to lecture at the University of El Litoral in Sta. Fe, I left with Maria and Laurita for Rosario in a private car provided by the National Railways. When we arrived that evening at nine or ten o'clock we were met by the Mayor, the Governor, the president of the university, and a number of leading citizens. The platform was thickly strewn with leaflets, and the Mayor and Governor hurried me away to the other end of the platform where there were fewer. I soon learned they were caricatures of me as a great bully of a cowboy (Peron knew I was born in Montana) flourishing revolvers at a poor little gaucho standing beside me—a clever appeal to chauvinism (of which *Fortune* thought well enough to reproduce it later in a rather unfriendly and half-baked article).

That afternoon the principal streets of Buenos Aires had been inundated with the same leaflets. That night a theater in the center of the capital was opened to the public where speeches by notorious Communists were made attacking the United States and myself. More vicious than the leaflets or the speeches were placards, posters, and imitation newspapers all filled with pictures of the corpses, and the widows, children, and other relatives of 400 miners who had died in a fire at the Braden Copper Company in Chile. They were all splotched with red ink in imitation of dripping blood, and more screamer headlines:

"The Name Braden Means Death and Destruction in Chile."

It was years since I had owned stock in any South American enterprise, but that fact was of course widely unknown among the people of Argentina. And yet the attacks seemed to backfire. In Rosario we were magnificently entertained, then drove in a motorcade to Sta. Fe. The auto in which I was to ride had been tampered with, but fortunately this was discovered in time. There, in a huge auditorium, I addressed the entire student body, the faculty, and many outsiders, to thunderous applause. (Here I should say that never, while in Argentina, did I criticize the government or any Argentine official. I did defend our record in World War II, and constitutional representative government.) It was a long block from the auditorium to the street. Yet the student body covered the entire lawn in front of the building and stood bareheaded in torrential rain as our party left.

That night the faculty entertained us at dinner. The next morning, Sunday, I went over to the University where some thirty or forty students were gathered, and had a *mano a mano* (a tough show-down or fight) with them over United States policy, internal and external.

On this entire trip we met with great cordiality and enthusiasm. At a small station just outside Buenos Aires on our way back the mayor and others came to pay their respects and to tell us to expect a big demonstration in the capital. As we reached the Retiro Station I was astonished to find some five thousand people gathered to demonstrate their repudiation of the vicious attacks on the United States and myself. Only with difficulty could we make our way to our cars—and, strangely, it was Saavedra Lamas who escorted Maria. We learned that the huge crowd had been assembled by telephone after three o'clock that afternoon. We also learned, to our regret, that when we had left the mounted police rode into the crowd and trampled several people. When we arrived at the Embassy a couple of hundred friends insisted on coming in to shake hands and express their solidarity with us. I tried to offer them some hospitality, but only a few remained.

We afterward obtained copies of telegrams sent to Chile by the Argentine Secretariat of Press and Public Information asking for the photographs of the fire at the Braden Copper Co. We also found that the entire costly attack had been planned and carried out by Communists working from the top floor of the Presidential Palace. I had strongly suspected Peron's collusion with the Communists. Here was definite proof of it.

I had not waited for proof before sending to Washington two cablegrams whose history—or lack of it—I find sinister.

Ambassador Quintana, who had served temporarily as President of Chile, and as Minister of Interior in charge of all police work, had an excellent intelligence service. He had confided to me his conviction that Peron and the Communists were working hand in glove and forming a menacing alliance. Therefore, on July 5 I sent a cable to Washington, with copies to Ambassadors Claude Bowers in Chile and Adolf Berle in Brazil, giving Quintana's information which confirmed my previous reports to the Department. I urged that at the forthcoming Potsdam Conference President Truman and Secretary Byrnes demand that Stalin tell them what he was up to in spreading Communism in Latin America, and playing footsy with Peron.

So concerned was I that I followed this cable with another on July 8 along the same lines. Both cables were "Top Secret' and addressed exclusively for the President and the Secretary of State, which meant that no one else should see them. Being purely informative, they did not require answers yet the information was so important that I was surprised to receive none. Only a year later, in Washington, I learned from Secretary Byrnes that neither of those cables was ever delivered. What happened to them, who withheld them from the President and Secretary of State, remains a mystery. They could have been stolen in the code room by a minor employee who was in sympathy with Communism or in Communist pay. The employee who handles incoming messages can, in a way, control the Department and sabotage government policy.

8

With the notable exceptions of the Bolivian and Brazilian Ambassadors, my Latin American colleagues stood shoulder to shoulder with me during this persecution. This was especially true of Ambassador Quintana, who nearly was declared persona non grata after attacking dictatorships at the ceremonies on the Chilean national holiday, September 18. The Bolivian and Brazilian Ambassadors served as espionage agents for Peron. At our unfriendly interview of June 30, Peron had pounded the table and declared that within five minutes of the time any conversation was held in Buenos Aires he knew it in detail, so magnificent were his sources of information. He concluded with the words, "One of your own diplomatic colleagues is one of my best informants."

The Brazilian Ambassador was soon recalled and was succeeded by my good friend, Cyro Freitas Valle, who subsequently had a distinguished career as Brazil's Ambassador in the United Nations.

Cyro refused to stand for Peron's antics, and was popularly known as "the Brazilian Braden." I was proud when he boasted of this title. However, his resistance to Peron resulted in his being declared persona non grata; whereupon the Brazilian Foreign Office acted with traditional skill by making him its Secretary General, the equivalent of our Undersecretary of State.

The dean of the diplomatic corps was the Papal Nuncio (later Cardinal), Msgr. Giuseppe Fietta, my friend since the Chaco Peace Conference; he had officiated at the wedding of my daughter Maruja in 1937. After the attack on me through leaflets, posters, and speeches he called to express his solidarity and his contempt for such methods.

For some years Msgr. Fietta had been a close friend of Bishop Miguel de Andrea, who had organized a rather extraordinary federation of women workers. Thanks to his efforts their situation was greatly improved, notably that of the sewing women who had worked under sweatshop conditions at starvation wages. But there was nothing demagogic about his leadership. When the workers for the telephone company (a subsidiary of Sosthenes Behn's International Telephone & Telegraph Company) wanted to go on strike Bishop Andrea persuaded them that their working conditions and pay were too good to warrant it.

The federation owned a large building in the center of Buenos Aires, with comfortable bedrooms, meeting rooms, a library, and a dining room where members could lunch for the equivalent of five cents. There I attended, on the Bishop's invitation, a session of its annual meeting. We sat on a dais overlooking separate tables each of which was occupied by the officers of one of the unions, were served an excellent tea, and listened to an animated discussion.

The Bishop was a humanitarian in the best sense of the word, therefore of course no Peronista. Neither were the members of the federation, which refused to accept Peron's control of their various unions—a fact that infuriated him, since an important element in his strength was his success in getting control of labor as well as the military. His distaste for me was augmented by my attendance at a meeting of this recalcitrant organization.

It was augmented much more by the continuing popular demonstrations provoked by the curious indirect return to freedom of the press that I have described. These took place in various cities, above all in the capital. Demonstrators were sometimes severely injured. Alberto Maria Candioti, who as Argentine Ambassador was my colleague in Bogota, was confined to his bed after being beaten with the flats of their swords by the mounted police.

The tension steadily mounted, while troops with military bands were kept marching continuously around the city, especially and rather ostentatiously in the streets near the Embassy. It finally culminated, just before I left, in the greatest demonstration of all, a "March of Liberty and Constitution" participated in by at least one hundred thousand people and led by society women such as Mrs. Bemberg (whose family owned a large brewery) arm in arm with workingmen.

Whenever I appeared in public I met with great enthusiasm. I spoke at a large luncheon at the Hotel Plaza, and the crowd overflowed into the lobbies and halls and even into the street, straining to get some word of what I was saying. I was entertained at a big dinner, and some eight or ten of the leading dance bands in Buenos Aires, knowing how fond I was of dancing, volunteered to leave their places of employment in order to play an hour or two in my honor.

I need hardly say that this acclaim was not directed to me personally; I am not the popular hero type. It was an outpouring of enthusiasm for the principles I stood for as American Ambassador and defended in all my speeches: the traditional American principles of freedom and constitutional representative republican government. Years later my good friend Dr. Alberto Gainza Paz, editor and publisher of the famous newspaper *La Prensa,* expressed the Argentine sentiments of that moment in words I have quoted publicly before and cannot improve on here:

"Argentina, as you know, has never been very friendly toward the United States. There has been some jealousy perhaps; certainly we have strong national pride. And we have had economic differences. Argentines have long resented the implied insult when your country forbade the importation of Argentine meat because it was 'unsanitary.'

"Well, when you went down to Argentina as Ambassador and began to speak in friendly frankness to us, many decent, liberal Argentines changed their minds about the United States. We respected you. We knew where we stood and where you stood.

"But let me tell you what has happened since the policy you initiated has been abandoned by Washington. The United States has lost all the friends it ever had in Argentina."

9

In mid-August—midwinter in South America—I was in bed with a severe cold when Secretary James Byrnes telephoned. He and President Truman wanted me to return to Washington to become Assistant Secretary of State in charge of American Republics Affairs.

We traded objections and rebuttals. I told him I did not wish to supplant Nelson Rockefeller. He explained that Nelson was already out. Still, I protested, I didn't want Nelson to feel I had been gunning for his job. Jimmy insisted there would be no such feeling. I said that in my opinion I could be much more useful in Argentina. My friends believed my being there and continuing to speak out for representative, constitutional republican government in the name of the United States might help to resolve that situation favorably for us.

Byrnes was insistent, and after a long conversation practically ordered me to accept the so-called promotion. I was compelled to acquiesce. The only concession I could get was a postponement of my departure for six weeks.

Before leaving I had a conversation with the British Ambassador, an able and experienced diplomat who had been one of those recalled in 1943.

Sir David told me that United States foreign policy baffled him. We had meekly taken a beating from Ramirez. Then, suddenly annoyed, we not only withdrew our own ambassador but insisted that the Allies and the American Republics withdraw theirs. With no perceptible change in Argentine behavior, we sent down Warren and Brett, apparently to offer Peron anything he wanted—a distinct preference over the countries that had stood by us during the war. A couple of weeks later I arrived and not only cut off the promised aid but even refused to discuss it until the Chapultepec conditions were met. What kind of foreign policy was all that supposed to add up to?

It was not easy to answer my British colleague; and neither was it necessary. He knew as well as I that it added up to utter confusion.

After I left, Peron renewed the "state of siege" and threw some 2,000 people into jail. The result of this action and the brutality that accompanied it was the Putsch from which he barely escaped with his life. He went into hiding, and a provisional government was slated to take over; my friend from the time of the Chaco Conference, Dr. Isidoro Ruiz Moreno, was to be Foreign Minister. It was immediately dubbed "the octogenarian Cabinet" (Ruiz Moreno was in his seventies and the rest well along in years) and popular opposition due to the age of its members facilitated Evita's magnificent demagogic performance in bringing about Peron's return to power, October 17, 1945.

Peron blamed me for the uprising that so nearly cost him his life. From that time until his fall he attacked me frequently in the most scurrilous terms. I answered only once. He accused me of "controlling Wall Street," and I offered to settle for ten cents on the dollar.

Chapter XXXI

A FEW days after our conversation Secretary Byrnes announced my appointment as Assistant Secretary, with a statement that before long would sound ironical. At the time it was perfectly sincere, I am sure:

"The appointment of Mr. Braden . . . is particularly a recognition of his accurate interpretation of the policies of this Government in its relations with the present government of the Argentine. As Assistant Secretary in charge of Latin-American affairs, it will be his duty to see that the policies which he has so courageously sponsored in the Argentine are continued with unremitting vigor."

The few weeks between this announcement and my arrival in Washington gave my enemies plenty of time to mobilize opposition to the confirmation of my appointment. I was blamed for the postponement of the conference scheduled for that autumn in Rio de Janiero to negotiate an inter-American treaty of military assistance. Certainly I was opposed to any such treaty while the Argentine government refused to carry out its solemn obligations. The appeasers argued that the President's decision on September 29 that we could not properly negotiate with the Argentine government at that time was really mine, and an affront to other American republics and a blow to the Good Neighbor policy. They were able to implant distrust in the members of the Foreign Relations Committee. Also, these Senators, with their wives, had arranged with the Navy for a battle cruiser to convey them to Rio. My putting off the conference annoyed them no end.

I arrived from Argentina on October 1. I found that Nelson Rockefeller and Avra Warren—especially Warren, had been lobbying against me on the Hill. Agents of Trujillo and Peron were getting in blows wherever they could. So were the Communists. The Pentagon, which was all out for military assistance to Peron, and among its other grudges, held against me my refusal to sanction the proposals of Brett and Warren, was bringing pressure to bear against my confirmation.

I immediately added to my offenses against the military. Nelson

Rockefeller had been negotiating with the Ecuadorian Ambassador, Galo Plaza, for a long-term lease of the Galapagos Islands, for use as an Air and Naval base. The Ambassador, who had made a trip to Quito to get his government's acquiescence, came in elated to report he had obtained it. Learning that Nelson had agreed to pay $20 million and to make certain dubious commitments, I was far from enthusiastic. Incidentally the Pentagon was asking me to assume the onus of going to Congress for the money instead of including it in its own budget.

At this point Gen. Henry H. (Hap) Arnold consulted me about a South American trip he was planning. As he was in command of the Air Force, I took advantage of the opportunity to ask him what military value the islands would have for the United States.

"None whatever," he answered. "Some years ago, yes, it would have been worth while to have an air base there as a sort of outpost; but with today's long-range planes we don't need it. Our planes can protect us just as well by taking off from the Canal Zone as from the Galapagos."

I told him I was pleased to have his assurance that the islands were valueless, because I couldn't for the life of me understand why it was proposed to pay Ecuador $20 million for them.

"Oh," said the General, "they're worth the $20 million."

"Wait a minute. You just told me they weren't worth a penny. How are they suddenly worth $20 million?"

"For public relations," he answered. "We can point to them on a map and say, 'See, we've got an air base there,' and that will have a fine effect on the public."

I refused to ask Congress for $20 million to finance a publicity stunt.

There was hostility to me among the business community. It lasted until Peron himself demonstrated that he had fooled the foreign businessmen in Argentina, many of whom believed that here was a dictator with whom they could do business quickly, smoothly, and profitably—just as some had thought of Hitler.

When I arrived in Buenos Aires I had at once made inquiries about Peron, talking perhaps to 100 people from all walks of life during my first 24 hours there. I got a composite picture that was far from reassuring. After further investigation, I called in the American businessmen and said, "To begin with, this fellow is a crook. He's fascist by temperament, and he hates the United States. Besides, his economic policy is unsound."

I advised them to be very careful about dealing with the regime.

Not long after, the representative of General Motors asked me whether I would advise his company to build a $5 million factory. I said I wouldn't invest my own money that way, because Peron might last a long time. If General Motors, I said, wanted to put in that much money and sit it out until Peron's fall, the country was rich enough for the investment eventually to pay off. But if GM wanted its money working, I advised against investing in Argentina at that time. General Motors built its factory. By 1949 it was closed. Even during the brief time it was producing, the company was unable to get its profits out of the country.

The head of the International Telephone and Telegraph subsidiary in Argentina, Wm. A. Arnold, completely disagreed with my view of Peron and my advising against investment there while Peron lasted. I had known Arnold in 1931 when he was the second ranking executive in the telephone company in Chile. I saw him later at the Montevideo Conference. He was then in the unhappy position of being in charge of the maddeningly inefficient Montevideo telephone system.

Bill, who had a friend very close to Peron, was in the dictator's good graces. Nonetheless he asked me for help in getting the company's rights recognized. I gave it. Neither our long acquaintance, however, nor my cooperation with IT&T, kept him from criticizing me to anyone who would listen. His view, which looked pretty silly as time went on, was that Peron was the great leader of a great people. He convinced Sosthenes Behn of this, and Behn also used to attack me violently. Indeed, I was informed that at one directors meeting Behn brought Arnold in to tell the other directors just how outrageous I was and what a noble soul I was attacking when I exposed Peron.

They made their attitude pay off. They were able to sell their Argentine company to the government for $90 million—a very profitable sale. To be sure, it reportedly cost them a "pay-off" of some fifteen million. On the other hand, they were able to get their Argentine manufacturing subsidiary, Standard Electric, a contract to supply equipment. When the government's indebtedness to Standard Electric reached $15 million, IT&T became alarmed, but once more they came out very well. The bill was paid (at least indirectly) by American taxpayers out of the loan of $125 million that Acheson's Assistant Secretary, Edward G. Miller, obligingly arranged for Peron with the Export-Import Bank.

This, of course, was much later. My confirmation as Assistant Secretary was so delayed that four weeks passed before I could take the oath of office, a fact not lost on my friends and enemies in Argentina. Their reactions were described by my old friend Enrique Gil the following April in an address to the Economic Club of Detroit:

". . . the reactionary forces in Argentina were exultant, and the democratic forces were abashed. It was then said, 'Well, once again Washington has taken the wrong turn in the wrong direction.' "

2

In my early days in Washington after returning from Argentina, we were obliged to move from one hotel to another. Permanent lodgings were exceedingly difficult to find and I wanted the right place. The "right place" turned out to be a five-story house on Connecticut Avenue that I rented. The service entrance was on a lower level but almost alongside the main entrance. The cook lodged in a large bedroom behind the kitchen.

To this house my daughter Maruja, her two children, and a Cuban nursemaid came to visit for several weeks. The visit precipitated an alarming discovery. Our Spanish cook was soliciting on the streets and bringing the men into her room where she and the Cuban nursemaid would entertain them, I presume for compensation.

In this manner was the Assistant Secretary of State running a house of ill fame on one of Washington's leading thoroughfares. Fortunately we rid ourselves of both cook and maid before the gossip columnists got wind of the story. They could hardly have been blamed for finding it a choice morsel.

I have already said that one of my first acts as Assistant Secretary was to bring Ellis Briggs back from Chungking and make him Director of the Office of American Republics Affairs in place of Avra Warren. I brought in Jim Wright as a Special Assistant.

On the Argentine desk I found Thomas C. Mann, very young and very able, whom I soon promoted to Chief of the River Plate Division, then made him my second Special Assistant. A graduate lawyer, he came into the Department during the war and served briefly in Uruguay as deputy to Carl Spaeth on the Commission to Study Nazi Activities in Latin America.

Just before I left the Department in 1947 Mann had an excellent offer from Gulf Oil. I think I influenced his decision to remain in the Department and go into the Foreign Service; I felt that the Service needed men of his integrity and ability. I wrote a citation to be placed in his record, in which I expressed my opinion that in him the Service had "gained an asset of great value."

He became an outstanding authority on Latin America, and it was a surprise and satisfaction to me when President Johnson, early in 1964, made him Assistant Secretary of State for American Republics Affairs and Special Adviser to the President: surprise that the President had withstood the pressures from the liberals around him, who certainly did not like Mann; satisfaction that he had placed our Latin-American relations in the hands of a man so informed, so honest, and so able.

Mann later was promoted to Under Secretary in charge of Economic Affairs. And I am still wondering whether I should have advised him one way or another, for I know he has had many frustrations over the years. The State Department is not always a happy environment for the American who puts his own country's interests first. If this should be taken to imply that there are many unhappy people in the Department, I answer that I don't see how it can be otherwise.

The Department, when I took office, was in the throes of infestation by the personnel of such wartime agencies as the Foreign Economic Administration, the Office of Strategic Services, the Office of War Information, and the Office of Inter-American Affairs. They swarmed in, almost five thousand of them. And they were so leftist that *Plain Talk* was moved to suggest some years later that the State Department establish diplomatic relations with the United States.

Already, so many people were entitled to a voice in every decision that a decision was hard to get. What was worse, these consultants, who appeared to have the same authority as the Assistant Secretary of State, and at times of the Secretary himself, were inimical to private enterprise and to Americans doing business abroad.

My first experience of this came shortly after I took office, when a strike at the American-owned tramway company in Havana led to a so-called "intervention"—actually seizure of the tramways.

I had set a precedent for the action I took. While I was Ambassador to Cuba an American-owned sugar mill at Tinguaro had burned down and the company, which had been losing money on it for years, did not want to rebuild; whererupon the government threatened to take over the property. I managed, acting as mediator, to stave off this action, but the following year the mill was seized. I then wrote a formal note stating that if the seizure was tantamount to expropriation my government expected adequate, effective, and prompt payment to the owners.

To my consternation the Office of American Republics Affairs refused to support me. They told the Cubans they were right to confiscate American property. Through vigorous insistence I was able to make my view prevail, and the matter was adjusted through the purchase of the mill at a handsome price by a group of Cubans.

When I learned about the seizure of the American-owned tramways I telephoned my successor, Ambassador Harry Norweb, suggesting that he look up my memorandum on the Tinguaro mill and hand the government a demand for compensation with the same wording. He asked for a cable confirming my instructions, which I immediately dictated. That evening the Chief of the Division of Liaison and Review, Mrs. Blanche Halla, telephoned me to say that various offices in the Department as well as the Department of Labor and other outside agencies had a say in the matter and the cable could not be sent unless initialed by all of them.

I knew what that meant. Sending around a messenger to all these divisions and agencies was the quickest way to gather the required initials—assuming no one balked. But even that would take time, and the matter was pressing. I assumed full responsibility and she graciously consented to send the wire. It arrived in time; within little more than twenty-four hours the company had its tramways back, and incidentally the strike was settled.

About a week later Ellis Briggs and Jim Wright came in and told me I had got myself into the worst possible jam. I had violated regulations by sending the telegram on my own, and the whole interdepartmental soviet was insisting on a protest meeting. I said, "Make an appointment, and I'll explain that the matter is satisfactorily settled and that my ignorance of regulations was the reason why I omitted their initials."

They came—at least twenty of them (I remember that one of them was Ralph Bunche). They had chosen a spokesman and two or three others to back him up. I began by saying, "All right, gentlemen, what is it you have in mind?"

Their spokesman made an indignant speech. He said that without consulting them I had arbitrarily interfered with the rights of Cuban labor. The chosen backers supported him, and they were pretty violent about my "intervention" against the striking Cuban tramway workers. When the last one stopped for breath, I asked, "Is that all?"

Yes, that was it, they said, to my great relief. They had me cold on the regulations, but on the defense of American property I was right. I made my own little speech:

"As Assistant Secretary of State it is my duty to protect American property rights. That I propose to do as long as I am here. I haven't mentioned labor. I didn't mention the strike either in my telephone instructions to Ambassador Norweb or in my telegram of confirmation. The subject never came up. You are wholly out of order. Good day, gentlemen. The conference is over."

They took it quietly enough. They thought I had merely won a battle, not a war.

3

A war I did win—for the time I remained in the Department—was that against permitting the horde of outsiders to get into the Office of Inter-American Affairs. The OSS insisted that it had been of indispensable aid in Latin America. I was able to prove that it had undertaken little in the field and performed less. While the fight was on an FBI report was circulated among the top officials identifying a number of government employees, including Harry Dexter White and Alger Hiss, as Communists. One of these was listed as slated for my Division. He never got in. He now resides in Moscow.

But I was never able, in spite of repeated efforts, to get any real discussion of the Communist peril while in the State Department. Just as my repeated warnings from the field had rarely elicited so much as an acknowledgment, so now my memos on the subject were met with evasion. I constantly had the feeling that I was shut up in a dark room vainly trying to catch a black cat.

Occasionally something happened that was hard to explain without a Communist hand acting in the shadows.

Ambassador Roberto Levillier, who had represented Argentina in Mexico and later in Uruguay, managed to smuggle a memorandum with a covering letter out to Montevideo and mailed to me from there. I sent my reply by diplomatic pouch to our Buenos Aires Embassy with instructions that it was to be delivered to Ambassador Levillier in person by one of the Embassy secretaries. Both my letter and his letter and memorandum somehow got into Peron's hands and were published in his newspaper.

It would have required some pretty fancy intelligence work for Peron to steal both Levillier's communication from the Uruguayan mails and my answer from our Argentine Embassy pouch. The logical assumption is that both communications were photostated in the State Department. It is quite unlikely that Peronists had infiltrated the Department; it is a well known fact that a few Communists had. Evidently the theft of those letters was an incident in the cooperation between the Communists and Peron of which I had warned

Jimmy Byrnes and President Truman in my two undelivered cables from Buenos Aires.

There were other disappearances, so highly selective that it would strain credulity to ascribe them to inefficiency, even granting that the Department's filing system went progressively from bad to worse (assuming that was due to inefficiency). A long memorandum on Communism that I had sent from Cuba disappeared from the files both in Washington and after I had left Cuba in the Havana Embassy, although there were several copies in each place. And while I am on the subject I may say that a high CIA official confirmed to me several years after I had left the Department an extraordinary disappearance not of one document but hundreds and not in the forties but in the mid-thirties.

At that time Hugh Gibson was our Ambassador to Brazil. After the suppression of Carlos Prestes' attempted Communist coup the Brazilian authorities arrested a man named Berger who was traveling on a probably fraudulent American passport. In his quarters they found over eight hundred documents of the first importance containing, among other information, the names, aliases, and addresses of Communist agents all over the hemisphere. Because of Berger's alleged American nationality, Gibson was able to borrow these documents and have them photostated, sending copies to the State Department.

Much later, in Washington, something came up in the Department about Communism in Brazil. Hugh said, "Let's get out those documents I sent up from Rio."

They were not to be found. They never could be found. The intelligence agencies familiar with the story were convinced that Larry Duggan had contrived their disapperance.

Years later I learned that Raymond Murphy, the Department's top specialist on Communism and Communists when I was there, used to take visitors into the hall to discuss any confidential matter. After my own experience I could well understand the precaution.

4

One day late in October 1945 I attended an urgent and important meeting held in Under Secretary Acheson's office. All the top echelons were there. I remember Donald Russell, Assistant Secretary for Administration; H. Freeman ("Doc") Matthews, Chief of the European Division, John Carter Vincent, Chief of the Far Eastern Division, and Loy Henderson, Chief of the Near Eastern Division—all three representing James Dunn, Assistant Secretary for European, Near East Affairs. The Economic Divisions were represented by Will Clayton who left early and was then represented by Willard L. Thorpe.

Dean Acheson opened the meeting by saying that after careful deliberation it had been decided to establish in the Department an Office of Research and Intelligence. Who had done the deliberating he did not vouchsafe. Certainly Loy Henderson and I had never heard of the idea before. On Dean's desk was a book that without exaggeration was six inches thick and nearly a foot long. He said, "It's all in here, what this office is, what it is to do, and what its powers are to be." It was to be staffed, as I recall, by 1,080 people drawn from OSS and other outside agencies, agencies under suspicion of suffering Communist infiltration.

The book, he said, was to go to the Hill that very afternoon, and we had been called in to be told about it. If we had any objections we had better take them right into Secretary Byrnes' office next door. His attitude was almost threatening. He said, "This is decided upon. If you have any objections they'll be thrown out by the Secretary. But if you insist on objecting, then you'll have to fight it out with him and God help you."

That was that, and we could take it and like it. Everybody else seemed prepared to do just that as far as I could see. I picked up the book saying, "I'd like to take a look at that."

I turned to the section on Latin American Affairs. I didn't have time to read it, but my skimming gave me a pretty clear impression, as Dean went on talking, about how unnecessary the proposed office was. I finally remarked:

"Now, wait a minute, naturally I've been rushed. I haven't had a chance to study this, but from the cursory examination I've made it is apparent to me that this is a complete duplication of what the Office of American Republics Affairs is doing today. The research and intelligence outlined here is nothing beyond what we do. This would be a duplication of personnel and expense, and would only create confusion. There's no reason whatever for this office, and I object."

At that everybody began to talk at once. But the only man in the room who looked at the book was Loy Henderson (now retired). I had always liked Loy, but I've liked him better ever since that day. He turned to the section on the Near East, for which he was responsible, and he said, "I feel the same way Spruille does about this. It looks to me as if it were a duplication."

By this time the behemoth that was to go to the Hill that afternoon, wasn't. It was to go to the Bureau of the Budget for approval before going to the Hill. That was pretty funny because, although we didn't know it, it had originated in Budget, abetted by Hiss and his boys. Nothing more was said about marching into Jimmy Byrnes' office with our objections. The meeting broke up with the matter subject to further consideration.

Next the proposal was sent to the Secretary's staff committee, composed of the Secretary, Under Secretary and Assistant Secretaries. These would sometimes bring along assistants to discuss special questions or send assistants to represent them when they were away. Since Jimmy Dunn was away often, Matthews, Vincent, and Henderson were at most of the meetings. Alger Hiss, Chief of the Office of Special Political Affairs, always participated. All discussion was supposed to be top secret.

In the staff committee the chief advocate of the projected Office was Col. Alfred McCormack, a lawyer who had been in military intelligence during the war and had been persuaded, I learned later, by Dean Acheson and George Schwarzwalder of the Bureau of the Budget (the same who tried to supplant J. Edgar Hoover), to come into the State Department with the title Special Assistant for Research and Intelligence, to head the new setup. Col. McCormack argued vehemently in favor of the plan and was strongly seconded by his chief, Leo Pasvolsky, Special Assistant for International Organization and Security Affairs, an influential adviser in the Department.

As the discussions went on they became more and more confusing, full of the most abstruse arguments and bewildering doubletalk. I could never get my teeth into the thing and even began to wonder whether I was just plain stupid. But I held my ground.

One reason, I think the Secretary's staff committee met less and less often and at last practically dissolved was the number of "papers" submitted. "Papers" are the bane of Washington existence and a principal explanation why committee government is inefficient and intolerable. Whenever anybody wanted to put something over he would write a "paper," sometimes fifty pages long. The agenda might include a half dozen subjects, and anyone who wanted to understand what they were about could sit up all night reading papers and then not finish.

Before each meeting on the proposed intelligence setup we were deluged with the usual papers. I arrived in Washington after several days absence just before a meeting and found a really vicious one among them. It referred to the opposition, especially myself, in the most abusive terms. I don't think the writer expected to persuade anybody with his name-calling. He was just giving vent to his anger because the proposal was losing.

Jimmy Dunn had returned and I immediately scheduled a meeting with him. By that time I had learned enough about Washington to know the importance of having allies. Jimmy agreed with me, and that brought his whole office along. Don Russell opposed a centralized intelligence office, and his objection had apparently brought about the meeting in Acheson's office. And since Don had charge of administration his opposition was not to be lightly dismissed. Besides, as Jimmy Byrnes' law partner he had Jimmy's complete confidence and was able to persuade him—inform is perhaps the better word, for it appeared that Byrnes had been sold a bill of goods on the thing and had not realized its implications.

Here I cannot forgo digressing to remark on the unfortunate effects, not only on State Department operations but on our foreign relations, of the peripatetic habits of our postwar Secretaries of State. A Secretary who is everywhere but in his office cannot possibly know how his Department is being conducted. Jimmy Byrnes was as intelligent as any Secretary who ever occupied the office. He was a good American and I always have admired him. But he was just too busy running around to meetings of the Council of Foreign Ministers and elsewhere to properly support the loyal officials who had to cope with the Communist and other left-wing infiltrators who came in with the influx of unscreened personnel from the wartime agencies to take over the Department.

When in 1952 the electorate turned out the Democrats, one of the reasons was popular concern over the Communist infiltration of the State Department that had been exposed by Congressional investigations and the two Hiss trials. But Mr. John Foster Dulles, certainly a loyal American, rushed around the world at such a pace that the hoped-for purge of Communists never took place. In his own actions Mr. Dulles tried to represent his country's best interests. But his country's best interests required that he stay at home long enough to clear treason, incompetence, and "do-goodism" out of his Department. For that he never found the time. I forbear to comment on what has happened since—or has not.

Over the proposed centralized intelligence office we had a real knock-down-drag-out fight, which was reflected in the press. But we won it. A modest central office of research and intelligence was set up according to a plan drafted in Don Russell's office; it preserved the autonomy of the geographic divisions in matters of intelligence and formulation of policy. The fight took six months, but the super duper duplicate department that had been devised to take us over was out.

Donald Russell had been ably seconded in the controversy by J. Anthony Panuch, whom Secretary Byrnes had brought in as Deputy Assistant Secretary of State for Administration to coordinate the merger of the wartime agencies into the Department. When Gen. George C. Marshall succeeded Byrnes, Dean Acheson sent for Panuch, said Marshall had given him, Acheson, carte blanche in matters of administration, and demanded that Panuch resign. Joe had already sent Marshall a pro forma resignation. Acheson instantly accepted it, effective at the close of business that day. Actually Dean, within minutes after Marshall had been sworn in at the White House, told a group of us that Panuch was already out.

At the time I thought we had won a good fight on a good, sound basis—proper organization, economical administration, and the elimination of some Communists and socialists. It was quite a time before I realized how really important it had been.

Joe Panuch, as Byrnes' chosen coordinator of the merger of the wartime agencies into the Department, was in as good a position as anyone to understand why the Department, which in 1943 employed 2,755 people, was swamped by the influx of almost 5,000 "inexperienced, untrained—and what is worse, unscreened—personnel," as he expressed it in his 1953 testimony before the Senate Internal Security Subcommittee. Panuch described the merger and the proposed intelligence setup as a Communist move to capture the Department no less. The merger was intended to get the Communist agents in; the intelligence scheme, to put them in control. And Alger Hiss, Panuch swears, had drafted the Intelligence and Research Plan.

At about the time the centralized intelligence plan was finally defeated, Leo Pasvolsky sent to the Secretary a plan by Hiss for reorganizing the Department that Panuch characterized as making the scheme for reorganization under the cloak of "intelligence" look "provincial and myopic."

This modest proposal would have changed the name of Hiss's setup to "Office for United Nations Affairs" and moved it into the office of the Under Secretary. Hiss, as its head, would have been the Under Secretary's deputy for United Nations Affairs, and as such would no longer have had to consult the heads of the geographic divisions. Since American relations with UN members would have been under his practically uncontrolled jurisdiction, and since we were committed to make the UN the cornerstone of our foreign policy, this adroit move would have placed Alger Hiss in control of American relations with all foreign governments except those not in in the UN, such as Franco Spain. In other words, Hiss was playing for domination of American foreign policy—that is, of the State Department. Fortunately Panuch was able to scotch this ambitious project with one sarcastic memorandum to Donald Russell.

5

Even without the power to dominate the Department, Alger His was one of the most influential men in it. He had charm; indeed actual sweetness appeared to be his outstanding characteristic. He had great influence with his chief, Leo Pasvolsky. And he was unfailingly supported by Under Secretary Dean Acheson, if my own observation and experience were any criterion.

The experience concerned the Republic of Panama, and specifically the Canal Zone. A prime Communist objective was and still is to ease the U.S. out of control of the Canal Zone.

One year after V-J Day, agitation began in Panama for the return of 134 bases, ranging in importance from observation and anti-aircraft outposts to the vast Rio Hato Airbase, which we had acquired from Panama under an agreement negotiated by Sumner Welles and Panamanian Foreign Minister Fabregat. The agitation developed into the kind of noisy demonstration by students and other groups, egged on by Communists, that took place in 1964. Before long it was echoed in the Panamanian Congress. In short, the situation was becoming ugly. It was especially unfortunate for us in its timing because the United Nations Assembly was to meet in New York that Fall. (Its timing was "not accidental," to use a favorite Communist cliché.)

I sent for the record and the documents and found that the bases were to be returned to Panama one year after the signing of the definitive treaty of peace. Welles had thought this provision so important that a memorandum was attached to the agreement stating that it meant exactly what it said: the "definitive treaty" of peace, not a cease-fire or a truce or an armistice. No treaty of peace had been signed. There was no legal basis whatever for all the agitation.

Nevertheless I suggested to the Pentagon that it return to Panama twenty-five or thirty of the insignificant and worthless outposts, with a maximum of publicity. This would save face for the Foreign Minister, Ricardo J. Alfaro, who was taking a leading part in the agitation, and perhaps restore a calm in which we could discuss the rest. The Pentagon answered that it needed every one of the bases, and I agreed to fight it out on that line. To my chagrin, it shortly returned thirty of them without giving me a chance to use their restoration as a trading point with the Panamanians.

Meanwhile the Governor of the Canal Zone made his annual report to the War Department. Soon two of my assistants, Wm. P. Cochran, Jr., who was in charge of affairs in that area of the Caribbean, and Murray Wise of the Panamanian Desk, were involved in an argument with Alger Hiss's office. Hiss insisted on sending the report to the United Nations, claiming as authority Article 73(e) of the UN Charter. Article 73 stipulates that UN members administering territories "whose people have not yet attained a full measure of self-government" do so in such a way as to ensure their political, economic, and cultural advancement, to promote self-government and take account of their political aspirations. Section (e) provides for the regular transmission to the UN of information on such territories.

Cochran and Wise consulted with the legal adviser's office, where Miss Anne O'Neill, a very competent lawyer whom I had known and admired since the Montevideo Conference, agreed with them that under no circumstances should the Governor's report be submitted to the UN. Hiss continued to insist, and at last they came to me and said, "You will have to enter this fight. We can't get any further with it."

We asked for an opinion from the Legal Adviser of the Department. Before long my assistants told me they feared he was veering over to Hiss's side. He didn't go all the way over, but he did avoid giving an opinion; so the matter went to Under Secretary Acheson.

I went in to see Acheson and found Hiss already there. Acheson listened to all Hiss had to say, and it was a lot. But when I tried to state my case he interrupted, saying he knew enough about the matter, and that Hiss was right. In effect, I was refused even a hearing.

All we could get out of Hiss's office was a statement that the Governor's report was to be submitted to the UN on a pragmatic basis for 1946 only. Of course that did not meet our objections, but Hiss had the Under Secretary on his side. There was nothing we could do.

The UN Assembly met in New York that Fall while Panama continued to seethe. Presently the Russians began to make the vitriolic speeches that so influenced and injured the innocents who had liked to think the Russians were our friends. They attacked us as aggressors because of our air bases all over the world. And of course the Panamanian demonstrations were made to order for them—literally, I do not doubt.

One day Jimmy Byrnes, who was heading our delegation, sent word to Washington that he had talked to Alfaro, found him to be right in his extreme view that we should give up all the bases forthwith, and told him so. Evidently Jimmy had not done his homework: he had never read the agreement about those 134 bases. Immediately I arranged for Murray Wise to see Byrnes in New York the next morning, with Col. (now Gen.) Charles Hartwell Bonesteel, Wise's opposite number in the Pentagon, and General George Arthur Lincoln, who had charge of the bases. I hoped they could get Byrnes out of the embarrassing situation he had got into with Alfaro, and that we could somehow tide things over until the Assembly adjourned and we could get Alfaro down to Washington for quiet discussion.

Late the next afternoon Murry Wise returned.

"Well," I asked, "how did you come out with Jimmy Byrnes?"

"We didn't even see Jimmy Byrnes."

I was astonished. "What do you mean?"

"I mean that we kept the appointment all right, but he didn't. He sent us word that unless we agreed with him he wasn't going to receive us."

To this day I don't know who had so influenced Jimmy Byrnes.

The furore continued, with Vyshinsky shouting himself hoarse and the Panamanians getting more and more obstreperous. Then one fine morning I picked up the Washington Post, to find on page one a story about our having made a report to the UN on occupied territories. Listed among those territories was the Canal Zone.

I knew we were in for real trouble. The Panamanians would be furious at being referred to as "an occupied territory" plus our refusal to admit they had any sovereignty over the Zone. The other American republics would be alarmed. Alfaro was certain to attack us in the UN, to the great satisfaction of the Russians. I tore down to the Department, called in Briggs and Wright, and demanded to know what was going on. Of course they knew no more than I did, and neither did Murray Wise. At last we learned what we already suspected, that the report had been sent in by the Office of Special Political Affairs—that is, Alger Hiss. We tried to find him but to no avail.

I went at once to Acheson's office and demanded that the report be withdrawn.

"We can't do anything about it," said Acheson. "Where is Mr. Hiss?"

Mr. Hiss was not to be found. He had left his home. He had not arrived at his office. He was supposedly attending some meetings, and his office telephoned to the places where presumably he could be found. He was not there. He had just disappeared. The whole day went by without action, and the delay was doing us no good.

At last, in the late afternoon, I learned that Hiss was in Acheson's office. Being tied up in a conference, I sent Ellis Briggs down to demand that the report be withdrawn. When he came back he told me that Hiss had been, oh, so apologetic. He had been very charming about it. Of course the Office of American Republics Affairs should have been consulted before the report was submitted to the UN. But it was just one of those things: a mistake had been made somewhere, and he was so *very* sorry. The "mistake" had obviously resulted from our fight over the Governor's report; he knew he would never get our consent.

However, he told Briggs, the report was now in, and it would do great harm to withdraw it. He did not say why. He did not need to: Dean Acheson sustained him. And that was that.

But that was not all. Alfaro made an angry speech in the UN, as we knew he would. To anyone ignorant of the facts it was an excellent speech. The Panamanian Foreign Minister speciously explained the legal basis on which the sovereign Republic of Panama had ceded the Canal Zone to the United States (without relinquishing sovereignty) for the sole purpose of constructing and operating the Canal. He pointed out that the whole indigenous population of the Zone had been removed in furtherance of that purpose; and that the people living there were not wards of the United States, yearning for cultural advancement and political autonomy. They were employees engaged in maintaining and operating the Canal.

Alger Hiss's interest was conspiratorial. If he could put over the fiction that the Zone was "occupied territory," the Russians would be able to demand that the UN have a voice in the operation of the Canal. It was worth the try. And if it failed, still his report would enrage the Panamanians and alarm the other Latin American Republics.

When Alfaro had finished his speech our delegation mistakenly admitted that the United States did not claim sovereignty over the Canal Zone. Later the State Department promised the Panamanian chancellery to abstain in future from reporting the Zone as occupied territory.

Hiss had done very well for the master he chose to serve. He had sown confusion and suspicion and created such difficulties with the

Panamanians that the outposts our armed forces considered so essential to the defense of the Canal were returned within a year, even though we had every legal right to retain them. As he himself had said admiringly of Stalin during the horrible Soviet purges, Hiss "played for keeps."

Chapter XXXII

AS I remarked in the previous chapter, on September 29, 1945, President Truman (on my urgent advice) decided it was impossible to go forward with the negotiation of mutual assistance treaties scheduled for that autumn at an Inter-American conference to be held in Rio. Dean Acheson, as Acting Secretary of State, therefore issued a statement saying the United States did not feel it could properly negotiate a treaty of military assistance with the Argentine government at that time, and announcing the intention of the United States to consult with the other American republics concerning the Argentine situation.

I arrived in Washington on October 1, and on October 3 took steps to provide documentation in support of this decision, to be made available to the other republics. I had a further motive. Our public officials, from President Roosevelt down, had rightly accused Peron and his clique of being Nazi sympathizers and collaborators. If those charges were documented, historians could not, as time passed, come to give to Peron's denials as much weight as to the truth.

Carl Spaeth, a classmate of Nelson Rockefeller at Dartmouth and a former Rhodes scholar, had served in Uruguay on the Inter-American Commission to Study Nazi Activities in Latin America. I made him my Special Assistant and put him at the head of a group to investigate the archives of the defunct Hitler *Reich* and interview former Nazi officials, to determine the actual extent of Argentine complicity in Nazi designs on Latin American countries. We had to work with utmost speed, since Peron was coming up for election as President of Argentina soon—as it turned out, at the end of February. I knew that by hook or by crook he would win (I won three bets to that effect), and once he was elected we could not bring out the evidence.

Spaeth (recently retired as Dean of the Leland Stanford Law School) and his group did a splendid job; in addition to many interviews, they had to sift through some five tons of documents. The result was a thoroughly documented and convincing picture of Nazi infiltration and designs in Latin America and of connivance between the Hitler government and the Argentines. Every charge against the Argentine government was based on its violation of an international agreement. We published our findings on February 11, 1946, under the title, *Consultation Among the American Republics With Respect to The Argentine Situation.* It immediately became known as the *Blue Book.*

If I had personally needed any proof of Peron's connivance with the Nazis, even after their defeat, I had had it shortly after my arrival in Buenos Aires, when it began to be rumored that German submarines were off the coast. Suddenly one day a German submarine came into Mar del Plata. At once I sent my Naval attaché, Capt. Walter W. Webb, and my chief legal attaché, James Joice, to interview the crew. For about forty-eight hours Argentine officials prevented them from so doing while the crew was carefully coached. Even so, Webb and Joice learned that the submarine had been some thousand miles northeast of Puerto Rico on V-E Day, when all U-Boat commanders were ordered to go to the nearest United States, British, or Canadian port and give themselves up or risk being treated as pirates—that is, shot—if captured. Disregarding the order, this submarine had risked the long journey to Mar del Plata.

A couple of weeks later another arrived. It had been in a Scandinavian port on V-E Day, the port where the Nazis were producing heavy water for their atom bomb research. The crew was very much reduced, and it seemed quite evident that the missing members had been supplanted by other persons or valued objects in order to prevent their falling into Allied hands. Later there were rumors, never verified, that a third U-Boat had appeared off the coast but had been ordered scuttled in order to spare the Argentine authorities further scandal. In view of the Allied order and the obligation of the Argentine government to turn over enemy agents to the Allies, these events sufficiently indicated on which side lay the interest and sympathy of Peron and his gang.

Characteristically, the appeasers in this country took very little interest in the revelations of the *Blue Book.* They preferred to treat it as my personal effort to defeat Peron (a view which they parroted from him), and to declare that Peron had defeated *me* in a "free election." And indeed the election was free if Army supervision of the polls and other persuasive government pressures on the electorate are conceded to be conditions for an uninhibited exercise of the right to vote. They also swallowed Peron's accusation, backed by a costly publicity campaign, that the *Blue Book*'s exposure of Argentine failure to comply with international obligations constituted interference in Argentine domestic affairs. By that criterion the United States interferes in Soviet domestic affairs every time it demands Soviet compliance with the UN charter.

On April 1, Secretary Byrnes submitted a statement of our views to the other American republics. When all except Ecuador had expressed substantial agreement he publicly stated, on April 8, that the United States and other American republics hoped the new constitutional government of Argentina would implement Argentine agreements under the Inter-American system, to the end that all Axis influence might be eliminated from this hemisphere. Firm and unequivocal performance, he said, would open the way to an Inter-American mutual assistance pact. "But there must be deeds, and not merely promises."

2

The Secretary of State did not take this action entirely on his own. Back of it lay an incident that made me realize the attempts to undermine my position had not ended with the delayed confirmation of my appointment as Assistant Secretary of State.

One morning early in 1946 I was outlining to Dean Acheson certain steps to be taken in the implementation of our Argentine policy. He stopped me with the words, "But that would be in contradiction to Jimmy Byrnes' agreement with the Senators."

"What agreement with the Senators?" I asked. "I haven't heard of any."

Dean was surprised that Jimmy had not told me of the agreement, and suggested that I speak to him myself. The Secretary was very apologetic for failing to tell me of a conversation he had had at Blair House ten days earlier with a group of Senators from the Foreign Relations Committee—Connally, Vandenberg, La Follette, Wiley, White, and some others—demanding changes in our Argentine policy to which he had agreed.

"In that case," I said, "I had better go upstairs and write my resignation."

He begged me to take no such drastic action; and our conversation ended in a compromise. Byrnes undertook to issue a statement completely confirming our Argentine policy as it had previously been agreed upon between us (his statement of April 8). For my part I agreed to the appointment of George Messersmith as Ambassador to Argentina.

Various candidates had been suggested for the post, among them

Gen. Matthew Ridgway. The naming of a military man would have been misunderstood in Argentina. I had suggested two career men, neither of whom was interested; also a thoroughly competent private citizen. But he was a Republican. I did not think George Messersmith well suited for the post. On the other hand, he had always professed agreement with my Argentine policy. And there was good reason for getting him out of Mexico.

The Mexican Ambassador had warned me that the incoming President, Miguel Aleman Valdes, would almost certainly want to declare Messersmith *persona non grata* after his inauguration because of Messersmith's repeated rudeness to him as a Cabinet official. That would have been embarrassing. Our policy was to demand sound reasons for recalling an ambassador. On the other hand, to have an ambassador accredited to the President of Mexico whom the President did not like would hardly make for cordial relations between the two countries.

I had only one brush with Messersmith, but it was prophetic.

It concerned a deal between the Mexican and Brazilian Ministers of Agriculture for the Mexican purchase of some Brazilian bulls. In the Department we had reason to believe the animals might have foot and mouth disease. I expressed to the Mexican Ambassador, and instructed Messersmith to repeat to the Mexican Minister of Foreign Affairs, our concern over Mexico importing diseased bulls. The infection would spread rapidly throughout Mexico and possibly into Texas. If that happened the situation would be extremely serious and might even affect relations between the two countries.

Messersmith took it upon himself to disobey my instructions. With his agreement the bulls were imported. The disease soon appeared in Mexico and was prevented from spreading into Texas only through our government's prompt financial and technical aid in fighting it. It was eventually stamped out in Mexico but not before Messersmith's insubordination had cost the American taxpayers considerably more than one hundred million dollars.

Following my interview with Byrnes, Messersmith was summoned to Washington, where on the President's behalf I offered him the Argentine post. During his stay in Washington, to my great annoyance, he was summoned to the White House for a conference with Truman and Byrnes. Acheson may have been present; I learned of the meeting from him. It was extremely unwise and also bad manners to exclude from a conference with an ambassador-designate the official to whom he would be directly responsible.

When Messersmith arrived in Argentina he was at first coolly received by the Peron government. But he soon made it clear that he had no intention to continue the policy of his predecessor—the policy President Roosevelt had laid down, to which Cordell Hull had adhered, and which Secretary Byrnes had reaffirmed on April 8. He laid himself out to be friendly to Peron, Evita, and their clique, openly aired his antagonism to my policies, and ignored my instructions. Moreover, he successfully demanded from Washington (though not through me) these concessions to Peron that I listed on July 12, 1946, in a memorandum to President Truman:

". . . we have yielded much of what Peron and his associates have demanded from us. We have removed restrictions on all exports to Argentina with the exception of those relating to arms and war material. Almost three quarters of a billion dollars of Argentine gold, which had been held here since 1944, has been released. At the special request of the Argentine Foreign Office, we have unblocked the accounts of two large Argentine banks. These latter steps have been taken on Ambassador Messersmith's recommendation."

This July 12 memorandum, by the way, I wrote at the President's request, after he had asked me to come to the White House for a review of the Argentine policy. During our conversation he expressed complete agreement with my views and recommendations, and I returned to my office elated. Dean Acheson asked me how the interview had gone. I answered that it could not have been better; that the President had confirmed my policy in every particular. I was shocked when he said, "Well, I wouldn't count on that too much, Spruille."

The memorandum for which the President had asked reviewed the behavior of Argentina: its refusal to cooperate with the other American republics during the war; its collaboration with the Nazis; its signing of the Chapultepec Agreement solely in order to gain admission to the United Nations; its subsequent failure to comply with the conditions of the agreement by eliminating Nazi influences and turning Nazi agents over to the Allies; and its demand, as early as 1943, for arms not to fight the common enemy but to build up its power vis-à-vis its neighbors against whom it traditionally harbored aggressive designs. If we gave military assistance to Argentina on its own terms of non-compliance, I told the President, we would be rewarding its recalcitrance at the expense of those republics that had loyally stood by us during the war, and would invite their suspicion and distrust. By such an abandonment of principle we would incur the contempt of the Argentines and of all those peoples who looked to us for moral leadership.

A short time later Secretary Byrnes was taking off for an international conference, and we all went out to the airport to see him off. I found myself standing close to the President, and as I greeted him I remarked that I hoped my memorandum was what he wanted.

"It is exactly what I wanted," he replied. "It is letter perfect. We will stand on that policy even if they take the hide off us."

3

Messersmith's insubordination continued until at last I sent Thomas Mann to Buenos Aires with memoranda recapitulating his instructions, in an attempt to bring him into line. That did no good. He did not confine himself to attacking me in Buenos Aires. He wrote endless letters (he was known in the Department as "Forty-Page George") to Henry Luce, Arthur Sulzberger of the *New York Times,* various senators and congressmen, and even to members of my own staff.

In my files are three interesting documents from that period.

There is a cable of August 5, 1946, to the Department from Jefferson Caffery, then our Ambassador to Paris, quoting the Brazilian Foreign Minister on the subject of Peron's campaign to sow distrust of the United States.

The Foreign Minister referred to a report he had received shortly before leaving Rio for Paris, from his Ambassador to Argentina. Peron had called in the Ambassador and told him that "the United States is now being disloyal to Brazil as it has in the past to Argentina, by preparing for war against the Soviet without taking you into its confidence."

Peron's efforts, the Foreign Minister had told Caffery, were now directed at sowing American fear of a possible Soviet penetration of southern South America, in order to improve the Argentine bargaining position. He added a warning that the maladministration and corruption within the Argentine government had reached new heights.

The second document is a memorandum, dated September 4, 1946, of a conversation with the Italian anti-Fascist leader and one-time Foreign Minister, Count Sforza, who called on me at the end of a Latin American tour.

Count Sforza likened the atmosphere in Argentina to the tensions and repressions of the early Fascist dictatorship, "before Mussolini started killing people." He characterized Peron as the "perfect dictator type" and cited his seeking to take over the whole national life of Argentina, step by step, to the end of establishing a totalitarian state. He contrasted Mussolini and Peron at length and declared Peron to be by far the more determined and dangerous man. And he concluded that in his opinion the Argentine situation was fraught with serious menace.

Such was the appraisal, by one who spoke with authority, of a dictator on whom the United States Ambassador was at that moment fawning and to whom he was demanding that we give whatever he wanted—*on his own terms.*

The third document is a letter to a friend in the State Department from the late James I. Miller, former head of the United Press for Latin America but at that time in business in Buenos Aires. Writing on December 21, 1946, the day after Messersmith left on a trip to Washington for consultation, Miller said many people in Buenos Aires feared that Ambassador to Brazil Wm. D. Pawley, and Senator Brewster, who had just been there, would do all they could to get me removed.

"If Spruille leaves," he went on, "and if Messersmith's policy of appeasement is followed the carrying out of the plan to make this a one hundred per cent Nazi system will proceed at an accelerated pace. I don't think there is any doubt about this . . .

"The impeachment of the Supreme Court is scandalous . . . When the Supreme Court goes all liberty in this country goes with it. Anything Peron proposes will then go through without a hitch. The only thing that holds him back in his designs is Braden. Peron wants to be invited to the Rio conference. He wants arms and both Pawley and Messersmith think the U.S. should arm him to help him remain in power. He knows that Braden is watching him but when and if Braden goes he will start on his real program which will be worse than anything we have yet seen . . . it seems to me that Spruille has a lot of people working against him. He is entirely right in his policy and some day it will be generally recognized but it may be too late by then."

I have quoted this letter at length because it was written by an experienced reporter from on-the-spot observation. It shows what was at stake in the struggle between myself and those people—of whom Messersmith was only one though in a unique position to do harm—who were pressuring the President and Secretary of State to yield to Peron's wishes throughout my twenty months as Assistant Secretary.

When Messersmith arrived in Washington for consultation I confronted him with the fact of his letter-writing campaign against me.

He swore it was not true, and especially that he had not tried to undermine me with my own staff. Then, as he sat nervously taking his own pulse (he did so more or less continuously), he suddenly turned to me and said, "Have you seen any letters to members of your staff from me?"

"Yes, George," I answered, "I have read them myself."

That silenced him—for the moment. The predictable soon happened: his insubordination and intrigue became public knowledge and were commented on in the press, especially in *Time*. George went on a *Time* cover. At last I went to the President and told him that unless Messersmith were fired I should have to resign. Truman seemed almost as angry as myself and observed that George was an s.o.b. and would certainly be fired. It was not done. On the day when General George C. Marshall was sworn in as Secretary of State succeeding Byrnes, as those who had witnessed the ceremony were filing out of the President's office he beckoned me out of the line. He wanted to repeat his intention to fire "that s.o.b." Messersmith.

After Gen. Marshall had had a few days to get acquainted with affairs in the Department, he asked me to come in and discuss the Argentine problem with him. Dean Acheson was present. At one point Marshall asked me what I thought was Messersmith's motivation. I answered that I was no mind reader, but that Messersmith—rightly or wrongly—had probably got the impression from the President and Secretary Byrnes that he and not I had their backing. That he did indeed think so is borne out in a passage from James Miller's letter, quoting Messersmith as having told the Chamber of Commerce in Buenos Aires:

". . . that he will recommend to Washington the policy to be followed when Argentina has fulfilled the Chapultepec agreement, 'according to its interpretation of that agreement' and that 'Mr. Truman and Byrnes, *and no one else,* will decide on his recommendations.' "

Subsequently it was intimated to me through Jim Wright that the highly influential "theys" who were so enormously powerful in the Department wanted me out of the Assistant Secretaryship, and that as a consolation I could become High Commissioner to Korea. I sent them back word that I was just as eager to leave the post as anyone could be to get me out of it; but that I would not accept the Korean appointment with its connotation of being eased out. I intended, I said, to leave with dignity, honor, and all flags flying. If any attempt was made to shove me out, then I would fight with everything I had and they knew from my record that I could put up a pretty nasty fight—with no holds barred. (Besides, at that time I still had a considerable public following.)

4

A series of discussions followed. Messersmith was to be summarily fired, and a few weeks later I would resign with an exchange of cordial letters between the President and myself that I was to draft for his approval. But two things happened to disrupt this timing.

Here I must again bring in the military brass, which never relaxed its pressures against me. The officers with whom I had to deal were unfailingly hostile with only two exceptions: Generals Vandenberg and Eisenhower.

The Pentagon was determined that we should arm the Latin American republics, Argentina included. With the arms would go the kind of military missions I had refused to permit in Argentina. The reasons were not entirely altruistic. Neither were they entirely patriotic. Getting rid of obsolescent equipment to the Latin Americans would enable the military to go to Congress and plead shortages; shortages would lower Congressional resistance to demands for new equipment. And the military missions meant more colonels and generals and more prestige. They were a favorite military racket.

I was against our arming Latin America, for several reasons.

In a number of Latin American republics there was danger that any arms we sent would be used against the people, as our lend-lease tanks, planes, machine guns, and gas were later used in Guatemala to keep a government of Communist gangsters in power. I quoted to the military a Venezuelan friend of mine, a distinguished former Cabinet officer, who begged me, "For Heaven's sake don't send us arms. The Communists are likely to take over one of these days, and if they do they'll turn them against us."

They were unimpressed. They not only wanted to arm Peron; they were determined to send airplanes and machine guns to Higinio Morinigo, the Paraguayan dictator. My answer was, "I'm not going to give this dictator airplanes and machine guns with which to shoot down Paraguayans, for the Paraguayan people will later, and rightly, accuse the United States of having helped him."

I sent substantially that same answer to Trujillo, who had the effrontery to send his ambassador to me with a request for weapons. My official note in reply to the request was emphatic and damning. I said that so far as I was concerned the only possible use to which he could put such arms was against his neighbor Haiti. Or against his own long-suffering and exploited people.

Trujillo never liked me and with good reason. I recall the occasion when he had his stooge Congress pass a resolution changing the name of Dajabon to Presidente Franklin Delano Roosevelt. The implied sinister insult in this action will be evident only to those familiar with Dajabon. This place was the scene, in 1939, of a ghastly massacre of between 10,000 and 15,000 men, women, and children who had come over from Haiti to harvest the sugar crop. The awful deed was done with machetes.

I informed the Dominican ambassador in Washington, and had our chargé d'affaires in Ciudad Trujillo tell the Foreign Minister, that if he changed the name of Dajabon to that of any citizen of the United States, not merely Roosevelt, I would publicly denounce him.

It was clear that we would have a kind of arms race to answer for. Each country would think it had to have the equivalent or better than what every other country got. I ran into this kind of thing shortly after I became Assistant Secretary, when we distributed some surplus planes among them. The Colombians, very sensibly, asked for transport planes for use between Bogota and the Llanos. But when they learned that Peru was getting fighters and bombers, suddenly they needed fighters and bombers, too. When the Colombians got some tanks (which they would probably rarely use) the Peruvians at once had to have more tanks.

Then there was the special rivalry between Argentina, which had not qualified for arms during the war, and Brazil, which had. Peron was demanding that we reward Argentina's support of Hitler by bringing its military strength up to that of our loyal ally. I was opposed to that.

The question of costs didn't seem to be bothering anyone. Even at five cents on the dollar, the Latins could not afford to pay for all the war material the Pentagon was proposing to send them. I tried to find out how much that five cents would amount to. The Pentagon kept promising estimates but sent none. I asked about costs of maintenance, which I knew would be considerable. I was no more successful there.

It must have been an accident. Someone in the Pentagon must have slipped up badly. Just as I was about to give up all hope I did get an estimate on the cost of accessory equipment. For logistic transportation equipment, medical and office equipment—those things, in other words, that keep an army running—I received an estimate of $1,066,000,000 for ten years. It was broken down country by country. The amount assigned to Chile was $2,500,000. Poor little Chile could no more afford that amount for accessory equipment than I could afford a private yacht. The amounts assigned to the other republics were equally unrealistic. That item alone made the entire program demonstrably foolishly extravagant.

In my memorandum to President Truman I had discussed the great need of a higher standard of living throughout Latin America and suggested that we might better undertake to strengthen those countries through economic than through military assistance (but *not* by dollar grants). With the aid of American technical genius and know-how, I said, a rapid improvement in their industrial and agricultural techniques, sanitation, public health, and general well-being could be brought about while Peron and other demagogues were making empty promises. That program at least had the merit of practicability. But of course there was nothing in it for the military politicians.

While I was fighting it out with the Pentagon, Peron evidently decided that American surrender was imminent. He sent up his chief of staff, Gen. Carlos von der Becke. I had met von der Becke in Argentina. He was one of three brothers, all rabid Nazis. He was also amazingly stupid. Even George Messersmith, with all his adulation of Peron, called Peron's chief of staff "a dumb Prussian."

A Colonel at the Pentagon (he had slandered the Department and myself at a dinner in the Guatemalan Embassy and been called to order by the Ambassador) telephoned my office and said the military intended to send Gen. von der Becke up from Miami in a special plane. I gave orders that he was to be shown every courtesy, but allowed to finish his trip as he had begun it, by commercial plane. In direct disobedience of my order—a State Department order on a matter involving our foreign relations—Peron's Nazi general was flown to Washington by special plane.

Von der Becke was met in Washington by Gen. Hoyt S. Vandenberg and a clutch of three and two star generals. And he proceeded to demonstrate that even George Messersmith could be right. He managed to impress Gen. Eisenhower, who pronounced him "quite a guy." But he bored Dean Acheson to exasperation. Personally, I was interested in seeing just how stupid he could be.

He had with him a typewritten statement to the effect that relations between Argentina and the United States had been restored to a state of perfect amity. We loved each other dearly, and the United States was going to see to it that Argentina received large amounts of military equipment.

"Will you please have President Truman issue this statement," he said.

At the time I found it preposterous; also amusing. How could I know that Peron's dumb general had gauged the President's future course far better than I had?

5

In April 1947 Robert Patterson, Secretary of War, and James Forrestal, Secretary of the Navy, sent identical letters to Acheson as Acting Secretary of State (Marshall was in Moscow), repeating the Pentagon's demands. With the help of my assistants I drafted the reply, later signed by Acheson, laying down the policy that we opposed the arming of Latin America, which was to proceed no further, and giving our reasons why.

So far as I was concerned, the policy was set and that was that. But Marshall had hardly returned when, without consulting or even informing me, he put the question of arming Latin America under Maj. Gen. John H. Hilldring, who had been brought in as Assistant Secretary of State to handle the problem of displaced persons. Hilldring next drafted a bill embodying Pentagon policy, which was being sent to the Hill without consultation with me. I went to the fifth floor and told Marshall and Acheson that I was resigning forthwith. They begged me to wait; for reasons of their own they had never kept their promise to fire Messersmith and they wanted time to do so before I left.

Hilldring's bill was sent to Congress the next day, May 27; whereupon I wrote my resignation and drafted a reply for the President, as I had been asked to do. Marshall of course realized that Messersmith should have been fired long since; also that the way I had been doublecrossed about the arms bill would not look well in print. Not that he was sorry; but he knew that if there was any public comment on all this, I would not hold my peace, and when I spoke I would speak with the facts. This made him pretty uneasy.

Another incident just at this time may have added to his nervousness. John C. Dreier, who was acting for my office on the State, War, and Navy Committee, sent me a memorandum that the Pentagon had drafted and at its insistence had been accepted by the Committee. He attached a note saying he supposed there was nothing we could do except take it.

When I read the memorandum, which purported to represent the views of the three Departments on the Hilldring bill, I decidedly did something about it, for in effect it said:

"Every time we bring up the matter of arming Latin America, we find a great repugnance to the idea. Therefore, this bill must be handled in the Congress, both Senate and House, with great secrecy and in such a way as to discourage all editorial comment by either the press or the radio."

I sent the thing to Marshall and Acheson with a comment that seared the paper it was written on. If the American system of government, I told them, had declined to the point where legislation could be sneaked through Congress conspiratorially in order to prevent criticism from press or public, then the Republic was in a really bad way.

If the Department's treatment of me had become a matter of public discussion, this memorandum committing three Government Departments to deception of the American people about the bill responsible for my resignation would have created something of a scandal.

I say that the arms bill was the cause of my resignation. It was indeed the immediate cause. But I knew the Argentine policy would be reversed and it was imperative to have my resignation accepted before that happened. If the reversal had come before Hilldring's bill went to Congress instead of a few days after, it would naturally have caused my immediate resignation and given unwanted publicity to an odious policy change.

The reversal, when it came, was disclosed under peculiar circumstances.

Early in the year I had learned by grapevine that Senator Arthur Vandenberg was under pressure (from what sources I never knew) to go to Buenos Aires and talk with Peron. The argument was that if he did so, he could secure Peron's compliance with our demands within forty-eight hours. At once I invited the Senator and Mrs. Vandenberg to have dinner with Maria and me. They accepted. During dinner I added my own persuasions.

"Why not make a try?" I argued. "If you can put it over, that will be a great achievement."

He insisted he couldn't get away. I suggested he try to get former President Hoover to go, but for some reason he emphatically rejected that idea, alleging that the former President would not do the job successfully.

With Vandenberg's refusal to intercede, it was decided to take advantage of a visit the Argentine Ambassador was about to make to Buenos Aires. President Truman sent for him, and in the presence of Senators Vandenberg and Connally and Under Secretary Acheson, gave him a message for Peron. The United States, said the President, wished to reestablish friendly relations with Argentina, but Argentina must first discharge its obligations under the Chapultepec Agreement. Otherwise relations between the two countries must inevitably deteriorate still further.

The Ambassador's home visit was long. When he returned he was again called to the White House. There, in the presence of the same group and without waiting for him to give Peron's answer (assuming he carried one) the President told him that our relations with Argentina were once more completely friendly.

Who was responsible for this mysterious capitulation, who had pulled what strings, I never knew. It was the result of strictly secret diplomacy, and to speculate on its method or motivation would be idle. The important fact is that from that time until Peron was thrown out by the Argentine people in spite of our tacit support, the United States gave him whatever he demanded and intervened in his behalf throughout the hemisphere.

6

Since the President and Secretary appeared at last to be not only ready but eager to fire Messersmith, and fire him before I left the Department, I agreed to make my resignation effective officially on June 30. On June 3, I was to leave for Montana to receive an honorary degree from the Montana School of Mines. I proposed that the resignation be announced on June 13, when I would be somewhere between Butte and Chicago on my way back and difficult for the press to locate in case the news created any great stir. The timing would allow opportunity to fire Messersmith. After my return I would be presented with the Medal of Freedom (the highest civilian award).

All this was agreed upon. I left the Department on May 28. On June 3 Maria and I departed New York. As we had to wait for a night train out of Chicago, we took a room at the Drake Hotel. We were about to go down to lunch when the telephone rang. I was expecting a call from Ellis Briggs, and unhesitatingly answered, only to find myself talking to Bert Andrews, head of the *Herald Tribune* Washington bureau.

"I want to get confirmation of your resignation," said Andrews.

"What are you talking about?" I answered. "I don't know anything about my resignation."

"Oh, come come," he said. "I don't have to read you your own letter, but if you like I'll read you the President's reply."

Secretary Marshall had sent the two letters to the White House with a slip attached prohibiting their release before June 13 without his express permission. The White House press secretary had not bothered to read the Secretary's instructions, but released them to the press at once.

It was pretty embarrassing, especially for Marshall. He was enraged. He never could get used to the fact that civilian officials don't carry out orders with military precision. The mistake at the White House forced his hand; he shot off a telegram to Buenos Aires accepting Messersmith's resignation.

George proved intractable, being a civilian official. Also, he had been hoping for reward not punishment, after the about face on Argentine policy. He replied at great length that he had not resigned; that indeed he had no idea of resigning. Oh, yes, he had resigned, insisted Marshall. And the futile exchange continued until Marshall peremptorily ordered him to get out. It cost the Department a pretty penny to get rid of "Forty Page George," who was fired not because the tops disagreed with his policy (they had just adopted it) but because he had abandoned even the pretense of diplomatic discretion in his zeal to promote the interests of Peron.

When I returned to Washington I was presented with the Medal of Freedom, but not at the usual White House ceremony, with the President pinning it on. Instead, a ceremony was held in Acheson's office, and Dean pinned on the medal. Secretary Marshall rather surprised me later by saying that if he had known I was receiving the medal that morning he would have liked to present it himself.

Only one duty remained, my protocolar visit to the White House, to take formal leave of President Truman. The call lasted some ten or fifteen minutes, and the topic of conversation was a gabardine suit I was wearing.

On that trivial note my diplomatic service of thirteen years came to an end. Fortunately it had not been long enough to make me forget that there are worse fates than being out of office. Many people who knew the story of those last twenty months were indignant because I had, as they put it, been "outrageously doublecrossed." They marveled that I had refrained from making a scandal about it. But I had departed with dignity as far as the public was concerned, and I was content to leave it at that. After all, there had been times when I doubted whether I should be able to leave with a whole skin.

Entr'acte (2)

IN 1938 President Roosevelt issued an Executive Order prohibiting Ambassadors, Ministers, or Foreign Service officers from accepting foreign decorations. If a decoration had been presented, the beneficiary could receive it at the time but was obliged to return the decoration and accompanying diploma. The reasoning behind the order was that our representatives abroad might be influenced in favor of the donor country by the promise of or receipt of the honor.

This always has seemed to me an absurdity and an implied slur on our representatives abroad. If any are under suspicion as being open to such influence, they should be dismissed. And if the government does not trust even to that slight degree its representatives, our lot as a nation is sorry indeed.

The heraldry of such decorations is many centuries old. In most countries, notably in this hemisphere, the ranks that can be given are:

1—Knight. *This is a simple bronze medal hanging from a wide ribbon that can be pinned to the chest. It can also be represented by a narrow ribbon in the jacket lapel button hole.*

2—Officer. *This next highest rank is represented by the same medal as Knight only in silver and with a rosette on the ribbon. A rosette is worn in the buttonhole.*

3—Commander. *The medal is usually gold or gold plated and it is worn on a ribbon around the neck. It is represented by a rosette with two silver wings in the buttonhole. This is usually the highest rank given to anyone without official status.*

4—Grand Officer. *This rank is represented by a ribbon around the neck with a gold medal hanging from it, a plaque to be worn on the breast, and in the lapel a rosette with one silver and one gold wing. This is usually reserved for Ministers Plenipotentiary and other high officials of similar rank.*

5—The Grand Cross *consists of a wide ribbon worn across the chest from the right to the left side, with a medal suspended at the end that can be seen below the uniform or full-dress jacket as the case may be. It is worn from right to left because in former days a sword also dangled from the ribbon and could be more readily drawn. The rosette for the buttonhole has two gold wings. The rank is usually reserved for Ambassadors, Cabinet officers, Chief Justices of the Supreme Court, Field Marshals, and occasionally even Chiefs of State.*

But many countries have gone on to Grand Collar, *which is really a necklace with gold or gold plated links from which the medal hangs. It is reserved exclusively for Chiefs of State.*

In my youth, as a layman, I received the Officer of the Order of Merit of O'Higgins by Chile. Later, after the Seventh International Conference of American States and while I was out of the Service, the Chileans gave me the Grand Cross of the same order.

This I was able to keep even after the Executive Order of FDR. I was also able to retain the Bolivian order of the Condor of the Andes Grand Cross, as I received it before the Executive Order, but being Ambassador at the time I had to leave the decoration in the State Department safe.

Through the years a number of other countries wished to decorate me but in each instance, after explaining the reason, I refused the decoration. It was very gratifying, therefore, that following my retirement from diplomacy all of these countries excepting one, Panama, conferred their Grand Crosses on me. I say gratifying, because no longer having an official position I could look on the honors as reflecting genuine regard for me.

Paraguay and Guatemala, however, instead of giving me the Grand Cross made me a Grand Officer because at that time they did not have the Grand Cross. Several years later, when the Communist Arbenz regime controlled Guatemala, I attacked them energetically, particularly in a lecture on public events I delivered at Dartmouth College. At once the Guatemalan Congress passed a resolution urging the President to recall my decoration, and circularized all of the other Congresses in the American Republics advising them of the action and denouncing me.

At a later date the Communists were thrown out and Castillo Armas became president. I was promoted to the Grand Cross, which by then had been established. The cablegram from the President announcing the honor was so long that it nearly bankrupted me to send an adequate reply.

A few countries, among them Japan, instead of following this heraldry give decorations of the first, second, and third degree. I recall an episode involving one such decoration that shows how all is not ceremonial solemnity in these matters.

A young secretary in our Embassy was about to be transferred. The host country was very grateful for his many kindnesses and attention to their affairs, and the officials proposed to confer on him a decoration of the 2nd or 3rd degree. The young man explained the Presidential Order to the authorities, who were understandably disappointed. But one cleverer than the others remarked, "Surely there is no prohibition against your wife accepting a decoration." He allowed as there probably was not. The country proceeded to decorate his wife with the Order of Chastity of the Second Degree.

2

My feeling of affection for the Metropolitan Club in New York has its origins in my childhood. My father was a member and often I was with my mother when she would call for Father at the Club. I was about fourteen. She would send me in for my father rather than the chauffeur. I joined the Club in 1947. Since then I have served on the Board of Governors, as Chairman of the Admissions Committee, vice president, and since 1966 as president. During the Depression the Club had gone very much to seed. I was fortunate that my immediate predecessor Richard H. West had done a magnificent job and I had only to continue his good work.

The Metropolitan Club played an unexpected part in my continuing opposition to the dictator Juan Peron, which went on long after I had left my Argentine ambassadorial post. The incident developed around my old and dear Argentine friend Raul Lamuraglia.

Raul was very active in the internal efforts to dislodge Peron and his henchmen, working in collaboration with the Argentine Navy and other forces that ultimately succeeded in driving Peron from power. His activities on behalf of freedom forced him into exile, which he spent either in Uruguay or the United States.

He often would return to Buenos Aires to confer with his fellow conspirators, and on one of these occasions committed the disastrous folly of carrying two letters. One was from Alberto Gainza Paz, owner of the great newspaper, La Prensa, *and the other letter was from me. Peron regarded both Gainza and me as personal enemies. Either letter was enough to cause Raul's execution. While making his secret way back to Uruguay, he was apprehended and arrested. The cell his captors placed him in was totally dark, and so constructed that he could neither stand up nor lie down.*

Word of his arrest reached New York. Tito Gainza and I con-

ferred, agreeing that the first step was to publicize Raul's arrest. Thus, whatever Peron might have in mind could not be carried out in secret. This slight deterrent was all we had, for the moment. Casting about for additional pressure besides publicity, I came up with a possible answer.

I had obtained Raul's membership in the Metropolitan Club. I proposed at the next meeting of the Board of Governors that a telegram I had drafted be sent to Peron by the President on behalf of the Club, declaring that habeas corpus *was a treasured principle in the United States and made quite clear that the Club's total membership was deeply concerned by Peron's action in arresting and holding incommunicado our fellow Club member.*

We were fortunate in our timing. Peron at that moment was trying to arrange for a large loan from the U.S. Government. He felt he might help his cause by ingratiating himself with the distinguished members of the Metropolitan Club. What he failed to notice was my presence on the Board of Governors. This oversight was costly to him. The Argentine government released Raul from prison. The Metropolitan Club returned to its former unruffled existence.

Peron repeatedly intruded into my New York life. In 1953 a number of my friends in the Pan American Society were eager for me to be elected president of the Society, of which I was vice president and a member of the Council. Some of the corporations with interests in Argentina opposed the plan because they felt my election would antagonize Peron. A compromise was offered: I could serve as honorary president. I refused indignantly, stating furthermore that if the Society were so to prostrate itself before Peron I would resign my membership.

The result was that I was elected and served the constitutional limit of six years. I am happy to say they were a successful half-dozen years, with the Society gaining in prestige and building up a substantial amount in its treasury. I think that without exception I presided at every Society function given to honor visiting Presidents, Foreign Ministers, Ambassadors, etc.

These occasions provided opportunities frequently for amusing deceptions. Many of our guests would come prepared to orate for hours, as politicians will. This habit had to be thwarted: From our luncheons businessmen were impatient to return to their offices and from dinners to their homes. My tactic was to install microphones at the lectern, and inform our speakers that they were on the air not only in this country but Latin America—however only for fifteen minutes. This usually succeeded, although some speakers might run on to 30 minutes. But 30 minutes was an improvement over several hours.

The most interesting and, in a way, thrilling experience I had with the Pan American Society occurred the day after I was elected president and the announcement of my election had appeared in the morning papers. From the most reliable U.S. Government sources, I received confidential information about a responsible employee under the Society's secretary. I was told that this woman and her husband were high on the list cf the first ten people who, in the event of hostilities breaking out between the U.S. and any other power, would promptly be seized as security threats. I immediately acted to have the woman fired, giving her orders that she was to be out of the office within two hours. She and her husband had been among employees of the Office of Strategic Services supplying information in some detail of our affairs.

3

A man's life is not only composed of major exercises and assignments. He does many things for fun or because of a disinterested desire to help or, often, because he can be an intermediary where his cooperation serves to bring together in a mutually helpful enterprise many people who would otherwise remain disconnected.

This happened, for example, in 1955, when the Museum of the University of Pennsylvania sought my assistance. The institution was planning exploration at Tikal in Guatemala. Knowing of my cordial association with Guatemalan President Colonel Carlos Castillo Armas, they asked me to intervene on their behalf for airplane service and other essential facilities in Guatemala.

I supplied letters of introduction to influential Guatemalans and personally wrote to Castillo Armas. All the university's requirements were met. I was assured my intervention had been indispensable, and the exploration turned up much valuable information. It was only a slight sting when the honorary degree the university had mentioned was not acted upon. In any case it was pleasant to have been publicly associated with a major exploration effort of an important scientific institution.

Somewhere around the same time an idea of mine that even today seems somewhat inspired surfaced only to sink again without leaving a ripple. It occurred to me that a valuable alliance could be established between business leaders and the leadership of the nation's conservative farm organizations. To this end I invited the top officers of the Grange and the Farm Bureau Federation to a buffet dinner in my apartment along with some of my business friends. But, alas! Nothing developed, although I held the affair two years in succession.

However, in the light of the 1968 presidential election and the subsequent career of the man in question, one remark, made by a farm representative, is worth recalling today. We were in the midst of cocktails, which the farmers did not drink, and I speculated to one of them that Walter Reuther was perhaps the most dangerous man in the United States at the time. He disagreed. "Oh no," he said, "the most dangerous man in the United States is H. H. Humphrey. He is a dangerous demagogue and a charmer who can mesmerize the birds out of the trees with his oratory."

The Democratic Party's 1968 hopeful could only be ruefully amused by this comment, as he remembers how his charm and demagoguery failed at the critical time.

In 1958 I agreed to be chairman of the First Inter-American Music Festival in Washington, held April 18, 19, and 20, at which many works specially commissioned and written by composers of all the Americas were first played. My program for the occasion lists ten new works given their premiere performance. Seven additional compositions by Latin American composers received their first United States presentation at the Festival. It was effective proof, if proof were needed, that musical creativity in the Americas was vigorous.

Two years later I found myself briefly involved in a controversy over an opera proposed for production by the Metropolitan Opera Association. The work was to be based on the famous Sacco-Vanzetti case. The composer hoping for the commission was Marc Blitzstein.

As soon as I learned of this plan I took the matter up with my good friend Floyd Jefferson, then chairman of the Metropolitan Opera Association. On April 8, my files show, I wrote him the following letter.

> *Of course, a number of operas have been written around criminal activities. But since these two criminals, who committed murder while carrying out an armed robbery, have been glorified as martyrs* because they were Communists, *I feel it is particularly unfortunate in these times for the Metropolitan Opera Association to add fuel to the flames of the Communist penetration into our country.*
> *Incidentally, Marc Blitzstein, I understand, admitted under*

oath in testifying before a Congressional committee some years ago that he was a Communist.

I am happy to say Floyd Jefferson put a stop to this Communist intrigue.

A goodwill undertaking that I am pleased to be able occasionally to assist is the Bolivarian Society of the United States. I had to decline an offer to be president of the Society because despite my size there simply isn't an endless supply of me to go around. And I will not serve in any office without performing genuine duties.

However, in October 1968 the Bolivarian Congress, with delegates from Venezuela, Colombia, Panama, Ecuador, and Peru met in New York, and the members insisted I act as chairman of the meeting.

A business assignment I enjoyed during its tenure was being a trustee of the Dry Dock Savings Bank, later serving as well on several committees. As chairman of the Examining Committee I made extra and arduous work by insisting that the formerly brief reports be given depth and detail. As a result, I learned how a savings bank worked.

A suggestion was made at one time that bank trustees should resign at the end of the calendar year when they became 72. I quoted the old Spanish saying, "Mas sabe el diablo por ser viejo que por ser demonio." Which means that the devil knows more by reason of his age than because he is a demon. I voted for the ruling, though, little appreciating how quickly I would myself become 72.

President Roosevelt always was influenced greatly by the last person with whom he spoke. Therefore when I wanted an instruction from him, I always would endeavor to see him at the last possible moment before returning to my post; then got out of Washington as quickly as possible to put his instruction into action.

In this connection I do not pretend the following story about Franklin D. Roosevelt deserves even a footnote in the history books. It is amusing as well as pathetic, though, and shows how extraordinarily vulnerable the President of the United States is by virtue of the personal concessions he must make. I hope the situation today in the White House is not thus . . .

I was leaving Washington to return to my post in Bogota and had made an appointment with President Roosevelt for the day of my departure. General (Pa) Watson, the President's appointments secretary, had Senator Greene of Rhode Island with him when I entered his office. We were told it would not be long.

Shortly, two White House ushers entered bearing some intricate woodwork (wrought by a jigsaw) on pedestals, painted white and gold. The creations were quite without beauty. Following the set of objects was their maker, a small boy wearing a heavily gold braided uniform and medals, with his mother. The mother was corpulent, deferential in manner and speech, and for some reason I felt she was probably a cook. Accompanying them was a Congressman, his name long forgotten by me, full of pomp and importance, insisting his charges must get in to see the President forthwith.

Pa Watson protested the President's schedule was full and he simply could not see this child, who was also carrying a violin case. Pa pointed to Senator Greene and me and said our appointments were long-standing. Senator Greene stormed that an ambassador and a senator should not be thus wholly shunted aside. The Congressman raged: they would not be long: they must see the President. Pa finally relented and agreed, exacting a promise that the Congressman and his visitors would be no longer than a minute. The ornate wood structures were born in and placed on a side table in the President's room. The mother and boy followed.

In a moment we heard the song "God Bless America" drawn out in screeches and scratches from a violin. Beckoned over to the door into the President's office by Pa Watson, Senator Greene and I saw the little boy playing his violin at the corner of Roosevelt's desk. His mother stood beside him becoming visibly more emotional every minute. She looked as if she might grab at the President with her trembling hands.

As the tune ended another aide entered the room. Roosevelt looked over the knick-knacks on his desk and on the table and said, "What can I give him? I don't see anything here." The aide suggested the President autograph a piece of White House notepaper, but before Roosevelt could complete the action the boy said, "Shall I play it again?" And before anyone could say him nay, he started sawing away once again at the violin. The strains of a discordant "God Bless America" filled the room.

It was too much for the mother. She broke down completely, knelt beside the President's chair, and having grasped his hand began kissing it furiously, all the while weeping rivers of tears. It was perfectly apparent that Roosevelt was embarrassed and irritated but incapable of doing anything but sit there and wait out the dismal end. His braces were unhooked and he could not rise. Pa Watson at last dashed in and bore the mother and child out almost bodily.

Several years later, when Harry Truman was President, President Miguel Aleman visited Washington. The first big official dinner was given by Truman at the White House, the second by President Aleman at the Mexican Embassy. During the meal my companion at the table dropped her napkin, and when I leaned over to retrieve it I found myself stuck to the chair. The cane seats had been gilded recently and were not completely dry. What a symphony of ripping and tearing was heard when the company stood to respond to President Aleman's toast to the United States President. Derrieres all over the room were spotted with gold. The Chairman of the Foreign Affairs Committee of the House, I recall vividly, went over to the two Presidents to display his gilded bottom. There can be humor in diplomacy, and I can't now resist the temptation to paraphrase Shakespeare: The two Presidents doubtless had hoped to come before us with ungilded tales.

5

William D. Pawley was a sort of international merchant and entrepreneur when I met him in Cuba. He had made a fortune assembling and selling planes to the Chinese during the war, a high risk enterprise that was typical of him. Pawley's path and mine crossed more than accidentally a little later in my career and there is much in the record that needs setting straight.

While I was Ambassador to Argentina, Pawley was named to the same post in Peru. He was an ambitious man. He wanted to rise in the diplomatic ladder and his opportunity came when my move to Washington as Assistant Secretary of State became known. Soon rumors were circulating that Pawley would succeed me in Buenos Aires. An American friend of mine in charge of American and Foreign Power interests in Argentina shared his knowledge of Pawley with me, he had shared living quarters with Pawley in Miami. His information convinced me Pawley had no business being made Ambassador anywhere.

Pressure, however, paid off. Pawley was a large contributor to the Democratic Party and the National Committee was on his side. After long opposition, I was forced to yield to a compromise that made the man Ambassador to Brazil. I stood fast on my conviction that the Argentine situation was too delicate for an amateur to handle.

Sometime late in 1946, as I recall, the rumor mills had it that Pawley was gunning for my job. The campaign was so near the surface that Newsweek *reported efforts by Pawley to have me replaced by himself. Pawley had just returned to Washington from Rio de Janeiro. He saw the* Newsweek *item and reacted violently, de-*

manding a meeting with me and all my section chiefs and other divisional heads to protest the matter.

The demand was an outrageous presumption. The matter was between him and me and he had no right to insist on the other officers being present. However, realizing how silly he would look, I conceded, and on the following morning more than 20 of my assistants filed into the office with Pawley.

After he had demanded that Newsweek *be reprimanded in a letter from me denying the story, I expressed surprise at such a reaction after his experience in public life and said, "That kind of letter would enlarge and extend the controversy. You say you want to avoid publicity. The best thing is to ignore the article as I intend doing."*

Pawley wouldn't be satisfied. He protested that he had never had such a thought and had never expressed it to anyone. This was too much for me. I said that Henry Wallace had revealed Pawley's statements to me earlier and they duplicated Newsweek's *story. Pawley bluffed and blustered. I had more against him. "Bill, you told some of the senators on the Foreign Relations Committee the same intention." I chided him: "You should have known that one of the best ways to make something public is to talk as you did with those particular senators." Then I named the men in question.*

I concluded by quoting from Kipling's poem "If": "If you can bear to hear the truth you've spoken twisted by knaves to make a trap for fools—or being lied about don't deal in lies—you will be a man." This terminated the interview. Pawley left forgetting his hat.

From then on he was my sworn enemy. Several times friends of mine who knew Pawley would speak of him to me, and my reply was, I fear, always unprintable!

In 1962 Pawley appeared before Senator Thomas Dodd of the Senate Sub-Committee on Internal Security and wrote into the record an attack made on me by a young Army officer whom I had had to reprimand through my Military Attaché when I was Ambassador in Havana. He accused not only me but Ellis Briggs and others of my associates of being Communist sympathizers. This was the least likely of charges.

I immediately telegraphed the Sub-Committee protesting the publication of this testimony, which I said was untrue, excepting for one thing, viz: When he stated I had prevented his appointment as Ambassador in Argentina, that much was true. I urged the group to summon both me and my accuser for hearings under oath, the judgment of perjury then to be determined by the Sub-Committee and the Department of Justice. Nothing more was heard, and later Senator Dodd acknowledged to me that he had made a grievous error in admitting the testimony.

At that time President Truman was in Bermuda. He was twice interviewed, and each time stated that I had been an outstanding public servant. Pawley was, on another occasion, severely reprimanded by Secretary of State George Marshall and my successor Assistant Secretary of State Norman Armour for defamatory statements he made about me and Ambassadors Briggs and Butler before some press people at a Miami luncheon.

During my diplomatic career I had occasion to visit New Deal Washington from time to time. When Latin American affairs were discussed, I was frequently either amused or infuriated by the naivete exhibited by officials there.

On one such visit we were invited to a Sunday night supper and the private showing of an Argentine movie. We arrived late and the showing was under way. The film concerned a woman who in her eagerness to gratify her husband's desperate wish for an heir tried to palm off an adopted child on him as her own. She failed, and the ensuing family crisis was resolved only by the heroine's timely discovery that she was at last about to produce a genuine heir.

A happy ending and a turning up of lights revealed the Vice-President, the Director of the Budget, an ambassador or two, assorted New Deal agency heads and other prominent Washingtonians enjoying an evening of inter-American "culture."

We were shooed into another room, seated around a deluxe record-player and provided mimeographed copies of Latin American songs. The first song was announced by number, the disk put on and the assembly—in murderous Spanish—joined in. One after another song was lustily butchered, right up to the climactic number called Expropriación.

This was a Mexican song written shortly after the nationalization of the American oil properties—"We've expropriated the oil companies; now we'll expropriate (this and that), and then we'll expropriate the Atlantic Ocean." There sat a large sampling of top Washington officialdom loudly celebrating in execrable Spanish the theft of American property by the Mexican government.

Chapter XXXIII

AFTER my many years as Ambassador and Assistant Secretary of State, which followed my severe losses in the Depression, my finances were sadly depleted. Only a few securities rescued from the stock market catastrophe in 1931 kept me decently solvent. I say 1931 because my father and I survived 1929 fairly well. But seeing stocks of Anaconda and other companies dropping to values far below their true worth, we bought in again. Unwisely, though, we bought on margin, and in 1931 paid for our foolishness.

Also, when I threatened to sue the bankers who reneged on the financing of my apartment house project at Stonehurst I obtained a small settlement that helped tide me over.

Maria and I were in accord on not wishing to return to Chile and on seeing New York as the best source of opportunities for me. We took a summer lease on an apartment and in the fall by great good fortune—apartments were scarce as hen's teeth—we rented a small duplex on Park Avenue. In 1949 I purchased an eleven-room apartment on 72nd Street, where I still reside.

As my old friend Curtis Calder, chairman of the board of Electric Bond and Share, explained to me, the majority of U.S. businessmen, just as they had thought well of Mussolini years before, felt they could do business profitably with Peron. Hence my disputes with him, which were so widely publicized, made my name more or less anathema on Wall Street, at least for a year or so, although I am happy to say the situation completely cleared later on.

Nevertheless, I felt my best opportunity was to act as a consultant and not to try to get a permanent job with any corporation. I filled in during this period with a series of lectures at $2,000 each. A large publisher offered me a $10,000 advance against my memoirs. This I refused, being convinced it would consume so much time I could not meet my consultant obligations.

About this same time I negotiated with Con Kelley, chairman of the Anaconda board, settlement of my father's estate with respect to properties he had either developed or acquired for Anaconda. I had such complete confidence in Kelley and the Anaconda officials that I thought it wisest to leave it to them in each case to set the figure rather than bargaining. I could see no other way to deal with such outstanding men and my confidence was fully justified. Later, Mr. Kelley engaged me as a consultant for Anaconda with a substantial retainer. Also, I was retained as a consultant by American Foreign Power, Lone Star Cement, United Fruit, and several other corporations.

Thanks to these assignments, and some fortunate investments, I have been able measurably to reconstitute my personal finances.

Also my activity in a number of organizations, like the Foreign Affairs Committee of the National Association of Manufacturers, brought Maria and me expense-free to many parts of the country on speaking programs. As an independent consultant, I was able to come out frankly, often criticizing the authorities. This the corporate representatives could not do in NAM or other meetings lest they antagonize the powerful Washington bureaucrats with whom they had to deal.

A Canadian-American Conference on Foreign Relations met at Niagara Falls, Ontario, from May 31 to June 5, 1951. I was asked to head the U.S. delegation to this off-the-record discussion of related policies of the two governments: How the United States and Canada were confronting economic and political problems in Europe as well as the Far East, the organization of the Free World for defense and security, in particular to improve U.S.-Canadian relations, and a wide range of subordinate topics under these headings.

In my delegation, as also in the Canadian, a full spectrum of political opinion could be found. On the right, there was Christian A. Herter, then Congressman from Massachusetts; Charles E. Salzman, former Assistant Secretary of State; George Wolf, president of the United States Steel Export Co.; and myself. Over to the left were John Kenneth Galbraith, Harvard economist, recently Ambassador to India, and president of the Americans for Democratic Action; Lincoln Gordon, now president of the Johns Hopkins University; some professors, labor union officials, and farm spokesmen. Nearer the middle was Joseph E. Johnson, president of the Carnegie Endowment for International Peace, one of the sponsoring organizations, and U.S. Army Colonel George E. Martin.

The minority of conservatives in the U.S. delegation was balanced by a majority in Canada's. The discussions consequently divided not according to country, that is vertically, but horizontally with Canadian and U.S. conservatives joining forces and the more radical Americans seeking their liberal Canadian counterparts.

I became involved in a heated debate with Charles A. Millard, the national director of the CIO Steel Workers of Canada and a member of the Ontario legislature. He had charged that Canada suffered grievously from absentee ownership and management at the hands of large U.S. corporations. He specifically cited the Aluminum Company of Canada, Westinghouse of Canada, Ford, and several others.

My answer was that no absentee management existed. Ray Powell, I pointed out, the chairman of the board of the Aluminum Co., though born in the United States had lived a large portion of his mature life in Canada and become a Canadian citizen. There was no more patriotic Canadian than he. In all these corporations Canadians not only occupied high as well as subordinate positions but all Canadians were at liberty to purchase stock. Before a coffee break interrupted us, I numbered the advantages Canada derived from these huge investments of U.S. capital.

After the brief intermission, we continued on with our agenda, the next topic being the St. Lawrence Seaway. It must have been intuition that prompted me to ask Mr. Millard what was the attitude of his union on the matter. He replied that he could not tell because they had not yet received instructions from Pittsburgh. That is Pittsburgh, U.S.A.! I won the debate hands down, as all present roared with laughter.

All in all, I think the Conference was a success, particularly in bringing about conversations between Canadians and Americans. Although it did not pretend to heal all of the breaches in policy and differences between the two countries.

2

Earlier in 1951 I had been invited by a group of prominent, civic-minded citizens to become Chairman of the New York City Anti-Crime Committee. Discussions of the offer continued for some time. I argued against accepting the position because I had no experience in fighting crime. Some of the principal backers replied to this by citing the many public speeches over many years in which I had declared that perhaps the gravest problem facing this country, and for that matter the world, was the breakdown of morality in all walks of society. So serious was this, I had stated repeatedly, that it constituted a threat to our national security, because of the growth of organized crime at home and because the worst known form of immorality was Communism.

Therefore, my colleagues argued, I was qualified to lead the independent citizens' group against crime.

We were particularly disturbed by the moral collapse as it was evidenced in New York City. Commencing in 1949, and continuing through 1950, a series of investigations had revealed corruption in the various municipal departments of our city. Frank Hogan and Miles F. McDonald, district attorneys of New York and Kings Counties, were particularly energetic in conducting these investigations. Similarly, in 1950 the United States Senate appropriated funds and named a committee (the Kefauver Committee) to investigate organized crime in interstate commerce.

The investigations confirmed the worst fears of those of us who were at all familiar with the situation. The Kefauver Report listed gangster infiltration into more than 100 different types of legitimate business. Competent authorities unanimously concluded that the situation could be changed only by an informed and aroused public opinion exercising its will at the municipal level in each community. Our committee was to serve this purpose in New York.

Prior to accepting as chairman, I proposed certain guiding principles for the committee. It must, I said:

1—Be permanent.

2—Work at the local level.

3—Be non-partisan.

4—Be supported wholly by private contributions.

5—At all times be as anxious to uphold the honest and competent law official as to criticize and condemn the negligent, incompetent, or worse.

6—Allow no public office holder nor any one with political ambitions to be a member.

7—Function through a trained professional staff with policy directed at all times by an unpaid board of directors.

These principles were accepted and approved by the board and the committee proceeded to its multiple tasks.

We set as our goal meticulously, systematically, and purposefully to observe the functioning of the police, the courts, and all agencies responsible for the administration of justice. We were determined to support and would endeavor to aid, in the proper discharge of their duties, honest and competent authorities, keeping the community informed of the results of our observations. Thus law enforcement officers who, through ineptitude or worse, failed in their trusts and obligations we hoped would be exposed surely and rapidly to the flame of an outraged public opinion. That flame should reduce to ashes all whom it touches.

Then, as now, this nation had become increasingly angered by the breakdown in morals and manners shown to exist among, or close to, the highest authorities at the Federal, State, or Municipal levels. Ethical standards often appeared to have been forgotten by an officialdom oblivious to all the finer sensibilities of correct conduct and unable to distinguish between what is proper or improper, honest or dishonest.

I believe in Thomas Jefferson's aphorism: "The whole art of government consists in the art of being honest."

Montesquieu once said: "The tyranny of a Prince in an oligarchy is not so dangerous to the public welfare as the apathy of a citizen in a democracy." This is true. History tells how all too often empires and civilizations disappeared because of the citizens' apathy to moral issues. However, apathy works in two directions. If it permits crime and corruption to flourish, the collapse of morals and manners in high places causes the public to lose confidence in the authorities and to look upon their so-called leaders with contempt, to despair of corrective measures being taken, and, in short, to become apathetic. Public apathy is both cause and effect of corruption in high places. To break this vicious circle, and to keep it broken, was an essential objective of the New York City Anti-Crime Committee.

After the staff was organized, my board of directors elected Sloane Colt, president and later chairman of the board of the Bankers Trust Co., chairman of the finance committee and treasurer. Alec Lewitt, the prominent manufacturer, was vice chairman. Included on the board were such distinguished New Yorkers as John Hooper, president of the Lincoln Savings Bank; General William Donovan of World War II fame; Win Smith, managing partner of Merrill, Lynch, Pierce, Fenner and Smith Inc., and many others of equal stature. Our Finance Committee was composed of Barney Balaban, Lee Bristol, William M. Chadbourne, Percy Chubb II, Jarvis Cromwell, Clarence Francis, William S. Gray Jr., Charles B. Harding, John W. Hooper, General Ephraim F. Jeffe, Roy E. Larsen, James Linen, Laurence M. Marks, Major Benjamin H. Namm, Leroy A. Petersen, and Thomas J. Watson Jr.

I found the job (unpaid) I had accepted interesting but time consuming. I was a working chairman. I visited the committee's offices daily. I did my homework so that I could face squarely and effectively the many challenging problems, to draft statements and speeches, to direct the carrying out of policy, and otherwise do all that was necessary.

The first principle I set forth was that of permanency. This depended on the fourth principle—support by private contributions. I had received assurances from many prominent citizens, including all of my directors, that the support would come. However, from the moment the committee was formed, money was our biggest problem.

The board of directors authorized an annual budget of $250,000. But in only one year were we able to collect as much as $100,000. The annual average in our seven-year existence was $70,000. We sought foundation aid, but were unable to obtain it in any sizeable amount; and we were successful at all on only two occasions.

Despite my initial refusal to engage in fund-raising, I personally had to solicit some 50 to 60 per cent of the money brought in. Twice the committee contracted bank loans with the implicit obligation of repayment resting on the directors individually as well as collectively. The third time this necessity arose, we decided that as we could not obtain adequate public contributions, especially from business, our greatest beneficiary, we must close down.

But that moment was still to come . . .

At the start, on my insistence, the committee's work was placed in the hands of a competent and experienced staff rather than, as some directors had believed adequate, the traditional executive secretary.

James D. Walsh turned out to be our man and fortunate we were to have him. Jim Walsh was born and bred in New York City. He had worked his way through college driving a truck in every borough and through law school as a patrolman and detective in the New York Police Department. He either knew where the stenches were or he could quickly locate them and the individuals involved. He had been an assistant attorney both for the city and for the Federal Government. Also he had taken part in the Nuremberg trials.

As his principal assistant we employed John O'Mara, whom I had known during the war when he was an FBI agent in Costa Rica; and William Keating, who had served for years as an assistant district attorney in New York.

In addition we hired a number of investigators, some of them remarkably competent operators. During an investigation of the numbers and narcotic rackets in Harlem, they used a harmless-looking delivery truck to take photographs of "pushers" or others making deliveries of narcotics or of policy tickets without their realizing they were on camera.

One of the informers also employed in this investigation would receive telephone calls on a wall pay phone located adjacent to the front window of a bar and grill. One day he was called to the phone, and as he took the message he was shot through the window and killed. The call very evidently had been made to set him up for the slaying.

With this staff and in spite of the limitations of our budget, in short order the committee won the confidence of law enforcement agencies at all levels and the support of the news media.

Nevertheless I found myself under increasing pressures from the fund raisers to have the professional staff furnish them with sensational or dramatic achievements to help sell the committee to potential benefactors. They also wanted to raise money through a big dinner at the Waldorf. Nothing could have brought the committee more quickly into low repute than such futile expedients. The committee sought neither notoriety nor popularity but respect, and that it had won widespread esteem and confidence was demonstrated by the daily parade of public officials of integrity, journalists, the representatives of industry and labor, and many others, to our office.

Keen interest in our activities was expressed in many quarters. Jim Walsh and I were invited to speak frequently, and having been asked, we helped form a crime committee in the city of New Orleans. Our group cooperated with other crime committees in Chicago, Detroit, St. Louis, and elsewhere. The committee measurably induced Governor Dewey's establishment of the New York State Crime Commission, which subsequently recommended creating the Waterfront Commission of New York Harbor.

I am particularly proud of our investigation highlighting the misconduct of the International Longshoremen's Association, which brought about the union's ouster from the American Federation of Labor.

In this assignment we were effectively assisted when the Columbia Broadcasting Company put on a public service radio program entitled "Crime on the Waterfront." We supplied the documentation and, as witnesses, longshoremen who had been beaten badly and threatened with death and the widow of a dock worker who had been murdered. This program won the 1951 Peabody Award and was rebroadcast in answer to public demand.

I concluded the program by summarizing the gravity of the dock situation, but I was irked because I could not at that time announce the name of the man known as "Mr. Big," who actually was the power behind all the waterfront crime and corruption.

Fortunately, at that time the editor of *Collier's* magazine, a courageous man, was willing to publish an article describing the whole waterfront scandal with a box containing a statement by me. *Collier's* publicly called Mr. Big by his real name. Mr. Big's only riposte was to curse and swear that our committee was a group of ignorant dilettantes and that he had never been either east or west of Fifth Avenue. Mr. Big was a millionaire several times over who because of his charitable donations was often invited to sit on the dais at large banquets. At one of these he approached Mr. Colt and asked if he was not a director of the New York City Anti-Crime Committee. When our distinguished treasurer replied affirmatively, Mr. Big cried, "Well, I don't like you!"

The waterfront investigation was the result of many weeks of arduous labor by our staff. But the inquiry, culminating in a telegraphic report to Governor Dewey, was vehemently assailed. We touched some very prominent tender spots. Joseph P. Ryan, life-time president of the I.L.A., damned it as "evil slander," "malicious and unwarranted attacks," and "a rumor campaign." Mr. Big, William J. McCormack, waterfront tycoon, blasted those who "dream up Captain Kidd lurking in the shadows of our piers." He added that the distortions were the "work of experts whose knowledge of the waterfront must have been gained during a ferry ride to Staten Island." Edward F. Cavanaugh Jr., Commissioner of Marine and Aviation of the City of New York, took sharp issue with individuals who "with little or no knowledge of the facts and for purposes of their own find the New York waterfront a 'cesspool of iniquity.' "

An ironic footnote to the committee's career at that time; we had hired a public relations firm to assist us in raising funds. Only due to the alertness of the committee's manager did we learn in time that Mr. Big and other similarly notorious but affluent social pretenders were being solicited for funds. We nipped that potential embarrassment quickly.

The attacks from vested interests in waterfront corruption continued for a while, but the committee was complimented rather than discouraged. And, of course, the sordid situation was shortly dramatized for the entire nation in Budd Schulberg's award-winning film, *On the Waterfront.*

3

During the very first days of the New York City Anti-Crime Committee we were successful in having one stupidly corrupt magistrate removed from the bench. Also we attacked the lack of efficiency and hard work by other magistrates. At the time I expected that the Chief Magistrate, John Murtaugh, would protest but, on the contrary, he welcomed our assistance in correcting the failings amongst his subordinates. He was a fine man.

The ousted magistrate subsequently sued the Committee, me personally, and the *Herald Tribune,* which had published our findings, for $3,000,000. This man was a branded character thereafter. The suit over the course of a few years fell of its own weight and never came to court.

Our inquiry into racketeer control of union welfare and insurance funds brought about the original investigation into the situation by several congressional committees as well as New York State and New York County investigations. On May 26, 1956, the late Robert F. Kennedy, then chief counsel for the U.S. Senate Sub-committee investigating crime, wrote to me:

> "Recently a staff member of this subcommittee secured considerable information from the New York City Anti-Crime Committee files relating to the infiltration of the racketeering element into the garment industry.
>
> "I would like you to know that we have found this information to be most valuable in conjunction with the Subcommittee's current investigation into the procurement of clothing by the military services.
>
> "May I express my sincere appreciation for your making material available, as well as for the most courteous treatment afforded by Mr. Thomas J. Donlan and Mr. Edward Jones [of our staff]."

Also around this time, U.S. Attorney Paul W. Williams' office conceded it was getting most of its information about racketeers from the New York City Anti-Crime Committee. We inspired disclosure in the press of racketeer control over distribution in the servicing of cigarette vending machines in the New York area. Similarly, we went after other industries, calling attention to collusion in the building trades, the harness racing scandals, the racketeer control of certain union welfare and insurance funds, and the "numbers rackets."

We pointed out that an apparently "innocent" bet with a bookmaker, when multiplied by the thousands who do it daily, is in fact supplying organized crime with huge resources with which to corrupt law enforcement officers, to buy immunity from punishment for all manner of offenses, to make drug addicts of our children, and generally to prostitute society.

The Committee was the first organization—long before anyone else had acted—to bring to the light of day the activities of James R. Hoffa, then a vice president of the Teamsters Union. He was the real power, although Dave Beck was its international president. This helped to precipitate the hearings held by the United States Senate Investigating Committee.

Our information in this matter was given in my annual report for 1955, which I read at our annual meeting during a luncheon in the Commodore Hotel, with much subsequent publicity. I received a telegram from Hoffa's attorneys demanding a copy of my report. I expected litigation, such as the magistrate had brought. Therefore, taking the bull by the horns I sent them three copies. No more was heard from them.

What I then said and published publicly was:

> "Over the years, the underworld in its attack on any area of industry had proceeded on the premise that he who controls the means of distribution, in effect controls the industry.
>
> "Louis 'Lepke' Buchalter, the late head of Murder, Inc., accordingly acquired substantial control in the men's garment industry in the 1930's by first getting control of the trucking companies and their employees. He thus controlled the servicing of the garment industry.
>
> "Otherwise, the efforts of the racketeers to get control of the remainder of the trucking industry in New York have not been too successful. A major barrier has been the virtual autonomy of the locals in the International Brotherhod of Teamsters, particularly in the eastern part of the United States. The result has been that here in New York a few bonafide honest labor leaders have, through the control of their locals, been able to withstand the onslaught of the racketeers and to preserve a hard core of honest trade unionism. Thus, in general, the trucking industry in this City has only to a certain extent felt the influence of the underworld.
>
> "At the present time, however, an intensive effort is being made to break down that autonomy and to gain control over the teamster locals. Regional organizations are being used to accomplish this end. The resultant centraliza-

tion of control, in the opinion of experts, will facilitate the efforts of racketeers to dominate the trucking industry in any area, provided they are able to get control of the regional office of that union.

"In a recent city-wide trucking strike in New York, the accepted spokesman of the trucking unions in this community was replaced by order of James R. Hoffa of Detroit, a Vice President of the Teamsters. Hoffa put in as spokesman a man who has been a lifelong associate of the worst gangsters in this city. The strike was settled on terms dictated by Hoffa. This is the same man whose activities in the field of union-welfare funds was the subject of disclosures by this Committee and later by a Congressional Committee. He, himself, is a friend and associate of several major figures in the ranks of gangsterdom. His activities, though well publicized, have not as yet developed in Dave Beck (president of the Teamsters) any visible will to take vigorous and forthright action.

"The rise of Hoffa to a position of prominence in a union as large and powerful as the International Brotherhood of Teamsters is due in large measure to the backing of a few nationwide trucking firms who have purposely played into his hands. Hoffa's plans for New York City, though not publicized by him, have been uncovered by your Committee's investigations.

"Any trucking firm desirous of favored treatment can easily get it by retaining one of a few select labor relations firms and by going along with suggestions as to what insurance agencies will handle the union-welfare and insurance funds.

"Certain leaders in the New York City trucking industry have already been approached with this proposition. Some of them cannot make up their minds. They are bothered by the realization that one major weapon of Hoffa's is a plan which will ultimately relegate the local trucker to a very minor status in the industry. Other leaders have decided to combine their efforts in order to fight Hoffa and his racketeer allies. These men, unlike their colleagues, realize the truth of the statement that 'You employ the racketeer on Monday—he is your partner by Wednesday—and your employer by Friday.' "

Another of our most important investigations was in connection with wire tapping and various electronic listening devices. I personally was astonished when I learned of the efficiency of these apparatae. If a small microphone could be hidden under a desk or elsewhere in a room, the listener could sit in an automobile several blocks away and overhear every word that was said.

The staff did a most excellent job and our exposition of the facts created quite a sensation. Although we did have one contretemps because one of our employees idiotically made a statement to some correspondents that District Attorney Frank Hogan had employed wire taps to further his own political ends. I was enraged and immediately apologized to the district attorney, who is one of the finest men and most distinguished public servants I have ever met. I fired the talkative employee.

My dismissal of this man provoked a dispute within the board of directors, details of which kept leaking out to the press. Finally at one meeting one of my directors proposed that at the end of the meeting nothing, but absolutely nothing, be said to the press waiting in the hall outside. This was unanimously approved by the board. A crowd of reporters assailed me as I left the Board Room; I would only reply "No Comment." This occurred on a Friday evening. Saturday morning the newspapers had the full story of what had happened in our board meeting.

Fortunately, one of our most responsible directors had overheard the director who had called for privacy tell the reporters the full details of our session, within moments after our adjournment. Some of our employees also heard him, and a few of the reporters confessed that they had gotten the story from him.

At a meeting the following Tuesday, Sloane Colt inquired how on earth this information had leaked out. I said: "I am glad you asked the question because our fellow director, Mr. X (who was seated at the table) gave it out." This man vehemently denied that he had done so. I observed that it was bad enough for him to have broken his word but that he should not add lying to his other sin.

During the committee's life considerable pressure, overt and covert, was brought to bear, not only against members of the committee and its board of directors, but in one case almost forced the National Broadcasting Company to cancel a program on labor racketeering on which we had cooperated and furnished much of the reference material.

The program was based in the main on material prepared by the committee's staff. The script pulled no punches; it pinned the label of racketeer on individuals who had earned it. It named one of the foremost racketeers in the ladies' garment industry, Ben Levine, ex-convict, ex-Lepke partner, and wealthy manufacturer. Levine, who had learned of the tenor of the program, was powerful enough to bring terrific pressure on the committee and NBC in an effort to cancel the program. He was able to call on the services of lawyers, misguided labor leaders, and businessmen. The committee would not back down.

NBC, after learning from reputable sources in the garment industry that Levine was all that the script labeled him, stood fast. Levine could not cancel the program. However, through the intensity of the pressure, he did move the moderator of the program to agree to delete his name and substitute "Mr. X." That agreement was made in good faith by a man who feared that otherwise the program would be cancelled. The program went off as scheduled despite what was regarded as one of the most concentrated efforts to spike a television program in the history of the industry. NBC and the committee were both rewarded by the enthusiasm and acclaim.

Our investigators at one point discovered that there was to be a species of international gangster conference to be held on one of the cays off the coast of Florida. A number of leading U.S. gangsters, particularly those engaged in gambling and narcotics and those associated with Cuba, were to meet with some Cuban gangsters (the heads of La Casa Marina, a famous house of prostitution in Havana), a brother of the President, and Lucky Luciano was to come over from Italy.

Our information was passed on to the Federal authorities here, but the whole conference was broken up before they could act by Batista's overthrow of the Cuban regime.

Despite the committee's splendid record over the years, it was forced to cease operations because of the utterly inadequate incoming funds. At times there was barely one month's operating revenue available.

I can boast of the committee's achievements because the most dangerous and hardest work was done by the staff. Maria used to fear for my personal safety, but I reassured her and truly felt that I was the safest risk in New York. I was the one person the gangsters would not dare attack, because accusing fingers immediately would be pointed at them.

After the committee closed shop our files were stored where no one could get at them except our manager and a trusted employee, both subject to my approval. At that time Robert Kennedy, counsel for the Senate Committee investigating organized crime, telephoned to me. I most cordially referred to the time when he and his brothers and sisters used to come to my place in Riverdale to play with my children. Despite his previous praise of the committee he brusquely thrust my remembrance aside, to demand that the committee's files be delivered to him. I politely explained that in those files, along with the facts in many cases, was much rumor and unsubstantiated material, so we could not turn them over to anyone. I said we would give him data on any particular case he was interested in. But he was adamant, he wanted all of them. He pushed so hard that finally I had to tell him in very positive terms that we would deliver only a specific file. He finally gave in and he got the file he asked for.

The New York City Anti-Crime Committee in its method of operation was unique among all the crime committees of the country. It was the only one that did not seek publicity, but instead sought to enlighten and arouse the public; so that by its power it could obtain immediate remedial action. The committee collated and kept information that it furnished to all the media, as well as to law enforcement authorities. It was the only source of such information. Moreover, it did not concern itself with the day-to-day minor malfeasance of the police and the courts. In this city, with rare exceptions, that kind of activity was adequately handled by the elected officials or the higher appointed officers, such as the Police Commissioner. Organized crime and its infiltration into the labor, business, and political life of the city composed our field. I believe sincerely that the committee's demise was an irreparable loss and the failure of business and industry and private citizens to maintain it shortsighted. The committee in its brief 5½ years life left its mark on law enforcement and set a high standard indeed for some future committee to follow.

I was disappointed but not too downcast when the committee was unable to continue its work. Its achievements were solid. It succeeded in bringing about several reforms, and, even more, in showing the need for such a citizens' group provided it is operated on the seven principles I have set forth.

4

The texture of a man's life is composed much the same way as a carpet's. In addition to the main configurations, essential but less conspicuous strands of activity, commitments of various kinds, and responsibilities run through the overall pattern. They support one's major endeavors and often reflect personal concerns of great moral import without being sensational. In recent years, such activities for me were primarily in private, voluntary associations dedicated to causes that touched on the well-being of Latin America and its relations with the United States. As was, and is, the Avenue of the Americas Association.

This group was first formed as the Sixth Avenue Association, to promote the beauty and prosperity of that thoroughfare. Surely one of its notable accomplishments was the removal of the elevated railway that disfigured the avenue and drastically retarded its progress. Property values promptly soared; assessed values rose over 230 per cent in eight years. The creation of a subway station at 57th Street, largely due to the association, similarly promoted the economic health of the avenue.

This dream of a great central thoroughfare must be credited to V. Clement Jenkins and the move was engineered through Mayor La Guardia, Grover Whalen, Robert Moses and by Farris A. Flint. The association was responsible for changing the name Sixth Avenue to Avenue of the Americas in 1945, an effort to unite all the Americas for American hemispheric security by a fuller neighborly understanding and sounder economic relations. Because of its name, I went on the association's board of directors and was named chairman of its coat of arms and inter-American committees.

Each year around Columbus Day, Day of the Americas, the association gives a dinner of over 1,200 people at one of the avenue's principal hotels, and presents awards to those judged to have played a decisive role in developing the avenue and to have been active in promoting inter-American relations.

Another group forwarding friendship between the American republics that I have been honored to belong to over the years is the Americas Foundation, established October 12, 1943, the 450th birthday of the Americas.

Laboring always without substantial funds, the foundation because of the energy and initiative of its founders has done a remarkable job. It was the catalyst in bringing into being the Inter-American Press Association, which has grown to great size and exercises a tremendous influence throughout the hemisphere, especially in defense of freedom of the press.

It played a similar role in the formation of the Inter-American Education Association. The inspiration for this group lies in the fact that most scholarships bringing students from Latin America to the

United States have been to support college work at the undergraduate or graduate levels.

When I was president of the foundation I felt that a better plan was to "catch 'em young," as I reported at the time, and teach them the fundamentals of economics. Our first step was to hold a two-day meeting for thirty private secondary school principals from the several republics, including the United States, to acquaint them with the Foundation's purposes. This was in October 1961, at the University Club in New York City. The association now has between 500 and 600 members. I am proud to be an honorary member.

The Americas Foundation through the contributions of individual members has helped finance the IAEA. In particular Messrs. Farris A. Flint, James S. Copley, Paul Mellon, Harold A. Fitzgerald, Dr. Alberto Gainza Paz, Wickliffe B. Moore, Joshua B. Powers, and James G. Stahlman have done yeoman service in benefit of the Foundation and therefore of the American republics.

At the foundation's annual dinner, given on or about the Day of the Americas in such major capitals as New York, Washington, Buenos Aires, Rio de Janeiro, Mexico City, San Diego, an award is presented to some person who pre-eminently has contributed to develop friendship and understanding between all the republics of the hemisphere. In 1957 my name was added to such dignitaries as Juan T. Trippe, Helen Keller, Dr. Nicholas Murray Butler, and Herbert Hoover among many others.

Subsequently, I served as president of the foundation for six years, to be succeeded by James S. Copley of the Copley Press.

The needs for ameliorating disagreements among the American republics are, of course, many and not always easy to sort out. Commercial disputes loom large in this area and I have recorded earlier in these pages my work at the VIIth International Conference of American States at Montevideo in forming the Inter-American Commercial Arbitration Commission that was designed to deal with such matters. The commission was organized under my chairmanship. Later, due to my absence from the United States on diplomatic missions, I was elevated to the honorary chairmanship and was replaced as active commission chairman by Tom Watson Sr. of IBM.

Tom Watson was interested in arbitration through Miss Frances Kellor, a brilliant and charming woman who, I always said, would have been chairman of the board of United States Steel or some other large corporation had she been a man. From Watson and many other important and wealthy men Miss Kellor obtained sizable contributions. But after some years and handsome assistance Tom Watson appeared to be losing interest in the subject. To revive it, and put the ideals of arbitration before the public, we decided it was necessary to give a big dinner in his honor and present him with a gold medal.

He accepted the idea, with the provision that General Eisenhower, then president of Columbia University, should be the principal speaker at the dinner along with the president of Lafayette College.

I visited Ike on Morningside Heights. At first he showed reluctance to accept. He did not want to speak, he said. Because of all the talk of his becoming President of the United States, too many people were trying to ride his coattails to glory. I told him I thought the remark was unjust, because many citizens sincerely wanted him in the White House, and after some more conversation, he agreed to speak.

After I departed the Washington scene, Miss Kellor insisted that I become president of the American Arbitration Association. Overcoming considerable reluctance, I accepted, laying down certain guiding principles for the association:

1—In labor matters the association should only arbitrate the interpretation of labor-management contracts.

2—The association should no longer be dependent for its financing on the wealthy supporters who Miss Kellor was able so skillfully to enlist in its behalf. It should increase its charges on arbitrations and make a drive for a vastly larger contributing membership.

3—The organization should take on some business executives to relieve Miss Kellor of these organizational and financial responsibilities. Martin Butler Gentry, a top executive of Freeport Sulphur Company, was made vice president and Harry Derby, a leading businessman, agreed to serve as a consultant on the Board of Directors.

I believe it is fair to say that during my time as president I was able to establish the confidence both of labor and management in the purposes of the association. We attracted numerous new members who not only supported my principles but also were important financial contributors. Nevertheless, as we were getting under way Miss Kellor revealed her unwillingness to relinquish her virtually dictatorial control of the association. She tangled badly with Gentry. My first two conditions were hardly given the time of day. Then there were some other complicating factors.

After several conversations, I took the stand that she was "Miss Arbitration" and that under no circumstances would I enter into the slightest dispute with her. Harry Derby and I resigned our positions. Despite the internal dissension, I do want to emphasize what a remarkable woman Miss Kellor was. She made an enormous contribution to the cause of arbitration in this country. Soon after our differences arose, Miss Kellor was stricken with a deadly disease and died shortly thereafter.

Noble Braden, a fine man (no relative of mine) took over and achieved much during his presidency. He was succeeded by Paul Herzog Jr., a good friend, and finally by Donald Strauss, who has completely reorganized the American Arbitration Association with astonishing efficiency and success. As a former president I remain on the executive committee.

There is sufficient evidence, to my mind, that the Inter-American Commercial Arbitration Commission could, and should, play a significant role in settling commercial disputes between the different republics. It requires adequate moral and financial support. This it is now receiving, thanks to Donald Strauss, ably abetted by Jay Parkinson, Chairman of the Anaconda Company and Mr. Martinez de Hoz of Argentina. I am proud to have been associated with IACAC.

In 1967 it was evident that a small but influential State Department clique had plans to give up United States control of the Panama Canal. Charles Edison, former Secretary of Navy and Governor of New Jersey and myself organized the American Emergency Committee on the Panama Canal to block this blatant giveaway, which was incorporated in three draft treaties. The Johnson Administration had hoped to rush the treaties through the Senate before the American public had time to notice what was happening, much less to protest.

A little background; the Panamanians have repeatedly come to the State Department asking for amplifications and many other favors in connection with the treaties we have made with them. I have related earlier how when I was Assistant Secretary of State they appealed to me and I absolutely refused to discuss the matter with them. My reason was that the last time we had acceded to their requests Sumner Welles attached a memorandum to our copy of the treaty stating that the Panamanian foreign minister and ambassador had agreed the new treaty fully met every possible request they might ever make. They therefore renounced further changes.

The committee received heartening moral and financial support from hundreds of thousands of our fellow citizens who endorsed our petition to the Congress. The proposed treaties were subsequently shelved.

No one can say, of course, if these treaties or variations thereof may be revived in the future. The danger always will exist, and so the committee, which was organized as an ad hoc emergency group, has been merged with the Citizens Committee for a Free Cuba, of which

I am chairman. Both Mr. Edison and I felt that this group could carry out the objectives of our temporary committee within its broad program.

5

Many of my activities following my departure from government service in 1947 were the product of my devotion to the free enterprise system and my inalterable hostility to any and all intents or endeavors to subvert it. Chief among these, to be sure, is the Communist conspiracy. But I also include in this category socialism and any and all efforts to dilute the national integrity of the United States.

In this regard I recall the controversy I willingly became involved in over the publication of an iniquitous book called *The Shark and the Sardines* in 1961. It was written by a former president of Guatemala, Dr. Juan Jose Arevalo. It was the worst kind of pro-Communist, anti-U.S.A. propaganda, translated by a woman who was subsequently arrested in Guatemala carrying Communist literature and who admitted to having been a $1,000-a-month employee of the Cuban Communist government.

The book was promoted in a number of full page advertisements (as Communist as the book itself) in *The New York Times,* the *Washington Post,* and other papers. Together with Henry Balgooyen, vice president of the American and Foreign Power Company, and John Moore, vice president of W. R. Grace and Company and now Ambassador to Ireland, a number of us protested to *The New York Times* for their accepting an ad for this calumnious piece of trash. Our protest did no good. The *Times* alleged that to have interfered with the advertisements would have violated freedom of the press. I also protested to the Council on Foreign Relations for promoting the book in its publication *Foreign Affairs.* My response there was similarly without real substance.

What caused our astonishment as much as anything was the credence given this book in the light of its publisher's previous performance. Lyle Stuart (the publisher) was a specialist at that time in anti-Catholic, pro-Communist, and pornographic literature. Such titles as *Diary of a Nymph, Crime and the Catholic Church, Pleasure Was My Business, Sex Without Guilt,* and *Strange Lovers* would not have encouraged me to take anything from Lyle Stuart very seriously. His whole operation was suspect.

This incident alone demonstrates why I have so often in conversation facetiously referred to *The New York Times* as the "Mid-Town Daily Worker" and/or the "New York Tass."

Quite a few of my anxieties about the directions the country was taking converged on the island of Cuba, particularly since its domination by the Castro-Communist dictatorship. I became more personally implicated in the Cuba situation in April 1963 in response to a call from Freedom House for a group of qualified Americans to investigate the problem of Cuba. This group met at Ardsley-on-Hudson for three days, studied all aspects of Cuba, and concluded that the lodgement of Soviet power in the Western hemisphere posed a direct threat to the security of the United States. From this three-day meeting emerged the U.S. Citizens Committee for a Free Cuba that, it was agreed, would research and publish regularly a newsletter and, less frequently, special studies on the Cuba problem.

The committee was fortunate to obtain the services of Paul D. Bethel as executive director. Paul is an experienced newsman and a former Foreign Service officer with experience in Germany, the Far East, and Latin America over a period of eleven years. His last post was in our Havana embassy, as press attaché. The years he served there (1958 until the break in relations with Cuba on Jan. 3, 1961) I always felt specially qualified him. He recently published an authoritative book, *The Losers,* on this whole situation. It is "must" reading for anyone wanting to know the complete story.

A little later, I took over as chairman of the committee. From this time on I spoke on Latin American affairs not only as former ambassador, former assistant secretary of state, and a consultant to many firms as a Latin American expert, but as chairman of a committee of prominent American citizens. My own extensive personal sources of information were materially supplemented by those of Paul Bethel. Paul, responsible for operating the committee's offices in Washington, D.C., and Miami, has a continuous flow of facts coming to him from sources in Cuba, constant radio monitoring of the island, and several other means to acquire Cuban intelligence. More importantly, he has excellent sources to judge the extent Communist subversion is being exported to Latin America and other areas of the world from Cuba.

Even before the Citizens Committee was formally established, Paul was issuing his own newsletter, which was the basis for the committee's monthly publication, *Latin American Report.* On January 30, 1962 at the Rotary International Conference in Bermuda, I announced that the Soviets had installed missile pads and submarine pens in Cuba. Paul also had found incontrovertible evidence that Soviet troops and missiles were in Cuba. This was confirmed on August 7 in a radio interview conducted by Dr. Salvador Lew, a colleague of Paul. Doctor Lew produced an eyewitness to Soviet troops and missiles moving around the Province of Matanzas in the early morning hours under cover of darkness.

These findings were later reconfirmed by Kenneth B. Keating, then senator from New York, who made the same declarations as Paul and I. The reports were officially and publicly denied by the Administration; only at a later date were they acknowledged to be true.

Our *Latin American Report* goes to every member of the House and Senate and to some 3,000 schools, libraries, news media, etc. throughout the country. In addition, it is sent to other thousands of individual contributors both here and abroad. It has played an important role in educating the American people, appearing in lead editorials in major newspapers and in the *Congressional Record.*

Many times Paul and his competent staff have brought out the facts about the Tricontinental Conference, the Latin American Solidarity Conference, and the purpose of their formation: namely, to lodge the tentacles of subversion in Latin America and even in the United States. The Citizens Committee was the first to link "black power" groups in the U.S. with Russian-Cuban subversion and to prove that a major Communist target was the U.S. Commonwealth of Puerto Rico. This has provided proof positive that the premise on which the committee was formed—that Cuba posed a direct security threat to the United States—was indeed sound.

The United States, from 1961 to 1968, has created a sanctuary for the Communist conspiracy to spread its guerrillas, espionage net, and propaganda barrage throughout the hemisphere. It is an irrefutable fact that the Kennedy Administration was responsible for the steady encroachment of Communism on the bodies politic of Latin America and for gratuitously destroying the Monroe Doctrine.

I feel a sense of personal betrayal in the way our government facilitated the advent of Castro's rule in Cuba. After I retired from the State Department I made several visits to Cuba and was active in various business negotiations with the government there. Batista and I made up our differences, in fact so thoroughly that he broke all precedent by having me to luncheon with him and several key aides. I was astonished, for when he had again seized power in his 1952 coup I said in a widely circulated interview that Batista could make a great name for himself only if he remembered that he had been in his first term Cuba's youngest president, that he had all the wealth anyone could desire, and that an honest government under him would raise him above all Cuban presidents and make him a hero to his country. Of course, he went in the opposite direction.

Nevertheless, to choose Batista over Castro was no difficult decision to make so far as I was concerned. In the middle of 1957, about 18 months before Castro descended from his hideout in the hills, I wrote and spoke much against United States policies toward Castro and Cuba. My argument was that should our government continue on its present course we would surely bring "Castro, chaos, and Communism" to Cuba.

On October 4, 1957 I was discussing United States policy with Terry Sanders, head of the South American Division of the State Department. We had refused to sell Batista any arms, and had even refused to ship a large order of arms bought and paid for by Batista's government at the behest of our Military, Naval, and Air Missions and a smaller shipment of anti-riot and police weapons bought and paid for by Batista on his own. Reminding Terry that my dealings with Batista when I was ambassador in Cuba demonstrated I had no bias in his favor, I said our denial of arms to Batista would inevitably become public knowledge and undermine Batista's position. Particularly would this happen, as simultaneously we were permitting shipments of arms clandestinely to Castro in the hills. It was perfectly clear to me that as these facts became known to the Cuban public, they would be construed to mean the United States was backing Castro and seeking Batista's downfall.

Terry Sanders advised me that he had conveyed my views to Secretary of State John Foster Dulles. One month later, early in November, Dulles gave me his answer in a press conference, during which he said, "There is no danger of Communism in Latin America."

Do I need to say that my continuous battle against the Cuban Communist dictatorship has won me the everlasting enmity of the Communists including Castro. Recently I used train rather than plane when travelling to and from Palm Beach, out of a very realistic fear that my plane would be seized by hijackers and diverted to Havana. This is not a bad dream. On a trip to Colombia in 1962 I had planned to fly Avianca. And would have done so had not two good and well-informed Cuban friends warned me that underground information had my flight due for hijacking so that Castro could get me.

After some hesitation, I cancelled the flight. If the Communists were able to lay hands on me, that would be my end for Washington does little anymore to defend an American citizen. The days of Teddy Roosevelt's ultimatum demanding Perdicaris (who only had his first papers) alive or Raisuli dead within 24 hours have gone forever, I fear, considering the government's handling of the Pueblo seizure.

The cancellation was apparently wise. On the day of my scheduled flight a plane to Guantanamo was forced down. I must confess that it was good to learn that my activities against Communism were taken seriously by the enemy.

My opposition to Communism, in this hemisphere or anywhere else on the globe, runs just a little bit ahead of my opposition to the mismanagement of American resources, chiefly, I would say, in the distribution of our foreign aid.

Earlier in these memoirs I mentioned some of the crazy schemes the United States public was forced to support. In this group can be found the forerunner to the whole foreign aid program that, incidentally, was given tremendous impetus by the Marshall Plan for European recovery.

In this connection, the last time I testified as assistant secretary of state before the House Appropriations Committee on aid to Latin America, I supported a program of five million dollars for the entire hemisphere. Please note: millions not billions. I said I was doing this because we had outstanding commitments made by my predecessor in this amount but I could assure the committee members this sum would be reduced to three million the following year and later to zero if I still were assistant secretary of state. If the Latinos would go to work as the West Germans and the Japanese did after World War II they could pull themselves out of their economic doldrums.

Let me say unequivocally that I did not and I do not oppose all foreign aid. I am vehemently against the extravagance, inefficiency, false idealism, and, not too seldom, the corruption its vast sums have generated. Accordingly, I continued fighting this battle after leaving the State Department, working with several gentlemen of like mind. We formed the Citizens Committee on Foreign Aid.

I am on record in these pages for having a strong distaste for fund-raising. Therefore I worked to obtain the best man I could think of to take over this duty. Finally we succeeded in getting Walter Harnischfeger, head of the Harnischfeger Corporation. His company for years has done a worldwide as well as national business in heavy machinery, and has prospered greatly. Walter himself has travelled all over the face of the globe, and continues to do so. He is courageous, forceful, and informed.

The committee was organized with Walter as chairman and assisted by General Bonner Fellers and such equally informed gentlemen as Robert E. Pabst, Dr. Elgin Groseclose, Clarence Manion, Charles Edison, J. Howard Pew, A. G. Heinsohn Jr., and T. Coleman Andrews.

Through the years I have appeared several times as a witness before both the Senate and House Committees, as have most of my associates. Messrs. Harnischfeger, Fellers, and some of the others have rendered better service than I. This past year our efforts met with substantial success in getting a reduction in the appropriations for foreign aid.

My testimony at Congressional hearings was not always popular. In 1958 I appeared before the Senate Appropriations Committee and tackled the International Cooperation Administration for its actions involving properties confiscated by the then Marxist Bolivian government. The properties, gold placers, belonged to the Aramayo Company and the ICA had offered investment guarantees as an inducement for an American company to take over the operation of the properties. I charged that in doing so the United States government became what was tantamount to being the receiver of stolen goods. Furthermore, I felt it was shameful for the United States to lend any support whatever to a dictatorial regime guilty of murder and various kinds of terrorism.

A letter from a deputy director of ICA, L. J. Saccio, challenged my testimony in terms both impertinent and ill-informed. I contested his assertions about the non-Communist quality of the Bolivian regime and the property expropriation with facts. I said that the evidence showed the property was confiscated, not nationalized, and added, in my reply, "To my mind, confiscation without due process of law for a dominating public purpose, and without adequate effective and prompt compensation, is stealing." Mr. Saccio had no response to my presentation.

My preference for improving the economies of underdeveloped countries has been and is for private investment over huge infusions of foreign aid. I put this conviction into a telegram to President John F. Kennedy in 1961. It concisely states my central views in the matter. Part of that telegram's text follows:

> "Not only foreign investors but the nationals in other American republics have become so alarmed that they are withdrawing billions of dollars of their investments whenever possible and refusing to make new ones due to their fears of:

> "1—Precedents set by confiscations of private properties by Bolivian Marxist and Cuban Communist governments, not to mention numerous indirect expropriations elsewhere.
>
> "2—Communist infiltrations, subversions, and resulting political timidity and instability throughout the hemisphere.
>
> "3—Apparently permanent entrenchment of Communist regime in Cuba.
>
> "4—Failure by U.S. government during recent years effectively to protect legitimate rights and interests of many of its citizens who have been operating or have had investments abroad.
>
> "5—Rapidly increasing domination of socialistic principles and programs in Washington.
>
> "Foreign aid and Alliance for Progress never more than fractionally can replace these huge investments, now either running for cover or which will not be made until confidence is restored."

I had concluded my letter to Mr. Saccio with these words: "I urge that you [ICA] take a stand in defense of private property rights and stop encouraging and financially supporting Socialist and Communist governments." My distaste for these debasing methods of interfering in the affairs of a nation's citizens and its economic life, always a constant in my own philosophy, brought me into sharp conflict with my alma mater Yale. In the middle 1950s I felt obliged to cease my contributions to the Yale Alumni Fund, which I had been accustomed to make regularly over the 43 years since leaving the university.

The matter at issue for me was the rapid drift towards the endorsement of various forms of socialism and other collectivist tyrannies by Yale. The endorsement appeared in the courses taught, in public statements and attitudes by Yale faculty members, and in the mounting professorial appointments of teachers noted for their leftist philosophies. Later on, my profound disappointment with Yale was fed by the university's opposition to a loyalty oath from students supported by Federal (that is to say taxpayers') funds. I was convinced, as I wrote in 1957 to Edward N. Allen, the former lieutenant governor of Connecticut and my class agent, that Yale should "take a public and forceful attitude against socialism and collectivism . . . teach the fundamental principles of economics and constitutional representative government laid down for us by the Founding Fathers

. . . rid itself of the left-wing professors and instructors." Until it did these things I could not see that it deserved being called a great university—or my financial support.

Contrary to what was widely believed at the time, I was not advocating suppression of dissenting views at Yale or any kind of dogmatized teaching. I refined my position in a 1958 letter to Ned Allen. "I am anxious to have the facts," I said, "but I mean the *facts,* about Communism and socialism taught in our schools and at Yale. But I object to these ideologies being taught as ideals to be implanted in the United States."

Furthermore, I wrote, "You say that you believe we should not 'hamstring what our college professors should say, believe, or teach, and (that) to insist that they limit their teaching and preaching only to what we would ourselves believe they should say would very quickly spell the end of all our freedoms.' Here I take issue with you, because the young, flexible, absorbent minds of undergraduates instinctively respect their elders, and accept what their professors teach as true. Hence, grievous harm can result to our youth and the nation when the Rostows and scores of other Leftists teach socialism or communism, and ignore or preach against the noble, tried and proven principles laid down by the Founding Fathers."

I was against loading the scales by not teaching all sides of a question. I still am. Students were not being exposed to a variety of doctrines and allowed to choose. They were being indoctrinated. This is not education. It is a form of brainwashing and I could not in conscience support it by contributing to the institution practicing such tactics.

My position in the matter of loyalty oaths was similar. As recently as 1967, after more than ten years of opposition, I wrote to Ned Allen and said "that it is disgraceful for Yale University not to insist on a loyalty oath for those students who are being supported by taxpayer's money in getting their education, particularly when all of the boys who have and are giving their everything for the country are proud to take the loyalty oath . . ." Yale's decision to stand by while its faculty members visited Hanoi and gave comfort to our enemies and while its chaplain advocated draft card burning and insurrection did nothing to change my mind.

This long and, to me, unpleasant episode terminated with correspondence between Yale President Kingman Brewster and me. I believe the last paragraphs from my final letter to Doctor Brewster are worth quoting here:

"In order effectively to serve a free society, it first must be preserved. As an integral part of this essential objective, our students must be protected by the universities, insofar as possible, not only from incitation to anti-U.S. activities and false preachings, but also from puerile sentimentalisms, apathy, and ignorance which now abound on all sides.

"As you will see from the foregoing, it is my firm belief that a great university such as Yale must not countenance the type of 'Trojan Horse' infiltrations I have referred to [represented by left wing faculty members] and which have caused me to stop my contributions to the Alumni Fund."

6

It has been convenient for many of my enemies to try to tarnish my character by treating my opposition to Communism as some kind of abnormality, a defect of judgment that blinded me to other styles in political aberration. I can only say that my loathing for tyrannies of the right is no less than that for leftist tyrannies. I cherish individual liberty and individual initiative and find detestable any and all force that interferes with them.

How clearly this was known to dictators other than Communist is shown in earlier portions of this memoir, in connection with my public hostility to the regimes of Peron in Argentina and Trujillo in the Dominican Republic. In fact Trujillo, whose power had a dreadful longevity, intruded his hatred of me into my years of retirement and created several interesting episodes.

On August 25, 1953, the dictator Trujillo had a law passed (no. 3643) by his puppet Senate and Chamber of Deputies authorizing the erection of two plaques attacking international Communism, its organization, and the infamous and depraved conspiracy conducted by its despicable agents. It was evidently a move designed to curry favor among Latin American republics likely to be sympathetic with the anti-Communist sentiments who were not sympathetic to Trujillo and his bandit regime.

Among the names memorialized on these plaques as Communist agents were Ellis Briggs, George Butler (formerly ambassador in the Dominican Republic and at the time a State Department officer), and myself, along with Romulo Betancourt, Ramon Grau San Martin, Juan Jose Arevalo, and Gustavo Doran.

The motivation was evident. Trujillo had never gotten over my action in respect of him when I was assistant secretary of state, particularly when I stood against giving him the enormous quantity of arms he had requested from the U.S. government.

I immediately protested the Trujillo slander to Secretary of State Dulles. The names of Briggs and Butler were removed from the list because they were U.S. government employees, and Doran's because he was with the United Nations. My name remained. I intensified my objections and finally my name, too, was deleted.

The delay over my name was explained to me by Bob Woodward, who at the time was deputy assistant secretary of state for American republic affairs. When Dulles first instructed our ambassador in Ciudad Trujillo to make representations protesting the Dominican action, according to Woodward, our ambassador there professed reluctance to do so because: "He was just becoming friendly with Trujillo." I later came to know the ambassador in question and he denies taking the stand Woodward recounted to me. In any case, the matter was adjusted.

This was not my only encounter with the dictator. In the mid 50s Ken Redmond, president of United Fruit Company, one of the firms retaining me as consultant, asked Maria and me to accompany him and his wife on a trip through the Caribbean, visiting Panama, Costa Rica, and the port of Salvador on the north coast of the Dominican Republic.

We readily accepted. The company had a number of new ships, constructed in Germany, with most comfortable accommodations of two big double staterooms and two single staterooms, with a bar, lounge, and aft deck. It was the equivalent of sailing a huge private yacht and we had a most enjoyable trip.

About two days out from Salvador, the United Fruit Company manager in the Dominican Republic shot us a hysterical cable stating his fears of what might happen upon my arrival in the republic. He suggested I cable the "Benefactor," the Dominican ambassador in Washington, and to the U.S. ambassador in Ciudad Trujillo to make amends for Trujillo's and my differences in the past.

I willingly agreed to telegraph Trujillo himself and our ambassador, but I would not telegraph the Dominican representative in Washington. Accordingly I sent word to our ambassador in Ciudad Trujillo that I was going to visit the republic and since I would not be travelling to the capital I was paying my respects by wire.

To Trujillo I telegraphed declaring my great admiration for the beauties of the island, its great natural wealth, its fine people, and that I further understood that there had been many public works erected, but nary a word otherwise.

Everybody was extremely nervous at the time of my arrival, but the Governor of the Province came down specially to welcome me to the Republic in the name of the "Benefactor." I had no trouble or embarrassment while there. But I was shocked at a big dinner party that was given for Ken Redmond and myself when the United Fruit manager made a speech of adulation in the most shameful fashion for Trujillo.

Present at the dinner was a leading banana grower who sold his crop to the company. After the dinner, as we were returning to the boat, this man, way out in the middle of a long pier, began to tell me of the outrageous deeds committed by Trujillo. His wife went into panic telling him for God's sake to shut up as someone might hear him. There was not a chance in the world of anyone hearing him, but she was near hysteria.

The "Benefactor" never ceased his attempts to reinstate himself in my favor, though I was long out of government service. In late 1958 Trujillo's jovial and simpatico ambassador in the United Nations, called on me in person, to present an invitation to Maria and myself to visit the Dominican Republic. We would be the President's guests from the time we left New York until our return. I was to indicate how long we would stay. We would occupy the suite de luxe in the hotel or, if I preferred, a private home. I should indicate our leisure preferences: golf, fishing, tennis, riding, the choices were ours to name. It was a most open-handed and cordial invitation.

I deferred giving an answer for a long time on one excuse or another. Then the "Benefactor" was shot and killed, relieving us of what may have proved to be an unwelcome decision in any case.

Subsequently President Beranguer invited my new wife and myself to attend his inauguration as his guest. This, due to other commitments, I was unable to accept.

However, in the latter part of April and early May 1967 I did accept an invitation from President Somoza of Nicaragua for his inauguration. He and his wife Hope, a beautiful and attractive woman, had been guests at our home in New York a couple of times as well as at the Metropolitan Club. The board of the club voted him honorary membership and I presented the gold card to him during my stay in Managua, where Mrs. Braden and I could not have been treated more royally.

It is perhaps pertinent to recall that Tacho Somoza (father of the president, who is known as Tachito) was really the man who financed and equipped Colonel Castillo Armas so that he was able to overthrow the Communist regime of Arbenz in Guatemala.

Castillo Armas, even with Somoza's help, was having a tough time of it until a group of Latin American ambassadors called on the then Under Secretary of State General Bedell Smith to point out the dangers of the situation. They stated that if Arbenz and the Communists won out the malignancy would spread throughout Central America, and it was important that the U.S.A. give its assistance through Tacho. Bedell Smith was persuaded and arms were sent to Somoza. The Communists were driven out of Guatemala, at least for the time being.

In 1959 I was invited to deliver three lectures at the University of Chile. Accordingly we embarked for that country looking forward with much anticipation to seeing Maria's family and our many old friends. However, when we arrived in the port of Antofagasta in northern Chile, I received word from my friends in Santiago that the Communists were planning a demonstration against me. Amongst other things they proposed to picket our ship when it arrived in Valparaiso.

In order to avoid a disagreeable incident Maria and I hastily disembarked. My original plan was to return north from Santiago to visit the properties of the Chile Exploration Co., Andes Copper Mining Co., both controlled by Anaconda, and incidentally the important nitrate fields. Instead, we made these visits during this first week in the north, taking the next ship to Valparaiso.

The Communists appeared pretty ridiculous as they proceeded with their plans for picketing my arrival on the first ship. They released streams of propaganda stating that I was sent to Chile to control the Interamerican Foreign Minister's Conference scheduled to open there shortly. They declared that disguised as a tourist I actually was going to be the corner stone of the conference. Their other charges were equally nonsensical. I had (they said) forced down the price of sugar while I was Ambassador to Cuba; in Argentina I almost brought on a revolution, and 150,000 persons there had asked for my departure; I was responsible for troubles in Bolivia; and at the behest of the United Fruit Company I had overthrown President Jacobo Arbenz of Guatemala.

The anti-Communist public and press ridiculed the Communists for all of their efforts, when no Braden showed up on the boat. They had not had the sense to find out what had happened to me.

When I did arrive on the second boat, there were no demonstrations. I thought there might be some at the university when I gave the first of my three lectures, but everything there was completely peaceful, although the gallery usually occupied by students was largely empty. A student leader approached me after the first lecture to say that he and a few others had found it interesting. He assured me that there would be full attendance at the two subsequent lectures. This was precisely what happened, and my remarks were loudly applauded by the students as well as by all of the others attending.

Also I received most favorable press comment, the Communist newspapers remaining silent. Shortly thereafter I was asked to give another lecture at the University of Concepción, which went off equally well. My comments on the advantages of private property and enterprise failed to impress, as proved by the subsequent outrageous seizure of majority holdings of U.S. copper companies and even some Chilean corporations in 1969. They will ruin the Chilean economy and impoverish the nation—except for U.S. grants and loans, direct or indirect.

Curiously enough Andre Malraux, French Minister of Culture, who had himself been a Communist in his youth, gave a lecture two weeks later in the same University of Chile and had a disagreeable time of it with hissing, catcalls, and booing.

7

After our return to New York from Chile Maria developed a heart condition that in January 1960 resulted in a serious coronary. She was hospitalized for five weeks and only recovered at all because of her great courage and willpower. In early 1961 she had a complete and most distressing stroke, paralyzing her entire right side and adversely affecting her speech. Despite every precaution and the best medical assistance she finally passed away in May 1962.

Needless to say, I was completely desolated and only was able for many months to keep going with anti-depression and sleeping pills. I prayed God to take me too.

But the Lord in his wisdom brought me my second wife, with whom I fell in love the moment I saw her. She was Mrs. Verbena Hebbard, a charming and beautiful lady a few years younger than I. I met her due to the kindness and hospitality of my friends the Clyde Weeds and Richard Wests, and immediately proceeded to pay court to her, which soon culminated in our engagement and marriage on May 29, 1964.

For one man to have had two such wonderful wives is a miracle indeed. I thank God for His extraordinary blessing.

Verbena and I for our honeymoon took a trip around South

America. I felt as Mrs. Braden she should know that part of the world. Moreover I wanted all my friends in Latin America to know what a charming wife I had acquired.

Verbena similarly several times has taken me to California, where I have become very attached to her many friends and to Beverly Hills, her former home.

Chapter XXXIV

IT would be totally unlike me to draw these memoirs to a close without distilling some conclusions from them. Necessarily, these conclusions derive primarily from my years of public service. I have never felt that I knew everything as I began each new phase of my career. Observation was imperative to me. And I gave much thought to what I observed. My analyses often found our government wanting, but never so seriously that errors could not be corrected in time. I offer the following remarks in the spirit of timely correction, hoping there is still time for us to be wise and practical and, above all, moral.

When I was appointed Ambassador in the Chaco Peace Conference I found there was no system for briefing new Ambassadors. I had to have files located and produced, and as I went through them I gleaned further hints as to what I should look into. For a couple of weeks of long days and late nights I instructed myself on the background and the negotiations to date in the Peace Conference that had been carried on by my predecessor Ambassador Hugh Gibson.

As a result, in one of the early sessions in Buenos Aires even Saavedra Lamas complimented me on my intimate knowledge of everything that had transpired. I was able to discuss and even argue competently with the two delegations from Bolivia and Paraguay.

I followed the same procedure before going to Colombia, although the State Department was uninformed on SCADTA, the Nazi dominated airline.

I had greater difficulties concerning the White mission in my preparations for Cuba.

By the time I went to Argentina I found obstacles to having the files broken out; they simply could not be found. This was particularly due to the growth of the State Department and partly to plain inefficiency.

Similarly in each of my posts I insisted on travelling all over the country where I was accredited. Even so I never felt that I had everything completely under control until I had been in the country a couple of years; and this despite my being bilingual in Spanish.

The usual procedure had been for an ambassador-designate to spend a couple of weeks in so-called consultations in Washington, but this period largely consisted of being entertained by the ambassador of the country to which he was being accredited and by others, with very little time spent in the Department.

As Assistant Secretary of State I inaugurated a new system, which I believe has endured to this day.

I had the ambassador-designate spend several days going over existing problems and files with the desk man for the country to which he was going. Then he would move up to the chief of the area division, then to the deputy director of the office and finally to the director of the Office of American Republics Affairs. At the end I would have the new Ambassador in for a briefing on what our policies were to be. During these conversations I would insist on the new ambassador following my procedure of travelling over the country, visiting the leading industries and getting acquainted with all walks of life.

There are many varieties of such adequate preparation. I learned that before an important international conference there should be fairly definitive agreement among the principals on what was to be done at the forthcoming conference. This meeting of the minds could go as far as agreeing upon drafts of the various treaties, conventions, and resolutions on the agenda. To take part in a conference with a total lack of understanding—as in the case of the Vietnam peace negotiations in Paris—is foolhardy.

Too often delegates have to depend upon instructions drafted in the Department that might or might not coincide with the views of the other nations represented. This can make matters very difficult for a delegate appointed from outside the Department and Foreign Service, who would feel impelled to follow such instructions to the very letter, thus losing valuable flexibility, such as I had in the VIIth International Conference of American States and other conferences: For instance, in respect of the definition of an immigrant, and several other topics recited earlier in this book, and on which I had the advantage of long experience in Latin America.

Also the chairman of each delegation should be the absolute boss of the delegation, and not be subject to embarrassment through interference from other members, as can readily happen if authority is not clearly defined.

Delegations should have proper representation expenses so that they can entertain at least on an equal scale with the others present. Our delegates, for example, at the VIIth International Conference of

American States were limited to half a bottle of wine a day for their guests and themselves.

If at all possible, the delegates should know the language in which speeches and debate will be carried on.

I grew up with Spanish as a second language; I always was sorry for the official who did not enjoy this advantage. In a Montevideo conference (Chapter XVII) I overheard a delegate of one of the smaller republics, whom everybody thought would vote against our proposal, in a low voice emphasize in Spanish to the man sitting next to him a point that he regarded of utmost importance to his country. It was a point to which we had no objection. When I next spoke I incorporated the idea with praise into my words and so gained the vote without even a need for discussion.

Far beyond the diplomatic field, especially in Latin America, it is important to be able to introduce a humorous note into whatever one is saying. Even a risqué story, although it may be as old as the hills in the United States, can be translated into Spanish or Portuguese and make a hit. It is like telling a risqué story in the presence of a lady; if one uses the proper language and approach, it is quite surprising how far one can go.

The other countries of this hemisphere would like to look up to the United States with respect, and there is no real reason they should not. But in late years we have only given them bad examples. It is our blundering and shilly shallying, our inflation, extravagance, and other errors that have been emulated by the other Republics.

The United States government frequently has been motivated by weak sentimentalism and unwillingness to take a firm stand. The most outrageous example of this was our handling of the Communist seizure of Cuba.

Another aspect of this same problem is the fear of criticism. President Johnson once met this fear head on when he courageously sent our armed forces into the Dominican Republic when the Communists were trying to take over that country. I congratulated him but warned him that the very people in Latin America who might publicly criticize his action, actually in their hearts and privately in conversation would be enthusiastic for it. In other words, we must stand on principle, and if we are right go full steam ahead and to hell with the torpedoes.

This failure on our part has been one of the difficulties vis-à-vis the Russians.

In this connection it is interesting to note that Karl Marx (of all people!) when warning Europe against Russian expansionism said:

"Russia's diplomatic game consisted 'of doing nothing, and creating for others a situation hard to endure which made them finally inclined to compromise,' the while they exploited fear in the outside world." The Soviets certainly learned their lesson from the czars.

Of late years it has become a custom to send the Secretary of State gallivanting all over the earth to attend conferences. Even the President has been compelled to do far too much travelling.

We should have an ambassador on the ground in any given country who under the President's policies and the broad instructions of the Secretary of State can handle any important matters in accordance with our official policy. If he is unable to do so then he should be fired and replaced by someone who can. Too frequently the Department has attempted from a distance to spell out minutely what the ambassador should say or write in representing the U.S. to the host-nation's Foreign Office, dangerously limiting his maneuverability.

The Secretary of State and the President, if they go abroad, have to endure a long and tiring air trip, frequently arriving exhausted, and have little if any immediate knowledge of the Chief of State, Foreign Minister, and other officials with whom they may have to deal. They are at once at a disadvantage; again there may be a language barrier. Then within a few days they are supposed to settle a whole series of important matters. The consequent rush breeds further confusion.

As an old friend of mine used to say, "It is always good to have a bad partner at home." This cannot be done when the Secretary of State, and still more the President, are doing the negotiating.

Let me explain; time and again in the process of negotiating as ambassador I have held out declaring that I knew the Foreign Minister's proposals were unacceptable to the State Department. Then I would use the Secretary of State as the "bad partner," later the President, and finally the Congress. In other words, having gained everything possible speaking as Ambassador, I would use these further obstacles to advance our position to the maximum. Occasionally I would telegraph to the Department requesting them to send a cable (which I could show) back to me with some further specific conditions that I deemed desirable.

I might add that the same procedure applies to many businesses operating abroad. The chairman of the Board or the president will fly off to carry on discussions that might better be left to the manager on the job; and as I have said before, either have a good manager or fire him.

One of the shibboleths promoted by Woodrow Wilson, which had a great sentimental and popular appeal to the uninformed, was "Open covenants openly arrived at." This is totally wrong. Our open diplomacy should consist of treaties and conventions secretly arrived at but then thrown open to confirmation by the Senate and public discussion, so that if they are deemed unsatisfactory they will not be confirmed and will thus be inoperative.

In speaking of the State Department as a witness before Congressional committees and otherwise I have often referred to an anonymous "THEY." Particularly when I served as Assistant Secretary of State, "THEY" were in the wings on the Washington scene and State Department, pulling wires, influencing policy and its execution, preventing action on things they were against, and promoting causes that were not official U.S. policy.

Often they are initiated and guided by some one or more persons down the line, and other than their duly elected or appointed superiors.

It is these unidentifiable "THEYs" that the Communists have utilized so often and so effectively.

After leaving the State Department I testified for the Senate Internal Security Subcommittee that in my opinion, while in such a large body of employees as the State Department's there must be some bad apples in the barrel, there were relatively few Communists. I felt, however, that these few located themselves in strategic positions—just as Alger Hiss and Harry White had, where they could exercise their influence on a myriad of people, such as misguided but well intentioned idealists, plain sentimentalists, some Socialists, and even a few Marxists who were opposed to the Soviet on the grounds that the Kremlin had abandoned real Marxism.

In some ways the Socialists and misguided idealists, while not advocating violence, were as dangerous as the Communists because of their goal to socialize the world under a single centralized government, using the United Nations to this end. In other words, one global entity operating under the international socialistic system. Their loyalties were to this objective and not to the United States. These people likewise have infiltrated educational institutions, the press, radio, TV, and even some Churches. Thus they can bring down what purports to be the wrath of public opinion on any official opposing their connivings.

It is these people who seriously have advocated that the United States reduce its military potency to a level equal to that of the Soviets. Their vain hope is to entice the Soviets to abandon their ambitions for a world hegemony, which actually would adhere to all

Communist policy and procedure. These same people, amongst many other things, have been responsible in a considerable measure for our extravagant, excessive, and even corrupt foreign aid.

"THEY" are destroying U.S. foreign policy. "THEY" make it necessary for our Government to tax the American people to the very limit of toleration. In other words "THEY" constitute an international conspiracy almost rivaling the Communists in danger to the survival of the United States.

The ignorance of this amorphous group is really astonishing, since history proves that to become workable at all Socialism in the end must resort to a dictatorial government made effective only through force—i.e., some form of totalitarianism, whether it be Nazism, Fascism, Falangism, the "New Left" or some like ideology. Curiously enough, "THEY" never seem to recognize their top position on the list for extermination if, as, and when the Communists take over.

I remember a few years ago speaking with a foreign equivalent of our "THEY," a former President of a Central American Republic. He chided me for my ultra-conservative opposition to the Communists. I replied: "Don't you realize that when the Communists take over you will be one of the first—long before me—to be bumped off?" He blanched because in his heart he knew I was right.

It is also important, I have always felt, for our diplomacy in regard to existing dictatorships and other disreputable governments to be conducted more realistically than is usually the case. We are often cordial and helpful to the wrong governments. I reported to the State Department on April 5, 1945, in the following words on this subject:

> ". . . we must not ignore what, as I have frequently reported, may prove in the post-war era to be the most dangerous and insidious threat of all to the American mode of life and to democracy—Communism. And it is well to bear in mind that the laws of action and reaction cause the dictators of every ilk to prepare the most fertile soil for that disruptive ideology.
>
> ". . . since it may well be that in the post-war era, after we have laid down our military arms used in defense of democracy, we will be confronted with an even more dangerous attack, which our enemies may well camouflage in the spurious robes of a false democracy.
>
> "Therefore, even implicitly to evidence an apparent approval of the dictators may not only entrench them but may serve to spread the system elsewhere and so discourage

> the people as to induce the acceptance of 'anything for a change,' be it Nazism, Falangism, social democracy, socialism, or Communism."

2

So often the average layman if not actually sneering at protocol is critical of it, regarding it as stilted and unnecessary. Actually, protocol is just doing things in an orderly fashion and avoiding misinterpretations and heart burnings.

A properly regulated protocol prevents rivalries between ambassadors and other officials, and enables one to know exactly not merely where they are to be seated at a dinner or any other ceremony, but what is their real position in the community.

If I knew in advance who would be the guests at a given party, I could tell exactly where Maria and I would be seated. This frequently enabled me to coach her in advance as to any thoughts I wished her to convey to her dinner companions or what information to try to extract from those seated on either side of her. Ambassador's wives are thus an essential part of the diplomatic team and should be considered in judging the ambassadorial appointments.

It is not the individual ambassador that is insisting on his personal seating; but rather as the representative of his government he must insist on due respect for that government. A favorite way to test a new ambassador frequently is to misseat him or his wife at some function. If he takes it, then other tricks can be tried on him, for he will have shown himself to be weak in defense of his government on this question of seating.

If one is misseated there are three recognized ways of handling the situation: 1) Suddenly pretend sickness and go home; 2) walk up and down the length of the table and when the hostess or someone else says: "Oh, Mr. Ambassador you are seated here," by standing at the position you are entitled to, reply: "Oh no, I cannot be" and remain standing where you should be seated. The hostess usually apologizes, gives in, and shifts the table. 3) Accept the misseating but touch no food and go home as soon as the meal is concluded.

I have employed the second and third methods but never the first.

When the wife of the British Minister tried to repeat the misseating twice, I protested to the Chief of Protocol at the Foreign Office, and the following day the British Minister called on me to apologize.

Often I have remarked that ambassadors are a dime a dozen.

The trend toward making every chief of a diplomatic mission an ambassador was started by Sumner Welles in the early 1940s, when he decided that all of our legations in this hemisphere should be raised to embassies.

Apparently he felt this was a fine democratic move. Actually it only served to make the conduct of foreign relations more complicated and lengthy.

An ambassador is the personal representative of the Chief of State accredited to the Chief of State and Government of the foreign country where he is located. As such he is supposed to have rapid access to the Chief of State, Foreign Minister, and other officials of that government. A Minister, on the other hand, is only accredited to the Government and cannot demand the same courtesies and speed of action as an Ambassador, a Chargé d'Affaires still less.

The system originally intended to have ambassadors exchanged between countries of importance having much business with one another. For instance, I might arrive at the Foreign Office and be shown in to the Foreign Minister immediately, even though some Ministers Plenipotentiary and Chargés d'Affaires who had arrived before me would have to wait. This was logical because the business I had to transact almost always was of far greater importance than theirs.

Today, some 126 or more ambassadors are in Washington. The President cannot possibly receive them all, and now we have added delegations to the United Nations and the Organization of American States, with several ambassadors on a single delegation.

I know of one small Republic with five ambassadors on its delegation to the United Nations, at least one other in the Organization of American States, and the ambassador on post in Washington. As many of these countries were being supported by grants and low interest loans from the United States, the U.S. taxpayer was actually paying for these people with their plush jobs and large entertainment allowances.

Another misconception of the public is that an ambassador need only be a dilettante attending social functions.

Actually an ambassador should be a man of responsibility, and must have a wide range of experience and knowledge so that he can supervise properly the work of his diplomatic mission, which aside from negotiations on a wide variety of subjects will include economic and military matters, information, and cultural affairs.

He must be an acute observer and reporter, a public speaker able to play a prominent role in the host country. He must be a good executive and manager in order to control the staff operating under him.

Usually a career ambassador is better equipped than a political appointee for the manifold duties and responsibilities of the office.

The State Department can help or hinder the ambassador according to the confidence it displays in him. Too often it hinders by proceeding as if he weren't there, going off on tangents on its own, undermining his position.

Another State Department failing is its frequent tendency to convert the ambassador into merely a messenger boy. A strong ambassador, of course, will not stand for this.

A Foreign Service officer who served with me once put the difference between career and political appointees very well. He stated that as a career officer he liked to see some political appointees come in as Chiefs of Mission, because if they were good they brought in new thoughts and methods and genuinely helped develop our diplomatic service, whereas if they were bad they were usually so bad that they made the incompetent career men look good in comparison.

3

The subject of intervention or non-intervention by one country in another country's internal or external affairs is such a mish-mash of inconsistencies that one feels a bit like the young sultan who had just inherited his father's harem: he knew what to do but not where to begin.

First of all, over the last 35 years we have become increasingly accustomed to the centralized government in Washington, abetted by the Supreme Court and a slavish Congress, intervening in our local, municipal, and even personal affairs. This demagogic sentimentalism, or as my good friend Clarence Manion puts it, ". . . this soft, unprincipled, materialistic humanism has given us crime without punishment, rights without responsibilities, rewards without risk, wages without work," and now two wars (Korea and Vietnam) without victory. Simultaneously we have deliberately and progressively decreased our national defenses in the face of increasing Soviet and Communist intervention all the way from Latvia, Estonia, and Lithuania to the Far and Middle East, Hungary, East Germany, recently Czechoslovakia, and most dangerous for the U.S.A., Cuba only 90 miles off our shores.

Many diplomats complain petulantly if someone hints that personal moral standards should be applied to statecraft. Basically, many of us go along with this idea, for patriotic, religious, or other real or quasi reasons. To extend this anomaly, everyone, as an individual, refuses knowingly to brook any interference with what he thinks are his rights; at the same time if he does not like something he will not hesitate to shout that "There ought to be a law"—one which often infringes the rights of others. Too many, like the Duchess in *Alice in Wonderland,* feel that others have "Just about as much right" to think "as pigs have to fly."

Intervention and non-intervention sound simple, but each one clearly is the antithesis of the other: like the villains and heroes in a professional wrestling match, intervention popularly is adjudged to be bad, and non-intervention good.

This is metaphysical tommy-rot. The handsome, clean gladiator "non-intervention," may foul things up for everyone concerned just as much as his allegedly scurvy opponent "intervention." And in the maze of foreign relations there is nothing more muddled, self-contradictory, and generally confused than the theory and practice of intervention and non-intervention. I should add that the task of differentiating between them is not made any easier by the gusty sentimentalisms of the U.S. public as reflected in Washington.

For instance, there is the devotion to a barren welfare-statism, the "Great Society," and their off-shore twin, foreign aid or "Quickly give away as much as you can, getting little or nothing in return." We have an ardent desire to be loved; we fruitlessly try to buy it by hand-outs of billions of our hard-earned tax dollars. But we entirely forget that the *sine qua non* for the successful conduct of foreign relations is *Respect.* Certainly the peoples suffering under totalitarian police states can neither love nor respect us as we pour billions into the pockets of their dictator-masters, thus helping to keep them in power. By this addled type of intervention, we antagonize friends in the vain hope of making friends of enemies.

Then there is an overweening yearning to reconstruct the rest of the world in our own image. No matter if it does not always look pretty or that our system and ways are unadaptable to, and unwanted by, other peoples.

We insist that other nations adopt democracy. They often are incapable of practicing it or do not want it anyway. Only a very wealthy and absolutely secure nation can afford the expensive luxury of democracy. I am not sure how much longer we ourselves can "take it."

Typical of this intrusiveness have been trips to Latin America by some of our officials and legislators who, ignoring the advice of responsible leaders in those countries and instead consorting with demagogues and left-wingers, have urged intellectuals, students, and workers to revolt against their present social systems.

An innocent inquisitiveness by the Pentagon and other Washington agencies a couple of years ago aroused charges of intervention in Chile, Colombia, Peru, and even Canada, because of the public opinion polls our officials tried to take in those countries. All of these things coagulate in a sort of crusading spirit that causes many worthy citizens, especially along the Potomac, to see ourselves as the chosen apostles to lead the rest of mankind into the best of all worlds. This is an impossible task for any nation with only 5 per cent of the globe's population.

Curiously enough, we simultaneously indulge in a guilt complex and cry *mea culpa* for much that goes wrong anywhere on earth or even in outer space. You can't blame Johnny when the teacher tells him that the control of the U.S.A. is all over the globe.

It is impossible to detail the large number of United States interventions in Latin America, such as the famous Baltimore incident with Chile, our declaration of war against Paraguay, the pursuit of Villa and his troops into Mexico, and so on down the line. However, it is pertinent to mention the following:

William Henry Harrison, who died one month after he was inaugurated as President, previously had served as United States Minister in Bogota. There he instigated Cordoba's revolt against Bolivar. At the Colombian government's request, he was withdrawn.

It is not far from this incident to Theodore Roosevelt's intervention when, as he expressed it, he "took Panama" from Colombia. There was right and wrong on both sides, but the major responsibility lay with the United States which flagrantly intervened. The fault was partly redeemed because the Canal greatly benefited both countries, the entire west coast of South America, and the world as a whole (specifically, it helped insure the safety of the U.S.). Moreover, two of Colombia's most distinguished presidents, one a conservative and the other a liberal, declared to me that the separation of Panama was most fortunate politically for their country.

Theodore Roosevelt's much censured corollary to the Monroe Doctrine was promulgated when, to prevent European intervention, he promised we would maintain order in the Dominican Republic—an intervention to prevent intervention.

Intervention has been damned and non-intervention upheld repeatedly in conference after conference beginning with the VIIth International Conference of American States in Montevideo, where as a delegate in 1933 I signed a solemn pact committing the U.S.A. to non-intervention. My only excuse is that I was young and innocent. Within the Organization of American States (OAS) alone there have been more than a dozen solemn agreements condemning the "direct or indirect intervention by any country in the internal or external affairs" of any of the other parties to countless treaties and conventions, resolutions, declarations, and proclamations. Similarly, there have been innumerable debates and resolutions in the United Nations (UN).

A flagrant example of UN intervention was when Secretary General U Thant went to Cuba to tell Castro that he should not permit on the ground or on the ships inspections of missile sites or missiles by the United States since to do so would be infringement of Cuban sovereignty. He should have been severely rebuffed by us.

All of which may be edifying to international jurists and diplomats. But the average man becomes perplexed when he finds that out of all this endless discussion there has never emerged any clear-cut definition of what constitutes an intervention or why it is bad, whereas "collective action" by the UN, OAS, or other international groupings doing the same things axiomatically is acclaimed as good. Which is like saying that to break the Ten Commandments is no sin, providing you do it collectively.

Intervention can no more be defined accurately than can aggression, and that has been attempted without success in the League of Nations and elsewhere for at least half a century. In fact, "aggression" and "intervention" often are linked together in the OAS, UN, and other discussion groups and documents.

Probably about as close as we may expect to get to a definition is what the U.S. Secretary of State on July 4, 1952 told the Brazilian Chamber of Deputies:

> "The essence of the inter-American system is collective responsibility plus absolute non-intervention in the affairs of other states. The United States intends to abide by both the letter and spirit of these inter-American commitments."

This appears to be a concise and categoric enunciation of a "noble and humane policy." It is in keeping with the UN and OAS charters. It would be fine except that:

(1) It is inaccurate.

(2) We could not carry it out if we wished to.

(3) The attempt to do so often would be both unwise and immoral.

The Secretary's dictum (for years it has been a State Department theme song) is simply an obtuse cliché. Figures of speech that do not coincide with reality augment confusion, cause people eventually to lose confidence in their leadership, and to label diplomats as practitioners of the "craft sinister." This hardly makes for an effective foreign policy.

It is inexact to say that any country has in the past, or even now, abided by the "letter" and "spirit" of "absolute non-intervention." The United States, both wittingly and unwittingly, continuously has intervened in the affairs of other nations.

Forgetting the many armed interventions of the 19th and early 20th centuries, we landed the Marines in the Dominican Republic in April, 1965. But, let me emphasize, we did so at the request of the military junta, who promptly held a solemn Mass when our troops disembarked. The Red rebels did not like our action so well: but then, they do not go to masses anyway. This intervention was fine and constructive, it saved hundreds of lives, and then and there prevented a Communist "take-over." I telegraphed my congratulations forthwith to President Johnson. To have had another Caribbean island go down the drain as had Cuba would have been intolerable. I emphasized to the President that the Latinos who were most vocal in their protests, off-the-record were delighted.

Having done our good deed for the day in Trujillo's old bailiwick, we reversed the field and intervened *against* the Dominican people by proceeding, in company with the OAS, to protect the Communist and fellow traveller "rebels" against the anti-Communist military. General Wessin y Wessin, who forthrightly had stood shoulder to shoulder with us against the Communists, was seized bodily by our troops and under guard flown to Miami from where he was not allowed to return to his native land. This change in policy, characteristically, was induced by one of our "gusty sentimentalisms." Like babes in the wood, we were led astray by would-be reformers who generalizing think "military" is a naughty word and that Army and Navy officers who have risked their lives for their countries must be off-loaded to make room for do-gooders, socialists, and even Communists. As a result, the focus of infection on the Island of Española still is large and dangerous.

In the old days *The Nation, The New Republic,* and Leftists as a class used to rant vociferously against the interventions of Grover Cleveland, Teddy Roosevelt, and Woodrow Wilson. But they overlooked with the greatest of ease what former President Carlos Davila of Chile later wrote: "The remarkable thing about United States' interventions in Central America and the Caribbean is not that it went in, but that it voluntarily got out."

Now, having acquired great influence in government, the Leftists and demagogic agonizers have become just about the greatest little interveners on the loose, prying into other folks' affairs in the name of either sweet charity or democracy.

The charity, known as foreign aid, has cost the U.S. taxpayers approaching $160 billion. Now this is no mean sum, if one considers that it is the equivalent of our having given away probably more than 75 to 100 of our largest cities, because the assessed valuation of all real property in the 65 largest cities comes to only $118 billion. An open-handed distribution of such huge sums often does little good and frequently harms the recipient nation morally and otherwise. As per Plutarch's aphorism, the real destroyer of the liberties of any people is he who spreads among them bounties, donations, and largesses.

Alleging humanitarian motives and "informed self-interest," not only have we set up our own Gargantuan foreign aid bureaucracies but the U.S.A. also picks up the tabs for the United Nations and other international organizations who, imitating us, often try to interfere with the internal as well as external affairs of nations. In so doing, like our government, they frequently ignore the advantages of private endeavor, thus discouraging individual investment and enterprise, developing an avaricious incompetence amongst the local politicos, and destroying the people's liberties. Truly, these foul blows are enough to make a villain out of any hero wrestling in the international arena.

I do not know whether it is a natural or a cultivated ignorance, but it is not very bright to advise the Latin Americans to seize and divide their agricultural holdings and increase taxes, when not infrequently larger farms would produce more food and the taxes often are as high as our own which nullify many wholesome economic incentives. We discourage farming abroad by giving away our wheat and other foodstuffs. This causes the peasants to stop farming and drift into the cities where they become public charges, and to avoid starvation receive more aid and food from Uncle Sam. Foreign aid further interferes with the finances of other countries by creating excessive bi-partite funds. All of these antics supported by our huge governmental grants have built up the U.S.A. balance of payments deficits, which in turn are not helped by the President imposing "voluntary" restrictions on private investments overseas. This of itself is an indirect intervention.

The Leftist reformers in and out of Washington have gotten the U.S.A. into hot water all the way from the Congo to Laos, from the Arctic to the Antarctic. Their interpositions may lie in such piddling absurdities as spending over $200,000 to subsidize cigarette advertising in Japan, Thailand, and Austria, while the Federal Government at home, because of the danger of cancer, runs anti-smoking campaigns. Their activities become much more serious when they have supported and financed Marxist regimes in Poland, Yugoslavia, Bolivia, and elsewhere.

The worldwide "population explosion" is a serious matter. But does that justify our having population officers attached to each diplomatic mission in Latin America and allocating $2,000,000 per year to birth control in that area? No more sextuplets for the Aymara and Quichua Indians! Or should we give the "pill" to the Hottentots so they won't get so hot and have so many tots.

Sometimes we are accused unjustly of intervening, as I was while serving as ambassador in Buenos Aires. I was charged with speaking against Peron. The details of my position and of Peron's conduct are in Chapter XXX. If this be intervention, so is every diplomatic utterance. And it will be a sad day indeed when a United States ambassador cannot defend and speak out for free, constitutional representative government.

Also it is fitting to observe that other governments, including those of some very small countries, often intervene in the domestic affairs of the United States. They may do this through lobbyists and propaganda. They probably have been most effective when working through blocs of our citizens who are linked to them by racial, national, or religious ties, and who hold the balance of voting power in certain parts of this country.

My second point about the Secretary of State's declaration was that, even if the United States wished to, it could not abide by the "letter" and "spirit of absolute non-intervention."

Such has been the power and wealth, prestige, and influence of the United States (at least in the 20th Century), that whatever it does or does not do or say, insofar as any other nation is affected, inevitably constitutes an intervention.

If one nation depends economically upon another, it may assert itself only to a limited extent. Its disposition will be to remain in the good graces of the other and to follow its lead and even whims. The same thing may occur when a weaker country depends upon a stronger one for defense against a possible aggressor: in other words, for its independence and security. United States economic and military commitments in Europe, Latin America, and elsewhere are so intimately interwoven with the domestic affairs of the countries in those areas as to make our interventions unavoidable. "Collective responsibility" and "absolute non-intervention" are not easily reconcilable.

Our complete inaction and silence may be tantamount to an intervention because they are interpreted as lending implied consent, if not actual approval, to given circumstances or developments. Our failure to speak or act may entrench the bad and dispossess the good. Many a rogue in this hemisphere has remained in power, to exploit his people, because the other republics have said and done nothing.

On the other hand, while Perez Jimenez was President of Venezuela, we decorated him with the highest military order given to foreigners. When he was overthrown and took asylum here, we broke all precedents by packing him off to Caracas to go on trial, perhaps even for his life. In other words, while he was an authoritarian chief of state, we intervened in his favor; when he became an exile, we intervened against him. We demonstrated that friendship for and with Uncle Sam is not always rewarding. It would have been well for General Wessin y Wessin in the Dominican Republic had he remembered this lesson.

Paradoxically, by complete abstention we may be able to intervene for a good cause. I vividly recall that evening of June 3, 1944 when, as ambassador to Cuba, I was implored by several Cuban officials to have the United States intervene immediately, with our armed forces, to prevent a revolution at that very moment being hatched by a group of generals and colonels. My judgment not to intervene is described in Chapter XXXI. It stopped the revolution in its tracks.

My third point on the Secretary's pronouncement was that often it would be both unwise and immoral not to intervene.

Cuba's independence from Spain would have been impossible without intervention by the United States in Spanish affairs. Our Latin American neighbors gave high praise to that intervention. In 1898 a Joint Resolution of the United States Congress declared: "Cuba is, and by right should be, free and independent." What has happened to that pledge today? It is lost in a mire of mawkish sentimentality about "non-intervention." The Soviets' and Castro's outrages are infinitely more cruel and numerous than were those of Weyler, the Spanish general, that so enraged the American people that they went to war to free Cuba.

If we grant that the Monroe Doctrine was an intervention by us in the affairs of the other American republics, for more than a century it at least preserved our several sovereignties and independence and prevented intervention from without the hemisphere. To this extent, it was a brilliant diplomatic accomplishment.

In April, 1961, the United States intervened against the Cuban people when by stupidity and even intrigue 1,200 patriotic Cubans were led into the Bay of Pigs debacle. That miserable affair momentarily seemed to have been redeemed in October 1962, by President Kennedy's magnificent confrontation of Khrushchev in the missile crisis. But, alas, this brave victory quickly was converted into a Khrushchev-Castro triumph and an all-out defeat for the Monroe Doctrine, as without any formal request from Khrushchev, the President offered on October 27, 1962, not to permit by ourselves or any other American republic, an invasion to rescue our Cuban friends from Communism. This was a peculiarly bad intervention because the U.S. government exclusively recognized Soviet sovereignty over Cuba, totally ignoring that of the Cuban people. It created a sanctuary under which Russian missile and submarine sites have been established, although Moscow never fulfilled its part of the bargain. Also, the United States further insures this unholy Soviet sanctum sanctorum by preventing, with our armed forces, Cuban patriots from attempting even to harass the usurpers of their homeland. The United States government intervenes by having our Revenue cutters capture Cuban patriots, confiscating their ships, arms and equipment in international waters, as far as 43 miles off the mainland; this is piracy on the high seas. Thus we block a courageous attempt by these Cubans to help free their nation. This is counter to our mistaken but clearly official position that the Cubans themselves must liberate their country. It further directly negates U.S. policy in the Orient where thousands of our boys are fighting and dying for Vietnamese freedom and self-determination. No international law justifies our protecting the Communist-Soviet-Castro sanctuary from attacks by Cuban Freedom Fighters.

Under the umbrella of this sanctuary, the representatives of Communist parties from 82 countries met in Havana at the end of January 1966, in the Tri-Continental Solidarity Conference. This "Hate the U.S.A." meeting was the largest gathering of guerrillas in history. There the Moscow-Peking axis openly boasted that Havana had been established as the general staff base for world and especially Latin-American infiltration, subversion, and insurrection by armed force. This was the culmination of seven years of Soviet bloc intervention in this hemisphere. Yet, the U.S.A. has done nothing effective about it!

On February 7, 1966, all the Latin American members of the UN, excepting Mexico, filed a formal protest with Secretary General U Thant, against the intervention proposed by this Tri-Continental parley. At which point all pretense of collective action and responsibility ended. The Mexican abstention is interesting because that country always denounces any hint of intervention, although the Central American republics are not so convinced of the purity of its motives. I recall a discussion with a distinguished Mexican ambassador to Washington, when he finally agreed intervention could be imperative and a good thing. But, he pleaded with me, "Just find another name for it."

Through our adherence to a profusion of multilateral agreements, we have imposed a long series of self-denying ordinances upon ourselves. We appear to have rendered ourselves impotent and ceded large chunks of our sovereignty to the UN and OAS. Positive and worthwhile action comes only in the rarest instances from such bodies. Decisions are usually reduced to the lowest common denominator of the most timid or reluctant member. This is precisely what has happened with respect to Cuba. For more than seven years the American republics have been so vacillating and pusillanimous that no effective action has been taken against this Communist invasion of the western hemisphere.

Yet, while the United States has appeared to be emasculated and ham-strung under international law, it is not as much so as some of the Latinos and the State Department would have us believe. There are ample authorizations under the Charter of the Organization of American States signed in Bogota, Colombia, in 1948, confirming many previous commitments which give all of the American republics the right to intervene directly or indirectly, and by force if necessary, for any reason in the internal or external affairs of another.

Although the Charter and these several agreements clearly require collective action to thwart the Communist invasion of this hemisphere, the sole compliance so far has been that the United States along with a majority of the American republics have broken diplomatic relations with the Communist regime in Cuba.

By its inaction, the U.S.A. also has failed to keep its pledged word under the Monroe Doctrine and the 1898 Joint Resolution of Congress. Simultaneously we have appeased the Soviet and its Communist allies and by so doing have encouraged terror and aggressions in

Vietnam and elsewhere. We have permitted the Kremlin to establish a strongly fortified military and naval base only 90 miles from our shores, equipped with missile sites and underground submarine pens, imperiling the very survival of the United States and the independence of all the American republics.

It would seem that Washington has learned nothing since Mr. Dulles in 1957 declared there was ". . . no danger of Communism in this hemisphere." Tragically, it is like a circus going full blast with a large coterie of clowns and nobody noticing that the big top is collapsing over their own and the spectators' heads.

The only way we can get out of this desperate situation is for the United States, with or without the concordance of the other American republics, to throw the Russian, Chinese, Ghanian, and local Communists bodily out of Cuba by a properly planned, all-out invasion. This is an imperative and moral intervention in the best sense of the word, and one which, if we act in time, with God's help still can succeed. Such a victorious intervention could lay the groundwork for that world peace for which mankind so anxiously longs.

4

A few years ago Jesse Grover Bell requested me, along with a number of other gentlemen, to epitomize my advice to the youth of the country on how to have successful and happy lives. The messages were to be published as a book called *Here's How by Who's Who.*

The contributors included such distinguished citizens as Herbert Hoover, General Mark Clark, Senator Everett Dirksen, Charles Edison, Barry Goldwater, Billy Graham, Richard Nixon, Norman Vincent Peale, Ronald Reagan, J. Edgar Hoover, Eddie Rickenbacker, and many others of similar standing.

I replied that the counsel I had given my own children was applicable and, in my opinion, the qualities needed for a successful happy life are:

> "1. *Complete honesty.* I have discovered in a long life that not only is honesty the 'best policy,' but the ONLY policy.
>
> "2. *Judgment.* While some judgment may come intuitively, largely it must be acquired through long hours of careful thought and deep concentration. It will help to put one's conclusions in writing before attempting to express them.

"3. *Energy*. Unless one is willing to put forth his maximum effort at all times, and to work long, hard hours, he will get nowhere. Initiative is part and parcel of this formula.

"4. *Tolerance*. No matter how right we may believe ourselves to be, we must try to put ourselves in the other fellow's position and make allowances for his opinions.

"In the exercise of these qualities and carrying them through to a conclusion, one inevitably will arrive at the fifth condition—*a belief in God*."

As I have said, it is my belief these principles of private morality are applicable to public morality and in diplomacy. While foreign policy necessarily may change according to circumstances, times, and place, through the years I have laid down four other principles that I believe are essential for the wise conduct of this nation's foreign relations. In fact, during the latter part of my diplomatic career I always kept them in mind as a measuring rod to guide me in the solution of any specific problem and my determination of the policy or policies I should pursue. They are:

1. *Respect* is the *sine qua non* of all foreign relations. Quite apart from every other consideration and under all conditions, the United States must demand and get respect. To do so we must first have self-respect and exact from our own and other governments respect for their obligations and the sanctity of agreements. Without the former we cannot expect the latter.

2. The sole reason for the existence of the State Department and Foreign Service is to protect and advance the legitimate interests of the United States, including its citizens. If ever they should become illegitimate then they are unworthy of this great nation and should not be supported.

3. Every policy and action must be moral. Leaving ethics to one side, only in this way will we win and hold the confidence and respect of other countries, which are so essential for a solid and enduring amity between peoples.

4. While never attempting to impose our way of life or form of government, our ideas or even our moral standards, on others, we should ourselves stand unswervingly for and practice the system of republican, constitutional, representative government laid down for us by the Founding Fathers in the Declaration of Independence, the Constitution, and the Bill of Rights.

We can adhere to these principles and help save our civilization by following the precepts announced by George Washington in his Farewell Address—the finest statement ever made on both domestic and foreign policy. If with moral fibre we will dedicate ourselves to the pursuit of these principles then, with God's help, the United States will defeat Communism along with many other immoral forces. We will preserve our freedoms and insure peace for our children and grandchildren in what may not be the best of all worlds but will at least be a much better world than the present.

Appendix

A so-called Liberal publisher that originally was scheduled to publish my memoirs had requested that this series of vignettes not be included. When I decided to publish with Arlington House, they requested that this Appendix be added because they felt that it was too important and interesting to be left out.

During recent visits to Ireland, where we were guests of one of the most gracious and hospitable hosts I have ever known, John H. Mulcahy, I looked into the origin of the name Braden, and found that while the family came from England, through Scotland, and thence into Ireland, various spellings developed; as for instance, O'Bradain, Breadon, Breydon, O'Bradden, but the earliest record in Ireland was Brodon, which is gaelic for salmon.

Therefore, I like to point to this fact as the reason why when visiting the Mulcahy home in Waterville, although never having fished before, I had the extraordinarily good luck (with the able assistance of our host's gilies) to kill 36 salmon in 9 days on one occasion, and 16 on another.

I also obtained the Braden coat-of-arms, which shows three salmon, which we now display as a knocker on our entrance door, and woven in the upholstery of a settee.

Father died as I think he would have wanted to die—in the field looking at mines. He was stricken as he had just finished examining a property he was interested in outside Reno, Nevada, in July 1942. I was Ambassador to Cuba at the time, and Messmore Kendall telephoned me at noon one day to tell me that Father was in a Reno hospital. I was making arrangements to fly to Reno when Larry Duggan called me from the State Department and told me Father had died.

I have always felt that I was right in urging him to get back into mining, away from the boredom of his New York life. Even though he felt keenly the loss of his fortune, I still think his last ten years were far happier than the preceeding decade. He was too brilliant, resourceful and energetic to be really content to "be in retirement".

To my mention of my mother's pride of family and being related to half the statuary in New England (sic), I should add that one of our ancestors, Hannah Dustin, is immortalized in a statue outside of Concord, New Hampshire.

As the reader will perhaps remember, she, a young boy servant and her baby were kidnapped by the Indians. The baby's brains were bashed out on a rock.

But that night while the Indians slept she loosened the ropes binding her and, along with the boy they then proceeded to scalp the Indians and they escaped, bearing the scalps. There was a bounty for each Indian scalp. Hence Hannah, being a frugal soul, was meticulous on this point.

A good friend attributed my mother's undoubted fortitude and what she alledged was my courage to our inheritance from Hannah. But it must be remembered that Hannah's husband and older sons hid behind the barn while the savages carted her, the boy and baby off. Mr. Dustin was as much our ancestor as Hannah, and I doubt that my mother and I can attribute much bravery to our descent from him or his progeny.

Amongst my mother's very good friends were the Donald Bacons. He was President of the Tennessee Coal and Iron Company. Mrs. Bacon had a society friend, Mrs. Peck, who asked for the loan of Mrs. Bacon's drawing room in order to receive her lawyer in afternoon conference. She had several meetings behind closed doors in the drawing room until before an overly inquisitive servant, peeking through the keyhole having ushered in the "lawyer," Woodrow Wilson, then President of Princeton University, saw what was going on. Needless to say Mrs. Bacon did not again lend her drawing room, and Wilson acquired the nickname of "Peck's bad boy."

My advise to at least two of my granddaughters resulted to their detriment. The first one, Kimie, my oldest daughter's daughter, a student at Miss Chapin's, was to write an article on the colonization of the United States. I asked if she wanted fantasy or the facts. She said, or course, the facts. Well, I said, let's begin with the Puritans. They were so obnoxious to the British that they were shipped over to Holland. The Dutch shipped them back to England and finally the problem was solved by putting them on the Mayflower. After they disembarked at Plymouth Rock they formed a communist state. Under the communist regime they were all about to starve until Governor Bradford did away with the communism, so that each man and family could work for themselves and sell their product or buy from others. I understand from my granddaughter that she was reprimanded for writing such a shocking article.

Several years later my granddaughter Mia, my oldest son's daughter, came to me to get help on an article she was writing on Cuba. This was when Castro first came into power and there was a lot of silly sentimentalism about him rife in this country. I told her the facts about Castro and the Communists. Castro was a murderer and a thoroughly despicable character. She put these and other facts I gave her down and I guess nearly got expelled for her pains.

Many years ago a young reporter and author interviewed not only me but members of my family and friends in order to prepare an article in the *New Yorker* about me. I am told that one of my daughters-in-law, a beautiful and charming girl, (whom I dearly love), when asked what kind of a man I was, replied, "He will not be content with a piece of cheese, but wants to eat the whole cheese." I've always said I was descended from a long line of rodents.

My refusal for several years to contribute to the Yale Alumni Fund, and my reasons therefor (pages 407 and 408) have been reinforced further by a great deal of other news emanating from New Haven, such as:

a) President Kingman Brewster's proclamation that Black revolutionaries cannot get a fair trial in the United States [sic] and that President Nixon's election was "a Hucksterized Process".

b) Chaplain Coffin of Yale's antics including his permitting so called young Activists to light their draft cards on his altar.

c) Professor Lind's visits to Peiping and Hanoi and so on ad nauseaum.

I have exchanged frank letters on these topics with Kingman

Brewster. I doubt that I changed his thinking any more than he did mine.

Incidentally, pictures of the Black Panthers and all the others of the "radical left" always are shown with raised clenched fists. I cannot fathom why the American public has not awakened to the fact that this, at least since Lenin's time, has been the Communist salute.

Eleanor Roosevelt had a capacity for frankness. As the wellknown author, Martha Gellhorn (at one time wife of Ernest Hemingway, who did such a valuable job for me in getting $184,000 for the internment of Nazis in Cuba) told me, once when visiting the White House she was seated next to Mrs. Roosevelt at a table of about 20, when the first lady of the land called to the President at the other end of table: "Franklin, you must listen to this little girl who has studied and can tell you all about prostitution in the South."

During my tour of duty as Ambassador in Cuba, Mrs. Roosevelt paid us an overnight visit, including a reception which we offered her at the Embassy, and a dinner given by President Grau.

In the summer of 1944 on my next visit on consultation to Washington, Maria and I received what was practically a command to spend the weekend with her at Hyde Park. We were already obligated to go to Connecticut, so we only spent Friday afternoon and evening and Saturday morning with her, before our friends called for us.

One interesting incident occurred while Maria and I were having cocktails on the south terrace of the Roosevelt home with her, a cousin of hers and the President's by the name of Hooper, and her secretary (the President was on a trip to the Pacific).

We discussed the recently held Democratic convention, during which pursuant to the President's orders, Wallace had been jettisoned as a candidate for Vice President, first in favor of Jimmy Byrnes, Alvin Barkley, and finally Truman.

Mrs. Roosevelt made one of the strongest tirades against the President I have ever heard. She said he had completely double-crossed Wallace, that it was the dirtiest kind of politics, and he should be made to pay for it. It certainly would lose him the Negro vote, which she hoped it would, and this would jolly well serve him right. All of us were aghast.

To my remarks on page 420 in respect of protocol, I should add two observations:

1) When a new Ambassador arrives on the job, the Government to which he is accredited usually tries to find out of what kind of timber he is made. A common practice is to begin with some small breach in protocol, such as misseating him or his wife. If he takes this, they will try something a little worse, and continue on until they discover the breaking point.

One of the worst breaches of protocol I have seen was committed in Washington.

President-elect Grau San Marten of Cuba, the invited guest of the United States President and Government, with his staff, was lodged at Blair House. Roosevelt gave a large luncheon in his honor at the White House. Naturally, all of his retinue and I, as Ambassador in Cuba were supposed to be invited.

But I was shocked to learn from the Cuban Ambassador late in the morning of the luncheon that one of Grau's new Cabinet officers who, also was Vice President of the Cuban Chamber of Deputies, had not received his invitation. I apologized and assured the Cubans that of course there had been some mistake, which would be remedied promptly.

I scurried down to the Protocol office, only to be informed that there was no mistake. It appeared that President Roosevelt wished a teenage grandson to be at the luncheon; as a result the Cuban official had been shunted aside since there was no room at the table for both him and the grandson. I appealed to George Summerlin, Chief of Protocol, who confirmed the reasons why F.D.R.'s grandson was to be given preference.

Getting nowhere with Summerlin, I appealed to the Acting Assistant Secretary of State in charge of American Republic Affairs. He was as shocked as I, but could do nothing with Summerlin.

The Cuban dignatary, being disinvited to the White House, forthwith moved out of Blair House to a hotel.

I grabbed Cordell Hull after luncheon and demanded that he get an autographed photograph of President Roosevelt in a silver frame, and that he as Secretary of State accompanied by me call on the Cuban to make an adequate apology. This was done and friendly relations re-established.

George Summerlin was well overage for retirement, but was kept on as Chief of Protocol because he had the greatest store of risque and even worse stories I have ever heard. For this reason the President, who enjoyed these racy tales, kept Summy on. (Incidentally, as First Secretary of our Embassy in Chile, although years older than I, Summy attended my bachelor dinner in 1915).

Another amusing anecdote occurred when a British nobleman who, during a visit to Chile, was most hospitably entertained by the President, decided to write his bread and butter letter in Spanish. He found in his dictionary what he thought was an appropriate protocolor conclusion (which should only to be used when addressing a lady): "Beso sus manos"—I kiss your hand. Since he was writing the Chief of State, he decided to improve on this expression and instead wrote, "Beso sus pies, etc., etc."—I kiss your feet, etc., etc.

When Evita Peron returned to Argentina from Europe where she had been snubbed, as for instance when she hoped to obtain a high decoration from the Pope and received nothing (which led her to throw her shoes in rage at Dodero—a very important Argentine shipping man—who had accompanied her as sort of an aide on her trip through Europe) she stopped in Brazil hoping to address an inter-American Conference then in session in Quitandinha. When she entered the assembly hall the Brazilian Foreign Minister, who was presiding, was too quick for her. He forthwith called a recess, inviting all the delegates to adjourn to another room to imbibe a glass of champagne with her, but no speech! Again, she was enraged.

I have recounted some of my experiences how both as Ambassador and Assistant Secretary of State interventions, when the seizure of U. S. owned properties was attempted, I put an end to them by forthwith cancelling all credits, loans, grants and other favors. Every time the result was almost instantaneous and as I have told a couple of times, if the interventions came as a result of strikes, the strikes likewise promptly were called off. In short, I did not need the Hickenlooper amendment.

If our Ambassadors and the State Department would take such

attitudes we would not now have to suffer the many serious confiscations that have taken place in Latin America.

For instance the Peruvian Government seized International Petroleum properties as well as others belonging to Americans, such as Grace & Co. sugar mills. By this time the Hickenlooper Amendment prohibiting the granting of loans or grants to governments acting in this fashion was in full force. Instead of obeying this U.S. law, we practically acquiesced in these seizures—actually thefts—by twice delaying enactment of the Hickenlooper amendment and letting it die on the vine.

The Chileans witnessing our timidity in Peru emulated the Lima Government by taking over first 51% of the American copper companies, and now Allende, the Marxist President of Chile promises to seize the balance and all other U.S. industry, banks, etc. He also threatens his own country's capitalists.

As a leading Colombian attorney, who contributed substantially to the establishment of the United Nations—although he now declares it should be done away with—offered to bet me recently that our pussy-footing will bring Communism to all of Latin America within ten years. I am afraid he is right.

The United States should remember that the second world war could not have been won without copper from Chile and oil from Venezuela.

During trips which I made around Latin America in 1959 and 1964 I observed that in many of the countries I found the responsible people fearing the Christian Democrats as much as they did the Communists. That they were right in their prognostications has been proven by the fact that Tomic, the former Chilean Ambassador in Washington and recently defeated as a candidate for the Presidency of that country, was more violent in his animosity towards the United States and all foreign investments than even the Communists. Curiously enough, Allende, the winning candidate is a socialist and he too is more ferocious against the United States and private investment than even the Communists, threatening the confiscation of all foreign property in Chile. Of course, these left wingers have been aided and abetted as I have remarked by our attitude in the cases of confiscation of American property first in Peru, then in Chile, and finally in Bolivia while the State Department refused to obey U.S. law in the form of the Hickenlooper Amendment.

Despite our huge grants and loans at very low interest to these countries they are violently against us. For instance, the President of another Republic recently told me of his experience. He sent 15 army officers and 50 non-military technicians of one kind or another to Chile for training. Ten of the 15 officers returned inculcated with thoroughly leftists ideas as did over half of the technicians. For this reason, therefore, a friend of mine who has twice served as Ambassador to Washington, as Foreign Minister of his own country and who helped greatly in the organization of the United Nations, which he now thinks should be thrown out the window.

Aside from the much-publicized Bay of Pigs and Missile Crisis in Cuba, it should be known that that island is underlain with huge caverns. The Soviets have taken advantage of this fact to put in two-lane underground highways in many places throughout the island, which are employed for transporting missiles, which are installed from underneath instead of from on top of the ground, and can be so camouflaged that therefore they could not be spotted from high-flying airplanes.

Also, some of these caverns have been converted into submarine pens so that submarines can enter underwater from the ocean without being seen. The foregoing information has been uncovered by the Executive Director of the Citizens Committee's for a Free Cuba, of which I am Chairman, from the Committees many Cuban and other informants.

More recently, however, the Soviets have been charged by the United States Government with building a submarine base on the southern shore of Cuba in Cienfuegos. Moscow, of course, denies this but there is positive proof that it is true. As a part of this installation, a huge thermoelectric power plant for use by the submarine base has been installed in the area of Cienfuegos. Also, thought should be given to the fact that there is being delivered to the Soviets a 22,000-ton tanker, named "7th of November". It is said that two more tankers are to be added to Cuba's merchant marine, which now is six times larger than in 1959. With these tankers Cuba could ship oil from Trinidad and even Venezuela. Such a plan would suit Prime Minister Eric Williams of Trinidad-Tabago since he has openly called for the "economic integration" of Cuba into the Carribbean trading area.

Recently he welcomed a Cuban trade or agriculture mission. This oil would provide enough fuel for the thermoelectric power plant for the submarine base.

There is one rather risque anecdote that should be told about Doris Stevens (pgs. 120–121), who as I have described led what now is called the "Woman's Liberation Movement"—a typically communist expression—in opposition to Eleanor Roosevelt's program not for "equal" but for bigger and better rights for the fair sex.

She and a French girl companion, and a reporter whom she later married were on board the ship with us when we went to the VII International Conference of American States in Montevideo.

One evening when Jimmy Dunn and I had concluded an after-dinner consultation with Secretary Hull in his suite, with our wives we came down to the deck to have some champagne. It was a lovely, balmy, tropical evening with the stars and the moon shining down upon us.

As Doris Stevens passed our group, I invited her to join us for a glass of champagne. Whn she sat down I told her that I had known her husband, Dudley Field Malone, and did not understand why she had divorced him. (She was his second wife.) She replied it was because they had no children, and then proceeded to tell me: "You may recall that when Dudley went to the opening night of the Ziegfield Follies he was in white tie and tails with a white butonniere, and would wait until the last minute before the lights were dimmed; then he would be ushered down the aile with great eclat. Everyone would whisper: 'there goes Dudley Field Malone.' "

Similarly, if he went to a nightclub he would have a ringside table, and the same comments would be uttered.

I said I was puzzled by her account—what had it to do with her divorce? She replied that he simply could not perform without an audience.

Some months later at a dinner party of a dozen or so, Dudley (who had been blessed with child by his third wife) asked me if the story about Doris was true. When I replied in the affirmative, he said he could present evidence that Doris had falsified about his inability to cooperate in producing a baby; whereupon he pulled a baby's knitted shoe out of his wallet! Rather tenuous evidence?

While in Bogotá Maria and I were invited to a dinner being given in honor of the governor of the Department and his wife at the Mexican legation. The various living rooms and dining rooms fronted on a main great hall but a few steps lower. The guests of honor were about an hour late in arriving. Finally cocktails were served, but before that I had noticed a stream of some kind of liquor seeping out of the butler's pantry and flowing down the stairs to the main hall. The butler tried to persuade me that I was seated on the other side of the table from where I was supposed to sit, but since I knew where protocol would place me, I refused his direction and went to the place in which I belonged. The dining room had a beautiful marble floor but when serving the fish course some of the sauce was spilled directly behind our host's chair. Then came two huge turkeys, one for each side of the table. One servant hit the place where the sauce had fallen, his legs went up as he sat down with a bump and the turkey went spinning down the length of the dining room. It was retrived. (I do not know whether it was taken to the pantry to be cleaned and reserved.) Then came some red wine. This time the butler hit the skiddy place, but clutching the bottle of wine, went down again. The result was a red geiser, which gushed over a beautiful silk dress of the Japanese minister's wife. By this time our hostess was so embarrassed as to be almost hysterical. All of her guests tried to pass it off with laughter. But then came the ice cream, in a large silver platter. As the platter was passed over Maria's head she suddenly saw a white waterfall in front of her eyes. The ice cream had melted during the delay in the dinner.

When we got to the main hall, the Foreign Minister, who was standing a few steps up, slipped as he started down. Fortunately, I was able to catch him before he fell. The evening ended when the Governor's chauffeur, taking him home, drove into and smashed the stone gateposts at the exit driveway.

When I spoke earlier of my two top-secret cablegrams for the President and the Secretary of State *only*, I might add that they could have been stolen in the code room by a minor employee who was in sympathy with Communism or in Communist pay. The employee who handles incoming and outgoing messages can, in a way, control the Department and sabotage government policy.

My secretary, Mrs. Ethel Blake, who was with me both in Buenos Aires and Washington, as I dictated this Appendix, gave me her impressions as follows:

Demonstrations were taking place in Buenos Aires—some directed against the United States. Fire bombs were being thrown everywhere. Ambassador Braden decided to dismiss the staff of the Embassy Chancellry in mid-afternoon. However, he asked Counselor of Embassy John M. Cabot, two Secretaries of Embassy, one of his three secretaries, a member of the Code Room, and the Marine Guards to remain in order to draft a cable to Washington about Peron's latest move, and the riots. As we all tried to concentrate on the composition of the cable, we gazed at the Ambassador. He was the picture of composure, and business-as-usual while Buenos Aires was burning. An impressive figure sitting at his desk immune to the noise and the flames from the fire bombs, which made the rest of us jump out of our seats and look nervously at one another each time they exploded.

When will the Ambassador decide to go home? This was the question asked many a time by the exhausted Military and Naval Aides and one of his secretaries whenever we were at a social affair. The Ambassador loved a good party, and stayed and stayed, while the rest of us did tire of keeping up to his pace, and were ready to go home, but could not until he did so.

After the famous Chamber of Commerce luncheon, in which the Ambassador spoke frankly about Peron, a group of distinguished Argentine men and women telephoned the Embassy, saying that they wished to call on the Ambassador to express their gratitude. The calls were so many, and the hours of the day not enough to receive each individually, that I suggested to the Ambassador we receive them at the Embassy. We promptly organized an afternoon reception thinking about 100 would come. We returned each call for an appointment stating that the Ambassador and Mrs. Braden would receive them at the Embassy. Somehow in a matter of hours, the word spread through Buenos Aires, and we were faced with an impressive demonstration of friendship to the Ambassador and Mrs. Braden and the United States consisting of hundreds of people. The social secretary and the housekeeper were kept hopping, asking more members of the Embassy staff to come to the Embassy to help receive, not to mention encouraging the butler and the chef to keep supplies of liquid and solid sustenance moving. (I believe this is the time you were presented with a beautiful, antique English silver bowl (about 10″ high by more than a foot in diameter). It had been displayed in a jewelry store window and was purchased by small contributions from hundreds of individuals.)

Our recent Presidents have adopted the procedure of having

special advisors on all manner of subjects, but particularly in respect of foreign relations.

To such extent has this custom grown that while once the little white building adjacent to the White House could accommodate the President and all of his immediate aides; now the "General Grant Period" huge atrocity across the street, which formerly housed the Department of State, War and Navy is entirely devoted to adjuncts of the White House.

Of course, our Government has grown, and an increase in staff has become necessary. But I cannot believe that such a multiplication in advisors and employees ever was necessary.

As I look back, this mushroom growth began with Woodrow Wilson when he made Colonel House his alter ego. His successors Harding, Coolidge and Hoover, were more restrained and used their Cabinet and sub-Cabinet members as advisors, despite the heavy burden of work falling on them.

Parenthetically I recall one Saturday afternoon when I was in the upstairs office in the White House talking with President Roosevelt, a pile of documents 2 feet high was brought in for his signature I commented that it was unfair to load the President with this manual labor. F.D.R. replied: "Oh, I'm not the hardest working President by any means. I have made a study of my predecessors: the hardest working was Hoover, the amount he did was unbelievable. On the other hand, probably the laziest was Taft, who was able to take an automobile ride in the park every afternoon".

F.D.R. to begin with had Louis Howe his personal secretary as a staunch advisor. In fact I believe that if the latter and Will Woodin, the Secretary of the Treasury, had lived, Roosevelt would have followed a conservative line. But, alas, when these two men died, he gathered together a corps of advisors typified by Harry Hopkins, with some pretty unsavory characters amongst them.

Truman, had his poker and other cronies, but did his own thinking. Perhaps that is the reason why he was one of the abler Presidents we have had since Cleveland.

Ike, at least in foreign relations, depended on Foster Dulles, who while he made mistakes—as for instance his statement which I quoted about there being no danger of Communism in this Hemisphere—was, I believe, patriotic, constructive and a good Secretary of State.

In contrast John Kennedy had a phalanx of special advisors. Perhaps they, with his brother Bobby, are the ones responsible for so disastrously confusing him in respect of the Bay of Pigs, and later inducing him to back down in the missile crisis after 36 hours of standing by his first courageous and correct demands on the Russians. Vacillations on these two matters in my opinion place him in the category of being one of, if not the worst President the U.S.A. ever had.

Johnson had his Fortases and other advisors, but he compensated for them in part by having as his principal advisor on Latin America, Tom Mann, who wisely steered him to prevent the Communists taking over the Dominican Republic. For this we can thank God —and Tom.

Now President Nixon, unquestionably able, has as his principal advisor for foreign affairs Dr. Henry Kissinger, who reportedly has a staff of over 100 in the White House. Kissinger, although a Liberal, is brilliant and the President naturally is very much influenced by his opinions, which apparently outweigh those of Secretary of State Rogers, who is inexperienced in the foreign field. Needless to say this dual leadership does not make for efficient operations.

Cordell Hull would never have accepted such a duality of leadership. He knew that too many cooks spoil the broth. Hull successively got rid of such presidential advisors as Ray Moley, George Peek and Sumner Welles.

I have described how I used Mrs. Roosevelt and Harry Hopkins to get the $184,000 I needed for the incarceration of the Nazis in Cuba. This illustrates how diplomats have to use Presidential advisors as well as the State Department.

Where I speak of the President's unofficial advisors, I recall one case when the advisor purchased a home adjacent to the President's country home, frankly admitting that he had done so so that he could be with and influence the President at all times.

I have remarked on the breakdown in morals across the board in the United States and, for that matter, throughout the world, observing that perhaps the worst form of immorality was communism. I began preaching this whole thesis 40 years ago. Since then the breakdown in morals has increased and my opinions become fully vindicated by what we now see surrounding us—the crime, violence, the Black Panthers, hippies, SDSers, Weatherman and similar organizations. God help our country if this trend continues, as otherwise the prophecy of Thomas Babington Macaulay of over 100 years ago will be realized "that America would never be conquered from without, but would collapse from within because of the deterioration of the character of its people."

Of course our disintegration from within is completely in accord with Lenin's declaration:

> First, we will take eastern Europe, then the masses of Asia, then we will encircle the United States which will be in the last bastion of capitalism. We will not have to attack. It will fall like an over-ripe fruit into our hands.

and followed by Stalin's:

> That is why it is essential that the triumphant proletariat of the advanced countries should render aid, real and prolonged aid, to the toiling masses of the backward nationalities in their cultural and economic development; that it should help them to rise to a higher stage of development and to catch up with the more advanced nationalities. Unless such aid is forthcoming, it will be impossible to bring about the peaceful co-existence and fraternal collaboration of the toilers of the various nations and peoples within a single world economic system that are so essential for the final triumph of socialism.

And such observations as Manuilski's:

> The capitalist countries, stupid and decadent, will rejoice to co-operate in their own destruction. They will leap at another chance to be friends. As soon as their guard is down, we will smash them with our clenched fist.

Eastern Europe and most of Asia have been lost, as have large sections of South Africa and the near East. Now the Communist envelopment of the United States is proceeding through the Marxist control of governments in Cuba, Chile, Bolivia and Peru. George Dimitrov declared:

> . . . let our friends do the work. We must always remember that one sympathizer is generally worth more than a dozen militant Communists. A university professor, who without being a party member lends himself to the interests of the Soviet Union, is worth more than a hundred men with party cards.

and our pretended friendship with Marshall Tito counts for little in view of his statement that:

> . . . the capitalist forces constitute our natural enemy despite the fact that they helped us to defeat their most dangerous representative. It may happen that we shall again decide to make use of their aid, but always with the sole aim of accelerating their final ruin.

Rodriguez Alves became convinced that Saavedra Lamas intended to postpone a territorial settlement in the Chaco until he had first insured maximum Argentine influence in both Paraguay and Bolivia, and especially Argentine control over Santa Cruz and the oil fields; and he urged his government to counter the Yacuiba-Santa Cruz railway project by building a railway from Corumbá to Santa Cruz. Felix Nieto suspected Saavedra Lamas of designs on the Magallanes area of southern Chile. And both Chile and Brazil became concerned about Argentine military expansion and began to increase their own military establishments.

As for the ex-belligerents, even while they intrigued with Saavedra Lamas to obtain such advantages as they might, at the same time they feared and distrusted him. Above all, they came increasingly to suspect that peace between them was not their adjoining neighbors' primary concern at the Peace Conference.

With reference to the final boundary which we established betwen Bolivia and Paraguay, one may notice a slight protrusion of Paraguay towards the West. This tiny bit of territory the Paraguayans insisted on having because it encompasses Fortin (fort) Huey Long. Senator Long, for some reason, perhaps because he had swallowed the tale about Bolivia being supported by the Standard Oil Company of New Jersey, in many speeches in the Senate and elsewhere defended the Paraguayan cause and therefore became a hero to them. Actually, Fortin Huey Long, when our military observers got in to see it, was nothing more than an adobe oven for baking bread.

When discussing the accomplishment of the Chaco Peace Treaty I omitted to say that a special session of the Pan American Union (now the Organization of American States) was summoned specifically to celebrate the signing of the Peace Treaty.

Secretary Hull in his speech, amongst other things, said:

> "No other event could have had such a happy and fruitful effect on Inter-american relations than the definitive and peaceful solution of the old Chaco controversy."

I reported to the State Department several times on the rivalry—really animosity—existing between ex-President Lopez and President Santos, as the two leaders of the Liberal Party in Colombia.

Unfortunately, the State Department 25 years after the events have occurred issues copies of dispatches and telegrams from various diplomatic posts. This would be all right if they would consult the Ambassadors who had forwarded the dispatches and telegrams at the time, but instead the duty of gathering, selecting and publishing this information devolves upon some junior Secretary utterly unfamiliar with all the details and background—probably an officer not even in the service at the time of the events.

This procedure was very unfortunate in my case, because without consulting me, my dispatches and telegrams commenting on the Lopez-Santos rivalry and stating that the latter, Santos, was afraid of the former, Lopez, were issued in full. The press re-published the State Department's quotations of my reports.

Santos rightly was enraged and despite my apologies it came very near to breaking our friendship.

On page 214 and elsewhere I have criticized our extravagant and largely futile foreign aid programs, which have cost the U.S. tax payer in excess of $180 billion.

We engaged in all of these "give-aways" because a fundamental of our foreign policy has been that we so ardently wish to be loved. Love can never be bought, and the surest way to make an enemy is to lend or give someone money. This is precisely what we have been doing. The result is that governments to whom we have given or loaned (at infinitesimal interest rates) hundreds of millions or even billions of dollars dislike us, seize our properties and investments, vote against us in the U.N. and are generally disagreeable *vide* Chile, Peru and many others.

So great an admirer was I of President Somoza of Nicaragua that I likewise became a friend of his son, Anastasio Somoza. In fact, on my motion he was made an honorary member of the Metropolitan Club.

Three years ago, he was kind enough with his beautiful and charming wife, Hope, to invite Verbena and me to attend his inauguration as President in Managua, where we were given the most royal hospitality. I should add that he is a man of high intelligence and courage and does not pussyfoot when it comes to handling the Communists.

Some years ago, when a group of Communists from Cuba tried to invade Nicaragua, he captured a dozen or so of them who were inciting to riot and had them shot. Another half-dozen or so were able to escape and returned to Havana. If there were more heads of government such as he, this hemisphere would be far safer and far more secure.

While serving as President of the American Arbitration Association and Honorary Chairman of the Inter-American Commercial Arbitration Commission, I attended the United Nations in an attempt to expand arbitral procedures in international affairs. In this connection I am happy to quote the following from the Inter-American Commercial Arbitration Commissions third quarterly report for 1970:

> *United Nations Convention.* On September 30, 1970, the United States deposited its instrument of ratification of the United Nations Convention on the Recognition and Enforcement of Foreign Arbitral Awards, thus joining Ecuador and Trinidad and Tobago as ratifying countries in the Western Hemisphere. The Convention of June 10, 1958, now acceded to by thirty-six nations, recognizes the validity of an agreement in writing to submit differences to arbitration. It also provides that, under specified conditions, each contracting state shall recognize arbitral awards as binding and enforce them in accordance with the rules of procedure of the territory where the award is relied upon.
>
> Early accession to the Convention by all nations of the Western Hemisphere would give a great stimulus to the expansion of foreign trade by providing a solid legal framework for the settlement of international commercial disputes and the enforcement of the resulting arbitral awards.

When I speak earlier of the Coordinator's Office I should say that I was not in Washington when this superflouous and wasteful Agency was created; but the story I got about it was so characteristic of President Roosevelt that I never doubted it. Like so many outside agencies, it originated in the mind of Harry Hopkins, who knew and catered to the President's love of the novel and the grandiose. In this case Hopkins also played up to Roosevelt's inexplicable animosity toward the State Department.

The Department, in a way, had asked for it, by failing to take the stand that foreign affairs were its exclusive concern and that no United States Department or Agency was to do anything in a foreign country without its knowledge and consent. It even carried its namby pamby attitude to the point of permitting representatives of Agriculture and Commerce to sit on its personnel board. (When I became Assistant Secretary I proposed to make this privilege reciprocal, but I was not there long enough to get beyond irritating some of the officials in those two Departments.) In the field I always laid down the rule—and enforced it—that as Ambassador I was in charge of United States affairs and no official American activities were to be initiated without my knowledge and approval. But the Department was in no very strong position to combat the Hopkins proposal that there should be a coordinator of all United States activities in the American Republics; it had shirked its responsibility to coordinate them itself.

Having put over the idea with Roosevelt, Hopkins, who was by that time enjoying a luxurious social life among people of great wealth, happened to run into Nelson Rockefeller somewhere, and recommended him for the job. I was never able to learn what qualifications Nelson had for it beyond having once made a trip around Latin America, presumably to look over Standard Oil interests. But what he lacked in knowledge he made up in eager willingness to squander the taxpayer's money on harebrained schemes. Like so many men brought up in great wealth, he never seemed to realize how hard it is to earn and keep a dollar.

From time to time I have commented on the low calibre of some of our political appointees to posts as Ministers or even Ambassadors. I recall, not too many years ago, that we appointed a theatre ticket broker as minister to Bolivia. When he presented his credentials he was attired in full dress evening coat, a colored vest, string necktie, striped trousers, and yellow shoes. He could not be dissuaded from this costume by his staff.

Of course, a worse case occurred in or around 1910 when our Minister to Bolivia became involved in such shady deals that he had to disappear. Disappear he did, a report being arranged that he had died, but actually he was smuggled out of the country and the coffin at his funeral reportedly was filled with stones.

On page 339 I refer to an announcement issued by Secretary of State Byrnes on my appointment as Assistant Secretary. It was as follows:

> The appointment of Mr. Braden . . . is particularly a recognition of his accurate interpretation of the policies of this Government in its relations with the present government of Argentina. As Assistant Secretary in charge of Latin-American affairs, it will be his duty to see that the policies which he has so courageously sponsored in Argentina are continued with unremitting vigor.

This statement became somewhat ironical in the light of later developments.

The attitude of our government departments toward the national security has often—I might even say more often than not—been extremely frivolous. Most recently we have witnessed the inexcusable blundering or worse in respect of Cuba.

It was 1939. I was Ambassador to Colombia. Colombia was adjacent to the Panama Canal. It swarmed with Nazis. The Second World War was clearly imminent. As Ambassador to one of the most strategically important countries in the world to the United States, I had not one penny from my government to finance the gathering of intelligence, nor any agreement that intelligence was important. If this situation were not so common it might be called fantastic.

My Naval attache, Toby Munn, was allowed a munificent $1500 a year by the Navy Department to pay informants. It was paid in monthly installments for six months, then suddenly discontinued. From there on, where intelligence was concerned, I was strictly on my own.

Further to the remarks given on page 364 for my opposing the over-arming of Latin America, I should add that the question of costs didn't seem to be bothering anyone. Even at five cents on the dollar, the Latins could not affard to pay for all the war material the Pentagon was proposing to send them. I tried to find out how much that five cents would amount to. The Pentagon kept promising estimates but sent none. I asked about costs of maintenance, which I knew would be considerable. I was no more successful there.

It must have been an accident. Someone in the Pentagon must have slipped up badly. Just as I was about to give up all hope I did get an estimate on the cost of accessory equipment. For logistic transportation, equipment, medical and office equipment—those things, in other words, that keep an army running—I received an estimate of one billion and sixty-six million dollars for ten years. It was broken down country by country. I remember that the amount assigned to Chile was two and a half million dollars. Poor little Chile could no more afford that amount for accessory equipment that I could afford a private yacht. The amounts assigned to the other republics were equally unrealistic. That item alone made the entire program demonstrably idiotic.

I have recited the events which caused me to resign from Government. Among them, as set forth on page 368, was "the State Department's treatment of me". Often I have attributed this to the left-wing dislike of me and my policies, and both in testimony before Congressional committees and speeches and in other ways I have referred to my Departmental enemies as the "unidentifiable Theys".

I handily defeated them as they knew I would stage a knockdown-dragout fight if necessary. Others have received the same kind of treatment as was recounted in a book called the *Ordeal of Otto Otepka* (Arlington House), who was Chief of the Division of Evaluation in the Office of Security. Fortunately, I was more powerful than he and so was able to avoid such nasty attacks—searching files, tapping telephones, etc.—as were made on him, brought on by his legally testifying before a Senate Committee about some of the security risks who were part of the Kennedy Administration. The assaults on his character were especially scurvy. He fought and withstood all of these things with extraordinary valour, until finally Richard Nixon was elected President, and appointed him head of the Subversive Activities Control Board, thus absolving him from the accusations made against him, and re-establishing Otepka as an honest and patriotic citizen.

One of the Latin American Ambassadors to the United Nations, before Goldberg retired as our Ambassador to that body, invited me to a sumptuous luncheon at the "21" Club.

On my arrival I found that Goldberg was the guest of honor. I was seated at his right.

Our host, with what to me seemed a unique degree of indiscretion, introduced Goldberg at the end of the luncheon by saying that he had retired from the Supreme Court on President Johnson's request with the promise that if he would fill in the interim by serving in the U.N., Johnson would have him as the running mate candidate for the Vice Presidency in the forthcoming election (1968). But then Johnson ran out on Goldberg, and the latter, according to the Latino diplomat, was very much irritated.

I have since had this story confirmed to me from another and reliable source.

Immorality and Communism

ADDRESS BY THE HONORABLE SPRUILLE BRADEN
AMERICANISM EDUCATIONAL LEAGUE AWARD DINNER

January 15, 1965
Beverly Wilshire Hotel
Beverly Hills, California

Mr. Chairman, Distinguished Guests, Ladies and Gentlemen:

From the depth of feeling with which I say we thank you, I trust everyone here will sense how grateful Mrs. Braden and I are for the hospitality of the AMERICANISM EDUCATIONAL LEAGUE, and for the special award given me yesterday by it's Trustees. Also, I am indebted to the Knightly Order of St. Brigette for the presentation to me of it's Grand Cross.

Thus to be honored and to find ourselves in this distinguished company ordinarily would suffice to make us optimists, seeing the bright side as opposed to pessimists looking for gloom. (Parenthetically, I reject the definition of an optimist as one who doesn't care what happens so long as it doesn't happen to him—and a pessimist as one who lived all of his life alongside an optimist.) Instead of pretending that all events are ordered for good in the best of all worlds, I prefer to be a realist, a bit cynical perchance, and even an extremist, who believes in Thomas Jefferson's dictum made in 1791: "We prefer war in all cases to tribute under any form and to any people whatever". In short, I am not a romanticist who believes that good always automatically conquers evil anymore than I believe that evil, because of its dirty and foul blows has an invincible edge. If we will protect ourselves in the clinches and slug it out with the Devil, we can win.

Speaking of the Devil, an old Spanish aphorism is pertinent: "The Devil knows more by reason of his age than because he is a demon." While the passing years have not given me, I hope, any Satanic tendencies, I have acquired quite an experience in fighting a variety of demons. Among them have been a motley crew of shady characters, Latin American dictators, and communists. Also, as Chairman of the New York City Anti-Crime Committee, crooks in general along with some elite gangsters striving for anomimity. But, even these latter, when they are so careless as to wind up behind bars are socially very choosy—quite high hat; in prison they look down on the communists who may be their fellow tenants as below the salt and a despicable lot with whom they will have no truck.

It has been said that at first we are kids and then we kid ourselves. Well, at least on two things I do not kid myself:

1. For many years I have declared that the gravest issue facing humanity is not nuclear warfare and all the horrible death-dealing weapons science has produced; the insidious dangers of inflation; budgetary and balance of payments deficits; the undermining of the private enterprise system; nor even the gradual erosion of our freedoms. Nor is it aggression and the threats thereof; or socialism which inevitably leads to some form of totalitarianism, usually communism in our day. No. The major threat to mankind is the breakdown in morality everywhere, including government, where morality, like memory, seems to fade with the passage of time. I further hold that the worst of all immoralities is COMMUNISM.
2. I have reiterated time and again that while I hoped to live out my life in relative tranquility, due to the twin evils of immorality and communism, I was sorry for my children and much sorrier for my grandchildren. Now, these malevolent forces have expanded and spread so rapidly that I no longer am sure that my declining years will be unperturbed and peaceful.

It is rash for a layman to dive into the subject of morals, which even in ecclesiastical hands can be very dreary. Also, morals vary widely according to time and place. A multiplicity of wives is highoy respectable in some parts but not in others—at least not legally. As the Duchess said to Alice: "Tut, tut, child, everythings got a moral, if you can only find it."

I shall not now try to find and comment on generally accepted morals or flagrant immoralities. Most of us know what are good morals even if we don't always practice them assiduously. Instead, I shall point to a few random governmental actions and influence which are viewed widely with little or no criticism, but which I believe to be measurably immoral because they harm the whole community, individually and collectively.

1. Every responsible citizen is for the maximum possible equality of opportunity. But, to equate freedom and equality recently has become a popular pastime, especially by a galaxy of demagogues. This never can be done and to attempt to do so is silly, because given full equality, men stagnate, whereas given

liberty they soon become unequal, energetic and progressive; incentives take hold; hard work replaces feather-bedding; sciences, technology and the arts advance; income becomes proportionate to production; and honesty is self-imposed until it becomes almost automatic as one sure-fire essential for success. All of which make for the spiritual and material well-being of the public under the capitalist system.

2. Government is immoral when by excessive and discrimnatory taxes and spending coupled with an autocratic and large bureaucracy, it claims to create "economic growth". Actually, it does no such thing, but on the contrary, robs Peter to pay Paul, hampers or destroys free, private, competitive enterprise which gives men the opportunity to develop their individual potentialities. Under a paternalistic and centralized government, men in all walks of life and of every calling increasingly seek aid or subsidies from the bureaucratic power; the inappropriate and indelicate, or even outright corruption seep in at all levels of society; pride of craftsmanship degenerates; people want something for nothing and "Give me Liberty or Give me Death" is reduced to a simple "gimme".

   I do not consider it ethical for any government—such as we have experienced in the U.S.A. over the last three decades—to resort to the worn-out and discredited ideas of a welfare state; i.e. in a word Socialism, which the famous ex-socialist, Max Eastman, characterized as the "Flop of the Century".

3. Washington should not cover its confusion, lack of knowledge and blunders by employing thousands of public relations experts and spending hundreds of millions of dollars each year to write and feed self-serving stories, or enervating myths to the public, whose complacency in the face of serious problems too often flows from this type sedation known as "Managed News". This is a prime example of kidding ourselves.

4. Even our language under this process is distorted. "A curbstone guess" is dignified as "A calculated risk". "Human rights" are described as being far superior to and in conflict with "property rights", when in fact without "property rights" there can be no other "rights", human or otherwise. Only free men, and never slaves, have "property rights".

5. Our farmers are called "independent" although the Federal Government tells them what and how much to produce, in what fields to plant, and determines their income. If they disobey they are fined and even sent to jail. In the end, when people are thus told when to sow and when to reap, they will lack for bread.

6. "Free Workers", with governmental sanctions and legislative support, are compelled to join a Union and pay dues. I question

the ethics of this system. True, a Union officer misappropriating funds may be brought to trial. But is it an any less heinous immorality for labor leaders to use both the power of their Unions and the dues for their own aggrandizement and to back politicians and policies to which, as individuals, the workers are indifferent or even opposed?

The few transgressions committed or licensed by the government itself, which I have listed, at first glance may appear relatively insignificant; but they alarm me because not only do they harm the community and therefore are immoral, but still worse they:

a. Typify the usages which have destroyed nation after nation through all history;
b. Are precisely what the Communists try to inveigle us into doing because if we comply they hope to take over;
c. Weaken the U.S.A. domestically and thereby expose the country to conquest, at least by alien ideas and eventually militarily from abroad.

The Hammurabi Code promulgated earlier than 2,000 B.C. by imposing controls over wages, prices, production, consumption and all the rest of the economy, wrecked Babylonia. Governmental extravagance and a bloated bureaucracy killed individual initiative and led to the fall of ancient Greece. A planned economy of state maintenance for the slothful and excessive taxation brought the collapse of the later Roman Empire and regression of a civilized society into the Dark Ages. The Welfare State of the Incas became so debilitated as to become easy prey for Pizzaro and his "Conquistadores". In its turn, the great Spanish Empire broke when the throne so regimented every activity that no one could earn a living except by being a public employee, a priest, or a sailor. So Portugal, in its day, the richest empire in the Western World, disintegrated. For the same reasons the British Empire is now dissolving before our eyes. God forbid that the U.S.A. follow any further down these disastrous trails than it already has!

The details of recorded history may be full of falsehoods, just as romance is of truths. But it's broad movements over long periods of time prove that only nations committed to the principles of individual initiative and ownership of property have risen above penury, produced science, art and literature and promoted the general welfare. Moreover, no major civilization ever perished primarily because it was murdered by an external enemy. In each case, the victim first was weakened fatally by its own internal measures; in effect, it really committed suicide.

We must heed these cruel lessons of the past lest we be condemned to live them again.

Amidst all of the confusions and surprises of the modern world, a bang-up blunder may work out well—but only very rarely and by accident—after all there was the flier, "One-Way Corrigan"—who took off for California but landed in Europe. However, some of my less than favorite orators in the U.N. seem to feel that by following the absurd, better results will ensue than from logic. For instance, they denounce the U.S.A. and Belgium for humanely rescuing hundreds if not thousands of black and white hostages from the Congo, in the face of an official report to the U.N. that:

> "Witnesses attended scenes in which victims were dismembered, disembowelled and the heart later used for a ritual food."

Thus do Moscow, Peiping, Belgrade and other communist capitals make common cause with savages and cannibals.

As Tallerande said of the trial of the Duke of Enghein: "This is not merely a crime. It is much worse; it is an imbecility."

Those words about size up the Communist Conspiracy. It is not merely a gross immorality and a crime, but an imbecility. Communism while pretending to march toward progress actually is a reversion to a primitive system of tribal life and the morals of the ant-heap. Never in the many times it has been tried through all history has it benefitted either its subjects or humanity. Basically, it is stupid in its impracticability and evil in ideology, performance and effect.

Its system of government and way of life have been one long record of blunders, depravity and atrocities. Under this obscene conspiracy, there have been committed every known crime; broken promises and treaties, lies heaped on lies, thefts and tortures and individuals and mass murders.

Yet in our epoch, because of mankinds' ignorance, apathy and unwillingness to think, Communism has grown in less than 50 years to its present size, huge power and vast wealth.

By their iniquitous but shrewd intrigues, the Communists have contributed measureably to the civilized nations weakening themselves. They have subverted the U.S.A. and other countries into adopting many of the socialistic regulations, regimentations and laws which have been corroding our fundamental freedoms.

Aiding this huge conspiracy have been countless innocent although well-intentioned sentimentalists or idealists. Stalin baptized these groups as "useful idiots". Even the Chairman of the Policy Planning Staff in the State Department has advocated in writing what Senator J. Glenn Beal of Maryland called "an amazing plea for the destruction of our national sovereignity and our existence as a nation".

Starting from practically zero in 1917, the Communists have come to control about one-third of the earth's surface. Since 1946 they have been taking over and enslaving peoples at the rate of seven thousand per hour—mind you per hour—not per day or week. This paradox, that an absurd and cruel failure opposed to all logic should spread to the degree it has, justifies, I believe, my contention that Communism is the worst of all immoralities.

An essential ingredient of the Communist Conspiracy at all times has been to humiliate and weaken the U.S.A., causing it to lose the respect of the world and to suffer ridicule as a rather cowardly "paper tiger". Beyond the many serious incidents such as in Korea where somewhere between five and six thousand of our boys taken prisoners were brutally murdered, there have been the Berlin Wall, Vietnam and Cuba. Moreover, the Commies, like the Bongo drummers, keep up an incessant rat-a-tat-tat of both minor and major annoyances and worse, to embarrass our government.

It has become an international sport—almost a monthly occurrence for mobs inspired by the local governments to storm and virtually wreck our Embassies and other establishments abroad. The Kremlin a few months ago set up a so-called "Solidarity Fund" with $100 million to finance student agitations, riots and insurrections throughout the Americas. To these ends, Castro's Cuba is serving as an educational center and sort of clearing house. Eight thousand students from all over this hemisphere already have been trained in these subversion schools. While serving as Ambassador in Argentina, then under the police state dictatorship of Peron, I told a true story of an Ambassador who appealed to the Foreign Minister for protection of his Embassy building. When the latter offered to send more police, the Ambassador begged: "Don't send more police, but fewer students". Perhaps the antics of a very small number of students in Berkeley last month may be relevant.

A favorite Communist trick is to kidnap U.S. citizens, including our military. Our "no win" policies have prevented effective protests being made in these cases by Washington. The State Department has jettisoned an 1860 ruling of the Supreme Court that "the great object and duty of government is . . . the protection of the lives, liberty and property of the people . . . whether abroad or at home . . . and any government failing in the object of the performance of the duty is not worth preserving".

My personal experience has taught me that the sole thing Communists respect is effective strength greater than their own. Accordingly, Moscow knows that for its conquest of the world, the U.S.A. first must be encircled and defeated, preferably from within. The Communists prefer to resort to armed conflict only as an extreme measure, when and if they are conviced they can win an easy victory. But the encirclement of the U.S.A. is taking place exactly as per Lenin's specifications. Eastern Europe, the Middle East, Asia and Africa either have fallen, or are in danger of doing so. But the gravest threat to the security of our country lies in the Communist infiltration, espionage and insurrection throughout the Western hemisphere and particularly in Cuba.

For a time the U.S. public was wrought up at the thought of a communist bastion on that island, only ninety miles off our shores. Lately, however, due either to the indifference of our leaders or their unwillingness to face and give the public the facts, this Cuban menace, despite the Bay of Pigs and the October 22, 1962 missile confrontation, has been lost in the shuffle of world events and pushed off the front page, radio and T.V. by Vietnam, the Congo, and other faraway trouble spots.

I am compelled to say the meanest thing that can be said, "I told you so," because several times in respect to the growth of Communism throughout Latin America I have issued the strongest warnings, only to have them ignored. In 1945 I told about Peron along with his anti-U.S. attitude, as he collaborated with the communists. In 1952 I spoke out against the Guatemalan communist regime of Arbenz and the Marxist one in Bolivia. Finally, nearly a year and a half before Fidel Castro came down from the hills on January 1, 1959 to take over in Cuba, I warned that our then policies would lead to chaos and communism on that island. I alerted the State Department six months before the tragic Bay of Pigs defeat that, as then planned, it would fail. Far in advance of the October 22, 1962 confrontation, I declared publicly that there were missiles on the Island of Cuba.

Frankly, I am tired of being a Cassandra and only recite these facts because I am convinced that my sources of information are just as accurate now as they were before. I am convinced there still are many missiles. at least of short and intermediate range, hidden on the Island of Cuba and that there are submarine bases or pens, including those in underground caves opening on the surrounding waters.

King Phillip of Spain said: "He who controls Cuba controls the Americas." President Jefferson expressed the same thought, as did our own famous strategist, Admiral Mahan, when he declared the Carribean was vital for the defense of the U.S.A.

Therefore, I make so bold as to say that unless the Communists are driven out of Cuba, that island, under Moscow and Peiping direction, more than any other part of the world, will continue to be a cancer eating out the very innards of the Western Hemisphere. The Cubans cannot save themselves; they cannot go up against machine guns, tanks and gas unarmed. Hence, I maintain that the only way to drive the communists (including Russians, Chinese and African troops) out is by an invasion by patriotic Cubans, supported by other Latin-American contingents, but with the main effort and responsibility falling on the U.S. Army, Navy, Air Corps and Marines.

If we will take this positive action it will show that we mean business and so restore to us the respect of other nations and help galvanize free men everywhere into action to regain their liberty. The encouragement thus given to our allies in southeast Asia and Africa might even bring victory and independence to them. Many neutralist nations well might throw out their Kremlin bosses and flock to our side because a brave and successful action in Cuba would convince them that ours was the winning side.

Never before has the U.S.A. feared to fight for justice and freedom. Never have we paid tribute as in the case of the Cuban prisoners taken at the Bay of Pigs; nor ransom to bail out our citizens and soldiers from communist prison camps. If the U.S.A. is to survive it is high time to stop being timid and once again to hold cowardice to be utterly immoral.

Ladies and Gentlemen, in many ways I have drawn a gloomy and pesimistic picture. Yet, in the words of the South Pacific song, I remain a "cockeyed optimist", provided the U.S.A. returns to and stands firmly on certain unchanging principles, which for years past I have enunciated—i.e. whenever I could get anybody to listen to me:

I have maintained that foreign policy necessarily may change according to circumstances, times and place, but that there are certain immutable principles which always must outweigh policy. These principles are:

I. Respect is the *sine qua non* of all foreign relations. Irrespective of every other consideration and under all conditions, the U.S.A. must demand and get RESPECT. To do so we must first have self-respect and exact from our own and other governments respect for their obligations and the sanctity of agreements.

II. The sole reason for being of the State Department and Foreign Service is to protect and advance the legitimate interests of the U.S.A. If ever they should become illegitimate, then they are unworthy of this great nation and should not be supported.

III. Every policy and action must be moral. Leaving ethics to one side, only in this way will we win and hold the confidence and respect from other countries which are so essential for a solid and enduring amity between peoples.

IV. While never attempting to impose our way of life or form of government, our ideas or even our moral standards, on others, we should ourselves stand unswervingly for and practice the system of republican, constitutional, representative government laid down for us by the Founding Fathers in the Declaration of Independence, the Constitution, and the Bill of Rights.

We can adhere to these principles and help save our civilization by following the precepts set forth by George Washington in his Farewell Address, the finest statement ever made on both domestic and foreign policy. If with moral fibre we will dedicate ourselves to doing these things then, with God's help, the U.S.A. will defeat communism along with many other immoral forces. We will preserve our freedoms and insure peace for our children and grandchildren in, if not the best of all worlds, at least in a much better one than the present.

Statement by
The Honorable Spruille Braden

BEFORE THE
INTERNAL SECURITY SUBCOMMITTEE OF
THE UNITED STATES SENATE

July 17, 1959

Gentlemen:

I appreciate more than I can express adequately the invitation to appear before the Internal Security Subcommittee of the Senate, because not only has this Committee, through the years, performed a great and patriotic service, but it has proven itself to be one of the best safeguards and defenses of the United States.

In the interests of brevity, and because already in previous testimony, before this Committee I have given details of my experiences in Latin America in diplomacy, business and otherwise, I omit any curriculum vitae now.

Perhaps as a chopping block leading to questions and discussion, I best may summarize my opinion in respect of Cuba and the Caribbean area generally by saying that in all of my many years of intimate contact, since early childhood, with Latin America, never have I seen the situation so dangerous as it is now for the defense of the United States.

The principal threat to our security of course is Communism and its ever present weapon Anti-Americanism. But this menace is aided and exascerbated by other Marxist influences, by socialism, misguided idealism and unsound nationalisms, all of which, unless eradicated at an early date, will convert the Caribbean into a Red lake.

So grave is the situation, that I pray with all my heart, body and soul, that the Communists and their most useful tool to date, Fidel Castro, may be ejected from their control of Cuba. Unless this is done soon—very soon—the United States, for its own security, may be catapulted into an armed intervention. This would be a major catastrophe for the inter-American system and the United States. It is precisely what the Communists wish to accomplish.

This Committee will recall my testimony before it when on December 22, 1953 and March 25, 1954, I described how I had been able in Cuba, as Ambassador of the United States,

1) to destroy the Communist organization known as "El Frente Nacional Anti-Fascisti" (National Anti-Fascist Front), and put an end to their meetings;
2) to block the machinations of Harry Dexter White, Assistant Secretary of Treasury of the United States, and Lawrence Advisor to the Secretary of State, in respect of an insidious scheme to establish a Central Bank and Cuban currency on such conditions as inevitably would have led to financial chaos in that country, thus opening the way for the Communists to get a foothold there.

In the aforementioned testimony, while expressing a high regard for the vast majority of the Career Foreign Service, their integrity and intelligence, I also detailed the infiltration of the Department of State by, as I christened them, "Unidentifiable THEYS". I described Alger Hiss' intervention in connection with our bases in Panama, and the attempt—which I blocked—to put over on the State Department an organization of 1080 persons, under the name of "Research and Intelligence". This plot, hatched in Alger Hiss' office, had extremely dangerous implications.

In that testimony, I gave documentary evidence of the warnings about Communist infiltration in this hemisphere, which repeatedly I had sounded from Havana, when I was Ambassador there, just as I had in "Top Secret" telegrams sent in July, 1945, to the President and Secretary of State from Buenos Aires, where I was then Ambassador. These telegrams described the serious Communist threat to this hemisphere and how Peron was working hand-in-glove with the Kremlin. I urged that President Truman and Churchill at the Potsdam Conference, confront Stalin with these facts and demand that an end be put to these Moscow contrivings. So far as I have been able to ascertain, neither of these telegrams, sent directly to the President and the Secretary of State of the United States, by a United States Ambassador, were ever delivered. It therefore does not surprise me when some of our Cuban and other Latin American friends are convinced that Castro and other anti-U.S. leaders are tipped off by friends within our own Government, as to just how far they can go with impunity.

I recited to this Committee with documents, the oft-repeated instructions which I had given in my capacity as Assistant Secretary of State in Washington to my staff, about the utter immorality of Communism and the perils we faced from it in the Americas. In short, gentlemen, time and time again I warned, with the citation of concrete cases, of the danger of Communism to the security of the American continents.

Similarly, I submitted to this Committee copy of speech delivered by me at Dartmouth College on March 12, 1953, sounding the alarm in respect of Communist infiltration in Guatemala.

Unfortunately, my many warnings were ignored, but subsequent events proved them to be absolutely accurate.

In early or mid-1957, I gave an interview to HUMAN EVENTS, in which I told of Fidel Castro's (now Prime Minister of Cuba) activities in respect of the Communist-inspired insurrections in Bogota during the Inter-American Conference held in that city in April, 1948, and I declared that he was either a Communist or their tool, and that his victory would bring political and economic chaos and the tyranny of Communism to Cuba.

Because these warnings were futile, on October 4, 1957, at a meeting of the U. S. Council of the Inter-American Council of Commerce and Production, where the main speaker was to be Mr. Terry B. Sanders, Director of the South American Division in the State Department, who had served under me in Colombia, I sent through him a most emphatic message to the higher echelons of the Department. I requested Terry to tell all of the high officials, up to and including the Secretary of State, that:

> The State Department was thoroughly familiar with the fact that no Ambassador had ever had a more violent collision with a Chief of State than I had had with Fulgencio Batista, when I was in Cuba. Therefore, I had no preconceptions or delusions in respect of him. I knew his bad points and I knew his good points. But I observed that when the United States, in the face of the solid support against the Soviet and Communism given us by the Batista regime, refused to ship arms to that Government (bought and paid for by it, frequently on the recommendations of our Military, Naval and Air Missions), it inevitably would convince the Cuban people that we were supporting Castro and opposed to Batista. I said that this interpretation would lead to Castro's victory, which would result in chaos throughout Cuba, which in turn would lead to Communist control of that island.

This is exactly what happened. A Communist reign of terror now overwhelms Cuba. My message was delivered by Sanders to the higher echelons of the Department, but it was ignored. As a result, we now are reduced to the extremity of trying to close the barn door after the horse has been stolen.

Practically every development in the Pearl of the Antilles since January 1, 1959 has confirmed the increasing domination by the Communists in government and every other sphere of life in that country, with the result that today the government of Cuba is completely Communist-controlled, and every non-Communist citizen of that country fears for his own life and that of his loved ones. Of course, like every other Communist regime, they deny this fact, which can be proven readily by a series of incidents and events, as in their public declarations, they pretend to be, as they call it, "democratic".

I request that a speech which I gave before the Rotary Club of New York on April 9th, and repeated before the Long Island Federation of Women's Clubs on April 10th, be made a part of the record. (With your permission, now I shall read to you the last few pages of that address, beginning on page 7 thereof.)

The foregoing statement I hope will elicit questions, not only to me, but to such distinguished Cuban patriots as Emilio Nunez Portuondo, former Cuban Ambassador in the United Nations, and the most staunch defender of the United States and Anti-Communism ever to appear in the meetings of that body; former Prime Minister Jorge Garcia Montes; former Finance Minister Garcia Reyneri; the former Chief of Cuban Intelligence, Col. Mariano Faget, and many others, including such distinguished businessmen as Sr. Cajigas.

Gentlemen, anything that has happened in respect of Communist penetration in the Far or Near East or elsewhere in the world, from the point of view of the United States, sinks into insignificance alongside of this threat from the Caribbean. Unless summary action is taken promptly, I dread to think of what may happen to these United States. Unless we take immediate and strong measures, Khrushchev may—as he has announced—bury us. The very life of the United States is at stake.

ADDRESS AT ANNUAL BANQUET OF THE SONS OF THE REVOLUTION WASHINGTON'S BIRTHDAY, 1952

Waldorf Astoria

The Honorable Spruille Braden
Former Ambassador and Assistant Secretary of State
Chairman, New York City Anti-Crime Committee

THE FAREWELL ADDRESS— A SIMPLE AND BRAVE FOREIGN POLICY

To be asked by the Sons of the Revolution on this anniversary and before so distinguished a company, to respond to the Toast to George Washington, is an honor for which I am profoundly grateful.

As I rise to respond, I must confess to being somewhat overwhelmed by the task assigned me. I am confronted with a perplexing paradox: It would seem that everything which can, or should be said of George Washington, has already been said and often superlatively well said—certainly more eloquently than I ever could. On the other hand, so far do the man's achievements and character surpass the powers of expression, that one may reasonably conclude that nothing adequate has yet been said, or for that matter can be said, of him.

In either case perhaps silence for me now would be the better part of discretion. Nevertheless, I am emboldened by the compliment of your invitation, very humbly, to attempt to draw from Washington's life and his Farewell Address a few lessons which may help in the solution of some of the problems presently besetting this Nation.

George Washington was a dazzling star, even in such a brilliant galaxy as was that of Jefferson and Hamilton, Franklin and Adams, together with all the other Founding Fathers. Just as competent navigators on calm as well as tempestuous seas take their bearings from the sun as often as may be possible, so our Ship of State will continue to sail safely and well, in both fair and foul weather, so long as its course is set by the light which comes down to us from Washington's wisdom.

Accustomed to extraordinary responsibilities from early youth, he learned the vagaries, the good and the evil of human nature. He came to know equally well the powerful and the weak and the rich and the poor. Through long and diverse experiences, his noble instincts were sharpened, as simultaneously he acquired a vast store of knowledge. An undaunted courage and intensity of spirit always were guided, in him, by an incisive and balanced mind and moral self-control.

Washington's military genius, acclaimed by experts in the old, as well as in the new world, won him the appellation of the "American Fabius." Yet with such splendor was his every civilian task acquitted, that Patrick Henry was led to say of his service in the Continental Congress: "If you speak of solid information and sound judgment, Colonel Washington is unquestionably the greatest man upon that floor."

Indeed, "the greatest man upon that floor," or upon any other floor past or present, in the history of these United States, George Washington combined an incorruptible integrity and rare wisdom, an inexhaustible energy and extraordinary ability in statecraft, with kindliness, patience and the many other virtues which made up the soul of this exalted patriot.

Every action and statement by Washington demonstrated his undeviating devotion to God and Country. But, his country, for him, never was restricted to the narrow limits of the thirteen colonies. As John Fiske says, "From an early age he had indulged in prophetic dreams of the coming civilization of America." Because he visioned the growth here of a great and strong nation, he aided Pitt's scheme for over-throwing French power in North America. In his prescience, he not only studied water connections for possible means of transportation between East and West, but he personally bought extensive tracts of land beyond the mountains.

And so, it is entirely understandable, that the parting counsels of this inspired and far-seeing leader of men should have made the "strong and lasting impression" on the American people Washington desired. For many decades, his advice served, as he hoped it would, to "prevent our Nation from running the (unhappy) course which has hitherto marked the destiny of (other) Nations." It is appropriate and timely to observe that so long as we have been guided by the principles of the Farewell Address, this country has lived in peace and prospered greatly.

When we failed to preserve that unity of government, which constitutes us one people (sic), we suffered the tragedy of the Civil War. Twice, when we implicated ourselves in the vicissitudes of

European politics and the "combinations and collisions of her friendships and enmities," we were drawn into World Wars I and II.

I am not arguing whether our actions in these instances were right or wrong; whether, on those two last mentioned occasions, we should or should not have ignored Washington's counsel; or whether his views have been rendered obsolete by science and modern transportation; I merely point to the fact that each time we have abandoned the precepts of the Farewell Address, trouble, serious trouble, has ensued.

I submit that, based on this record, the exercise of a modicum of common sense would indicate that our foreign policy—and all our other policies for that matter—should be reassessed promptly and thoroughly from the viewpoint of Washington's parting advice to the Nation.

Such a proposal, I realize, will be an anathema to many sentimentalists and "One Worlders," having the best of intentions, as well as to those false prophets who of recent years have spread over the land preaching new isms, mostly pink or red in hue. Amongst these people are many who blithely think that Communist dictatorships, fascist police states and other governments of dubious antecedents and usages, can be counted on to defend what they like to call the "Free World." Such are the people who, in a misdirected or pretended zeal for the good of the nation, revile as "Isolationists" all who defend the irrefutably successful principles of the Farewell Address as the best way to cultivate peace and harmony with all.

The American public has been induced by these same people, at least temporarily to accept certain things as axiomatic when actually they are nothing of the kind. For instance, we have been told officially and repeatedly that the one paramount objective of our foreign policy is Peace—world wide Peace.

Everyone wants Peace. The question is how to get it? Certainly not by appeasement nor by financing, in effect hiring, others to fight our battles. Rome's doom was sealed when she began to employ foreign mercenaries for her defense.

George Washington wanted peace so fervently that he fought for it, and planned for it in his Farewell Address. But far more, for his fellow citizens he wanted the only things which can make an enduring peace. He wanted Freedom and Honor, Decency and Honesty. These, together with the defense and advancement of the legitimate interests of the United States and its nationals, still remain, I believe, the main goals the American people instinctively seek to reach through the conduct of their foreign relations.

Once foreign policy has been determined and commitments made thereunder, every honorable man will adhere to Washington's admonition, rigorously to meet these obligations, irrespective of whether or not we like them. This makes it all the more imperative that our policies be formulated with maximum wisdom, and only after the most meticulous analysis and exhaustive thought and discussion.

For the people—who under our system must establish the broad patterns of policy—to reach sound conclusions, they must be fully and truthfully informed. To this end, there must be in the Congress and the press and by the public, the most ample and searching debate possible on every facet of our foreign affairs before definitive commitments are consummated. Thus, without in the slightest contravening Washington's warnings against an excessive or reckless factionalism, to explore and argue every aspect of each problem to a finality will strengthen the Nation. Not to do so may well stir partisan venom and recriminations, such as have resulted from Yalta, and weaken the Nation.

The Jeffersonians annoyed President Washington greatly by their opposition to his policy of reaching an understanding with Britain instead of pushing for a rapprochement with France as they wanted. Even under this pressure, which imperiled the success of his plan, the President made no attempt to restrict debate or to conceal the issues, nor did he suggest a bipartisan policy. Were he alive today, I am sure he would condemn any bipartisan policy were it, in ever so small a degree, to suppress or elude open and vigorous criticism.

Even John Foster Dulles has declared that our so-called bipartisan policy should be used "only sparingly."

To this I say "Amen" and add the following comments:

1. Domestic and foreign affairs and policies are so inextricably linked each to the other and so inter-react on one another that whatever we do or say within this country has profound and wide reverberations abroad, and, therefore, on our foreign policy. Similarly, our foreign policies will in considerable measure influence domestic affairs.

Yet, I take it that no thinking person would propose a domestic bipartisan policy.

But can we have bipartisanship in foreign affairs and avoid it domestically? Irrespective of how cautious we may be scrupulously to restrict bipartisanship to foreign affairs, the resultant policies will repercuss internally. To the extent that that bipartisanship is thus injected into the domestic field, it will tend to destroy the two party system which, I think everyone will agree, is essential for the successful working of our kind of democracy. One party government is the essence of totalitarianism. The consequentces of permitting bipartisanship to spread into domestic affairs could be disastrous.

The inter-play of foreign and domestic policies is apparent already in our waging of the cold war. Even if we grant that the NATO and its predecessor or accompanying agreements are essential, they require such huge expenditures as to make equally imperative compensating economies at home in respect of luxuries and, if needs be, some necessities. In other words, our government should proceed, just as a prudent man does when taking out insurance. It should economize on a long list of domestic expenditures having to do with social and welfare legislation, agricultural, labor, business and other subsidies, and all the many varieties of paternalism, which demoralize the people and destroy their hardihood by teaching them to try to get something for nothing.

Our failure precisely to follow sound economic and financial policies at home will so seriously weaken this Nation as to imperil not only our domestic well-being but also the entire foreign situation. If, as a result, the United States goes down, the world will fall with it.

In short, we arrive at the conclusion that the Republicans, who claim to be the defenders of sound economic and financial principles, before agreeing to go along on ECA and NATO, logically should have demanded the abandonment of many spending programs and "fair deal" proposals. Examples could be multiplied across the board of foreign policy to demonstrate that unless bipartisanship is employed "only sparingly" it must inevitably be extended into the domestic sphere.

2. The attempt to formulate a bipartisan policy necessarily leads to the committee type of accord or compromise, i.e., watering down to the least common denominator. Thus, due to the number and variety of opinions which must be consolidated, bipartisanship will in general lead to weaker rather than stronger policies and action, even though, when once determined, the policies acquire some degree of strength from the unanimity with which they appear to be supported.

3. A further evil effect of a bipartisan policy is that it destroys dicipline within each party. Adherents of both the Administration and the Opposition in Congress and elsewhere become inclined to go off on their own particular tangents and in effect to form splinter groups. Thus, instead of the organized, concentrated, intelligent and constructive criticism of an opposition party, there results a heterogeneous, haphazard series of criticisms by individuals. This is ex-

emplified presently by the divisions within both parties on foreign policy. More bewildering than the occasionally savage denunciations of an opposition Senator, is the fact that leading Democratic Chairmen in the Senate not infrequently have made pronouncements in direct contradiction to the policies announced by the President and the Secretary of State.

As a result, both parties, the supporters of the bipartisan policy and the opposition thereto all appear often to be going around in circles. Worse still, the public is presented with so many divergent views that it either becomes confused or accepts without adequate scrutiny the most intensive propaganda to which i' may be subjected (usually from governmental or bipartisan sources). In each instance we are deprived of the judgment of an informed public opinion, which, even if it existed, would be unable—due to bipartisanship—to express itself at the polls. Again we see how the two party system is broken down.

A collateral danger is that such superior wisdom is attributed to the bipartisan policy that people become timid about questioning it, lest they be linked to reactionaries or charged with unpatriotic or communistic sympathies. Such a state of mind does not make for an effectively functioning democratic republic.

4. In an attempt to get concurrence for a bipartisan policy in one area, policies elsewhere may be debilitated or sacrificed entirely.

When this happens—as it has in recent years—it has lessened respect for the United States and gravely harmed us in other ways. I would add that Respect is the élan vital—the essential impulse—in the conduct of foreign relations.

Of course, in the event of war or other imminent danger, when the chips are down, we Americans will close ranks, hoping that our country is in the right, but always "our country, right or wrong!"

Also, as we have so often seen, a certain amount of bipartisanship will develop automatically on many issues having to do with foreign affairs. Under the circumstances, I wonder if it would not be best to leave it at that, excepting for the rare times when it should be used "only sparingly." Why not follow the old system which has served us well in the past, even with the knock-down drag-out fights that it involves in the Senate and House, the press and elsewhere?

A basic tenet of the Constitution is that it is the President's responsibility with the advice and consent of the Senate, to direct our foreign affairs. Let him assume that responsibility. He must neither shirk it nor shift any part of it to others, thus putting the burden on two or more masters, whom no man can serve well. Already in our National Capitol we have too much committee government—a veritable young Soviet.

Probably the two most brilliant examples of successful foreign policy and action in our history—the Louisiana Purchase and the Monroe Doctrine—were not bipartisan. On the contrary, in each case the President acted unilaterally in keeping with his responsibilities. Not only was Jefferson opposed by the Federalists on the Louisiana Purchase, as he was also in the War of 1812, but he and his advisors had serious doubts themselves as to whether or not he had gone beyond the limits of the Constitution. As for the Monroe Doctrine, if it had been submitted to the Senate, it probably would have received popular bipartisan support due to the fact that this Nation was just beginning its period of enthusiasm for "Manifest Destiny." A less dramatic example of strictly partisan policy is that the Democrats in 1854 strongly favored the annexation of Cuba—vide: The Ostend Manifesto—however, the Republican opposition finally won the fight on this red hot issue. This situation subsequently was reversed when Cleveland, supported by the Democrats, opposed the annexation of Hawaii. The Republicans were for it and in the end they won.

When I say that respect is the essential impulse in the conduct of foreign relations, I mean that in order to enjoy the confidence and friendship of other nations and to exercise the leadership which is ours, there must be mutual respect and that cannot exist unless there be self-respect on both sides. This thought is implicit in everything that Washington ever said or did.

If we are to maintain our self-respect and the respect of others, we must always insist upon being treated with the utmost consideration and dignity, even in what at the time may appear to be insignificant or inconsequential matters.

Let me illustrate my point by repeating what I said to this esteemed Society on April 19, 1948:

"I hope that we as a nation soon will recognize the validity in human relationships of the old saying, 'Give a knave an inch, he'll take an ell'." This verity works in geometrical progression; if you let the knave take an ell, then he'll take a mile and soon more and more, until he has enveloped the globe and there is nothing left to give or take. The only way is to stop him in his tracks at the first inch, or so soon thereafter as possible.

In this connection, I would cite two recent incidents: 1. On January 14, 1948, two uniformed United States Army officers, attached to our Legation in Budapest, were illegally and unwarrantedly arrested in Hungary by Soviet troops, deprived of their small arms, kept incommunicado and as prisoners transported to Austria, where they were released the next day at the intervention of American military authorities there. It was not until February 7th that we mildly protested to Moscow—and, apparently, that is all we have done about it.

2. Recently an American soldier in Vienna, simply because he would not get off the sidewalk into the gutter in front of a Russian headquarters, was beaten down by a rifle butt and shot in the shoulder with a dum-dum bullet by a Soviet guard. He lay in that gutter unaided for forty-five minutes. To date, I have seen no mention in the press of even an official protest.

Incidents of this kind confront us with extremely difficult decisions. On the one hand, if we refuse to tolerate such indignities and forthwith exact adequate apoligies and assurances that they will not be repeated, we must be prepared to enforce our demands. Our ultimatum may lead to war. On the other hand, failure to take summary action will enhance the aggressor's prestige and increasingly encourage him to commit further and worse affronts until a point will be reached when our tardy ultimatum will not be accepted at full value, will cause the aggressor to become more reckless and ruthless, and so will be rejected. Then, for a self-respecting people, the only course is to fight. Hence, in cases like these, we must recognize that whatever is our decision, it may bring war. However, a protracted sufferance of such incidents will make war well-nigh inevitable; whereas, there may be at least some hope of avoiding it, if at an early moment we firmly demand that our rights be respected. The surest way to keep the peace is to stop these things at their beginnings."

Our government by deliberately shutting its eyes to those bad beginnings, by giving those two short inches to the Soviet in Hungary and Vienna, paved the way for a crescendo of abuse and indignities which have been heaped on the United States and its citizens and which include the Berlin Blockade, the swallowing of Czechoslovakia, the imprisonment of Vogeler and Oatis, and Korea!

The inches have become ells and lengthened into miles which have now cost us more than 105,000 battle casualties, not to mention the recent humiliation of paying ransom for the four flyers seized by Russian officers in Hungary just as were the two Lieutenant Colonels four years ago.

What has come over the United States that it tolerates such outrages? Have we lost our virility? We, the greatest and strongest nation in all history, appear to fear the U.S.S.R. more than does her little neighbor, Finland. We removed one of the greatest generals of our history and of our times from his command because, so far as I can discern, he wanted to win—and that we did, forsooth, because we feared the criticism of our so-called allies and other UN members.

> "Fear admitted into public councils,
> Betrays like treason."

By accepting a stalemate and the inglorious truce negotiations in Korea, we have lost face throughout the Orient, possibly invited further aggression in South Eastern Asia or elsewhere, and perhaps lost an opportunity to eject Mao and his Communists from the control of China. I say this because the records demonstrate that despots who are willing to shoot down their own people can only be unseated by bloody revolution or war, as happened with Hitler and Mussolini.

Instead of stopping things at their beginnings, there has been chatter about "good old Joe" and how close we were to peace in the late Spring of 1950. Meanwhile the Kremlin has extended its domination over hundred of millions of people and vast areas of the earth. This alarming expansion has now reached into the Western Hemisphere. Due to our negligence and timidity the Communists with some of their gangster pals now largely control Guatemala, less than 1000 miles from the Panama Canal. There is danger that they may do the same in some of the other American Republics.

Since we have made Europe's primary interests our own and ceded sovereignty to the UN, NATO, and other international organizations, how shall we answer Washington's querry: "Why quit our own to stand on foreign ground?" In reply, I suggest that our first consideration always must be the United States. When it is so strong as possible economically, militarily and every other way, we may turn to our immediate community, the Western Hemisphere. Only when it likewise is impregnable should we look overseas. By this procedure we will, in Washington's words, "remain one People, under an efficient government, . . . (then) we may defy material injury from external annoyances; . . . belligerent nations, under the impossibility of making acquisitions upon us, will not likely hazard giving us provocation, we may choose peace or war, as our interest(s) counsel."

We still are trying to do the impossible; to buy friendship, by scattering our taxpayers' hard-earned dollars all over the globe in gifts and loans, which frequently promote socialism or communism and are so wasteful as to do more harm than good even to the recipients. In return, we are "being reproached with ingratitude for not giving more."

We eschew George Washington's counsel "to cherish public credit" and "to avoid the accumulation of debt" as we bankrupt large sections of our own citizenry with governmental extravagance and exorbitant taxes.

Both at home and abroad, we have dangerously undermined confidence in and respect for our Country by permitting corruption to spread widely throughout the Federal, State and local governments. We ignore the proposition in the Farewell Address that "Providence" has "connected the permanent felicity of a nation with its virtue."

We have subverted Religion and Morality, which Washington called "the indispensable supports of prosperity," the "great pillars of human happiness," and the "firmest props of the duties of men and citizens."

From this distressing, though incomplete recitation, it is evident that Respect no longer is the essential impulse in the conduct of our foreign relations.

If this Nation is to pull out of the mire in which presently it is thrashing about, it must recapture its self-respect and the respect of others. It must stop at their beginnings every assault on or affront to our Country and its citizens. It must eliminate bipartisanship and those sentimentalisms which only create confusion, emasculate our foreign policy and impede or prevent effective action.

If these United States of America are to survive in liberty and prosperity, our government and people must again act with Honor and Vigor, self-reliance and dignity. There must be a return throughout the Country to Morality. As Washington declared, "Virtue or Morality is a necessary spring of popular government."

Flexibility in a changing world is often desirable but that we stand inflexibly for the spiritual values, for the "Virtue or Morality" demanded by Washington is imperative.

In that extraordinary document, the Farewell Address, is the ultimate proof of Washington's greatness because his words live on, his counsel is as sound and true, as simple and brave today as 156 years ago.

I pray that it be consulted by this Nation, at every turn, in plotting the difficult and perilous course which lies ahead.

INTRODUCTION OF THE HONORABLE ELLIS O. BRIGGS AT AMERICAS FOUNDATION DINNER METROPOLITAN CLUB

October 12, 1966

Annually, for 23 years, on October 12, the Americas Foundation has given its award to a non-official citizen of this hemisphere, who vigorously and effectively has promoted friendship between the several republics. The more than worthy recipient this year is a distinguished diplomat and author, the Honorable Ellis O. Briggs.

A phenomenon of the 1960's is the number of ambassadors cluttering the earth's scenery, in representation of 140-odd nations (and some of them really are odd), located in the world's capitols, the U.N. and elsewhere. There are so many of them that the going rate should not exceed a dime a dozen. In contrast, it is a pleasure tonight to have with us an ambassador of the old school, trained, experienced and of the highest caliber. A representative of whom we should all be proud. Mr. Briggs from the 20's through the 50's has been worth many times his weight in gold to the USA government and people. Hence, this truly is a diplomatic occasion deluxe.

October 12th was chosen for this annual affair because it is the "Day of the Spanish Race" or "Day of the Americas"; better known to us as "Columbus Day". Of course, Christopher Columbus was not a Spaniard. Neither did he have the remotest thought that there ever was or could be an America—sometimes ignorance is bliss. For that matter, both the Scandinavians and the Welsh claim their boys got to America first. Anyway, Christopher proved himself a diplomat by inducing Queen Isabella, at a time when Inquisitions 4½% Bonds were selling way below par, to hock her jewelry and finance his excursion into far out space. Her husband, Ferdinand, was unenthusiastic but accepted the idea because it might spread the true faith, greatly extend Spanish territory and its welfare-state system, as well as enhance his own image. But Ferdinand's particular vintage of great society was Anti-Deluvium. He was disinterested in creating a Peace Corps to civilize the then highly civilized Chinese or a Foreign Aid Administration to arm and industrialize the Aztecs. He did not even propose to give ballets and other performances at public expense, for the culturally deprived children of the Incas. Instead of handing out billions of his taxpayers gold as we do in a futile attempt to buy friendship, he set out to grab all he could of the other fellows' precious metals.

Such was Christopher's diplomatic mission, when he bid Signora Colombo arrividerci and set sail in his caravels; like Bobby Kennedy in his recent Latin American and African tours, full of paternalistic admonitions and a burning desire to tell the rest of humanity how to run their affairs. Christopher didn't know where he was going, where he was when he got there and never did know where he had been—and all at the taxpayers expense. Even the combined efforts of the State Department, Aid (The Administration for International Development) plus the army of bureaucratic intellectuals encamped along the Potomac could not beat that record.

Nevertheless, Columbus was a pretty good emmissary to an unknown and unknowing people. Perhaps he had a premonition of Secretary of State, John Ray's aphonism that diplomats and crabs when they seem to be going are coming. (sic)

Christopher had the diplomatic skill to take something from the Indians and act as if he were giving it to them. Thus exactly reversing our Twentieth Century Alliance for Progress program.

He convinced Isabella that a woman looks better without jewelry. Similarly he probably sold his wife on the theory that she would look stout in a mink coat.

He was the type of diplomat who would call a girl a "vision" and not a "sight". He would whisper: "as I gaze upon your countenance time stands still," instead of saying that her face would stop a clock.

The way to get to the top in diplomacy is illustrated by the story of the astrologer who profesied: "oh, Sultan Great, woe is nigh. Thou shalt live to see all thy kindred die". The Sultan ordered, "off with his head". A second astrologer said "rejoice, Great Sultan, joy to win, for thou shalt out-live all thy kin". He was made Secretary of State.

This circuitous route leads me back to our guest of honor and a story told of his tour as Ambassador in Czechoslovakia. An American reporter was arrested as a spy for taking photographs without a permit; Ellis got the man out of prison, but when he pled with the Foreign Minister for the return of the journalist's valuable camera which had been confiscated, he was told that any instruments or weapons involved in a crime became the property of the state.

"Does that apply to every crime?" The Ambassador inquired.

"Yes," replied the minister, "to every crime of every description".

"Oh," said Briggs, "if I can name a crime to which this law does not apply, will you release the camera?"

"Yes," answered the Czech dignitary, "I will."

"Well," remarked Ellis, "what about rape?"

He got the camera.

If I have dared to be facetious so far tonight, it is because I am so happy to be in the company of a dear friend and colleague. In over 44 years of intimate association with the Ambassador we have fought many a diplomatic battle shoulder to shoulder—and may I add we won them all. It is only natural therefore that I have acquired an abiding affection and admiration for him and his charming Senora, Doña Lucy.

What I now tell you is not a "commercial", but a recommendation that you read the Ambassador's books, "Farewell to Foggy Bottom" and "Shots Head Around the World." He is a vastly entertaining author who gives solid facts and thought-provoking views with a punch more decimating than Mohamed Cassius Clay's best punch.

Ellis Briggs is simpatico, there are none more so. His hard-fisted, straight-thinking common sense is applied with suavity and a scintillating wit. Above all he is a man of integrity and a patriot. Always he fights for the USA.

Ambassador Briggs is one of the most experienced and expert diplomats I have known in over half a century. He has improved our friendships and good relations with all the republics of this hemisphere. I can think of no one more highly deserving of the Americas Award for 1966.

Index